# ST...
# EU...
# GUIDE

## Statto

HEADLINE

First published in 1996
by HEADLINE BOOK PUBLISHING

Cover photographs: European Championship trophy (*Action Images*);
Statto (*Avalon Television Limited*).

10 9 8 7 6 5 4 3 2 1

ISBN 0 7472 5527 X

Typeset by
Letterpart Limited, Reigate, Surrey

Printed and bound in Great Britain by
BPC Paperbacks Ltd
A member of The British Printing Company Ltd

HEADLINE BOOK PUBLISHING
A division of Hodder Headline PLC
338 Euston Road
London NW1 3BH

# CONTENTS

# ACKNOWLEDGEMENTS

I hope that you find the following 288 pages a useful addition to your enjoyment of the greatest sporting event to be held in England since the 1996 World Cup finals.

A project like this inevitably involves lots of research and could not have been completed alone. Chris Rhys has given me a great deal of assistance, and, as one of the most respected men in the business, his help has been invaluable. Terry O'Neill has also worked overtime with the individual players' records and I thank him greatly for his contribution. Bob Harris has added his knowledge and experience of following the English national team over the last 30 years. Of course, a special thank you to all my foreign friends – Jan and Toy Buitenga from Dordrecht, Jurrian van Wessem from Monaco, Wolfgang Ley from Germany, and Oliver Lombard from the Cayman Islands.

To the Sheffield taxi driver from Jamaica who has driven me around the country at such competitive prices, including one epic journey to Southampton – I hope I have not bored you with all my stories going back to my first football match with a Sean Connery lookalike.

A big thank you to all at Thomas Kneale, Ray Spiller of the Association of Football Statisticians, and, of course, those at Headline including Alan Brooke, Ian Marshall and Celia Kent who have helped put together a *Euro 96 Guide* which I am proud to be associated with.

To all my working colleagues at Eurosport, *Fantasy Football*, Channel One, ESPN, the Bleeding Wolf, and all around the world: enjoy the following pages. I hope it gives you an extra insight.

NB: Facts and figures in this book are provided up to and including 1 April 1996 unless otherwise stated.

# PREVIEW OF EURO 96

France, even if their English-based outcasts Cantona and Ginola, do not participate, can emerge as the outstanding team in England this summer. They are more than just an outside bet for Euro 96 – I believe that they can set the tournament alight and go all the way to the final, where I fancy they will come up against the favourites Holland. As much as I would love to see England competing for the second most important football title in the world, I would not object to seeing these two fantasy football-playing teams exciting the viewers at home and abroad.

It will be even better if they do it in a trouble-free environment, with the hooligans banished to the shadows where they belong. Certainly the police, in co-operation with their European counterparts and the Football Association, could not have done more to present the best side of the beautiful game to the rest of the world. But they can only do so much. I predict that there will be little or no trouble within the confines of the super stadia where the Championships are staged, but it is hard to imagine that the Euro yobs won't cause some sort of chaos as they troop around the country. Though if it is contained, then the football should take centre stage where it belongs.

I'm holding my breath that we are blessed with an attacking tournament, although we may have to wait until the knockout stages for it to really catch fire. However, unlike the recent cricket World Cup, there are some scintillating games in the qualifying groups. From a domestic point of view, there is no more mouth-watering appetiser than England versus Scotland at Wembley on 15 June.

This is the first-ever 16-nation final and there is much, much more than the return to battle of the Auld Enemy. Indeed, England are more likely to see the Dutch as their great rivals after recent battles in World and European Championships. Their meeting at Wembley on 18 June should decide Group A.

My other predicted finalists, France, have their crucial battle with Spain in Leeds on 15 June and any slip-up there could blast my predictions apart, for my two finalists could finish up meeting in the quarters!

The best group sees Germany, Italy and Russia battling for the two places, and with the underrated Czech Republic thrown in for good measure, every game in Manchester and Liverpool will carry some considerable significance.

In Group D, I like the look of the clash between Croatia and Portugal, two of the tournament dark horses, to be played on 19 June in Nottingham. But, as good as those games are, they will not be able to compete with the raw excitement of the knockout section of Euro 96 when, for the first time, penalty shoot-outs will be replaced by sudden-death extra time. By then, the teams will be taking shape and many of the old faces will have been replaced as household names by the up-and-coming stars like Del Piero of Italy, Kluivert and Seedorf of Holland, and Zidane of France.

Guus Hiddink of Holland and Aime Jacquet of France – the two respective and respected coaches – have one thing in common, other than their love of good, passing football, and that is the way they have managed to bring their teams to the boil at the right time. Early on in the qualifying tournament when France had drawn four of their first five games 0-0, and Holland had slipped to a shattering defeat in Belarus, you could have enjoyed massive odds on either of them. But the Dutch won their last four games, including the play-off against the Irish, and France their last three to finish so strongly that both sides' odds were slashed. Indeed, the Dutch leapfrogged both Italy and Germany in the bookmakers' eyes.

It is an exciting prospect in every way: a month of top-class football unmatched in Europe before. Let's just hope that the fans are so distracted by the quality of what they are watching that they forget to fight.

# RESULTS CHART

## GROUP A MATCHES

| June | Venue | | Score | | Score | Crowd | H/T |
|---|---|---|---|---|---|---|---|
| 8 | Wembley | ENGLAND | ........ | SWITZERLAND | .......... | ....... | ...... |
| | *Goalscorers* | | | | | | |
| 10 | Villa Park | HOLLAND | ........ | SCOTLAND | .......... | ....... | ...... |
| | *Goalscorers* | | | | | | |
| 13 | Villa Park | SWITZERLAND | ........ | HOLLAND | .......... | ....... | ...... |
| | *Goalscorers* | | | | | | |
| 15 | Wembley | SCOTLAND | ........ | ENGLAND | .......... | ....... | ...... |
| | *Goalscorers* | | | | | | |
| 18 | Villa Park | SCOTLAND | ........ | SWITZERLAND | .......... | ....... | ...... |
| | *Goalscorers* | | | | | | |
| 18 | Wembley | HOLLAND | ........ | ENGLAND | .......... | ....... | ...... |
| | *Goalscorers* | | | | | | |

## GROUP B MATCHES

| June | Venue | | Score | | Score | Crowd | H/T |
|---|---|---|---|---|---|---|---|
| 9 | Elland Road | SPAIN | ........ | BULGARIA | .......... | ....... | ...... |
| | *Goalscorers* | | | | | | |
| 10 | St James' Park | ROMANIA | ........ | FRANCE | .......... | ....... | ...... |
| | *Goalscorers* | | | | | | |
| 13 | St James' Park | BULGARIA | ........ | ROMANIA | .......... | ....... | ...... |
| | *Goalscorers* | | | | | | |
| 15 | Elland Road | FRANCE | ........ | SPAIN | .......... | ....... | ...... |
| | *Goalscorers* | | | | | | |
| 18 | St James' Park | FRANCE | ........ | BULGARIA | .......... | ....... | ...... |
| | *Goalscorers* | | | | | | |
| 18 | Elland Road | ROMANIA | ........ | SPAIN | .......... | ....... | ...... |
| | *Goalscorers* | | | | | | |

## GROUP A RESULTS TABLE

| | P | W | D | L | F | A | Pts | Leading scorer |
|---|---|---|---|---|---|---|---|---|
| ENGLAND | | | | | | | | |
| SWITZERLAND | | | | | | | | |
| HOLLAND | | | | | | | | |
| SCOTLAND | | | | | | | | |

## GROUP B RESULTS TABLE

| | P | W | D | L | F | A | Pts | Leading scorer |
|---|---|---|---|---|---|---|---|---|
| SPAIN | | | | | | | | |
| BULGARIA | | | | | | | | |
| ROMANIA | | | | | | | | |
| FRANCE | | | | | | | | |

## QUARTER-FINALS

| June | Venue | Country | Score | Country | Score | Crowd | H/T |
|---|---|---|---|---|---|---|---|
| 22 | Anfield | 1B | ................ | 2A ...... | .......... | ....... | ...... |
| | *Goalscorers* | | | | | | |
| 22 | Wembley | 2B | ................ | 1A ...... | .......... | ....... | ...... |
| | *Goalscorers* | | | | | | |
| 23 | Old Trafford | 1C | ................ | 2D ...... | .......... | ....... | ...... |
| | *Goalscorers* | | | | | | |
| 23 | Villa Park | 2C | ................ | 1D ...... | .......... | ....... | ...... |
| | *Goalscorers* | | | | | | |

## GROUP C MATCHES

| June | Venue | | Score | | Score | Crowd | H/T |
|------|-------|--|-------|--|-------|-------|-----|
| 9 | Old Trafford | GERMANY | ........ CZECH REP | | .......... | ........ | ....... |
| | *Goalscorers* | | | | | | |
| 11 | Anfield | ITALY | ........ RUSSIA | | .......... | ........ | ....... |
| | *Goalscorers* | | | | | | |
| 14 | Anfield | CZECH REP | ........ ITALY | | .......... | ........ | ....... |
| | *Goalscorers* | | | | | | |
| 16 | Old Trafford | RUSSIA | ........ GERMANY | | .......... | ........ | ....... |
| | *Goalscorers* | | | | | | |
| 19 | Anfield | RUSSIA | ........ CZECH REP | | .......... | ........ | ....... |
| | *Goalscorers* | | | | | | |
| 19 | Old Trafford | ITALY | ........ GERMANY | | .......... | ........ | ....... |
| | *Goalscorers* | | | | | | |

## GROUP D MATCHES

| June | Venue | | Score | | Score | Crowd | H/T |
|------|-------|--|-------|--|-------|-------|-----|
| 9 | Hillsborough | DENMARK | ........ PORTUGAL | | .......... | ........ | ....... |
| | *Goalscorers* | | | | | | |
| 11 | City Ground | TURKEY | ........ CROATIA | | .......... | ........ | ....... |
| | *Goalscorers* | | | | | | |
| 14 | City Ground | PORTUGAL | ........ TURKEY | | .......... | ........ | ....... |
| | *Goalscorers* | | | | | | |
| 16 | Hillsborough | CROATIA | ........ DENMARK | | .......... | ........ | ....... |
| | *Goalscorers* | | | | | | |
| 19 | City Ground | CROATIA | ........ PORTUGAL | | .......... | ........ | ....... |
| | *Goalscorers* | | | | | | |
| 19 | Hillsborough | TURKEY | ........ DENMARK | | .......... | ........ | ....... |
| | *Goalscorers* | | | | | | |

## GROUP C RESULTS TABLE

| | P | W | D | L | F | A | Pts | Leading scorer |
|--|---|---|---|---|---|---|-----|----------------|
| GERMANY | ........ | ........ | ........ | ........ | ........ | ........ | ........ | ........ |
| CZECH REP | ........ | ........ | ........ | ........ | ........ | ........ | ........ | ........ |
| ITALY | ........ | ........ | ........ | ........ | ........ | ........ | ........ | ........ |
| RUSSIA | ........ | ........ | ........ | ........ | ........ | ........ | ........ | ........ |

## GROUP D RESULTS TABLE

| | P | W | D | L | F | A | Pts | Leading scorer |
|--|---|---|---|---|---|---|-----|----------------|
| DENMARK | ........ | ........ | ........ | ........ | ........ | ........ | ........ | ........ |
| PORTUGAL | ........ | ........ | ........ | ........ | ........ | ........ | ........ | ........ |
| TURKEY | ........ | ........ | ........ | ........ | ........ | ........ | ........ | ........ |
| CROATIA | ........ | ........ | ........ | ........ | ........ | ........ | ........ | ........ |

## SEMI-FINALS AND THE FINAL

| June | Venue | Country | Score | Country | Score | Crowd | H/T |
|------|-------|---------|-------|---------|-------|-------|-----|
| 26 | Old Trafford | QF1.............. | ........ | QF4.............. | ........ | ........ | ....... |
| | *Goalscorers* | | | | | | |
| 26 | Wembley | QF2.............. | ........ | QF3.............. | ........ | ........ | ....... |
| | *Goalscorers* | | | | | | |
| 30 | Wembley | .............. | | .............. | ........ | ........ | ....... |
| | *Goalscorers* | | | | | | |

# ANFIELD

11 June   Italy v Russia
14 June   Czech Rep v Italy
19 June   Russia v Czech Rep
22 June   1st in Group B v 2nd in Group A

**Address:** Anfield Road, Liverpool L4 0TH. **Telephone:** (0151) 263 2361. **Fax:** (0151) 260 8813. **Capacity:** 41,000.

**Home club:** Liverpool FC.

**Honours:** *European Champions Cup* – 1977, 1978, 1981, 1984. *UEFA Cup* – 1973, 1976. *League Champions* – 1901, 1906, 1922, 1923, 1947, 1964, 1966, 1973, 1976, 1977, 1979, 1980, 1982, 1983, 1984, 1986, 1988, 1990 (18 times – record). *FA Cup* – 1965, 1974, 1986, 1989, 1992. *League Cup* – 1981, 1982, 1983, 1984, 1995.

### Ground notes

Liverpool FC started as the remnants of Everton FC following a row between Everton and the owner of Anfield, John Houlding. Everton moved to Goodison Park at the other end of Stanley Park and Houlding started Liverpool FC at Anfield with a new team in 1892.

In 1895 a Main Stand was built to celebrate promotion to Division 1, and the Anfield Road Stand was added in 1903. The famous Kop was built in 1906 and named after the Spion Kop battle in the Boer War, after Ernest Edwards, then sports editor of the *Liverpool Echo*, suggested the name as a mark of respect to those who lost their lives in the battle.

The Kop was given a roof in 1928 and then had a capacity of 30,000. However, in May 1994, after a 1-0 defeat against Norwich City in front of 44,000 fans, this most famous stand in the land was pulled down, to be replaced by the new Kop, an all-seater stand for 12,500.

Nine World and British title fights were staged at Anfield in the 1930s and 1940s featuring Nel Tarleton and Ernie Roderick.

First *Match of the Day* on 22 August 1964 came from Anfield, when Arsenal were beaten 3-2. On 15 November 1969, the first colour transmission saw Liverpool v West Ham.

Liverpool lost championship at home to Arsenal on 26 May 1989 with almost the last kick of the season.

Rugby League's World Club Challenge was played at Anfield in 1991, when Wigan beat Penrith (Australia). The 1989 and 1990 Rugby League Charity Shield matches were also played at Anfield.

The New Zealand All Blacks Rugby Union side played the North at Anfield in 1993.

# CITY GROUND

11 June   Turkey v Croatia
14 June   Portugal v Turkey
19 June   Croatia v Portugal

**Address:** City Ground, Nottingham NG2 5FG. **Telephone:** (0115) 952 6000. **Fax:** (0115) 952 6003. **Capacity:** 30,500.

**Home club:** Nottingham Forest.

**Honours:** *European Champions Cup* – 1979, 1980. *League Champions* – 1978. *FA Cup* – 1898, 1959. *League Cup* – 1978, 1979, 1989, 1990.

**Ground notes**

Forest were the first club to play to a referee's whistle in 1878 (previously a handkerchief was used), and in January 1891 the North and South of Nottingham played the first match where goalnets were used.

Forest have had seven grounds, but have been at the City Ground since 1898.

The ground has undergone vast changes in the last few years. The brand new Trent End Stand now has seating for 7,000 and the Executive Stand has a capacity of some 15,000. The Executive Stand, which dominates the stadium, was opened in 1980 at a cost of £2.5 million.

The ground was flooded up to the crossbar in 1947 when the Trent burst its banks.

The first international for 86 years was staged at the City Ground in June 1995 with the meeting of Sweden and Japan in the Umbro Cup (2-2).

The City Ground features one of three sets of floodlights that can be seen on the horizon – from north to south the first is Meadow Lane (Notts County on the north bank of the River Trent), then the City Ground just across the river, and finally the Trent Bridge cricket ground, some 200 metres to the south.

# ELLAND ROAD

9 June    Spain v Bulgaria
15 June   France v Spain
18 June   Romania v Spain

**Address:** Elland Road, Leeds LS11 0ES. **Telephone:** (0113) 271 6037. **Fax:** (0113) 272 0370. **Capacity:** 39,000.

**Home club:** Leeds United.

**Honours:** *UEFA Cup* – 1968, 1971. *League Champions* – 1969, 1974, 1992. *FA Cup* – 1972. *League Cup* – 1968.

**Ground notes**

The original West Stand was burnt down in 1956 and replaced a year later at a cost of £180,000. An electrical fault was to blame. The South Stand (Scratching Shed) was completed in 1974 at a cost of £500,000. The East Stand – finished in 1993 – has the largest cantilever span (52 metres) of any construction in the world.

A brand new playing surface was laid prior to the start of the 1994-95 season in preparation for Euro 96.

The ground has hosted two Fairs/UEFA Cup finals – 1-0 v Ferencvaros (7 August 1968) and 1-1 v Juventus (2 June 1971).

Hunslet played all home Rugby League games at Elland Road between 1981 and 1994.

Elland Road staged the 1982 Rugby League Challenge Cup final replay, in which Widnes beat Hull.

Great Britain have played Australia three times and New Zealand twice in Rugby League internationals in recent seasons.

The Rugby Union Springboks played the North at Elland Road in 1994.

England and Sweden drew 3-3 in June 1995 in the Umbro Trophy.

# HILLSBOROUGH

9 June    Denmark v Portugal
16 June   Croatia v Denmark
19 June   Turkey v Denmark

**Address:** Hillsborough, Sheffield S6 1SW. **Telephone:** (0114) 234 3122. **Fax:** (0114) 233 7145. **Capacity:** 40,000.

**Home club:** Sheffield Wednesday.

**Honours:** *League Champions* – 1903, 1904, 1929, 1930. *FA Cup* – 1896, 1907, 1935. *League Cup* – 1991.

### Ground notes

When Wednesday moved to the present ground in 1899, the ten-acre site needed £5,000 of work to bring it up to standard. The Owlerton ground was renamed Hillsborough in 1912, but the club retain their nickname 'The Owls'.

The floodlights, installed for the Derek Dooley testimonial in 1955, are considered the best in the country.

The oldest part of the ground is the North Stand, finished in 1961, which was the first cantilevered stand to run the length of the pitch. The South Stand has been redeveloped in two stages – the first in 1992 when a new roof was fitted, followed in the 1995-96 season by the addition of 3,000 seats, executive boxes and banqueting facilities.

In the 1966 World Cup, Hillsborough hosted West Germany v Switzerland (5-0), West Germany v Uruguay (4-0), Spain v Switzerland (2-1) and Argentina v Switzerland (2-0).

The Leppings Lane end has been redeveloped after the Hillsborough tragedy, when 95 people died in the 1989 FA Cup semi-final between Liverpool and Nottingham Forest. Following the disaster, among other things, the Taylor Report recommended that top-division grounds should become all-seater.

The ground has hosted 33 FA Cup semi-finals.

# OLD TRAFFORD

9 June    Germany v Czech Rep
16 June   Russia v Germany
19 June   Italy v Germany
23 June   1st in Group C v 2nd in Group D
26 June   Winners QF1 v Winners QF4

**Address:** Old Trafford, Manchester M16 0RA. **Telephone:** (0161) 872 1661. **Fax:** (0161) 876 5502. **Capacity:** 53,000.

**Home club:** Manchester United.

**Honours:** *European Champions Cup* – 1968. *European Cup-Winners' Cup* – 1991. *League Champions* – 1908, 1911, 1952, 1956, 1957, 1965, 1967, 1993, 1994. *FA Cup* – 1909, 1948, 1963, 1977, 1983, 1985, 1990, 1994. *League Cup* – 1992.

### Ground notes

The ground first played host to the Manchester United v Liverpool game on 19 February 1910 – the visitors won 4-3 before 50,000 in an open stadium with just one stand (North Stand).

The ground was virtually destroyed on 11 March 1941, when German bombers scored a direct hit on the Main Stand, open terracing and cover. The pitch was also ruined. The War Damage Commission gave United £4,800 to repair the pitch and £17,000 to rebuild the ground, and the club returned in August 1949 after seven seasons at Maine Road.

The stadium has been rebuilt over the last 30 years – the new North Stand, costing £28 million, will be complete in time for Euro 96. The old stand housed the first private boxes at a British ground. The famous Stretford End was where the most fanatical supporters congregated. It was first covered in 1959, and in 1992 was demolished to make way for the all-seater West Stand.

In the 1966 World Cup, at Old Trafford, Portugal beat Hungary 3-1, Portugal beat Bulgaria 3-0 and Hungary beat Bulgaria 3-1.

The 1970 FA Cup final replay between Chelsea and Leeds was played at Old Trafford, where other FA Cup finals were staged back in 1911 and 1915.

Great Britain have hosted both Australia (three times) and New Zealand (once) in Rugby League matches at Old Trafford.

Rugby League Premiership finals have been played at Old Trafford since 1987.

The Rugby League World Club Challenge between Widnes and Canberra Raiders was played at Old Trafford in 1989.

Benn v Eubank II -- the drawn world super middleweight title fight was held here in 1993.

Manchester will host the 2002 Commonwealth Games.

# ST JAMES' PARK

10 June   Romania v France
13 June   Bulgaria v Romania
18 June   France v Bulgaria

**Address:** St James' Park, Newcastle-upon-Tyne NE1 4ST. **Telephone:** (0191) 232 8361.
**Fax:** (0191) 232 9875. **Capacity:** 36,500.

**Home club:** Newcastle United.

**Honours:** *UEFA Cup* – 1969. *League Champions* – 1905, 1907, 1909, 1927. *FA Cup* –
1910, 1924, 1932, 1951, 1952, 1955.

### Ground notes

St James' has been home to United since 1892, after two clubs amalgamated to form the
present club. The club is owned by the Freemen of the City and the City Councillors
rather than by the club itself.

The ground has been completely redeveloped since 1992, with former stands and
terracing removed, at a cost of £25.8 million.

The club have always had fine No. 9s, such as Jackie Milburn, Malcolm Macdonald,
Andy Cole and Les Ferdinand.

Several pop concerts have been held at St James' Park.

No FA Cup semi-finals have been played at St James' Park, which is not geographically
suitable.

# VILLA PARK

10 June   Holland v Scotland
13 June   Switzerland v Holland
18 June   Scotland v Switzerland
23 June   2nd in Group C v 1st in Group D

**Address:** Villa Park, Trinity Road, Birmingham B6 6HE. **Telephone:** (0121) 327 2299. **Fax:** (0121) 322 2107. **Capacity:** 40,000.

**Home club:** Aston Villa.

**Honours:** *European Champions Cup* – 1982. *League Champions* – 1894, 1896, 1897, 1899, 1900, 1910, 1981. *FA Cup* – 1887, 1895, 1897, 1905, 1913, 1920, 1957. *League Cup* – 1961, 1975, 1977, 1994, 1996.

**Ground notes**

Aston Villa first moved to Villa Park in their double-winning season of 1897.

The Holte End was covered in 1962 at a cost of £40,000, and the ground was extensively refurbished for the 1966 World Cup when the Witton Road Stand and the Trinity Road Stand were vastly improved. The cost was £89,000, of which £45,000 was met by a government grant.

There has been further recent redevelopment at a cost of £20 million, featuring the new North Stand and Doug Ellis Stand in Witton Lane, but the old Trinity Road façade remains a monument to the club's history. The final part of the restructuring at the Holte End will house the largest number of supporters behind the goal in any stadium in the country.

In the 1966 World Cup, Villa Park hosted Argentina v Spain (2-1), Argentina v West Germany (0-0) and West Germany v Spain (2-1).

In the 1981 League Cup final replay at Villa Park, Liverpool beat West Ham 2-1.

In June 1995 Brazil played Sweden in the Umbro Cup at Villa Park.

Villa Park is the most popular venue for FA Cup semi-finals, with 46 to date, including this year's game which saw Manchester United beat Chelsea.

Boxing events included Jack Bodell v Danny McAlinden, British heavyweight title fight in 1971; Dick Turpin v Vince Hawkins, British midddleweight title fight 1948; and other top fights featuring local boxers.

The Euro 96 draw took place in Birmingham.

# WEMBLEY

8 June    England v Switzerland
15 June    Scotland v England
18 June    Holland v England
22 June    2nd in Group B v 1st in Group A
26 June    Winners of QF2 v Winners of QF3
30 June    Final

**Address:** Wembley, Middlesex. **Telephone:** (0181) 902 8833. **Capacity:** 76,000.

**Home Club:** None.

**Hosted:** *World Cup final* – 1966. *European Cup final* – 1963 (won by AC Milan), 1968 (won by Manchester United), 1978 (won by Liverpool), 1992 (won by Barcelona). *European Cup-Winners' Cup* – 1965 (won by West Ham), 1993 (won by Parma).

**Ground notes**

Constructed initially for the 1924 British Empire Exhibition, it was first used for the famous White Horse final in 1923.

Wembley is also part of the 65-acre site which includes the Conference and Exhibition Centre and the Wembley Arena. Wembley Way was built in 1948 for the Olympic Games.

In its original form Wembley was uncovered at both ends. The covering of the stadium and both ends as it is today took place in 1963 at a cost of £500,000, the then capacity of 100,000 including 44,000 seats. The first international under the new roof was the game against Northern Ireland in 1963. The new floodlights were installed in 1973.

Wembley is bidding for a new national centre in which only the famous Twin Towers, now a listed building, would remain.

In the World Cup final at Wembley on 30 July 1966, England beat West Germany 4-2.

In the 1968 European Cup final, Manchester United became the first English club to win the trophy when they beat Benfica 4-1.

FA Cup finals from 1923 and League Cup finals from 1968 to date have been played at Wembley.

The first Cup final broadcast on TV was in 1938, and first final broadcast in colour on TV was in 1968.

Wembley staged the 1948 Olympics.

Wembley hosted the Live Aid concert, and many other top concerts.

The stadium has hosted the Rugby League Challenge Cup final since 1929, except in 1932 and 1941-45.

Frank Bruno outpointed Oliver McCall at Wembley in 1995 to win boxing's world heavyweight title at last.

London Monarchs played American Football at Wembley from 1990.

England beat Canada in the Rugby Union international, played at Wembley September 1992.

# RULES OF THE TOURNAMENT

The 16 teams are split into four qualifying sections of four, with the top two progressing to the knockout quarter-finals.

If two or more teams finish equal on points after all the group matches have been played, the following criteria shall be applied to determine the ranking:

1. Greater number of points obtained in the matches between the teams in question.
2. Goal difference resulting from the matches between the teams in question.
3. Greater number of goals scored in the matches between the teams in question (if more than two teams finish equal on points).
4. Goal difference in all the group matches.
5. Greater number of goals scored in all the group matches.
6. Coefficient of points from the last three qualifying rounds for the final rounds of Euro 92, USA 94 and Euro 96 (points gained divided by the number of matches played).
7. Fair Play conduct of the teams.
8. A drawing of lots by the European Championship Committee.

The winners and runners-up in each group shall play the quarter-finals over one match, as per the following table:

| | |
|---|---|
| B1 – A2 | B2 – A1 |
| C1 – D2 | D1 – C2 |

If at the end of normal time, a quarter-final match ends in a draw, extra-time shall be played until a deciding goal is scored ('golden goal'). This period of extra-time shall, however, not exceed 2 × 15 minutes. If a deciding goal is not scored by the end of this period of extra-time , the winning team shall be determined by kicks from the penalty mark.

The four winners of the quarter-finals shall play the semi-finals over one match, as per the following table:

Winners of B1 – A2 vs. Winners of D1 – C2
Winners of C1 – D2 vs. Winners of B2 – A1

If, upon completion of the statutory playing time, a semi-final match ends in a draw, the same system shall apply as in the quarter-finals ('golden goal', see above).

The winners of the semi-finals shall contest the final.

If, upon completion of the statutory playing time, the final match ends in a draw, the same system shall apply as in the quarter-finals ('golden goal', see above).

# TV AND RADIO SCHEDULE

| Date | Match | BBC | ITV | Eurosport | Radio 5 |
|---|---|---|---|---|---|
| 8 June | England v Switzerland | | 15.00-17.00 | 19.00-21.00<br>23.00-01.00 Rpt<br>07.30-09.00 Rpt | 15.00-17.00 |
| 9 June | Spain v Bulgaria | | 14.30-16.30 | 17.00-18.30<br>12.00-13.30 Rpt | 14.30-16.30 |
| 9 June | Germany v Czech Rep | 17.00-19.00 | | 22.00-23.30<br>09.00-11.00 Rpt<br>15.00-16.30 Rpt | 17.00-19.00 |
| 9 June | Denmark v Portugal | 19.30-21.30 | | 13.30-15.00<br>on 10 June | 19.30-21.30 |
| 10 June | Holland v Scotland | | 16.30-18.30 | 21.30-23.00<br>09.00-11.00 Rpt<br>14.30-16.30 Rpt | 16.30-18.30 |
| 10 June | Romania v France | 19.30-21.30 | | 19.30-21.30<br>12.00-14.00 Rpt | 19.30-21.30 |
| 11 June | Italy v Russia | 16.30-18.30 | | 21.30-23.00<br>12.00-14.00 Rpt | 16.30-18.30 |
| 11 June | Turkey v Croatia | | 19.30-21.30 | 19.30-21.30<br>09.00-11.00 Rpt | 19.30-21.30 |
| 13 June | Bulgaria v Romania | | 16.30-18.30 | 21.30-22.30<br>11.00-12.00 Rpt | 16.30-18.30 |
| 13 June | Switzerland v Holland | 19.30-21.30 | | 19.30-21.30<br>12.00-14.00 Rpt | 19.30-21.30 |
| 14 June | Portugal v Turkey | 16.30-18.30 | | 23.00-00.30 | 16.30-18.30 |
| 14 June | Czech Rep v Italy | | 19.30-21.30 | 19.30-21.30<br>11.00-12.30 Rpt | 19.30-21.30 |
| 15 June | Scotland v England | 15.00-17.00 | | 19.00-20.30<br>11.00-12.30 Rpt | 15.00-17.00 |
| 15 June | France v Spain | | 18.00-20.00 | 20.30-21.30 | 18.00-20.00 |
| 16 June | Russia v Germany | | 15.00-17.00 | 20.00-21.30<br>21.00-23.00 Rpt | 15.00-17.00 |
| 16 June | Croatia v Denmark | 18.00-20.00 | | 21.30-23.00 | 18.00-20.00 |

| Date | Match | BBC | ITV | Eurosport | Radio 5 |
|---|---|---|---|---|---|
| 18 June | France v Bulgaria | 16.30-18.30 or | | 23.00-00.30 13.30-15.00 Rpt on 19 June | 16.30-18.30 or |
| 18 June | Romania v Spain | 16.30-18.30 | | 09.00-10.30 on 19 June | 16.30-18.30 |
| 18 June | Holland v England | | 19.30-21.30 or | 19.30-21.30 15.00-16.30 Rpt | 19.30-21.30 or |
| 18 June | Scotland v Switzerland | | 19.30-21.30 | 21.30-23.00 12.00-13.30 Rpt | 19.30-21.30 |
| 19 June | Croatia v Portugal | | 16.30-18.30 or | 16.30-18.30 19.30-21.00 Rpt on 20 June | 16.30-18.30 or |
| 19 June | Turkey v Denmark | | 16.30-18.30 | 15.00-16.30 on 20 June | 16.30-18.30 |
| 19 June | Russia v Czech Rep | 19.30-21.30 or | | 19.30-21.30 09.00-10.30 Rpt | 19.30-21.30 or |
| 19 June | Italy v Germany | 19.30-21.30 | | 21.30-23.00 16.30-18.00 Rpt 09.00-11.00 Rpt | 19.30-21.30 |
| 22 June | 2nd in B v 1st in A | 1st choice 15.00-17.00 | 2nd choice 15.00-17.00 | 17.00-18.30 20.30-22.00 Rpt 08.00-10.00 Rpt | 15.00-17.00 |
| 22 June | 1st in B v 2nd in A | 1st choice 18.30-20.30 | 2nd choice 18.30-20.30 | 18.30-20.30 23.00-01.00 Rpt 10.00-12.00 Rpt 09.00-11.00 Rpt | 18.30-21.30 |
| 23 June | 1st in C v 2nd in D | 1st choice 15.00-17.00 | 2nd choice 15.00-17.00 | 17.00-18.30 | 15.00-17.00 |
| 23 June | 2nd in C v 1st in D | 1st choice 18.30-20.30 | 2nd choice 18.30-20.30 | 12.00-14.00 on 24 June 21.00-23.00 | 18.30-20.30 |
| 26 June | Winner QF1 v Winner QF4 | To be agreed 16.00-18.00 | To be agreed 16.00-18.00 | 18.00-19.30 21.00-22.30 Rpt 09.00-11.00 Rpt 16.30-18.30 Rpt | 15.00-18.00 |
| 26 June | Winner QF2 v Winner QF3 | To be agreed 19.30-21.30 | To be agreed 19.30-21.30 | 22.30-00.00 14.00-16.00 Rpt 21.00-22.30 Rpt | 19.30-21.30 |
| 30 June | Final | 19.00-21.00 | 19.00-21.00 | 22.00-23.30 09.00-11.00 Rpt 12.00-14.00 Rpt | 19.00-21.00 |

# INTERVIEW WITH TERRY VENABLES

## BY ANGUS LOUGHRAN

I think everybody's excited about Euro 96, it's getting very close. And really it's around the corner. I think it will whiz by.

I was very excited when the draw was made in Birmingham and Scotland came out. Even from being a young lad, it's our history. England v Scotland is one of the main fixtures on the calendar. You get the Cup final and England v Scotland. That was always something to look forward to at the end of the season. And we haven't had that at Wembley for eight years, and I think there's a lot of people, both English and Scottish, that would love to have the fixture back again. However, around the game the behaviour's got to be good, otherwise we won't get it back as a regular fixture. And I think the fans know that. They want it back so much I'm sure that the behaviour will be good, and the game is always exciting.

They're a very good side. Defensively I think they're second only to France in the competition leading up to qualifying. It's an outstanding record they've got. I think they've lost one goal in 10 games or something extremely good. They've got a solid all-round side. Craig Brown has got a good balance to the team. He's got some top individuals, too, so the side has improved, the same way as I feel we have.

The return of Ally McCoist, after three years out, can only help. I mean, he's a recognised striker, a bubbly character. He gets on well with the team, and he's always dangerous in and around the box. You can't rest or lose your concentration for a second.

All the matches in the group are important. The Dutch game, I think, is going to be the real artists' game, because tactically they're so good. Therefore it's important that we build up points before that game. It could be the all-important game, and that is why I've concentrated a lot on it, to ensure that we're ready for it.

Obviously, the side is now based round Ajax, after the team very nearly didn't qualify. They know that their original approach wasn't quite right. So they made a decision, and a good one, to put Ajax in orange shirts. And those that weren't at Ajax, like Seedorf and Bergkamp, have been. So they know what is expected of them, and they have developed into a very, very good team, but that doesn't mean they're unbeatable. Who knows, with Ajax now facing Juventus in the Champions League final in Rome, many players might be tired, and I think that may be helpful. Any little help we can get!

Of their players, Kluivert has been a class act for a long while. He did score the winning goal in the European Champions Cup final, against Milan, and he made the difference. Also, he's so physically mature, and mature in his mind too – the positions he takes up. Given his great finishing too, that's what makes him the star he is. He's someone to be feared and he constantly gets goals at the very highest level.

I think the De Boer brothers are particularly good, and they should not be underestimated. I'm sure in their own country they're not underestimated. And, of course, there is Overmars, who has been injured, but I think he's one of the best in his position in Europe. And I'm a great admirer of Blind. I think he dictates the pace of the game from the back.

Then there's the two playing in England, Dennis Bergkamp and Bryan Roy, who will report back on us. Dennis has done very well. So, too, has Bryan Roy. He is a player that could come in to the reckoning and, again, a very skilful, experienced player.

Since we last played Switzerland, they have changed their coach, but I think the past is the past. We had a good result and we played well. But that's one thing. The most important thing is the next game. Roy Hodgson did a very good job there. He played in a particular fashion, developed it and improved it. And now, I think that the new coach Artur Jorge will try and change it slightly. He doesn't want to make too many changes because he knows he's not got a lot of time with the players. So, he's got a dilemma, but he's a very shrewd, very good coach. He's done very well over the last 10 years. So, he is not a guy to be underestimated.

Obviously we want to open up with a win. It just gives that burst of confidence they're all waiting for throughout the country. But I suspect the competition will be like other European Championships and World Cups and be cagey to start with. Sides aren't going to open up and leave too many gaps. But, in saying that, I think there'll be teams, just like in the World Cup, that will be positive, a little more than they used to be. But there will still be that slight cageyness.

Regarding the England side, there has been a lot of pressure from the media on Alan Shearer, and the fact he hasn't scored for England for a while, but you can't weigh it up like that. You can have it the other way around, where people are scoring like mad leading up to a competition, and then you're full of confidence, but they dry up when it comes round. I've got to have confidence in what I think my players can do. I don't worry if someone's not doing this or that at this moment. It'd be nice if they're right in form. But you've actually got to have your instincts about your players and know that they'll come up for you on the night.

People wonder if I have a starting line-up in my mind for the first game against Switzerland, but this is something that I keep to myself. I've got to keep the players, all of them, on their toes, which they are. They're a good group. And they know there's hard, tough competition for places. Now we want to develop and improve right the way through, for it's very important that we do improve. Even if we don't win the games, team play has got to improve all the time until we get up there. And then I think the results will come.

The pre-Euro 96 tour to China isn't just about building the squad as a unit, but because I wanted more games as I'd been without them and it gives me a chance to get more games. Also the opposition is very good. I spoke about how good the Japanese were last year and everyone thought I was kidding. But they have proved to be a very good side, and they've improved even more since then. They beat Poland in a competition 5-0. And although a lot of people don't know much about Chinese football, it's come on leaps and bounds. It is tough opposition, take my word for it.

Some may wonder why we are going so far away for our build-up games, but the main problem with going to Europe, which would have been our first choice, was that you could possibly have trouble with people following you, which would be the last thing we want. The worst thing is to have problems from any elements of supporters marauding. And I think that that is something that we did not want. Furthermore, the players and myself did not want to be at the training camp for three weeks before another three and a half weeks. There's the risk of boredom setting in, and difficulties in filling the time.

We also felt South Africa would be a good option, because it's only one hour time difference, but we could get only one game, and I think there would have been a lot of other things for us to do, and expected of us. And that would have been tiring. So in the end, we chose, rightly or wrongly, to go to China.

The media's role in all of this plays a part. But it's not a matter of handling it, it's a matter of having to. They have to do what they've got to do. They've got their pressures, their jobs to do. And some of them are very good at it. Some of them are understanding. And some of them are knowledgeable. And some, there's a small group, that are not so good, or the pressures that they need to deliver for their papers is not good for the game or for the team. And for us, right across the board, it pressurises the situation. But to be an international footballer, or an international coach, you've got to be able to handle that pressure. That's what makes you an international. Taking the pressure is almost the same as having the ability. But some have got that mentality of rubbishing people, and I'm afraid there must be people that quite enjoy it, because they sell a lot of newspapers with those stories. You've got to have an attitude towards it. I find it ludicrous some of the things that are said. But I think we've got used to it, and the players have got used to it. They're going to get hardened to it.

Another problem with the press is making the players available to them. The press like to be able to speak to three or four players every day. And some players don't want to do that. I have to tell them that it's important that they do so as professionals, and that they're not just giving it to the press, they're giving it to the people of the country.

If some of the players get battered and treated unfairly, they say: 'See. What's the point of doing it? This is what they're doing to us.' So we've got to try and get a fairness if we can. And we've got to say: 'Yes, we're professionals. We've got to do this job.' But I think the press has a big responsibility to treat that information in an accurate fashion.

For me, I learnt much about coping with the press when I was at Barcelona. While I was there, I saw the changing of the press. Previously it had been at a certain volume, and, while I was out there, I used to go to the local hotel and get the English papers and have a beer. And I saw the ferocity of the press, in certain papers, get more demanding. And it got a lot worse. The Spanish press will hammer you professionally, about football. It's not really any other side of your life or whatever, that some players and some people have to deal with here.

Spain are very good, without a shadow of a doubt. I thought they had a good campaign in the World Cup. They got as far as playing Italy in the quarter-finals, and they were a bit unfortunate in that game, I felt, when they got knocked out by the odd goal. They had a lot of younger players then, and now they've had two years more experience. And I think they'll be better for it. They'll be one of the favourites. Their group, with France and Romania, will be fascinating. You can never tell with Romania, like they showed in the World Cup; they could beat the best and slip up against weaker opposition. It depends how they perform on the night. They're a very capable team.

Group C also has much to offer. The Czech Republic are a very underrated team. They had a good campaign coming through to England. Russia are also a very talented team, but they often disappoint on the big scene. I remember Bobby Charlton, World Cup after World Cup he used to tip Russia as his dark horse, and quite rightly, because they've got some great players. And you think, is it this time? But there's no doubt about it, they're a good side.

In Group D, although neither Turkey nor Croatia has any experience of a major tournament, I would say it would be foolish to underestimate them because it's always a powerful weapon, underestimation. And it always has been to lesser teams. But lesser teams are not around any more. You used to always get seven or eight in European Championships or World Cups that were weaker, but you still couldn't underestimate them, because you'd come unstuck. But now there are no weaker teams, there won't be

21

any more. There wasn't in the World Cup. There's not in this 16. The quality around the world is rising all the time, it'll just get tougher. Croatia are an excellent side. While the Danes have got the Laudrup brothers, who are outstanding. They're very talented and you can never drop your concentration for a moment with those two, because they've got great abilities.

I'm sometimes asked if being England coach was a boyhood ambition, but I can honestly say it wasn't really. I always had an ambition to be a manager and hopefully at the top. But the England job is one of those things you don't really feel is possible, that it's a bit outside your reach. But I'm delighted I've had the experience – it's been very good and interesting. It's given me a chance to get thinking time in. Whereas before I thought it a disadvantage that there weren't weekly games, I think you can turn that into an advantage for yourself as far as storing knowledge up is concerned. Though there is still the downside that I don't work every day and I miss that. I like working with players and I'm now doing it sometimes only three or four days in a month. And in the last two or three months, not even that. So I miss that. But on the other hand, as I said, at club management you're planning one or two games a week and so you don't really get a chance to sit down and think. Or travel, or get information in to you. At international level you do. So there's the up and the down side of both jobs.

There is time to relax and to be happy within yourself – there's got to be. I think you've got to concentrate on your job and take it seriously, but you've also got to have a bit of fun and time to relax. And you've got to try and get little breaks, so you're always fresh when the big game comes up.

It's all been said before about Paul Gascoigne. We've all seen him, in his high moments and lower moments. And he's had a very interesting career. But there's one thing for sure, it's not over yet. He has done magnificently well to get himself back to form. He's still got a couple of months to work at what he's doing. And he's a special sort of player, we all know that. He is unpredictable, and I like the unpredictable side of his football game. The other side, his discipline, has got to be more predictable and I thought he showed that against Bulgaria. Along with Paul Ince in the middle of the park, I thought they did very well for us. As far as I am concerned, the fact that Ince failed to make himself available for the Umbro Cup is now forgotten. The only part of history I'm interested in is the Bulgarian game. He came into the side having settled down in Italy, which took him a while – I knew it would, it's not easy. But they either go one way or the other. They either fall, when they're trying to settle down, or they ride on. And he's doing very well.

People wonder if we can repeat 1966 and win as hosts. Unfortunately, I haven't got a crystal ball. All I know is that all I can possibly do is to try to select the best players for what I want and try to get a blend. All the coaching staff work very hard to make sure we get the best out of players and prepare ourselves. And we hope that takes us into good results, and that everyone enjoys the games and behaves well and hope that we have great memories from this competition.

# EUROPEAN CHAMPIONSHIP 1996
# QUALIFYING ROUNDS

## GROUP ONE

Romania were the pacemakers from the start, thanks to France's succession of goalless draws. Coming up to the final hurdle, only six points separated the top five clubs, with only Azerbaijan seriously adrift. But it was France who finished with a flourish, including a 3-1 win over Romania, giving them a significant psychological advantage in Group B where the two are drawn together again.

*4 September 1994, Ramat Gan, Tel Aviv*    *3,500*

| | | | |
|---|---|---|---|
| **Israel** | 2 | **Poland** | 1 |
| R.Harazi [43, 58] | | Kosecki [80] | |

*7 September 1994, Bucharest*    *10,000*

| | | | |
|---|---|---|---|
| **Romania** | 3 | **Azerbaijan** | 0 |
| Belodedici [43], Petrescu [58], Raducioiu [87] | | | |

*7 September 1994, Bratislava*    *14,238*

| | | | |
|---|---|---|---|
| **Slovakia** | 0 | **France** | 0 |

*8 September 1994, Saint Etienne*    *31,744*

| | | | |
|---|---|---|---|
| **France** | 0 | **Romania** | 0 |

*12 October 1994, Ramat Gan, Tel Aviv*    *15,000*

| | | | |
|---|---|---|---|
| **Israel** | 2 | **Slovakia** | 2 |
| R.Harazi [25], Banin [33 pen] | | Rusnak [5], Moravcik [14] | |

*12 October 1994, Mielec*    *10,000*

| | | | |
|---|---|---|---|
| **Poland** | 1 | **Azerbaijan** | 0 |
| Juskowiak [44] | | | |

*12 November 1994, Bucharest*    *15,000*

| | | | |
|---|---|---|---|
| **Romania** | 3 | **Slovakia** | 2 |
| Popescu [16], Hagi [47], Prodan [81], | | Dubovsky [56], Chvila [79] | |

*16 November 1994, Zabrze*    *20,000*

| | | | |
|---|---|---|---|
| **Poland** | 0 | **France** | 0 |

*16 November 1994, Trabzon*    *3,000*

| | | | |
|---|---|---|---|
| **Azerbaijan** | 0 | **Israel** | 2 |
| | | R.Harazi [29], Rosenthal [50] | |

*13 December 1994, Trabzon*
| | | | | |
|---|---|---|---|---|
| **Azerbaijan** | 0 | **France** | 2 | 4,000 |

Papin [25], Loko [56]

*14 December 1994, Ramat Gan, Tel Aviv*
| | | | | |
|---|---|---|---|---|
| **Israel** | 1 | **Romania** | 1 | 40,000 |

Rosenthal [84]   Lacatus [69]

*29 March 1995, Ramat Gan, Tel Aviv*
| | | | | |
|---|---|---|---|---|
| **Israel** | 0 | **France** | 0 | 45,000 |

*29 March 1995, Bucharest*
| | | | | |
|---|---|---|---|---|
| **Romania** | 2 | **Poland** | 1 | 22,000 |

Raducioiu [45], Wandzik [o.g. 55]   Juskowiak [42]

*29 March 1995, Kosice*
| | | | | |
|---|---|---|---|---|
| **Slovakia** | 4 | **Azerbaijan** | 1 | 12,400 |

Tittel [35], Timko [40, 50],   Suleymanov [80 pen]
Dubovsky [45 pen]

*25 April 1995, Zabrze*
| | | | | |
|---|---|---|---|---|
| **Poland** | 4 | **Israel** | 3 | 5,500 |

Nowak [1], Juskowiak [50],   Rosenthal [37], Révivo [42],
Kowalczyk [55], Kosecki [62]   Zohar [77]

*26 April 1995, Nantes*
| | | | | |
|---|---|---|---|---|
| **France** | 4 | **Slovakia** | 0 | 26,000 |

Kristofik [o.g. 27], Ginola [42],
Blanc [58], Guerin [62]

*26 April 1995, Trabzon*
| | | | | |
|---|---|---|---|---|
| **Azerbaijan** | 1 | **Romania** | 4 | 500 |

Suleymanov [33]   Raducioiu [1 pen, 68, 76],
Dumitrescu [38]

*7 June 1995, Zabrze*
| | | | | |
|---|---|---|---|---|
| **Poland** | 5 | **Slovakia** | 0 | 20,000 |

Juskowiak [10, 72], Wiesczycki [58],
Kosecki [63], Nowak [69]

*7 June 1995, Bucharest*
| | | | | |
|---|---|---|---|---|
| **Romania** | 2 | **Israel** | 1 | 20,000 |

Lacatus [16], Munteanu [65]   Berkovitch [50]

*16 August 1995, Paris*
| | | | | |
|---|---|---|---|---|
| **France** | 1 | **Poland** | 1 | 40,496 |

Djorkaeff [85]   Juskowiak [35]

*16 August 1995, Trabzon*  
**Azerbaijan**      0

50
     **Slovakia**      1  
     Jancula [60]

*6 September 1995, Auxerre*  
**France**      10  
Desailly [13], Djorkaeff [18, 79],  
Guerin [33], Pedros [49],  
Leboeuf [53, 70], Dugarry [66],  
Zidane [68], Cocard [90]

15,000
     **Azerbaijan**      0

*6 September 1995, Zabrze*  
**Poland**      0

22,000
     **Romania**      0

*6 September 1995, Kosice*  
**Slovakia**      1  
Jancula [54]

7,810
     **Israel**      0

*11 October 1995, Ramat Gan, Tel Aviv*  
**Israel**      2  
R.Harazi [30, 50]

8,000
     **Azerbaijan**      0

*11 October 1995, Bucharest*  
**Romania**      1  
Lacatus [51]

25,000
     **France**      3  
     Karembeu [28], Djorkaeff [42],  
     Zidane [75]

*11 October 1995, Bratislava*  
**Slovakia**      4  
Dubovsky [32 pen], Jancula [68],  
Ujlaky [77], Simon [83]

12,000
     **Poland**      1  
     Juskowiak [19]

*15 November 1995, Trabzon*  
**Azerbaijan**      0

1,000
     **Poland**      0

*15 November 1995, Caen*  
**France**      2  
Djorkaeff [69], Lizarazu [88]

21,500
     **Israel**      0

*15 November 1995, Kosice*  
**Slovakia**      0

8,000
     **Romania**      2  
     Hagi [68], Munteanu [83]

# FINAL TABLE

|   |            | P  | W | D | L | F  | A  | Pts |
|---|------------|----|---|---|---|----|----|-----|
| 1 | **ROMANIA** | 10 | 6 | 3 | 1 | 18 | 8  | 21  |
| 2 | **FRANCE**  | 10 | 5 | 5 | 0 | 22 | 2  | 20  |
| 3 | Slovakia   | 10 | 4 | 2 | 4 | 14 | 18 | 14  |
| 4 | Poland     | 10 | 3 | 4 | 3 | 14 | 12 | 13  |
| 5 | Israel     | 10 | 3 | 3 | 4 | 13 | 11 | 12  |
| 6 | Azerbaijan | 10 | 0 | 1 | 9 | 2  | 29 | 1   |

Romania and France qualify for Euro 96 finals.

## TOP SCORERS

| | |
|---|---|
| Juskowiak [Poland] | 7 |
| R.Harazi [Israel] | 6 |
| Djorkaeff [France] | 5 |
| Raducioiu [Romania] | 5 |
| Lacatus [Romania] | 3 |
| Dubovsky [Slovakia] | 3 |
| Jancula [Slovakia] | 3 |
| Kosecki [Poland] | 3 |
| Rosenthal [Israel] | 3 |

# GROUP TWO

Spain dominated this group so much that they had already won their place in the finals by October. One of only three undefeated teams in the finals, they have developed into an outstanding side under Javier Clemente. Holders Denmark were locked in a battle with Belgium for the other place, but a fine finish by the Danes with three wins out of four saw them safely through, but without pulling up any trees.

*7 September 1994, Brussels*                                                    11,000
**Belgium**                    2        **Armenia**                            0
Krbachyan [o.g. 3],
Degryse [73]

*7 September 1994, Limassol*                                                    12,000
**Cyprus**                     1        **Spain**                              2
Sotiriou [36]                           Higuera [18],
                                        M.Charalambous [o.g. 26]

*7 September 1994, Skopje*                                                      22,000
**Macedonia**                  1        **Denmark**                            1
Stojkovski [4]                          Povlsen [86]

*8 October 1994, Yerevan*                                                       6,000
**Armenia**                    0        **Cyprus**                             0

*12 October 1994, Copenhagen*                                                   40,000
**Denmark**                    3        **Belgium**                            1
Vilfort [35], Jensen [72],              Degryse [31]
Strudal [86]

*12 October 1994, Skopje*                                                       30,000
**Macedonia**                  0        **Spain**                              2
                                        Julio Salinas [16, 25]

*16 November 1994, Brussels*                                                    17,000
**Belgium**                    1        **Macedonia**                          1
Verheyen [31]                           Boskovski [50]

*16 November 1994, Limassol*                                                    8,000
**Cyprus**                     2        **Armenia**                            0
Sotiriou [7], Phasouliotis [88]

*16 November 1994, Seville*                                                     38,000
**Spain**                      3        **Denmark**                            0
Nadal [41], Donato [57],
Luis Enrique [87]

*17 December 1994, Brussels*                                          25,000
**Belgium**                          1          **Spain**                          4
Degryse [7]                                     Hierro [29 pen], Donato [57],
                                                Julio Salinas [69],
                                                Luis Enrique [90]

*17 December 1994, Skopje*                                           12,000
**Macedonia**                        3          **Cyprus**                         0
B.Djurovski [14, 25, 90]

*29 March 1995, Limassol*                                            15,000
**Cyprus**                           1          **Denmark**                        1
Agathocleous [45]                               Schjonberg [3]

*29 March 1995, Seville*                                             27,000
**Spain**                            1          **Belgium**                        1
Guerrero [25]                                   Degryse [26]

*26 April 1995, Brussels*                                            13,000
**Belgium**                          2          **Cyprus**                         0
Karagiannis [20], Schepens [47]

*26 April 1995, Copenhagen*                                          38,888
**Denmark**                          1          **Macedonia**                      0
P.Nielsen [71]

*26 April 1995, Yerevan*                                             40,000
**Armenia**                          0          **Spain**                          2
                                                Amavisca [48], Goicoechea [62]

*10 May 1995, Yerevan*                                               12,500
**Armenia**                          2          **Macedonia**                      2
Grigoryan [22], Shakhgeidian [51]               Hristov [59], Markovski [70]

*7 June 1995, Skopje*                                    *Played behind closed doors*
**Macedonia**                        0          **Belgium**                        5
                                                Grun [15], Scifo [18, 60],
                                                Schepens [28], Versavel [43]

*7 June 1995, Seville*                                               20,000
**Spain**                            1          **Armenia**                        0
Hierro [63 pen]

*7 June 1995, Copenhagen*                                            40,199
**Denmark**                          4          **Cyprus**                         0
Vilfort [47, 52], B.Laudrup [59],
M.Laudrup [75]

28

*16 August 1995, Yerevan*                                                                22,000
**Armenia**                          0        **Denmark**                                2
                                              M.Laudrup [32],
                                              A.Nielsen [46]


*6 September 1995, Brussels*                                                             40,000
**Belgium**                          1        **Denmark**                                3
Grun [25]                                     M.Laudrup [19], Beck [21],
                                              Vilfort [65]


*6 September 1995, Skopje*                    *Played behind closed doors*
**Macedonia**                        1        **Armenia**                                2
Micevski [10]                                 Grigoryan [61],
                                              Shakhgeidian [78]


*6 September 1995, Granada*                                                              30,000
**Spain**                            6        **Cyprus**                                 0
Guerrero [45], Alfonso [51],
Pizzi [75, 80], Hierro [78],
Caminero [83]


*7 October 1995, Yerevan*                                                                5,000
**Armenia**                          0        **Belgium**                                2
                                              Nilis [28, 39]


*11 October 1995, Limassol*                                                             15,000
**Cyprus**                           1        **Macedonia**                              1
Agathocleous [90]                             Perides [o.g. 30]


*11 October 1995, Copenhagen*                                                           40,262
**Denmark**                          1        **Spain**                                  1
Vilfort [47]                                  Hierro [17 pen]


*15 November 1995, Limassol*                                                            10,000
**Cyprus**                           1        **Belgium**                                1
Agathocleous [18]                             De Bilde [76]


*15 November 1995, Copenhagen*                                                          40,208
**Denmark**                          3        **Armenia**                                1
Schjonberg [19], Beck [35],                   Petrossian [47]
M.Laudrup [58]


*15 November 1995, Elche*                                                               34,000
**Spain**                            3        **Macedonia**                              0
Kiko [8], Manjarin [73],
Caminero [79]

# FINAL TABLE

|   |         | P  | W | D | L | F  | A  | Pts |
|---|---------|----|---|---|---|----|----|-----|
| 1 | **SPAIN** | 10 | 8 | 2 | 0 | 25 | 4  | 26  |
| 2 | **DENMARK** | 10 | 6 | 3 | 1 | 19 | 9  | 21  |
| 3 | Belgium | 10 | 4 | 3 | 3 | 16 | 12 | 15  |
| 4 | Macedonia | 10 | 1 | 4 | 5 | 9  | 18 | 7   |
| 5 | Cyprus | 10 | 1 | 4 | 5 | 5  | 19 | 7   |
| 6 | Armenia | 10 | 1 | 2 | 7 | 5  | 17 | 5   |

Spain and Denmark qualify for Euro 96 finals.

# TOP SCORERS

| | |
|---|---|
| Vilfort [Denmark] | 5 |
| Degryse [Belgium] | 4 |
| M.Laudrup [Denmark] | 4 |
| Hierro [Spain] | 4 |
| Julio Salinas [Spain] | 3 |
| Djurovski [Macedonia] | 3 |
| Agathocleous [Cyprus] | 3 |

# GROUP THREE

At last the fanatical football country of Turkey came of age, chasing World Cup finalists Switzerland all the way to the finishing post and leaving fancied Sweden trailing in their wake in this five-team group. It is the first time in the finals for both teams, with the Swiss capturing their place in October. World Cup semi-finalists Sweden never recovered from early defeats by the two group leaders and finished with just nine points.

*7 September 1994, Budapest*                                             10,000
**Hungary**                                    2       Turkey                    2
Kiprich [4], Halmai [45]                               Hakan [66],
                                                       Bulent Korkmaz [70]

*7 September 1994, Reykjavik*                                            15,000
**Iceland**                                    0       Sweden                    1
                                                       Ingesson [37]

*12 October 1994, Berne*                                                24,000
**Switzerland**                                4       Sweden                    2
Ohrel [37], Blomqvist [o.g. 63],                       K.Andersson [5],
Sforza [80], Turkyilmaz [82]                           Dahlin [61]

*12 October 1994, Istanbul*                                             20,000
**Turkey**                                     5       Iceland                   0
Saffet [12, 29], Hakan [30, 60],
Yalcin [64]

*16 November 1994, Stockholm*                                           27,571
**Sweden**                                     2       Hungary                   0
Brolin [43], Dahlin [70]

*16 November 1994, Lausanne*                                            15,800
**Switzerland**                                1       Iceland                   0
Bickel [45]

*14 December 1994, Istanbul*                                            25,000
**Turkey**                                     1       Switzerland               2
Recep [40]                                             Koller [7], Bickel [15]

*29 March 1995, Budapest*                                               13,000
**Hungary**                                    2       Switzerland               2
Kiprich [50], Illes [72]                               Subiat [73, 85]

*29 March 1995, Istanbul*          20,000
**Turkey** 2    **Sweden** 1
Emre [65], Sergen [75]    K.Andersson [23]

*26 April 1995, Budapest*          10,000
**Hungary** 1    **Sweden** 0
Halmai [2]

*26 April 1995, Berne*          24,000
**Switzerland** 1    **Turkey** 2
Hottiger [38]    Hakan [17], Ogun [55]

*1 June 1995, Stockholm*          25,676
**Sweden** 1    **Iceland** 1
Brolin [16 pen]    A.Gunnlaugsson [3]

*11 June 1995, Reykjavik*          4,500
**Iceland** 2    **Hungary** 1
Bergsson [61], S.Jonsson [67]    Vincze [20]

*16 August 1995, Reykjavik*          10,000
**Iceland** 0    **Switzerland** 2
   Knup [3], Turkyilmaz [13]

*6 September 1995, Gothenburg*          18,500
**Sweden** 0    **Switzerland** 0

*6 September 1995, Istanbul*          35,000
**Turkey** 2    **Hungary** 0
Hakan [9, 31]

*11 October 1995, Reykjavik*          2,308
**Iceland** 0    **Turkey** 0

*11 October 1995, Zurich*          21,000
**Switzerland** 3    **Hungary** 0
Turkyilmaz [23], Sforza [56],
Ohrel [89]

*15 November 1995, Budapest*          3,000
**Hungary** 1    **Iceland** 0
Illes [55]

*15 November 1995, Stockholm*          11,700
**Sweden** 2    **Turkey** 2
Alexandersson [24],    Hakan [62], Ertugrul [72]
J.Pettersen [63]

# FINAL TABLE

|   |             | P | W | D | L | F  | A  | Pts |
|---|-------------|---|---|---|---|----|----|-----|
| 1 | **SWITZERLAND** | 8 | 5 | 2 | 1 | 15 | 7  | 17  |
| 2 | **TURKEY**      | 8 | 4 | 3 | 1 | 16 | 8  | 15  |
| 3 | Sweden          | 8 | 2 | 3 | 3 | 9  | 10 | 9   |
| 4 | Hungary         | 8 | 2 | 2 | 4 | 7  | 13 | 8   |
| 5 | Iceland         | 8 | 1 | 2 | 5 | 3  | 12 | 5   |

Switzerland and Turkey qualify for Euro 96 finals.

# TOP SCORERS

| | |
|---|---|
| Hakan [Turkey] | 7 |
| Turkyilmaz [Switzerland] | 3 |
| Halmai [Hungary] | 3 |

# GROUP FOUR

From the moment Croatia beat Italy away from home in November 1994, the rest of the football world stood up and took notice. The Croatians retained their edge over the Italians with a 1-1 home draw and would have won the group comfortably but for an inexplicable hiccup when they lost 1-0 in Ukraine as if to show that they are vulnerable. Italy had their early worries, as usual, when they drew their opening game in Slovenia, and then lost to Croatia, but, in the end, they had a cushion of seven points over Lithuania, leaving coach Arrigo Sacchi happy if not the tifosi.

| | | | |
|---|---|---|---|
| *4 September 1994, Tallinn* | | | 1,500 |
| **Estonia** | 0 | **Croatia** | 2 |
| | | Suker [45, 69] | |

| | | | |
|---|---|---|---|
| *7 September 1994, Maribor* | | | 18,000 |
| **Slovenia** | 1 | **Italy** | 1 |
| Udovic [14] | | Costacurta [15] | |

| | | | |
|---|---|---|---|
| *7 September 1994, Kiev* | | | 25,000 |
| **Ukraine** | 0 | **Lithuania** | 2 |
| | | Ivanauskas [53], | |
| | | Skarbalius [61] | |

| | | | |
|---|---|---|---|
| *8 October 1994, Tallinn* | | | 4,000 |
| **Estonia** | 0 | **Italy** | 2 |
| | | Panucci [20], Casiraghi [77] | |

| | | | |
|---|---|---|---|
| *9 October 1994, Zagreb* | | | 12,000 |
| **Croatia** | 2 | **Lithuania** | 0 |
| Jerkan [56], Kozniku [81] | | | |

| | | | |
|---|---|---|---|
| *12 October 1994, Kiev* | | | 12,000 |
| **Ukraine** | 0 | **Slovenia** | 0 |

| | | | |
|---|---|---|---|
| *13 November 1994, Kiev* | | | 500 |
| **Ukraine** | 3 | **Estonia** | 0 |
| Konovalov [29], Kirs [o.g. 45], | | | |
| Guseinov [72] | | | |

| | | | |
|---|---|---|---|
| *16 November 1994, Palermo* | | | 33,570 |
| **Italy** | 1 | **Croatia** | 2 |
| D.Baggio [90] | | Suker [32, 60] | |

| | | | |
|---|---|---|---|
| *16 November 1994, Maribor* | | | 2,500 |
| **Slovenia** | 1 | **Lithuania** | 2 |
| Zahovic [55] | | Sukristovas [64], Zuta [87] | |

*25 March 1995, Salerno*                                      35,000
**Italy**                         **4**      **Estonia**                    **1**
Zola [45, 65], Albertini [58],               Reim [71]
Ravanelli [82]

*25 March 1995, Zagreb*                                       30,000
**Croatia**                       **4**      **Ukraine**                    **0**
Boban [13], Suker [21, 79],
Prosinecki [71]

*29 March 1995, Vilnius*                                       9,500
**Lithuania**                     **0**      **Croatia**                    **0**

*29 March 1995, Maribor*                                       6,000
**Slovenia**                      **3**      **Estonia**                    **0**
Zahovic [39], Gliha [53],
Kokol [90]

*29 March 1995, Kiev*                                         10,000
**Ukraine**                       **0**      **Italy**                      **2**
                                             Lombardo [11],
                                             Zola [38]

*26 April 1995, Zagreb*                                       25,000
**Croatia**                       **2**      **Slovenia**                   **0**
Prosinecki [17], Suker [90]

*26 April 1995, Tallinn*                                         500
**Estonia**                       **0**      **Ukraine**                    **1**
                                             Guseinov [17]

*26 April 1995, Vilnius*                                      15,000
**Lithuania**                     **0**      **Italy**                      **1**
                                             Zola [11]

*7 June 1995, Vilnius*                                        6,000
**Lithuania**                     **2**      **Slovenia**                   **1**
Stonkus [47], Suika [70]                     Gliha [82]

*11 June 1995, Kiev*                                          8,500
**Ukraine**                       **1**      **Croatia**                    **0**
Kalitvintsev [13]

*11 June 1995, Tallinn*                                       2,000
**Estonia**                       **1**      **Slovenia**                   **3**
Reim [28]                                    Novak [37, 68],
                                             Zahovic [76]

*16 August 1995, Tallinn*                    *1,500*
**Estonia**                    0      **Lithuania**                    1
                                      Maciulevicius [48]


*3 September 1995, Rijeka*                   *25,000*
**Croatia**                    7      **Estonia**                    1
Mladenovic [3],                       Reim [17]
Suker [19 pen, 58, 90],
Boksic [29], Boban [42],
Stimac [81]


*6 September 1995, Udine*                    *30,000*
**Italy**                      1      **Slovenia**                    0
Ravanelli [13]


*6 September 1995, Vilnius*                   *5,000*
**Lithuania**                  1      **Ukraine**                     3
Maciulevicius [16]                    Guseinov [66, 71], Gusin [84]


*8 October 1995, Split*                      *40,000*
**Croatia**                    1      **Italy**                       1
Suker [48 pen]                        Albertini [29]


*11 October 1995, Vilnius*                   *2,000*
**Lithuania**                  5      **Estonia**                     0
Maciulevicius [8], Suika [13, 39],
Slekys [44], Ivanauskas [61]


*11 October 1995, Ljubljana*                 *4,000*
**Slovenia**                   3      **Ukraine**                     2
Udovic [50, 90], Zahovic [73]         Skrypnyk [24],
                                      Guseinov [44]


*11 November 1995, Bari*                     *50,000*
**Italy**                      3      **Ukraine**                     1
Ravanelli [21, 48], Maldini [54]      Polunin [19]


*15 November 1995, Reggio Emilia*            *30,000*
**Italy**                      4      **Lithuania**                   0
Stonkus [o.g. 51], Zola [65, 80, 82]


*15 November 1995, Ljubljana*                *15,000*
**Slovenia**                   1      **Croatia**                     2
Gliha [36]                            Suker [41 pen], Jurcevic [55]

# FINAL TABLE

|   |          | P  | W | D | L  | F  | A  | Pts |
|---|----------|----|---|---|----|----|----|-----|
| 1 | **CROATIA**  | 10 | 7 | 2 | 1  | 22 | 5  | 23  |
| 2 | **ITALY**    | 10 | 7 | 2 | 1  | 20 | 6  | 23  |
| 3 | Lithuania | 10 | 5 | 1 | 4  | 13 | 12 | 16  |
| 4 | Ukraine   | 10 | 4 | 1 | 5  | 11 | 15 | 13  |
| 5 | Slovenia  | 10 | 3 | 2 | 5  | 13 | 13 | 11  |
| 6 | Estonia   | 10 | 0 | 0 | 10 | 3  | 31 | 0   |

Croatia and Italy qualify for Euro 96 finals.

# TOP SCORERS

| | |
|---|---|
| Suker [Croatia] | 12 |
| Zola [Italy] | 7 |
| Guseinov [Ukraine] | 5 |
| Ravanelli [Italy] | 4 |
| Zahovic [Slovenia] | 4 |
| Suika [Lithuania] | 3 |
| Maciulevicius [Lithuania] | 3 |
| Reim [Estonia] | 3 |
| Udovic [Slovenia] | 3 |
| Gliha [Slovenia] | 3 |

# GROUP FIVE

This was a group in turmoil when the long-time leaders and World Cup finalists Norway suddenly fell by the wayside. The table was finally decided in a magnificent climax as Holland beat Norway 3-0 to take them into second place and a play-off against the Irish, which they won thanks to two goals from Kluivert at Anfield. The Dutch would have settled for that after losing sensationally 1-0 to Belarus. They had all but given it up until they heard that the Czechs had gone one better and lost to Luxembourg. The Czechs recovered magnificently from that reverse, drawing in Norway, beating the Norwegians at home, Belarus away and Luxembourg at home to win the group by a solitary point, with Holland and Norway level on 20.

*6 September 1994, Ostrava*                                             10,226
**Czech Republic**              6          **Malta**                        1
Smejkal [6 pen], Kubik [32],               Laferla [73]
Siegl [35, 60, 78], Berger [86]

*7 September 1994, Luxembourg*                                          8,200
**Luxembourg**                  0          **Holland**                      4
                                           Roy [23], R. de Boer [65, 67],
                                           Jonk [90]

*7 September 1994, Oslo*                                                16,739
**Norway**                      1          **Belarus**                      0
Frigaard [88]

*12 October 1994, Valletta*                                            4,000
**Malta**                       0          **Czech Republic**               0

*12 October 1994, Oslo*                                                22,293
**Norway**                      1          **Holland**                      1
Rekdal [52 pen]                            Roy [21]

*12 October 1994, Minsk*                                               5,000
**Belarus**                     2          **Luxembourg**                   0
Romashchenko [67],
Gerasimets [76]

*16 November 1994, Rotterdam*                                          40,000
**Holland**                     0          **Czech Republic**               0

*16 November 1994, Minsk*                                              8,000
**Belarus**                     0          **Norway**                       4
                                           Berg [34], Leonhardsen [40],
                                           Bohinen [52], Rekdal [83]

38

*14 December 1994, Valletta*                          *9,000*
**Malta**                      0      **Norway**                   1
                                      Fjortoft [10]

*14 December 1994, Rotterdam*                         *26,000*
**Holland**                    5      **Luxembourg**               0
Mulder [7], Roy [17], Jonk [40],
R. de Boer [52], Seedorf [90]

*22 February 1995, Valletta*                          *6,000*
**Malta**                      0      **Luxembourg**               1
                                      Cardoni [55]

*29 March 1995, Luxembourg*                           *3,000*
**Luxembourg**                 0      **Norway**                   2
                                      Leonhardsen [35],
                                      Aase [77]

*29 March 1995, Rotterdam*                            *34,000*
**Holland**                    4      **Malta**                    0
Seedorf [39], Bergkamp [77 pen],
Winter [80], Kluivert [85]

*29 March 1995, Ostrava*                              *5,549*
**Czech Republic**             4      **Belarus**                  2
Kadlec [5], Berger [17, 62],          Gerasimets [44 pen],
Kuka [68]                             Gurinovich [88]

*26 April 1995, Oslo*                                 *15,124*
**Norway**                     5      **Luxembourg**               0
Jakobsen [9], Fjortoft [10],
Brattbakk [23], Berg [46],
Rekdal [49]

*26 April 1995, Minsk*                                *13,000*
**Belarus**                    1      **Malta**                    1
Taikov [57]                           Carabott [70]

*26 April 1995, Prague*                               *20,000*
**Czech Republic**             3      **Holland**                  1
Skuhravy [49], Nemecek [58],          Jonk [17]
Berger [62]

*7 June 1995, Minsk*                                  *12,000*
**Belarus**                    1      **Holland**                  0
Gerasimets [27]

*7 June 1995, Oslo*         *15,000*
**Norway**    2    **Malta**    0
Fjortoft [43], Flo [88]

*7 June 1995, Luxembourg*      *1,500*
**Luxembourg**    1    **Czech Republic**    0
Hellers [89]

*16 August 1995, Oslo*      *22,054*
**Norway**    1    **Czech Republic**    1
Berg [27]    Suchoparek [84]

*6 September 1995, Prague*      *19,500*
**Czech Republic**    2    **Norway**    0
Skuhravy [6 pen], Drulak [87]

*6 September 1995, Rotterdam*      *17,000*
**Holland**    1    **Belarus**    0
Mulder [83]

*6 September 1995, Luxembourg*      *4,700*
**Luxembourg**    1    **Malta**    0
Holtz [44]

*7 October 1995, Minsk*      *9,500*
**Belarus**    0    **Czech Republic**    2
   Frydek [25], Berger [84]

*11 October 1995, Luxembourg*      *4,500*
**Luxembourg**    0    **Belarus**    0

*11 October 1995, Valletta*      *8,000*
**Malta**    0    **Holland**    4
   Overmars [52, 61, 65], Seedorf [80]

*12 November 1995, Valletta*      *2,500*
**Malta**    0    **Belarus**    2
   Gerasimets [82, 85]

*15 November 1995, Prague*      *20,239*
**Czech Republic**    3    **Luxembourg**    0
Drulak [35, 46], Berger [57]

*15 November 1995, Rotterdam*      *49,000*
**Holland**    3    **Norway**    0
Seedorf [59], Mulder [86],
Overmars [89]

# FINAL TABLE

| | | P | W | D | L | F | A | Pts |
|---|---|---|---|---|---|---|---|---|
| 1 | **CZECH REPUBLIC** | 10 | 6 | 3 | 1 | 21 | 6 | 21 |
| 2 | **HOLLAND** | 10 | 6 | 2 | 2 | 23 | 5 | 20 |
| 3 | Norway | 10 | 6 | 2 | 2 | 17 | 7 | 20 |
| 4 | Belarus | 10 | 3 | 2 | 5 | 8 | 13 | 11 |
| 5 | Luxembourg | 10 | 3 | 1 | 6 | 3 | 21 | 10 |
| 6 | Malta | 10 | 0 | 2 | 8 | 2 | 22 | 2 |

Czech Republic qualify for Euro 96 finals.
Holland play Republic of Ireland in a play-off in Liverpool.

# TOP SCORERS

| | |
|---|---|
| Berger [Czech Republic] | 6 |
| Gerasimets [Belarus] | 5 |
| Overmars [Holland] | 4 |
| Seedorf [Holland] | 4 |
| Drulak [Czech Republic] | 3 |
| Siegl [Czech Republic] | 3 |
| Mulder [Holland] | 3 |
| Jonk [Holland] | 3 |
| Roy [Holland] | 3 |
| R. de Boer [Holland] | 3 |
| Fjortoft [Norway] | 3 |
| Berg [Norway] | 3 |
| Rekdal [Norway] | 3 |

# GROUP SIX

This always looked to be a two-horse race, but who would have predicted that the Irish would slip from certain direct qualification to a disastrous losing play-off against Holland. Coasting along, the Irish lost their way after beating Portugal. They drew in Liechtenstein, lost at home and away to Austria and, after scraping a win against Latvia, were thrashed by group winners Portugal. Portugal, despite the loss to the Irish, were never in trouble and finished with an impressive 23 points, six ahead of the two Irelands who finished level on 17. Portugal impressed throughout after winning their first two games away from home in Northern Ireland and Latvia.

*20 April 1994, Belfast*                                                      7,000
**Northern Ireland**               4        **Liechtenstein**                   1
Quinn [4, 33], Lomas [25],                   Hasler [84]
Dowie [48]

*7 September 1994, Belfast*                                                   6,000
**Northern Ireland**               1        **Portugal**                        2
Quinn [58 pen]                               Rui Costa [8], Oliveira [81]

*7 September 1994, Eschen*                                                    5,800
**Liechtenstein**                  0        **Austria**                         4
                                             Polster [18, 45, 79],
                                             Aigner [22]

*7 September 1994, Riga*                                                      2,200
**Latvia**                         0        **Republic of Ireland**            3
                                             Aldridge [16, 75 pen],
                                             Sheridan [29]

*9 October 1994, Riga*                                                       2,000
**Latvia**                         1        **Portugal**                        3
Milevsky [87]                                Joao Pinto II [33, 72],
                                             Figo [73]

*12 October 1994, Vienna*                                                    20,000
**Austria**                        1        **Northern Ireland**               2
Polster [25 pen]                             Gillespie [3], Gray [36]

*12 October 1994, Dublin*                                                    32,980
**Republic of Ireland**            4        **Liechtenstein**                   0
Coyne [2, 4], Quinn [30, 82]

*13 November 1994, Lisbon*                                                   50,000
**Portugal**                       1        **Austria**                         0
Figo [67]

42

*15 November 1994, Eschen*     *1,300*

**Liechtenstein** 0     **Latvia** 1

Babichev [14]


*16 November 1994, Belfast*     *10,336*

**Northern Ireland** 0     **Republic of Ireland** 4

Aldridge [6], Keane [11],
Sheridan [38], Townsend [54]


*18 December 1994, Lisbon*     *30,000*

**Portugal** 8     **Liechtenstein** 0

Domingos [2, 11], Oceano [45],
Joao Pinto II [56], Fernando Couto [72],
Folha [74], Paulo Alves [75, 79]


*29 March 1995, Salzburg*     *5,500*

**Austria** 5     **Latvia** 0

Herzog [17, 59],
Pfeifenberger [40], Polster [71 pen, 90]


*29 March 1995, Dublin*     *32,200*

**Republic of Ireland** 1     **Northern Ireland** 1

Quinn [47]     Dowie [72]


*26 April 1995, Salzburg*     *5,700*

**Austria** 7     **Liechtenstein** 0

Kuhbauer [8], Polster [11, 53],
Sabitzer [17], Purk [84], Hutter [87, 90]


*26 April 1995, Dublin*     *33,000*

**Republic of Ireland** 1     **Portugal** 0

Vitor Baia [o.g. 45]


*26 April 1995, Riga*     *1,560*

**Latvia** 0     **Northern Ireland** 1

Dowie [67 pen]


*3 June 1995, Eschen*     *4,500*

**Liechtenstein** 0     **Republic of Ireland** 0


*3 June 1995, Oporto*     *40,000*

**Portugal** 3     **Latvia** 2

Figo [5], Secretario [19], Domingos [21]     Rimkus [51, 85]


*7 June 1995, Belfast*     *6,000*

**Northern Ireland** 1     **Latvia** 2

Dowie [44]     Zeiberlins [59], Astafayev [62]

*11 June 1995, Dublin*                                          33,000
**Republic of Ireland**                1       **Austria**                         3
Houghton [67]                                  Polster [70, 80], Ogris [74]

*15 August 1995, Eschen*                                        3,500
**Liechtenstein**                      0       **Portugal**                        7
                                               Domingos [25],
                                               Paulinho Santos [33],
                                               Rui Costa [41, 71 pen],
                                               Paulo Alves [67, 73, 90]

*16 August 1995, Riga*                                          2,000
**Latvia**                             3       **Austria**                         2
Rimkus [13, 59], Zeiberlins [88]               Polster [68], Ramusch [78]

*3 September 1995, Oporto*                                      50,000
**Portugal**                           1       **Northern Ireland**                1
Domingos [47]                                  Hughes [66]

*6 September 1995, Vienna*                                      24,000
**Austria**                            3       **Republic of Ireland**             1
Stoger [3, 64, 77]                             McGrath [74]

*6 September 1995, Riga*                                        3,800
**Latvia**                             1       **Liechtenstein**                   0
Zeiberlins [83]

*11 October 1995, Vienna*                                      40,000
**Austria**                            1       **Portugal**                        1
Stoger [21]                                    Paulinho Santos [49]

*11 October 1995, Vaduz*                                        1,100
**Liechtenstein**                      0       **Northern Ireland**                4
                                               O'Neill [36], McMahon [49],
                                               Quinn [55], Gray [72]

*11 October 1995, Dublin*                                      33,000
**Republic of Ireland**                2       **Latvia**                          1
Aldridge [61 pen, 64]                          Rimkus [78]

*15 November 1995, Belfast*                                     8,400
**Northern Ireland**                   5       **Austria**                         3
O'Neill [27, 78], Dowie [32], Hunter [53],     Schopp [56], Stumpf [70],
Gray [64]                                      Welt [81]

*15 November 1995, Lisbon*                                              *80,000*
**Portugal**                    **3**      **Republic of Ireland**          **0**
Rui Costa [59], Helder [78],
Cadete [89]

## FINAL TABLE

|   |                       | P  | W | D | L | F  | A  | Pts |
|---|-----------------------|----|---|---|---|----|----|-----|
| 1 | **PORTUGAL**          | 10 | 7 | 2 | 1 | 29 | 7  | 23  |
| 2 | **REPUBLIC OF IRELAND** | 10 | 5 | 2 | 3 | 17 | 11 | 17  |
| 3 | Northern Ireland      | 10 | 5 | 2 | 3 | 20 | 15 | 17  |
| 4 | Austria               | 10 | 5 | 1 | 4 | 29 | 14 | 16  |
| 5 | Latvia                | 10 | 4 | 0 | 6 | 11 | 20 | 12  |
| 6 | Liechtenstein         | 10 | 0 | 1 | 9 | 1  | 40 | 1   |

Portugal qualify for Euro 96 finals.
Republic of Ireland play Holland in a play-off in Liverpool.

## TOP SCORERS

| | |
|---|---|
| Polster [Austria]             | 11 |
| Aldridge [Republic of Ireland] | 5  |
| Domingos [Portugal]           | 5  |
| Dowie [Northern Ireland]      | 5  |
| Paulo Alves [Portugal]        | 5  |
| Rimkus [Latvia]               | 5  |
| Stoger [Austria]              | 4  |
| Rui Costa [Portugal]          | 4  |
| Quinn [Northern Ireland]      | 4  |
| Joao Pinto II [Portugal]      | 3  |
| Figo [Portugal]               | 3  |
| Quinn [Republic of Ireland]   | 3  |
| Gray [Northern Ireland]       | 3  |
| O'Neill [Northern Ireland]    | 3  |
| Zeiberlins [Latvia]           | 3  |

# GROUP SEVEN

Germany and Bulgaria went head-to-head from the off, with Bulgaria taking maximum points from their opening six games, including a dramatic comeback against the Germans when they won 3-2. But their chances of winning the group gradually slipped away as they drew in Albania, of all places, and went down in Georgia. It meant they went into the last round of matches level on points with Germany, but a 3-1 defeat and two goals from Jurgen Klinsmann put them in their place, albeit seven points ahead of third-placed Georgia. Germany's only other blemish was a home draw against second from bottom Wales, adding fuel to the critics who claim that the Germans are no longer the force they were.

*7 September 1994, Cardiff* 15,791
**Wales** 2 **Albania** 0
Coleman [9], Giggs [67]

*7 September 1994, Tbilisi* 40,000
**Georgia** 0 **Moldova** 1
Oprea [40]

*12 October 1994, Sofia* 45,000
**Bulgaria** 2 **Georgia** 0
Kostadinov [55, 62]

*12 October 1994, Chisinau* 12,000
**Moldova** 3 **Wales** 2
Belous [8], Secu [28], Speed [4], Blake [70]
Pogorelov [78]

*16 November 1994, Tirana* 20,000
**Albania** 1 **Germany** 2
Zmijani [34] Klinsmann [18], Kirsten [46]

*16 November 1994, Sofia* 50,000
**Bulgaria** 4 **Moldova** 1
Stoichkov [45, 85], Balakov [65], Clescenko [60]
Kostadinov [87]

*16 November 1994, Tbilisi* 45,000
**Georgia** 5 **Wales** 0
Ketsbaia [31, 49], Kinkladze [41],
Gogrichiani [59], S.Arveladze [67]

*14 December 1994, Tirana* 15,000
**Albania** 0 **Georgia** 1
S.Arveladze [19]

*14 December 1994, Cardiff*                                          20,000
**Wales**                           0       **Bulgaria**                  3
                                            Ivanov [5], Kostadinov [16],
                                            Stoichkov [51]


*14 December 1994, Chisinau*                                         20,000
**Moldova**                         0       **Germany**                   3
                                            Kirsten [7], Klinsmann [38],
                                            Matthaus [72]


*18 December 1994, Kaiserslautern*                                   20,310
**Germany**                         2       **Albania**                   1
Matthaus [8 pen], Klinsmann [17]            Rraklli [58]


*29 March 1995, Tirana*                                              20,000
**Albania**                         3       **Moldova**                   0
Kushta [32, 78], Kacaj [42]


*29 March 1995, Sofia*                                               60,000
**Bulgaria**                        3       **Wales**                     1
Balakov [37], Penev [70, 82]                Saunders [83]


*29 March 1995, Tbilisi*                                             75,000
**Georgia**                         0       **Germany**                   2
                                            Klinsmann [24, 45]


*26 April 1995, Dusseldorf*                                          45,000
**Germany**                         1       **Wales**                     1
Herrlich [42]                               Saunders [8]


*26 April 1995, Tbilisi*                                             20,000
**Georgia**                         2       **Albania**                   0
S.Arveladze [2], Ketsbaia [42]


*26 April 1995, Chisinau*                                            17,000
**Moldova**                         0       **Bulgaria**                  3
                                            Balakov [30], Stoichkov [57, 67]


*7 June 1995, Chisinau*                                              7,000
**Moldova**                         2       **Albania**                   3
Curtianu [12], Clescenko [17]               Kushta [7], Bellai [25],
                                            Vata [71]


*7 June 1995, Sofia*                                                 50,000
**Bulgaria**                        3       **Germany**                   2
Stoichkov [45 pen, 66 pen],                 Klinsmann [18], Strunz [44]
Kostadinov [69]


47

*7 June 1995, Cardiff*                                          *6,500*
**Wales**                          0         **Georgia**              1
                                             Kinkladze [72]


*6 September 1995, Tirana*                                     *10,000*
**Albania**                        1         **Bulgaria**             1
Rraklli [16]                                 Stoichkov [8]

*6 September 1995, Nurnberg*                                   *40,000*
**Germany**                        4         **Georgia**              1
Moller [39], Ziege [57], Kirsten [62],       Ketsbaia [28]
Babbel [72]

*6 September 1995, Cardiff*                                     *5,000*
**Wales**                          1         **Moldova**              0
Speed [55]

*7 October 1995, Sofia*                                       *35,000*
**Bulgaria**                       3         **Albania**              0
Lechkov [15], Kostadinov [80, 82]

*8 October 1995, Leverkusen*                                  *18,300*
**Germany**                        6         **Moldova**              1
Stroyenko [o.g. 16], Helmer [18],            Rebesha [82]
Sammer [24, 71], Moller [47, 61]

*11 October 1995, Tbilisi*                                    *45,000*
**Georgia**                        2         **Bulgaria**             1
S.Arveladze [3], Kinkladze [48 pen]          Stoichkov [88]

*11 October 1995, Cardiff*                                    *25,000*
**Wales**                          1         **Germany**              2
Helmer [o.g. 78]                             Melville [o.g. 75],
                                             Klinsmann [80]

*15 November 1995, Tirana*                                     *5,500*
**Albania**                        1         **Wales**                1
Kushta [4]                                   Pembridge [43]

*15 November 1995, Berlin*                                    *75,841*
**Germany**                        3         **Bulgaria**             1
Klinsmann [50, 76 pen], Hassler [56]         Stoichkov [47]

*15 November 1995, Chisinau*                                   *9,000*
**Moldova**                        3         **Georgia**              2
Testemicianu [3], Miterev [20, 61]           Dzyamashia [65],
                                             Kulibaba [o.g. 79]

48

# FINAL TABLE

| | | P | W | D | L | F | A | Pts |
|---|---|---|---|---|---|---|---|---|
| 1 | **GERMANY** | 10 | 8 | 1 | 1 | 27 | 10 | 25 |
| 2 | **BULGARIA** | 10 | 7 | 1 | 2 | 24 | 10 | 22 |
| 3 | Georgia | 10 | 5 | 0 | 5 | 14 | 13 | 15 |
| 4 | Moldova | 10 | 3 | 0 | 7 | 11 | 27 | 9 |
| 5 | Albania | 10 | 2 | 2 | 6 | 10 | 16 | 8 |
| 6 | Wales | 10 | 2 | 2 | 6 | 9 | 19 | 8 |

Germany and Bulgaria qualify for Euro 96 finals.

# TOP SCORERS

| | |
|---|---|
| Stoichkov [Bulgaria] | 10 |
| Klinsmann [Germany] | 9 |
| Kostadinov [Bulgaria] | 7 |
| S.Arveladze [Georgia] | 4 |
| Ketsbaia [Georgia] | 4 |
| Kushta [Albania] | 4 |
| Kirsten [Germany] | 3 |
| Moller [Germany] | 3 |
| Balakov [Bulgaria] | 3 |
| Kinkladze [Georgia] | 3 |

# GROUP EIGHT

Impressive Russia remained unbeaten throughout, joining France and Spain, and never looked in trouble after drawing in Scotland and winning in Greece in their first two away games. The former winners dropped only one other point, another draw with the Scots, and were able to watch the battle below them with distant interest. World Cup finalists Greece were second favourites, especially after beating Scotland, but while they fell away the Scots remained firm, and clever fixture-planning left them a run-in with away games in San Marino and Faroe Isles and home fixtures against Greece, Finland and San Marino. They won the lot to finish five points clear of the disappointing Greeks.

*7 September 1994, Helsinki*                                                          12,845
**Finland**                              0        **Scotland**                              2
                                                  Shearer [29], Collins [66]

*7 September 1994, Toftir*                                                            2,412
**Faroe Isles**                          1        **Greece**                                5
Apostolakis [o.g. 89]                             Saravakos [12], Tsalouhidis [17, 87],
                                                  Alexandris [55, 60]

*12 October 1994, Salonika*                                                          30,000
**Greece**                               4        **Finland**                               0
Markos [23], Batista [69], Mahlas [76, 90]

*12 October 1994, Glasgow*                                                           20,885
**Scotland**                             5        **Faroe Isles**                           1
McGinlay [4], Booth [34],                         Muller [75]
Collins [40, 72], McKinlay [61]

*12 October 1994, Moscow*                                                            20,000
**Russia**                               4        **San Marino**                            0
Karpin [43], Kolyvanov [64],
Nikiforov [65], Radchenko [67]

*16 November 1994, Helsinki*                                                         2,240
**Finland**                              5        **Faroe Isles**                           0
Sumiala [37], Litmanen [53 pen, 72],
Paatelainen [75, 85]

*16 November 1994, Athens*                                                           15,000
**Greece**                               2        **San Marino**                            0
Mahlas [20], Frantzeskos [84]

*16 November 1994, Glasgow*                                                          31,254
**Scotland**                             1        **Russia**                                1
Booth [19]                                        Radchenko [26]

*14 December 1994, Helsinki*                                        3,140
**Finland**                              4     **San Marino**             1
Paatelainen [24, 30, 86, 90]                   Della Valle [34]

*18 December 1994, Athens*                                         20,310
**Greece**                               1     **Scotland**               0
Apostolakis [18 pen]

*29 March 1995, Serraville*                                         1,000
**San Marino**                           0     **Finland**                2
                                               Litmanen [45], Sumiala [65]

*29 March 1995, Moscow*                                            25,000
**Russia**                               0     **Scotland**               0

*26 April 1995, Salonika*                                          30,000
**Greece**                               0     **Russia**                 3
                                               Nikiforov [36],
                                               Zagorakis [o.g. 78],
                                               Beschastnykh [79]

*26 April 1995, Serraville*                                         2,738
**San Marino**                           0     **Scotland**               2
                                               Collins [19],
                                               Calderwood [85]

*26 April 1995, Toftir*                                             1,000
**Faroe Isles**                          0     **Finland**                4
                                               Hjelm [55], Paatelainen [75],
                                               Lindberg [78], Helin [83]

*6 May 1995, Moscow*                                                9,500
**Russia**                               3     **Faroe Isles**            0
Kechinov [53], Pisarev [72],
Mukhamadiev [80]

*25 May 1995, Toftir*                                               3,452
**Faroe Isles**                          3     **San Marino**             0
J.C. Hansen [7], J.E. Rasmussen [9],
T. Jonsson [62]

*7 June 1995, Serraville*                                           1,400
**San Marino**                           0     **Russia**                 7
                                               Dobrovolski [20 pen], Gobbi [o.g. 38],
                                               Kiryakov [48], Shalimov [49],
                                               Beschastnykh [59], Kolyvanov [64],
                                               Cheryshev [86]

*7 June 1995, Toftir*                                                      *3,881*

**Faroe Isles**                       0        **Scotland**                       2

                                               McKinlay [25], McGinlay [29]


*11 June 1995, Helsinki*                                                   *7,000*

**Finland**                           2        **Greece**                         1

Litmanen [44 pen], Hjelm [55]                  Nikolaidis [6]


*16 August 1995, Helsinki*                                                *14,200*

**Finland**                           0        **Russia**                         6

                                               Kulkov [32, 51], Karpin [42],
                                               Radchenko [42], Kolyvanov [67, 69]


*16 August 1995, Glasgow*                                                 *40,000*

**Scotland**                          1        **Greece**                         0

McCoist [72]


*6 September 1995, Toftir*                                                 *1,792*

**Faroe Isles**                       2        **Russia**                         5

H.Jarnskor [12], T.Jonsson [55]                Mostovoi [10], Kiryakov [60],
                                               Kolyvanov [65], Tsimbalar [84],
                                               Shalimov [87]


*6 September 1995, Serraville*                                             *1,000*

**San Marino**                        0        **Greece**                         4

                                               Tsalouhidis [5], G.Georgiadis [31],
                                               Alexandris [61], Donis [81]


*6 September 1995, Glasgow*                                               *35,505*

**Scotland**                          1        **Finland**                        0

Booth [10]


*11 October 1995, Moscow*                                                 *40,000*

**Russia**                            2        **Greece**                         1

Kovtun [36], Onopko [71]                       Tsalouhidis [64]


*11 October 1995, Serraville*                                             *1,000*

**San Marino**                        1        **Faroe Isles**                    3

Valentini [52]                                 T.Jonsson [42, 45, 59]


*15 November 1995, Heraklion*                                            *12,000*

**Greece**                            5        **Faroe Isles**                    0

Alexandris [58], Nikolaidis [62],
Mahlas [66], Donis [75], Tsartas [80]


*15 November 1995, Moscow*                                                *6,000*

**Russia**                            3        **Finland**                        1

Radchenko [40], Kulkov [55], Kiryakov [70]     Suominen [45]

*15 November 1995, Glasgow*                                        *30,306*
**Scotland**                          5        **San Marino**            **0**
Jess [30], Booth [45], McCoist [49],
Nevin [71], Francini [o.g. 90]

## FINAL TABLE

|   |          | P  | W | D | L  | F  | A  | Pts |
|---|----------|----|---|---|----|----|----|-----|
| 1 | **RUSSIA**   | 10 | 8 | 2 | 0  | 34 | 5  | 26  |
| 2 | **SCOTLAND** | 10 | 7 | 2 | 1  | 19 | 3  | 23  |
| 3 | Greece       | 10 | 6 | 0 | 4  | 23 | 9  | 18  |
| 4 | Finland      | 10 | 5 | 0 | 5  | 18 | 18 | 15  |
| 5 | Faroe Isles  | 10 | 2 | 0 | 8  | 10 | 35 | 6   |
| 6 | San Marino   | 10 | 0 | 0 | 10 | 2  | 36 | 0   |

Russia and Scotland qualify for Euro 96 finals.

## TOP SCORERS

| | |
|---|---|
| Paatelainen [Finland]    | 7 |
| T.Jonsson [Faroe Isles]  | 5 |
| Kolyvanov [Russia]       | 5 |
| Radchenko [Russia]       | 4 |
| Booth [Scotland]         | 4 |
| Collins [Scotland]       | 4 |
| Litmanen [Finland]       | 4 |
| Mahlas [Greece]          | 4 |
| Tsalouhidis [Greece]     | 4 |

## PLAY-OFF

*13 December 1995  Liverpool*                                      *40,000*
**Holland**                           2        **Republic of Ireland**  **0**
Kluivert [30, 88]

Holland qualify for Euro 96 finals.

# ENGLAND

As host nation, England did not need to qualify for the final stages of the European Championships. The following is a record of all their matches since Terry Venables took charge of the side on 28 January 1994 up to 24 April 1996:

*9 March 1994, Wembley*                                      71,970
**England**                    **1**      **Denmark**               **0**
Platt [16]

*17 May 1994, Wembley*                                       23,659
**England**                    **5**      **Greece**                **0**
Anderton [24], Beardsley [37],
Platt [44 pen, 55], Shearer [65]

*22 May 1994, Wembley*                                       64,327
**England**                    **0**      **Norway**                **0**

*6 September 1994, Wembley*                                  38,629
**England**                    **2**      **USA**                   **0**
Shearer [33, 40]

*12 October 1994, Wembley*                                   48,754
**England**                    **1**      **Romania**               **1**
Lee [44]                                  Dumitrescu [37]

*16 November 1994, Wembley*                                  37,196
**England**                    **1**      **Nigeria**               **0**
Platt [41]

*15 February 1995, Dublin*                                   46,000
**Republic of Ireland**        **1**      **England**               **0**
D. Kelly [22]
*Abandoned after 27 minutes due to rioting*

*29 March 1995, Wembley*                                     34,849
**England**                    **0**      **Uruguay**               **0**

*3 June 1995, Wembley*                                       21,142
**England**                    **2**      **Japan**                 **1**
Anderton [48], Platt [88 pen]             Ihara [62]

*8 June 1995, Leeds*                                         32,008
**England**                    **3**      **Sweden**                **3**
Sheringham [44], Platt [89],              Mild [11, 37], K. Andersson [46]
Anderton [90]

54

| *11 June 1995, Wembley* | | | *67,318* |
|---|---|---|---|
| **England** | 1 | **Brazil** | 3 |
| Le Saux [38] | | Juninho [54], Ronaldo [61], Edmundo [76] | |

| *6 September 1995, Wembley* | | | *20,000* |
|---|---|---|---|
| **England** | 0 | **Colombia** | 0 |

| *11 October 1995, Oslo* | | | *21,006* |
|---|---|---|---|
| **Norway** | 0 | **England** | 0 |

| *15 November 1995, Wembley* | | | *29,874* |
|---|---|---|---|
| **England** | 3 | **Switzerland** | 1 |
| Pearce [45], Sheringham [56], Stone [78] | | Knup [41] | |

| *13 December 1995, Wembley* | | | *28,592* |
|---|---|---|---|
| **England** | 1 | **Portugal** | 1 |
| Stone [44] | | Alves [58] | |

| *27 March 1996, Wembley* | | | *29,708* |
|---|---|---|---|
| **England** | 1 | **Bulgaria** | 0 |
| Ferdinand [7] | | | |

| *24 April 1996, Wembley* | | | *33,650* |
|---|---|---|---|
| **England** | 0 | **Croatia** | 0 |

## LEADING SCORERS

| | |
|---|---|
| Platt | 6 |
| Anderton | 3 |
| Shearer | 3 |

# ENGLAND UNDER VENABLES

| Player | Club | DENMARK 1-0 | GREECE 5-0 | NORWAY 0-0 | USA 2-0 | ROMANIA 1-1 | NIGERIA 1-0 | REP OF IRELAND 0-1 | URUGUAY 0-0 | JAPAN 2-1 | SWEDEN 3-3 | BRAZIL 1-3 | COLOMBIA 0-0 | NORWAY 0-0 | SWITZERLAND 3-1 | PORTUGAL 1-1 | BULGARIA 1-0 | CROATIA 0-0 | Caps under Venables | Total Caps |
|---|---|---|---|---|---|---|---|---|---|---|---|---|---|---|---|---|---|---|---|---|
| David SEAMAN | Arsenal | GK | | | GK | | | GK | | | | | GK | GK | GK | | GK | GK | 11 | 23 |
| Gary PALLISTER | Manchester Utd | D | | D | D | D | | D | D | | | | D | D | | | | | 8 | 20 |
| Tony ADAMS | Arsenal | D | | D | D | D | D | D | D | | D | D | D | | | | M | | 11 | 39 |
| Paul PARKER | Manchester Utd | D | | | | | | | | | | | | | | | | | 1 | 19 |
| Graeme LE SAUX | Blackburn Rovers | D | | D | D | D | D | D46 | M | | D | M | D | D | | | | | 12 | 12 |
| David PLATT | Sampdoria | M | M | M | M | M | M | M | M | | S78 | D | | | | S79 | S76 | M | 12 | 57 |
| Paul INCE | Man Utd/Inter | M | M | M | M | | | | | | | | | | | | | | 6 | 18 |
| Paul GASCOIGNE | Lazio/Rangers | M66 | M62 | M76 | | | | | | S69 | S64 | S78 | M74 | | | | | | 9 | 37 |
| Darren ANDERTON | Tottenham H | M | M62 | M76 | M | | | | | M69 | M64 | | | | | | | | 9 | 9 |
| Peter BEARDSLEY | Newcastle Utd | M | M69 | M66 | M | | | M66 | M69 | M64 | | | | | S66 | | | | 9 | 58 |
| David BATTY | Blackburn Rovers | S66 | | | | | | | M78 | | | M78 | | | | | | | 3 | 17 |
| Matthew LE TISSIER | Southampton | S66 | S62 | S76 | M | | S78 | S78 | | M69 | | M78 | | | | | | | 6 | 6 |
| Alan SHEARER | Blackburn Rovers | A | A | A | A | A | A | A | A | A | A | A74 | A74 | A | A | M | M | A | 14 | 21 |

56

| Player | Club | DENMARK | GREECE | NORWAY | USA | ROMANIA | NIGERIA | REP OF IRELAND | URUGUAY | JAPAN | SWEDEN | BRAZIL | COLOMBIA | NORWAY | SWITZERLAND | PORTUGAL | BULGARIA | CROATIA | Caps under Venables | Total Caps |
|---|---|---|---|---|---|---|---|---|---|---|---|---|---|---|---|---|---|---|---|---|
| Tim FLOWERS | Blackburn Rovers | | GK | | | | GK | | GK | GK | GK | GK | | | | | | | 6 | 7 |
| Rob JONES | Liverpool | | D82 | D | D | D58 | | | | | | | | | | | | | 6 | 8 |
| Stuart PEARCE | Nottingham Forest | | S82 | | | S58 | | | D | D | M64 | D | | | | D79 | D | D | 9 | 64 |
| Steve BOULD | Arsenal | | D | D | | | | | | | | | | | | | | | 2 | 2 |
| Paul MERSON | Arsenal | | M | | | | | | | | | | | | | | | | 1 | 14 |
| Kevin RICHARDSON | Aston Villa | | M | | | | | | | | | | | | | | | | 1 | 1 |
| Ian WRIGHT | Arsenal | | S69 | S76 | S80 | A71 | | | | | | | | | | | | | 4 | 20 |
| Dennis WISE | Chelsea | | | | | S71 | | | M | | | | M | M68 | | M79 | | | 6 | 11 |
| Barry VENISON | Newcastle Utd | | | M | M | M | | M | | | | | | | | | | | 2 | 2 |
| John BARNES | Liverpool | | | | M | | | | | | | S74 | S74 | M | M | | A | A | 6 | 79 |
| Teddy SHERINGHAM | Tottenham H | | | | A80 | S71 | | | A71 | S76 | A | A78 | S74 | A | M | M79 | A | A | 12 | 14 |
| Les FERDINAND | QPR/Newcastle Utd | | | | S80 | S78 | | | | S76 | | | | | | A66 | A | | 3 | 9 |
| Robert LEE | Newcastle Utd | | | | | M71 | | M26 | | | | | S74 | M | M | | S76 | | 6 | 6 |
| Steve HOWEY | Newcastle Utd | | | | | | | | | | | | D | D | | | D | D | 4 | 6 |
| Neil RUDDOCK | Liverpool | | | | | D | | D | | | | | | | | | | | 1 | 4 |

| Player | Club | DENMARK | GREECE | NORWAY | USA | ROMANIA | NIGERIA | REP OF IRELAND | URUGUAY | JAPAN | SWEDEN | BRAZIL | COLOMBIA | NORWAY | SWITZERLAND | PORTUGAL | BULGARIA | CROATIA | Caps under Venables | Total Caps |
|---|---|---|---|---|---|---|---|---|---|---|---|---|---|---|---|---|---|---|---|---|
| Steve McMANAMAN | Liverpool | | | | | | S26 | | S46 | S69 | | | M | M | M | S79 | M | M | 9 | 9 |
| Warren BARTON | Wimbledon | | | | | | | D | | | D | S90 | | | | | | | 3 | 3 |
| Nick BARMBY | Tottenham/ M'boro | | | | | | | | S66 | | S64 | | A | A68 | | M79 | | | 5 | 5 |
| Andy COLE | Manchester Utd | | | | | | | | S71 | | | | | | | | | | 1 | 1 |
| Gary NEVILLE | Manchester Utd | | | | | | | | | D | | D90 | D | D | D | D | D | D | 8 | 8 |
| John SCALES | Liverpool | | | | | | | | | D | | | D | | | | | | 2 | 2 |
| David UNSWORTH | Everton | | | | | | | | | D | | | | | | | | | 1 | 1 |
| Stan COLLYMORE | Nottingham Forest | | | | | | | | | | D | S78 | | | | | | | 2 | 2 |
| Colin COOPER | Nottingham Forest | | | | | | | | | A76 | D | | | | | | | | 2 | 2 |
| Jamie REDKNAPP | Liverpool | | | | | | | | | | | | M74 | | M6 | | | M | 3 | 3 |
| Steve STONE | Nottingham Forest | | | | | | | | | | | | M | | S68 | M | M | M | 5 | 5 |
| Gareth SOUTHGATE | Aston Villa | | | | | | | | | | | | | | | S79 | | M | 2 | 2 |
| Robbie FOWLER | Liverpool | | | | | | | | | | | | | | | | S76 | A | 2 | 2 |
| Mark WRIGHT | Liverpool | | | | | | | | | | | | | | | | | D | 1 | 44 |

42 PLAYERS USED.

# GROUP A

## FIXTURES

## CONTENTS

59

# ENGLAND

### By Bob Harris

You would have to be a blind optimist to back England to win Euro 96 even though it is being played in their own backyard. Coach Terry Venables will need more than just his natural cunning and innovative coaching skills to turn round what has been an awful build-up for the host nation.

Such have been the personal pressures on Venables that he has already announced that he is to quit, never to return, on the conclusion of the summer tournament as he prepares for his forthcoming battles in court. He believes that the time he will spend in clearing his name in a minimum of five actions will leave him without the chance to devote his full attention to critical World Cup qualifying games.

Putting all that to one side for a moment, England and Venables have had precious little going for them. Europe has expanded the qualifying competition to such an extent that England, as hosts, couldn't get the quality or quantity of fixtures to prepare properly, leaving Venables with months-long gaps without getting his team together.

Not even playing at home guarantees success in this tournament. Only once in the past 24 years have the hosts won, when Michel Platini steered France to the title in 1984. Before that the Germans won in Belgium; Czechoslovakia were triumphant in Yugoslavia; the Germans won it again in Italy but lost it to the Dutch on their home turf and the Danes won against the odds in Sweden.

Injuries, such as that sustained by Darren Anderton, are a regular problem for every manager at whatever level, but far harder to work out is why one of the world's top goalscorers, Alan Shearer, dried up for over a year on the international front. Venables is hoping that Shearer, who takes the problem in his stride, will make up the lost time when it really matters – in Euro 96.

Shearer is not the only one who has kept his cool during those difficult months that have seen England slide down the world ranking lists into the also-rans, a fact emphasised by the bookmakers who make them outsiders behind the Dutch, Germans and Italians. Venables, remarkably, has retained his composure and his dignity in face of the problems on and off the pitch, all the time plotting and planning.

The respected former England manager Bobby Robson warned: 'The fact that Terry is quitting at the end of the Championships will concentrate his mind wonderfully on the job in hand. Instead of keeping one eye on the Europeans and the other looking forward to the World Cup, he need have no inhibitions. And he will want to leave with a bang. That's his style.'

Venables, now looking leaner and fitter, says: 'If you are mentally tough there is no limit to what you can achieve.' The 53-year-old Cockney has taken his luck where he can find it, such as making the most of not having competitive games to keep him and his players sharp. He explained: 'One thing I have not had to worry about is showing my hand. Other teams have had to make sure they qualify. We know how they play, their tactics, their best players and their dead-ball routines.

'Can any of them say they know what we will do? Not even my own players know the free-kick routines we will use in the Championships because I haven't told them yet. There has been no need.'

Venables is also relying on the obvious fact that performance percentages increase considerably when playing competitive football. No matter how important friendlies are perceived, they are still exactly that . . . friendlies. Subconsciously, footballers hold back because it doesn't, in the end, really matter. Euro 96 will be different; Venables will expect his players to run through walls for him and their country. A packed Wembley will expect no less.

The other hope is that teams tend to develop during these Championships, just as Robson's team did in Italia 90 when they went from mugs who were told they should come home, to within the width of the goalpost of reaching the final itself.

The England coach's first concern will be Switzerland in their opening group game at Wembley on 8 June. With two teams qualifying for the knockout round, a win in the opening game takes off all the pressure. The Swiss are not among the strongest teams in the finals and, indeed, England beat them 3-1 in November with one of their best displays under Venables. They have lost some of their momentum with the loss of their English coach Roy Hodgson and they must be considered there for the taking.

An unthinkable defeat by the Swiss would not knock England out of the tournament, but it would put them under the fiercest of pressures with their remaining games against the auld enemy Scotland and then the mercurial Dutch. They certainly wouldn't want to go in against Holland needing a win to qualify; history, not to mention the Dutch talents, would be against them. Two victories against the lesser nations, Switzerland and Scotland, would make the Dutch game a pleasant aside.

Venables said: 'I know quite a lot about all three teams in our group. But, remember, they know plenty about us, too! The Dutch are outstanding; the Swiss are well organised and we all know about the Scots and what an England game means to them.'

A place in the quarter-finals and anything can happen. Unfancied teams find themselves on a roll; favourites can be stricken with injuries and suspensions; unknowns emerge to fire their teams to new heights. Only then – hopefully – will we be able to judge Venables and assess England.

Maybe as the underdogs and with a low level of expectancy England can use the time together to develop and come good.

Only time will tell.


**NB: Figures in the England section are provided up to and including 24 April.**

# ENGLAND

*Formation:* 4-3-2-1
*Coach:* Terry Venables

Seaman

Neville          Adams          Pallister          Pearce

Stone          Gascoigne          McManaman

Platt          Sheringham

Shearer

| Player | Position | Club | Date | Caps | Goals |
|--------|----------|------|------|------|-------|
| Tim Flowers | G | Blackburn R | 3.2.67 | 7 | – |
| David Seaman | G | Arsenal | 19.9.63 | 23 | – |
| Ian Walker | G | Tottenham H | 31.10.71 | – | – |
| Rob Jones | D | Liverpool | 5.11.71 | 8 | – |
| Gary Neville | D | Manchester U | 18.2.75 | 8 | – |
| Stuart Pearce | D | Nottingham Forest | 24.4.62 | 64 | 5 |
| Tony Adams | D | Arsenal | 10.10.66 | 39 | 4 |
| Sol Campbell | D | Tottenham H | 18.9.74 | – | – |
| Ugo Ehiogu | D | Aston Villa | 3.11.72 | – | – |
| Steve Howey | D | Newcastle U | 26.10.71 | 4 | – |
| Gary Pallister | D | Manchester U | 30.6.65 | 20 | – |
| Gareth Southgate | D | Aston Villa | 3.9.70 | 2 | – |
| Mark Wright | D | Liverpool | 1.8.63 | 44 | 1 |
| Paul Gascoigne | M | Rangers (Sco) | 27.5.67 | 37 | 6 |
| Paul Ince | M | Inter (Ita) | 21.10.67 | 18 | 2 |
| Robert Lee | M | Newcastle U | 1.2.66 | 6 | 1 |
| Steve McManaman | M | Liverpool | 11.2.72 | 9 | – |
| David Platt | M | Arsenal | 10.6.66 | 57 | 26 |
| Jamie Redknapp | M | Liverpool | 25.6.73 | 3 | – |
| Trevor Sinclair | M | QPR | 2.3.73 | – | – |
| Steve Stone | M | Nottingham Forest | 20.8.71 | 5 | 2 |
| Dennis Wise | M | Chelsea | 16.12.66 | 11 | 1 |
| Darren Anderton | F | Tottenham H | 3.3.72 | 9 | 3 |
| Peter Beardsley | F | Newcastle U | 18.1.61 | 58 | 9 |
| Stan Collymore | F | Liverpool | 22.1.71 | 2 | – |
| Les Ferdinand | F | Newcastle U | 18.12.66 | 9 | 4 |
| Robbie Fowler | F | Liverpool | 9.4.75 | 2 | – |
| Alan Shearer | F | Blackburn R | 13.8.70 | 21 | 5 |
| Teddy Sheringham | F | Tottenham H | 2.4.66 | 14 | 2 |

# ENGLAND A-Z

**TONY ADAMS** (Arsenal)
*Born:* 10.10.66   *Caps:* 39   *Goals:* 4
Has already lifted more silverware than any skipper in Arsenal's history – six (two
League titles, two League Cups, one FA Cup and one European Cup-Winners' Cup).
Captained England in previous four internationals before the match against Bulgaria in
March when he was out of action through injury.

**PETER BEARDSLEY** (Newcastle United)
*Born:* 18.1.61   *Caps:* 58   *Goals:* 9
Rejoined Newcastle from Everton for £1.5 million in the summer of 1993. Began his
career at Carlisle then moved to Vancouver Whitecaps in 1981. A £300,000 move to
Manchester United in September 1982 went sour (made only one appearance) and he
returned to Vancouver six months later. Joined Newcastle for £150,000 in September
1983 and then Liverpool for £1.9 million in July 1987 (a British record transfer fee at the
time). Won two League titles and one FA Cup with the Anfield club. Joined Everton for
£1 million in August 1991, where he scored 32 goals in two seasons. Signed a new
three-year contract with Newcastle last summer, captaining them in their highly
successful 1995-96 campaign. Played in 1986 and 1990 World Cup finals.

**SOL CAMPBELL** (Tottenham Hotspur)
*Born:* 18.9.74   *Caps:* –   *Goals:* –
Versatile player capped by England at Youth, Under-21 and 'B' level. Member of the
England side that won the European Under-18 Championship in 1993. Signed a new
contract with Tottenham in August 1995.

**STAN COLLYMORE** (Liverpool)
*Born:* 22.1.71   *Caps:* 2   *Goals:* –
Joined Liverpool from Nottingham Forest for a British record fee of £8.5 million last
summer. Turned down Everton, even though the Goodison Park club had offered him a
better contract. Was unable to make the grade at Wolves and Walsall, moving to
non-League Stafford Rangers, then Palace. His career took off after joining Southend
from Crystal Palace for £150,000 in November 1992. He scored 15 goals to help
Southend avoid relegation before signing for Forest for £2.1 million in June 1993.
Scored 25 goals for them in 1994-95 (22 in Premiership). His striking partnership with
Robbie Fowler began to bear fruit in the second half of 1995-96.

**UGO EHIOGU** (Aston Villa)
*Born:* 3.11.72   *Caps:* –   *Goals:* –
This 6ft 2in central defender has established himself in the heart of the Villa defence. A
former England Under-21 captain (the first black player to captain England at any
level), he has been tipped by former Villa manager Ron Atkinson as a future England
senior captain. Signed a new four-year contract with Villa in August 1995. Cost only
£40,000 from West Bromwich Albion in August 1991. Won an England 'B' cap v
Republic of Ireland 'B' in December 1994.

**LES FERDINAND** (Newcastle United)
*Born:* 18.12.66   *Caps:* 9   *Goals:* 4
Joined Newcastle from QPR for a then club record fee of £6 million last summer. Was at
Rangers for eight years, but went on loan to Brentford and Besiktas in Turkey before
establishing himself under then QPR manager Gerry Francis and becoming their top
scorer for four seasons to 1994-95. Only 5ft 11in but can outjump almost all defenders.
Started his first game under Venables v Portugal in December 1995. PFA Player of the
Year in 1996.

**TIM FLOWERS** (Blackburn Rovers)
*Born:* 3.2.67   *Caps:* 7   *Goals:* –
Signed from Southampton for £2.4 million (a British record fee for a goalkeeper) in
November 1993. Began his career at Wolves but moved to Southampton in 1986 for
£70,000 and was Peter Shilton's understudy there. Was sent off after just 72 seconds v
Leeds in February 1995 (the fastest-ever sending off in top-flight English football).
Won a Championship medal in 1994-95.

**ROBBIE FOWLER** (Liverpool)
*Born:* 9.4.75   *Caps:* 2   *Goals:* –
Came through the club's School of Excellence, the A, B and reserve teams. A member
of England's European Under-18 Championship-winning side in 1993 (finished leading scorer with five goals). A former Under-21 international, he scored on his England
'B' debut v Republic of Ireland 'B' at Anfield in December 1994. Scored a hat-trick in 4
minutes 33 seconds v Arsenal on 28 August 1994 – the third fastest hat-trick in
top-flight League football. Voted the PFA Young Player of the Year for last two
seasons. Supported Everton as a boy.

**PAUL GASCOIGNE** (Rangers, Scotland)
*Born:* 27.5.67   *Caps:* 37   *Goals:* 6
Began his career at Newcastle and joined Tottenham in 1988. Spent four years at White
Hart Lane. Suffered a cruciate knee ligament injury in 1991 FA Cup final win v
Nottingham Forest which put him out of action for the whole of the 1991-92 season.
Joined Italian club Lazio for £5.5 million in June 1992. Had a pretty miserable time in
Italy and made only 41 league appearances in three years there, before his £4.3 million
move to Rangers last summer. Has had some disciplinary problems this season (sent off
in Champions League game v Borussia Dortmund), but is now returning to something
like his best form. Star of the 1990 World Cup finals, but missed the 1992 European
Championship through injury.

**STEVE HOWEY** (Newcastle United)
*Born:* 26.10.71   *Caps:* 4   *Goals:* –
Rated a potential Alan Hansen by Newcastle manager Kevin Keegan, he started his
career as a centre forward but switched to defence three seasons ago. Was dogged by
groin trouble and needed four operations in the 1993-94 season.

**PAUL INCE** (Inter Milan, Italy)
*Born:* 21.10.67   *Caps:* 18   *Goals:* 2
Combative midfielder who left for Italy at the end of 1994-95 having won two Premier-
ship titles with Manchester United. Originally played for West Ham United. In Italy, he

struggled early on to establish himself and also lost his England place, which he has only recently regained.

### ROB JONES (Liverpool)
*Born:* 5.11.71  *Caps:* 8  *Goals:* –
Signed from Crewe in October 1991 and won an FA Cup winners' medal in his first season at the club. Signed a new three-year contract at Anfield in August 1994. Yet to score in his Liverpool career (now played in over 200 games). Although normally a right-back, he has been playing at left-back of late.

### ROBERT LEE (Newcastle United)
*Born:* 1.2.66  *Caps:* 6  *Goals:* 1
Joined Charlton in 1983 and spent 10 seasons there before his £700,000 move to Newcastle in September 1992. Scored on his England debut (v Romania).

### STEVE McMANAMAN (Liverpool)
*Born:* 11.2.72  *Caps:* 9  *Goals:* –
Liverpool born. A former England Under-21 international (seven caps, one goal). Was captain of the Under-21s under Lawrie McMenemy. Agreed a new three-and-a-half-year contract in October 1994 which will keep him at Anfield until 1998. Supported Everton as a boy. Won FA Cup winners' medal in 1992 (was voted man of the match). Scored both goals in last season's League Cup final win v Bolton.

### GARY NEVILLE (Manchester United)
*Born:* 18.2.75  *Caps:* 8  *Goals:* –
Made his Premiership debut in final game of 1993-94 season (v Coventry). A member of United's FA Youth Cup-winning side in 1992 and also played in the European Under-18 Championship in 1993 which England won. Has played in last five internationals. Played in 1995 FA Cup final. Older brother of clubmate Phil, who joined the England squad for the first time against Bulgaria in March.

### GARY PALLISTER (Manchester United)
*Born:* 30.6.65  *Caps:* 20  *Goals:* –
6ft 4in central defender. Joined Manchester United from Middlesbrough for £2.3 million in August 1989. Won two League titles, one European Cup-Winners' Cup and two FA Cups with United. Has been plagued this season with a back injury.

### STUART PEARCE (Nottingham Forest)
*Born:* 24.4.62  *Caps:* 64  *Goals:* 5
Now in his 11th season at Forest, having signed from Coventry in a joint deal with Ian Butterworth worth £450,000 in May 1985. Forest skipper since 1987, he has led the club to victory in the 1989 and 1990 League Cup finals and 1989 Simod Cup final. Lost his place in the England side to Graeme Le Saux when Venables became coach. However, has started the last three internationals. He is currently in his testimonial season – his testimonial will be against Newcastle in May. Played in 1990 World Cup finals and 1992 European Championship.

**DAVID PLATT** (Arsenal)

*Born:* 10.6.66    *Caps:* 57    *Goals:* 26

Joined Arsenal from Sampdoria for £4.75 million last summer after a four-year exile in Italy where he played for Bari, Juventus and Sampdoria. Is now the most expensive player ever, having been involved in over £22 million worth of transfers. Has been dogged by knee injuries this season – has had to undergo two operations. He is England's top scorer under Terry Venables.

**JAMIE REDKNAPP** (Liverpool)

*Born:* 25.6.73    *Caps:* 3    *Goals:* –

Joined Liverpool from Bournemouth in January 1991. At 18, was the youngest player to represent Liverpool in Europe when he played v Auxerre in UEFA Cup in 1992-93. Captained the Under-21 team that beat Portugal to win the Toulon Tournament in June 1994. Son of Harry Redknapp, the West Ham manager. Signed a new three-year contract at Anfield in August 1994 despite having a year left on his current deal. Struggled for much of 1995-96 with a hamstring injury.

**DAVID SEAMAN** (Arsenal)

*Born:* 19.9.63    *Caps:* 23    *Goals:* –

After beginning with Leeds, and after spells with Peterborough, Birmingham and Queens Park Rangers, he joined Arsenal for £1.3 million in May 1990. Won one League title, one FA Cup, one League Cup and one European Cup-Winners' Cup with the Gunners.

**ALAN SHEARER** (Blackburn Rovers)

*Born:* 13.8.70    *Caps:* 21    *Goals:* 5

Prolific goalscorer for Blackburn since his £3.3 million move from Southampton in July 1992. Was the Premiership's leading scorer in 1994-95, with 34 goals as Blackburn won the League title. Won the 1994 Football Writers' Footballer of the Year award and 1995 PFA Player of the Year award. He became the first player to score 100 goals in the Premiership when he scored against Tottenham on 3 December 1995.

**TEDDY SHERINGHAM** (Tottenham Hotspur)

*Born:* 2.4.66    *Caps:* 14    *Goals:* 2

Signed from Nottingham Forest for £2.1 million in August 1992, where he lasted just over a season. Before that, he scored 93 goals in 220 league appearances for Millwall. Strong in the air.

**TREVOR SINCLAIR** (Queens Park Rangers)

*Born:* 2.3.73    *Caps:* –    *Goals:* –

A graduate from the FA School of Excellence, he began his career at Blackpool in August 1990 and helped them win promotion in 1992. Joined QPR for £750,000 in August 1993 after the record sale of Andy Sinton to Sheffield Wednesday. A former Under-21 international, he was a member of their squad which won the 1994 Toulon Tournament (scored in final v Portugal). Is the subject of constant transfer speculation, especially to rejoin former boss Gerry Francis at Spurs (also a target of Leeds).

**GARETH SOUTHGATE** (Aston Villa)

*Born:* 3.9.70    *Caps:* 2    *Goals:* –

Joined Villa from Crystal Palace for £2.5 million last summer. Has been converted by manager Brian Little from midfield to form part of Villa's three-man central defensive system. Was the Palace skipper and the youngest captain in the Premiership in 1994-95.

### STEVE STONE (Nottingham Forest)
*Born:* 20.8.71    *Caps:* 5    *Goals:* 2

The 1993-94 season was his first full season in the Forest first team – he missed only three games. Before 1993-94 his career had been ravaged by injury, including three broken legs in three years, playing for Forest's youth and reserve teams. Voted Forest's Player of the Year for 1995. Has had a dream season – made his England debut as a substitute v Norway in October 1995, scored v Switzerland in November after coming on for Jamie Redknapp after six minutes and then scored v Portugal in December in his first international start. Signed a new four-year contract with Forest in October 1995 worth £1.5 million.

### IAN WALKER (Tottenham Hotspur)
*Born:* 31.10.71    *Caps:* –    *Goals:* –

A former England Under-21 international and a former pupil of the FA National School of Excellence, he was also capped at Youth and Under-19 level. Son of former Norwich and Everton manager Mike Walker. Equalled Ray Clemence's club record in 1994-95 by keeping six successive clean sheets in league and cup. Signed a new three-and-a-half-year contract with Tottenham in February 1995. Was understudy to Tim Flowers in last summer's Umbro Cup.

### DENNIS WISE (Chelsea)
*Born:* 15.12.66    *Caps:* 11    *Goals:* 1

Chelsea captain. Now in his sixth season with Chelsea after a then club record £1.6 million move from Wimbledon in July 1990. Won FA Cup winners' medal with the Dons in 1988 and was a runner-up with Chelsea in 1994. Had a much-publicised case involving a taxi driver last year.

### MARK WRIGHT (Liverpool)
*Born:* 1.8.63    *Caps:* 44    *Goals:* 1

Central defender who played in 1990 World Cup, but injuries and loss of form meant that he was out of the England side from September 1992 to April 1996. In 1995-96 he was back to his best in a three-man central defence at Liverpool. Previous clubs include Oxford United, Southampton and Derby County.

### Coach: TERRY VENABLES
*Born:* 6.1.43

An inside forward or midfielder, he played for England at every level, from schoolboy, through amateur, youth and Under-23 to the senior side, where he won two caps. He captained Chelsea in the mid-1960s, and then moved to Tottenham with whom he won the FA Cup in 1967. As coach he began promisingly at Crystal Palace and Queens Park Rangers before joining Barcelona and guiding them to the Spanish League title in 1985. He returned to coach Tottenham where he won the FA Cup in 1991, but left the club in acrimonious circumstances following disagreements with club chairman Alan Sugar. He was appointed national coach in January 1994 in succession to Graham Taylor. By 1 May his England side had been beaten only once – by world champions Brazil.

## ENGLAND v BULGARIA

| Date | Venue | Score | Competition |
|---|---|---|---|
| 07-06-1962 | Rancagua (Chile) | 0-0 | WC finals |
| 11-12-1968 | Wembley | 1-1 | Friendly |
| 01-06-1974 | Sofia | 1-0 | Friendly |
| 06-06-1979 | Sofia | 3-0 | ENC qualifiers |
| 22-11-1979 | Wembley | 2-0 | ENC qualifiers |
| 27-03-1996 | Wembley | 1-0 | Friendly |

| | P | W | D | L | F | A |
|---|---|---|---|---|---|---|
| Home | 3 | 2 | 1 | 0 | 4 | 1 |
| Away | 2 | 2 | 0 | 0 | 4 | 0 |
| Neutral | 1 | 0 | 1 | 0 | 0 | 0 |
| Total | 6 | 4 | 2 | 0 | 8 | 1 |

* England met Bulgaria in 1979 in the European Nations Cup Qualifying round, winning 3-0 away, 2-0 at home, when Glenn Hoddle scored on his debut.

## ENGLAND v CROATIA

The two sides had never met until the game at Wembley on 24 April, which ended 0-0

## ENGLAND v CZECH REPUBLIC

*As Czechoslovakia*

| Date | Venue | Score | Competition |
|---|---|---|---|
| 16-05-1934 | Prague | 1-2 | Friendly |
| 01-12-1937 | Tottenham | 5-4 | Friendly |
| 29-05-1963 | Bratislava | 4-2 | Friendly |
| 02-11-1966 | Wembley | 0-0 | Friendly |
| 11-06-1970 | Guadalajara (Mexico) | 1-0 | WC finals |
| 27-05-1973 | Prague | 1-1 | Friendly |
| 30-10-1974 | Wembley | 3-0 | ENC qualifiers |
| 30-10-1975 | Bratislava | 1-2 | ENC qualifiers |
| 29-11-1978 | Wembley | 1-0 | Friendly |
| 20-06-1982 | Bilbao (Spain) | 2-0 | WC finals |
| 25-04-1990 | Wembley | 4-2 | Friendly |
| 25-03-1992 | Prague | 2-2 | Friendly |

|        | P  | W | D | L | F  | A  |
|--------|----|---|---|---|----|----|
| Home   | 5  | 4 | 1 | 0 | 13 | 6  |
| Away   | 5  | 1 | 2 | 2 | 9  | 9  |
| Neutral| 2  | 2 | 0 | 0 | 3  | 0  |
| Total  | 12 | 7 | 3 | 2 | 25 | 15 |

\* Czechoslovakia are one of only three teams that have knocked England out in the early stages of the European Nations Cup. France and Denmark are the other two. Czechoslovakia went on to win the tournament in 1976.

# ENGLAND v DENMARK

| Date       | Venue            | Score | Competition    |
|------------|------------------|-------|----------------|
| 29-09-1948 | Copenhagen       | 0-0   | Friendly       |
| 02-10-1955 | Copenhagen       | 5-1   | Friendly       |
| 05-12-1956 | Wolverhampton    | 5-2   | WC qualifiers  |
| 15-05-1957 | Copenhagen       | 4-1   | WC qualifiers  |
| 03-07-1966 | Copenhagen       | 2-0   | Friendly       |
| 20-09-1978 | Copenhagen       | 4-3   | ENC qualifiers |
| 12-09-1979 | Wembley          | 1-0   | ENC qualifiers |
| 22-09-1982 | Copenhagen       | 2-2   | ENC qualifiers |
| 21-09-1983 | Wembley          | 0-1   | ENC qualifiers |
| 14-09-1988 | Wembley          | 1-0   | Friendly       |
| 07-06-1989 | Copenhagen       | 1-1   | Friendly       |
| 15-05-1990 | Wembley          | 1-0   | Friendly       |
| 11-06-1992 | Malmo (Sweden)   | 0-0   | ENC finals     |
| 09-03-1994 | Wembley          | 1-0   | Friendly       |

|        | P  | W | D | L | F  | A  |
|--------|----|---|---|---|----|----|
| Home   | 6  | 5 | 0 | 1 | 9  | 3  |
| Away   | 7  | 4 | 3 | 0 | 18 | 8  |
| Neutral| 1  | 0 | 1 | 0 | 0  | 0  |
| Total  | 14 | 9 | 4 | 1 | 27 | 11 |

\* Denmark eliminated England from the 1984 European Championships in France. The decisive game was at Wembley where Denmark won 1-0 thanks to a Simonsen penalty. It is Denmark's only victory against England and their only goal at Wembley.

# ENGLAND v FRANCE

| Date | Venue | Score | Competition |
|------|-------|-------|-------------|
| 10-05-1923 | Paris | 4-1 | Friendly |
| 17-05-1924 | Paris | 3-1 | Friendly |
| 21-05-1925 | Paris | 3-2 | Friendly |
| 26-05-1927 | Paris | 6-0 | Friendly |
| 17-05-1928 | Paris | 5-1 | Friendly |
| 09-05-1929 | Paris | 4-1 | Friendly |
| 14-05-1931 | Paris | 2-5 | Friendly |
| 06-12-1933 | Tottenham | 4-1 | Friendly |
| 26-05-1938 | Paris | 4-2 | Friendly |
| 03-05-1947 | Highbury | 3-0 | Friendly |
| 22-05-1949 | Paris | 3-1 | Friendly |
| 03-10-1951 | Highbury | 2-2 | Friendly |
| 15-05-1955 | Paris | 0-1 | Friendly |
| 27-11-1957 | Wembley | 4-0 | Friendly |
| 03-10-1962 | Sheffield | 1-1 | ENC qualifiers |
| 27-02-1963 | Paris | 2-5 | ENC qualifiers |
| 20-07-1966 | Wembley | 2-0 | WC finals |
| 12-03-1969 | Wembley | 5-0 | Friendly |
| 16-06-1982 | Bilbao (Spain) | 3-1 | WC finals |
| 29-02-1984 | Paris | 0-2 | Friendly |
| 19-02-1992 | Wembley | 2-0 | Friendly |
| 14-06-1992 | Malmo (Sweden) | 0-0 | ENC finals |

| | P | W | D | L | F | A |
|---------|----|----|---|---|----|----|
| Home | 8 | 6 | 2 | 0 | 23 | 4 |
| Away | 12 | 8 | 0 | 4 | 36 | 22 |
| Neutral | 2 | 1 | 1 | 0 | 3 | 1 |
| Total | 22 | 15 | 3 | 4 | 62 | 27 |

* When France knocked England out of the 1964 European Nations Cup competition by 5-2 it was, and is, England's worst defeat in the competition.

# ENGLAND v GERMANY

| Date | Venue | Score | Competition |
|------|-------|-------|-------------|
| 10-05-1930 | Berlin | 3-3 | Friendly |
| 04-12-1935 | Tottenham | 3-0 | Friendly |
| 14-05-1938 | Berlin | 6-3 | Friendly |

*As West Germany*

| Date | Venue | Score | Competition |
|------|-------|-------|-------------|
| 01-12-1954 | Wembley | 3-1 | Friendly |
| 26-05-1956 | Berlin | 3-1 | Friendly |
| 12-05-1965 | Nurnberg | 1-0 | Friendly |
| 23-02-1966 | Wembley | 1-0 | Friendly |
| 30-07-1966 | Wembley | 4-2 | WC final |
| 01-06-1968 | Hannover | 0-1 | Friendly |
| 14-06-1970 | Leon (Mexico) | 2-3 | WC quarter-finals |
| 29-04-1972 | Wembley | 1-3 | ENC quarter-finals |
| 13-05-1972 | Berlin | 0-0 | ENC quarter-finals |
| 12-03-1975 | Wembley | 2-0 | Friendly |
| 22-02-1978 | Munich | 1-2 | Friendly |
| 29-06-1982 | Madrid (Spain) | 0-0 | WC finals |
| 13-10-1982 | Wembley | 1-2 | Friendly |
| 12-06-1985 | Mexico City | 3-0 | Friendly |
| 09-09-1987 | Dusseldorf | 1-3 | Friendly |
| 04-07-1990 | Turin (Italy) | 1-1 | WC semi-final |

*As Germany*

| Date | Venue | Score | Competition |
|------|-------|-------|-------------|
| 11-09-1991 | Wembley | 0-1 | Friendly |
| 19-06-1993 | Detroit (USA) | 1-2 | Friendly |

|         | P  | W | D | L | F  | A  |
|---------|----|---|---|---|----|----|
| Home    | 8  | 5 | 0 | 3 | 15 | 9  |
| Away    | 8  | 3 | 2 | 3 | 15 | 13 |
| Neutral | 5  | 1 | 2 | 2 | 7  | 6  |
| Total   | 21 | 9 | 4 | 8 | 37 | 28 |

* England's biggest defeat against Germany came in the 1972 quarter-finals of the European Nations Cup. They drew 0-0 in the away leg that year. That was the only time the two countries have met in this competition.

# ENGLAND v HOLLAND

| Date | Venue | Score | Competition |
|------|-------|-------|-------------|
| 18-05-1935 | Amsterdam | 1-0 | Friendly |
| 27-11-1946 | Huddersfield | 8-2 | Friendly |
| 09-12-1964 | Amsterdam | 1-1 | Friendly |
| 05-11-1969 | Amsterdam | 1-0 | Friendly |
| 14-06-1970 | Wembley | 0-0 | Friendly |
| 09-02-1977 | Wembley | 0-2 | Friendly |
| 25-05-1982 | Wembley | 2-0 | Friendly |

| Date | Venue | Score | Competition |
|------|-------|-------|-------------|
| 23-03-1988 | Wembley | 2-2 | Friendly |
| 15-06-1988 | Dusseldorf (Germany) | 1-3 | ENC finals |
| 16-06-1990 | Cagliari (Italy) | 0-0 | WC finals |
| 28-04-1993 | Wembley | 2-2 | WC qualifiers |
| 13-10-1993 | Rotterdam | 0-2 | WC qualifiers |

|  | P | W | D | L | F | A |
|--|---|---|---|---|---|---|
| Home | 6 | 2 | 3 | 1 | 14 | 8 |
| Away | 4 | 2 | 1 | 1 | 3 | 3 |
| Neutral | 2 | 0 | 1 | 1 | 1 | 3 |
| Total | 12 | 4 | 5 | 3 | 18 | 14 |

* Marco van Basten scored a hat-trick the last time England and Holland met in the European Nations Cup finals. England have never beaten the Dutch in a competitive match.

# ENGLAND v ITALY

| Date | Venue | Score | Competition |
|------|-------|-------|-------------|
| 13-05-1933 | Rome | 1-1 | Friendly |
| 14-11-1934 | Highbury | 3-2 | Friendly |
| 13-05-1939 | Milan | 2-2 | Friendly |
| 16-05-1948 | Turin | 4-0 | Friendly |
| 30-11-1949 | Tottenham | 2-0 | Friendly |
| 18-05-1952 | Florence | 1-1 | Friendly |
| 06-05-1959 | Wembley | 2-2 | Friendly |
| 24-05-1961 | Rome | 3-2 | Friendly |
| 14-06-1973 | Turin | 0-2 | Friendly |
| 14-11-1973 | Wembley | 0-1 | Friendly |
| 28-05-1976 | New York (USA) | 3-2 | Friendly |
| 17-11-1976 | Rome | 0-2 | WC qualifiers |
| 16-11-1977 | Wembley | 2-0 | WC qualifiers |
| 15-06-1980 | Turin | 0-1 | ENC finals |
| 06-06-1985 | Mexico City | 1-2 | Friendly |
| 15-11-1989 | Wembley | 0-0 | Friendly |
| 07-07-1990 | Bari | 1-2 | WC 3rd-place |

|  | P | W | D | L | F | A |
|--|---|---|---|---|---|---|
| Home | 6 | 3 | 2 | 1 | 9 | 5 |
| Away | 9 | 2 | 3 | 4 | 12 | 13 |
| Neutral | 2 | 1 | 0 | 1 | 4 | 4 |
| Total | 17 | 6 | 5 | 6 | 25 | 22 |

* England have met Italy only once in the European Nations Cup, that was in the finals in Italy back in 1980. England lost 1-0, and the scorer for Italy that day was Marco Tardelli, the goal coming in the 78th minute.

# ENGLAND v PORTUGAL

| Date | Venue | Score | Competition |
|------|-------|-------|-------------|
| 25-05-1947 | Lisbon | 10-0 | Friendly |
| 14-05-1950 | Lisbon | 5-3 | Friendly |
| 19-05-1951 | Everton | 5-2 | Friendly |
| 22-05-1955 | Oporto | 1-3 | Friendly |
| 07-05-1958 | Wembley | 2-1 | Friendly |
| 21-05-1961 | Lisbon | 1-1 | WC qualifiers |
| 25-10-1961 | Wembley | 2-0 | WC qualifiers |
| 17-05-1964 | Lisbon | 4-3 | Friendly |
| 04-06-1964 | Sao Paulo (Brazil) | 1-1 | Friendly |
| 26-07-1966 | Wembley | 2-1 | WC finals |
| 10-12-1969 | Wembley | 1-0 | Friendly |
| 03-04-1974 | Lisbon | 0-0 | Friendly |
| 20-11-1974 | Wembley | 0-0 | ENC qualifiers |
| 19-11-1975 | Lisbon | 1-1 | ENC qualifiers |
| 03-06-1986 | Monterrey (Mexico) | 0-1 | WC finals |
| 12-12-1995 | Wembley | 1-1 | Friendly |

| | P | W | D | L | F | A |
|------|---|---|---|---|---|---|
| Home | 7 | 5 | 2 | 0 | 13 | 5 |
| Away | 7 | 3 | 3 | 1 | 22 | 11 |
| Neutral | 2 | 0 | 1 | 1 | 1 | 2 |
| Total | 16 | 8 | 6 | 2 | 36 | 18 |

* Portugal have not been beaten by England since 1969 (five matches), drawing both games in the qualifiers for the 1976 European Nations tournament.

# ENGLAND v ROMANIA

| Date | Venue | Score | Competition |
|------|-------|-------|-------------|
| 24-05-1939 | Bucharest | 2-0 | Friendly |
| 06-11-1968 | Bucharest | 0-0 | Friendly |
| 15-01-1969 | Wembley | 1-1 | Friendly |
| 02-06-1970 | Guadalajara (Mexico) | 1-0 | WC finals |
| 15-10-1980 | Bucharest | 1-2 | WC qualifiers |
| 29-04-1981 | Wembley | 0-0 | WC qualifiers |
| 01-05-1985 | Bucharest | 0-0 | WC qualifiers |
| 11-09-1985 | Wembley | 1-1 | WC qualifiers |
| 12-10-1994 | Wembley | 1-1 | Friendly |

|        | P | W | D | L | F | A |
|--------|---|---|---|---|---|---|
| Home   | 4 | 0 | 4 | 0 | 3 | 3 |
| Away   | 4 | 1 | 2 | 1 | 3 | 2 |
| Neutral| 1 | 1 | 0 | 0 | 1 | 0 |
| Total  | 9 | 2 | 6 | 1 | 7 | 5 |

* England have never beaten Romania in England, nor have they ever met in this competition.

## ENGLAND v RUSSIA

*As USSR*

| Date | Venue | Score | Competition |
|------|-------|-------|-------------|
| 18-05-1958 | Moscow | 1-1 | Friendly |
| 08-06-1958 | Gothenburg (Sweden) | 2-2 | WC finals |
| 17-06-1958 | Gothenburg (Sweden) | 0-1 | WC finals |
| 22-10-1958 | Wembley | 5-0 | Friendly |
| 06-12-1967 | Wembley | 2-2 | Friendly |
| 08-06-1968 | Rome (Italy) | 2-0 | ENC finals |
| 10-06-1973 | Moscow | 2-1 | Friendly |
| 02-06-1984 | Wembley | 0-2 | Friendly |
| 26-03-1986 | Tbilisi | 1-0 | Friendly |
| 18-06-1988 | Frankfurt (Germany) | 1-3 | ENC finals |
| 21-05-1991 | Wembley | 3-1 | Friendly |

*As CIS*

| Date | Venue | Score | Competition |
|------|-------|-------|-------------|
| 29-04-1992 | Moscow | 2-2 | Friendly |

|         | P  | W | D | L | F  | A  |
|---------|----|---|---|---|----|----|
| Home    | 4  | 2 | 1 | 1 | 10 | 5  |
| Away    | 4  | 2 | 2 | 0 | 6  | 4  |
| Neutral | 4  | 1 | 1 | 2 | 5  | 6  |
| Total   | 12 | 5 | 4 | 3 | 21 | 15 |

* England lost badly to the USSR in the 1988 finals, having already failed to qualify for the semis. They did, however, beat the USSR in the third-place play-off in 1968.

## ENGLAND v SCOTLAND

See under Scotland, page 101-03.

# ENGLAND v SPAIN

| Date | Venue | Score | Competition |
|---|---|---|---|
| 15-05-1929 | Madrid | 3-4 | Friendly |
| 09-12-1931 | Highbury | 7-1 | Friendly |
| 02-07-1950 | Rio (Brazil) | 0-1 | WC finals |
| 18-05-1955 | Madrid | 1-1 | Friendly |
| 30-11-1955 | Wembley | 4-1 | Friendly |
| 15-05-1960 | Madrid | 0-3 | Friendly |
| 26-10-1960 | Wembley | 4-2 | Friendly |
| 08-12-1965 | Madrid | 2-0 | Friendly |
| 24-05-1967 | Wembley | 2-0 | Friendly |
| 03-04-1968 | Wembley | 1-0 | ENC quarter-final |
| 08-05-1968 | Madrid | 2-1 | ENC quarter-final |
| 26-03-1980 | Barcelona | 2-0 | Friendly |
| 18-06-1980 | Naples (Italy) | 2-1 | ENC finals |
| 25-03-1981 | Wembley | 1-2 | Friendly |
| 05-07-1987 | Madrid | 4-2 | Friendly |
| 09-09-1992 | Santander | 0-1 | Friendly |

|  | P | W | D | L | F | A |
|---|---|---|---|---|---|---|
| Home | 6 | 5 | 0 | 1 | 19 | 6 |
| Away | 8 | 4 | 1 | 3 | 14 | 12 |
| Neutral | 2 | 1 | 0 | 1 | 2 | 2 |
| Total | 16 | 10 | 1 | 5 | 35 | 20 |

* England have met Spain in two previous European Nations competitions and have never lost. In the 1968 competition, when Spain were the holders, England won both quarter-final matches [1-0 (h), 2-1 (a)]. In 1980 England won 2-1 in Naples.

# ENGLAND v SWITZERLAND

| Date | Venue | Score | Competition |
|---|---|---|---|
| 20-05-1933 | Berne | 4-0 | Friendly |
| 21-05-1938 | Zurich | 1-2 | Friendly |
| 18-05-1947 | Zurich | 0-1 | Friendly |
| 02-12-1948 | Highbury | 6-0 | Friendly |
| 28-05-1952 | Zurich | 3-0 | Friendly |
| 20-06-1954 | Berne | 2-0 | WC finals |
| 09-05-1962 | Wembley | 3-1 | Friendly |
| 05-06-1963 | Basle | 8-1 | Friendly |
| 13-10-1971 | Basle | 3-2 | ENC qualifiers |
| 10-11-1971 | Wembley | 1-1 | ENC qualifiers |
| 03-09-1975 | Basle | 2-1 | Friendly |
| 07-09-1977 | Wembley | 0-0 | Friendly |
| 19-11-1980 | Wembley | 2-1 | WC qualifiers |
| 30-05-1981 | Basle | 1-2 | WC qualifiers |
| 28-05-1988 | Lausanne | 1-0 | Friendly |
| 15-11-1995 | Wembley | 3-1 | Friendly |

|  | P | W | D | L | F | A |
|---|---|---|---|---|---|---|
| Home | 6 | 4 | 2 | 0 | 15 | 4 |
| Away | 10 | 7 | 0 | 3 | 25 | 9 |
| Total | 16 | 12 | 2 | 2 | 40 | 13 |

* England met Switzerland on the way to the quarter-finals in the 1972 competition. World Cup winner Geoff Hurst was one of the scorers in Basle.

## ENGLAND v TURKEY

| Date | Venue | Score | Competition |
|---|---|---|---|
| 14-11-1984 | Istanbul | 8-0 | WC qualifiers |
| 16-10-1985 | Wembley | 5-0 | WC qualifiers |
| 29-04-1987 | Izmir | 0-0 | ENC qualifiers |
| 14-10-1987 | Wembley | 8-0 | ENC qualifiers |
| 01-05-1991 | Izmir | 1-0 | ENC qualifiers |
| 16-10-1991 | Wembley | 1-0 | ENC qualifiers |
| 18-11-1992 | Wembley | 4-0 | WC qualifiers |
| 31-03-1993 | Izmir | 2-0 | WC qualifiers |

|  | P | W | D | L | F | A |
|---|---|---|---|---|---|---|
| Home | 4 | 4 | 0 | 0 | 18 | 0 |
| Away | 4 | 3 | 1 | 0 | 11 | 0 |
| Total | 8 | 7 | 1 | 0 | 29 | 0 |

* Turkey have never scored against England, and their 8-0 defeat at Wembley in the 1987 qualifying game equals their worst-ever loss. On that day, Gary Lineker scored a hat-trick.

## KEY PLAYER

## PAUL GASCOIGNE

*Date of Birth:* 27.5.67
*Current club:* Rangers
*Position:* Midfield
*Height:* 1.79 m
*Weight:* 77 kg

### CAREER RECORD

| Year | Club | League Apps | Goals | Int Apps | Goals |
|---|---|---|---|---|---|
| 1984-85 | Newcastle Utd | 2 | | | |
| 1985-86 | | 31 | 9 | | |
| 1986-87 | | 24 | 5 | | |
| 1987-88 | | 35 | 7 | | |

| Year | Club | League Apps | Goals | Int Apps | Goals |
|---|---|---|---|---|---|
| 1988-89 | Tottenham H | 32 | 6 | 5 | 1 |
| 1989-90 | | 34 | 6 | 12 | 1 |
| 1990-91 | | 26 | 7 | 3 | 0 |
| 1991-92 | | 0 | 0 | 0 | 0 |
| 1992-93 | Lazio | 22 | 4 | 7 | 3 |
| 1993-94 | | 17 | 2 | 2 | 1 |
| 1994-95 | | 2 | 0 | 3 | 0 |
| 1995-96 | Rangers | | | 5 | 0 |

## HONOURS

English FA Cup winner – 1991
PFA Young Player of the Year – 1988

| No | Date | Opponents | Venue | Score | Goals | Competition | Subbed Sub |
|---|---|---|---|---|---|---|---|
| 1 | 14.9.88 | Denmark | Wembley | 1-0 | 0 | Friendly | Sub pl 5 |
| 2 | 16.11.88 | Saudi Arabia | Riyadh | 1-1 | 0 | Friendly | Sub pl 10 |
| 3 | 26.4.89 | Albania | Wembley | 5-0 | 1 | World Cup, Q | Sub pl 23 |
| 4 | 23.5.89 | Chile | Wembley | 0-0 | 0 | Friendly | 90 |
| 5 | 27.5.89 | Scotland | Glasgow | 2-0 | 0 | Friendly | Sub pl 15 |
| 6 | 6.9.89 | Sweden | Stockholm | 0-0 | 0 | World Cup, Q | Sub pl 18 |
| 7 | 28.3.90 | Brazil | Wembley | 1-0 | 0 | Friendly | Sub pl 12 |
| 8 | 25.4.90 | Czechoslovakia | Wembley | 4-2 | 1 | Friendly | 90 |
| 9 | 15.5.90 | Denmark | Wembley | 1-0 | 0 | Friendly | 90 |
| 10 | 22.5.90 | Uruguay | Wembley | 1-2 | 0 | Friendly | 90 |
| 11 | 2.6.90 | Tunisia | Tunis | 1-1 | 0 | Friendly | 90 |
| 12 | 11.6.90 | Rep of Ireland | Cagliari | 1-1 | 0 | WC finals | 90 |
| 13 | 16.6.90 | Holland | Cagliari | 0-0 | 0 | WC finals | 90 |
| 14 | 21.6.90 | Egypt | Cagliari | 1-0 | 0 | WC finals | 90 |
| 15 | 26.6.90 | Belgium | Bologna | 1-0 | 0 | WC finals | 90 |
| 16 | 1.7.90 | Cameroon | Naples | 3-2 | 0 | WC finals | 90 |
| 17 | 4.7.90 | West Germany | Turin | 1-1 | 0 | WC finals | 90 |
| 18 | 12.9.90 | Hungary | Wembley | 1-0 | 0 | Friendly | 90 |
| 19 | 17.10.90 | Poland | Wembley | 2-0 | 0 | E Nations, Q | 90 |
| 20 | 6.2.91 | Cameroon | Wembley | 2-0 | 0 | Friendly | Subbed 67 |
| 21 | 14.10.92 | Norway | Wembley | 1-1 | 0 | World Cup, Q | 90 |
| 22 | 18.11.92 | Turkey | Wembley | 4-0 | 2 | World Cup, Q | 90 |
| 23 | 17.2.93 | San Marino | Wembley | 6-0 | 0 | World Cup, Q | 90 |
| 24 | 31.3.93 | Turkey | Izmir | 2-0 | 1 | World Cup, Q | 90 |
| 25 | 28.4.93 | Holland | Wembley | 2-2 | 0 | World Cup, Q | Subbed 46 |
| 26 | 29.5.93 | Poland | Chorzow | 1-1 | 0 | World Cup, Q | Subbed 79 |
| 27 | 2.6.93 | Norway | Oslo | 0-2 | 0 | World Cup, Q | 90 |
| 28 | 8.9.93 | Poland | Wembley | 3-0 | 1 | World Cup, Q | 90 |
| 29 | 9.3.94 | Denmark | Wembley | 1-0 | 0 | Friendly | Subbed 66 |
| 30 | 3.6.95 | Japan | Wembley | 2-1 | 0 | Friendly | Sub pl 21 |
| 31 | 8.6.95 | Sweden | Leeds | 3-3 | 0 | Friendly | Sub pl 26 |
| 32 | 11.6.95 | Brazil | Wembley | 1-3 | 0 | Friendly | Sub pl 12 |
| 33 | 6.9.95 | Colombia | Wembley | 0-0 | 0 | Friendly | Subbed 74 |
| 34 | 15.11.95 | Switzerland | Wembley | 3-1 | 0 | Friendly | 90 |
| 35 | 12.12.95 | Portugal | Wembley | 1-1 | 0 | Friendly | 90 |
| 36 | 27.3.96 | Bulgaria | Wembley | 1-0 | 0 | Friendly | Subbed 76 |
| 37 | 24.4.96 | Croatia | Wembley | 0-0 | 0 | Friendly | 90 |

# SWITZERLAND

Swiss coach Artur Jorge is on a hiding to nothing. The experienced Portuguese coach will need more than his two university doctorates and his command of half a dozen languages if the Swiss flop against England, Holland and Scotland.

The fans – not to mention some of the players – are still fuming over the decision to sack their hero, Englishman Roy Hodgson, who guided them to the World Cup finals for the first time in 28 years and to their first-ever European Championship finals. Although Hodgson was quite happy to divide his loyalty between Inter of Milan and the Swiss national team, the Swiss Federation were having none of it and, despite the public outcry, showed him the door.

Jorge, the former coach of the Portuguese national team, Paris St Germain in France, and Porto, whom he led to success in the European Champions Cup, was picked over Ivica Osim, Sven-Goran Eriksson, Arsene Wenger and Vujadin Boskov. It was not just his excellent coaching record, but the fact that he could speak all three languages – French, Italian and German – used by his multiracial, multilingual squad. They have settled on French as the common tongue for the dressing room and training pitch, which suits Jorge down to the ground as it is his favourite.

The fear for the Swiss fans is that Jorge will put the emphasis on defence, for he is known to be hot on discipline and organisation. Much will depend on whether his star striker, Stephane Chapuisat, regains full fitness after his long lay-off with cruciate ligament damage, suffered while playing for Borussia Dortmund. Chapuisat and Ciriaco Sforza form a threatening partnership, capable of taking on any defence in the world.

The bulk of this side were at the 1994 World Cup so many are well known, especially as they played England in November 1995. There is British interest in the side with Marc Hottiger, recently cleared to play for his new club Everton after protracted work-permit wrangling. Geiger is one of the 100-cap brigade, while Knup and Turkyilmaz have scored their goals at the top level – Turkyilmaz will be remembered as the player who gummed up the Manchester United works in the Champions League a couple of seasons ago with Galatasaray.

Their opening game against hosts England at Wembley will be the significant one. Jorge says: 'With that being the opening game of the Championship, it is a very big moment for me and my players. We know from our recent experience how difficult England can be at home, but anything can happen in football and if we can get a result against England who knows what might happen? We have worked very hard in our warm-up and we will be ready for England on 8 June. Holland are also a very fine team, while the Scots will not be easy, although my players know their players well.'

The Swiss will go into the group games as the outsiders and, with the pressure off, will be looking to cause a few upsets along the line. But any massive failure will rebound not only on Jorge but also on the Swiss Federation for the unanimous decision to axe Hodgson and look ahead to the World Cup.

# SWITZERLAND

*Formation:* 4-3-3
*Coach:* Artur Jorge

Pascolo

Hottiger          Henchoz          Geiger          Quentin

Ohrel                    Sforza                    Sutter

Knup                    Chapuisat                    Turkyilmaz

| Player | Position | Club | Date | Caps | Goals |
|--------|----------|------|------|------|-------|
| Marco Pascolo | G | Servette | 9.5.66 | 35 | – |
| Stephane Lehmann | G | Sion | 15.8.63 | 6 | – |
| Alain Geiger | D | Grasshopper | 5.11.60 | 110 | 2 |
| Dominique Herr | D | Sion | 26.10.65 | 52 | 4 |
| Yvan Quentin | D | Sion | 2.5.70 | 25 | – |
| Marc Hottiger | D | Everton (Eng) | 7.1.67 | 59 | 5 |
| Pascal Thuler | D | Grasshopper | 10.1.70 | 5 | – |
| Stephane Henchoz | D | SV Hamburg (Ger) | 7.9.74 | 15 | – |
| Ramon Vega | D | Grasshopper | 14.6.71 | 7 | 1 |
| Raphael Wicky | D | Sion | 26.4.77 | – | – |
| Christophe Ohrel | M | St Etienne (Fra) | 7.4.68 | 46 | 6 |
| Ciriaco Sforza | M | Bayern Munich (Ger) | 2.3.70 | 40 | 6 |
| Alain Sutter | M | Freiburg (Ger) | 22.1.68 | 61 | 5 |
| Sebastian Fournier | M | Sion | 27.6.71 | 11 | 1 |
| Stephan Wolf | M | FC Luzern | 31.1.71 | 1 | – |
| Marcel Koller | M | Grasshopper | 11.11.60 | 50 | 3 |
| Marco Walker | M | FC Basle | 2.5.70 | 1 | – |
| Christian Colombo | M | Lugano | 24.4.68 | 6 | – |
| Adrian Knup | F | Karlsruhe (Ger) | 2.7.68 | 45 | 26 |
| Marco Grassi | F | Rennes (Fra) | 8.8.68 | 21 | 2 |
| Kubilay Turkyilmaz | F | Grasshopper | 4.3.67 | 47 | 18 |
| Stephane Chapuisat | F | Bor Dortmund (Ger) | 28.6.69 | 45 | 12 |
| Dario Zuffi | F | FC Basle | 7.12.64 | 17 | 3 |
| Nestor Subiat | F | Grasshopper | 23.4.66 | 14 | 5 |

# SWITZERLAND A-Z

**STEPHANE CHAPUISAT** (Borussia Dortmund, Germany)
*Born:* 28.6.69    *Caps:* 45    *Goals:* 12
Returned to the Dortmund team after long-term cruciate knee ligament injury. Began his career with Lausanne, where he was top scorer for three seasons. Moved to Bayer Uerdingen in the Bundesliga and then on to Dortmund in 1991. Twice runner-up in Bundesliga scoring lists. His father, Pierre, won 34 caps as a rugged defender in the 1970s.

**CHRISTIAN COLOMBO** (Lugano)
*Born:* 24.4.68    *Caps:* 6    *Goals:* –
Usually a squad member rather than a first choice, and a useful player in his own First Division. He is a fine club servant having been with the south of Switzerland club since the age of 12.

**SEBASTIAN FOURNIER** (Sion)
*Born:* 27.6.71    *Caps:* 11    *Goals:* 1
Described by the Swiss press as a real find after scoring on his international debut in January 1994 in the USA, he went to the World Cup, but has had a less forward role since then. One of those who started at little Sion (pop: 27,000), the conveyor belt of good players.

**ALAIN GEIGER** (Grasshopper)
*Born:* 5.11.60    *Caps:* 110    *Goals:* 2
Joined Grasshopper in summer 1995 after the champions had offered him a playing role, plus continuing into a coaching position. He began his career with hometown club Sion back in 1978 before moving to Servette in 1981. He then moved on to Neuchatel in 1986, and then to France to join the leading First Division club St Etienne from 1988-90, where he was the captain. He returned to Sion in 1990 and was the captain of the team that won the league for the first time in 1992 and the Swiss Cup in 1991 and 1995. But just when it seemed he would finish his days at home – off he went again to Grasshopper. All this time he was quietly totting up international appearances – but is still short of Heinz Hermann's Swiss record of 117. Played all four games at World Cup finals to achieve lifetime ambition. Can play full back, sweeper, or midfield and, though he lacks pace, he is still a fine player.

**MARCO GRASSI** (Rennes, France)
*Born:* 8.8.68    *Caps:* 21    *Goals:* 2
Of Italian descent and with a multi-millionaire father, he came into the national squad early in 1993 after several impressive club displays. Is from the Italian region in the south of Switzerland and first played with FC Chiasso before joining FC Zurich in 1991 and thence to Grasshopper. Has been at Rennes since summer 1994 but fellow international Ohrel, who was also at the club, left in 1995 for St Etienne. Made several substitute appearances for Switzerland.

**STEPHANE HENCHOZ** (SV Hamburg, Germany)
*Born:* 7.9.74    *Caps:* 15    *Goals:* –
Capped at the age of 19 in 1993, and remembered by the international coaches
Hodgson and Stielike at Neuchatel as a player of huge potential. Was not included in
the 1994 World Cup squad though. He was snapped up by the Bundesliga club SV
Hamburg for £650,000 for the 1995-96 season. Previously at Neuchatel since 1991 and
they may have let him go too cheaply.


**DOMINIQUE HERR** (Sion)
*Born:* 26.10.65    *Caps:* 52    *Goals:* 4
Returned to the national side in March 1993 after a long spell out through injury. His
first club was FC Basle from 1983, then he was with Lausanne from 1988-92, before
moving to Sion with his international colleague Marc Hottiger in 1992. Noted hard-
tackling defender. Played all four Swiss games at 1994 World Cup, and won a 1995
Swiss Cup medal with Sion. Hardly missed a game since 1989.


**MARC HOTTIGER** (Everton, England)
*Born:* 7.1.67    *Caps:* 59    *Goals:* 5
First choice right back, he joined Newcastle from Sion in August 1994 for a snip at
£600,000, but for several weeks could not get a work permit for a £700,000 move to
Everton. Hardly missed an international since his first game for Switzerland and has
played in 59 of the last 64 internationals since he came into the side in 1989. He began
his senior career with Lausanne and then moved with his national team-mate Herr to
Sion in 1992. Will miss the first game through suspension.


**ADRIAN KNUP** (Karlsruhe, Germany)
*Born:* 2.7.68    *Caps:* 45    *Goals:* 26
His goal tally in internationals is excellent – yet to the end of 1994-95 he had only scored
57 league goals in 187 league games for FC Basle (1987-89), FC Luzern (1989-92) and
the two German Bundesliga clubs Stuttgart (1992-94) and Karlsruhe (1994-95 – six
goals in only 16 games). He has had injury problems, and was offloaded by the then
champions Stuttgart after failing to come to terms with the Bundesliga. He may well
return home if 1995-96 is a failure and Sion are favourites to sign him in summer 1996.


**MARCEL KOLLER** (Grasshopper)
*Born:* 11.11.60    *Caps:* 50    *Goals:* 3
Another one-club man, he joined Grasshopper at the age of 11 in summer 1972 and has
been there ever since, and has been a regular international for around a decade now.
Has won six League titles and four Cups with Grasshopper. Was not in the 1994 World
Cup squad – he was considered too old!


**STEPHANE LEHMANN** (Sion)
*Born:* 15.8.63    *Caps:* 6    *Goals:* –
Reserve keeper, who has been in the squad for some six years. He was No. 2 at the 1994
World Cup. Has been with Sion since his 1988 move from Second Division club
Schaffhausen, and has won the 1992 championship, and the 1991 and 1995 Swiss Cup
medals. Capable reserve.

**CHRISTOPHE OHREL** (St Etienne, France)

*Born: 7.4.68    Caps: 46    Goals: 6*

One of several trained bank clerks in the squad, he now plays for St Etienne in the French First Division after joining for the 1995-96 season from another French club Rennes. Went to France from Servette of Geneva and was formerly with the Lausanne club with whom he made his international debut. He left for France after gaining a 1994 championship medal with Servette. Has missed only three internationals (unavailable) in last three years but is playing for a once-famous club now in a rut.

**MARCO PASCOLO** (Servette Geneva)

*Born: 9.5.66    Caps: 35    Goals: –*

First choice goalkeeper through to the 1994 World Cup finals, but has had injury problems in 1995 and is only just back to his best. Regular in the national side since 1991, the same year he joined Servette from Neuchatel – when at Neuchatel he came under the coaching influence of Roy Hodgson.

**YVAN QUENTIN** (Sion)

*Born: 2.5.70    Caps: 25    Goals: –*

Another player developed by Sion. He made his debut for them in 1990 and was in the championship team of 1992. From there he progressed into the national squad. Was a long-term injury sufferer in part of the 1994-95 season and after playing in all four games at the 1994 World Cup, he was not called on again until the 1995 Swiss Centenary games. Won 1995 Swiss FA Cup medal. Under pressure for place from fans and media.

**CIRIACO SFORZA** (Bayern Munich, Germany)

*Born: 2.3.70    Caps: 40    Goals: 6*

Of Italian extraction and parentage, he was wanted by several clubs in Italy even after becoming a Swiss national in 1990, but has decided to pursue his career in the Bundesliga and – after joining Kaiserslautern from Grasshopper in 1993 – he signed in June 1995 for Bayern Munich for £4.2 million. First played for Grasshopper in the Swiss Division 1 at the age of 16 and is the new star of Swiss football.

**ALAIN SUTTER** (Freiburg, Germany)

*Born: 22.1.68    Caps: 61    Goals: 5*

Moved in November 1995 from Bayern Munich to fellow Bundesliga club Freiburg. Originally joined the Bundesliga club FC Nurnberg in the summer of 1993 from Grasshopper of Zurich for just £200,000 and thence on to Bayern Munich in summer 1994 for £1.4 million. His first club was Grasshopper, for whom he was a teenage prodigy in 1985. He spent a year on loan at Young Boys of Berne in 1987-88. He is easily recognisable with his long blond hair.

**NESTOR SUBIAT** (Grasshopper)

*Born: 23.4.66    Caps: 14    Goals: 5*

Argentinian born, his father was a top pro. He moved to France and played for Mulhouse (then in Division 1) and Strasbourg before crossing the border to play for Lugano in 1992. Now a Swiss national and has played for Grasshopper since 1994. Was in World Cup squad. Was top scorer in the club's 1995 Championship win with 21 goals in 26 games and was the Swiss Footballer of the Year. Spent much of the 1995-96 season with injury.

**PASCAL THULER** (Grasshopper)

*Born:* 10.1.70   *Caps:* 5   *Goals:* –

Has come through off the back of the fine 1994-95 season for Grasshopper, culminating in a championship medal. Took the place of the recuperating Quentin in the national side. Joined Grasshopper from St Gallen in 1993, and now establishing himself in the national squad. Wants to play in the Bundesliga as his mother was born in Germany.


**KUBILAY TURKYILMAZ** (Grasshopper)

*Born:* 4.3.67   *Caps:* 47   *Goals:* 18

Now back with Swiss champions Grasshopper after a spell in Turkey with Galatasaray. Missed the World Cup through an Achilles' injury, but after fine displays in the Champions League for Galatasaray, he was back in contention. He was the scourge of Manchester United with a couple of goals at Old Trafford in 1993-94. First played in the Swiss First Division for Bellinzona in the Italian south of the country, where he was league top scorer and spotted by then Serie A club Bologna. The Swiss were keen to sign up the son of Turkish immigrant parents. After Bologna's demise in 1993 he moved to Galatasaray for a Swiss record £1.8 million.


**RAMON VEGA** (Grasshopper)

*Born:* 14.6.71   *Caps:* 7   *Goals:* 1

Another player of immigrant parents (Spanish) whom the Swiss have tied to the mast very quickly – he was in the national side before the World Cup but did not make the final squad. Joined from junior club Trimbach in 1990 and has been in Grasshopper's 1995 championship team as a key defender. Will probably take over from Geiger.


**MARCO WALKER** (FC Basle)

*Born:* 2.5.70   *Caps:* 1   *Goals:* –

Has played for Basle since 1992 and gained his first cap as a sub in the Euro qualifier against Turkey in April 1995. Previously with Lugano and his brother Phillip has been a recent international keeper for Switzerland (11 caps to 1992).


**RAPHAEL WICKY** (Sion)

*Born:* 26.4.77   *Caps:* –   *Goals:* –

Another new member of the squad, he is also uncapped but it is only a matter of time before this right-sided midfield/defender earns his first cap in a spiralling career. Has been with Sion since the age of ten, and was a schoolboy/student only a few months ago. Has come through the youth and Under-21 set-up, and won a 1995 Swiss Cup medal, surely the first of many honours.


**STEPHAN WOLF** (FC Luzern)

*Born:* 31.1.71   *Caps:* 1   *Goals:* –

New to the squad and uncapped until coming on as sub at Wembley in autumn 1995, he is a defender/midfielder from the FC Luzern club, who has given consistent performances in the Swiss First Division since joining them in 1990.

**DARIO ZUFFI** (FC Basle)

*Born:* 7.12.64    *Caps:* 17    *Goals:* 3

Has not featured in the national side since 1990 after winning a string of caps 1988-90.
He played for Young Boys, Lugano and for Basle since 1993 and has kept in the eye of
the national selection with useful domestic performances.

### Coach: ARTUR JORGE

*Born:* 13.2.46

Former Portuguese coach Artur Jorge is on a hiding to nothing as the newly appointed
coach to the Swiss. He has to follow in the footsteps of the man who took the team to
the finals, Roy Hodgson, the Englishman who became a national hero when he guided
them to their first World Cup finals for 28 years. But if anyone can handle the pressure,
it is the intellectual Jorge, holder of two University doctorates and a linguist. Jorge is his
own man and will play to his own style, which may well mean the Swiss being more
defensive under him than they were under Hodgson. His record speaks for itself. He
was undefeated in his brief reign as manager of his native Portugal, with five wins and
three draws, while he gathered knowledge and experience as he coached in France and
Portugal. At his home club, Porto, he won three League titles, the domestic cup and
capped it all with the European Champions Cup in 1987. In France he was in charge at
Matra Racing Club in Paris and at Paris St Germain, where he again hit the jackpot
with the League title and the French Cup. Not a man to be underestimated.

# KEY PLAYER

## CIRIACO SFORZA

*Date of Birth:* 2.3.70
*Current club:* Bayern Munich
*Position:* Midfield
*Height:* 1.80 m
*Weight:* 76 kg

### CAREER RECORD

| Year | Club | League Apps | Goals | Int Apps | Goals |
|------|------|------|------|------|------|
| 1986-87 | Grasshopper | 21 | 1 | | |
| 1987-88 | | 29 | 3 | | |
| 1988-89 | | 16 | 1 | | |
| 1989-90 | FC Aarau | 22 | 3 | | |
| 1990-91 | Grasshopper | 28 | 1 | | |
| 1991-92 | | 26 | 4 | 6 | 0 |
| 1992-93 | | 21 | 2 | 10 | 3 |
| 1993-94 | Kaiserslautern | 29 | 8 | 12 | 1 |
| 1994-95 | | 32 | 7 | 7 | 1 |
| 1995-96 | Bayern Munich | | | 5 | 1 |

### HONOURS

Swiss champion – 1992
Swiss cup winner – 1988, 1989

| No | Date | Opponents | Venue | Score | Goals | Competition | Subbed Sub |
|---|---|---|---|---|---|---|---|
| 1 | 21.8.91 | Czechoslovakia | Prague | 1-1 | 0 | Friendly | 90 |
| 2 | 11.9.91 | Scotland | Berne | 2-2 | 0 | E Nations, Q | 90 |
| 3 | 9.10.91 | Sweden | Lucerne | 3-1 | 0 | Friendly | 90 |
| 4 | 13.11.91 | Romania | Bucharest | 0-1 | 0 | E Nations, Q | 90 |
| 5 | 23.1.92 | UAE | Dubai | 2-0 | 0 | Friendly | Subbed 87 |
| 6 | 27.5.92 | France | Lausanne | 2-1 | 0 | Friendly | 90 |
| 7 | 16.8.92 | Estonia | Tallinn | 6-0 | 1 | World Cup, Q | 90 |
| 8 | 9.9.92 | Scotland | Berne | 3-1 | 0 | World Cup, Q | 90 |
| 9 | 14.10.92 | Italy | Cagliari | 2-2 | 0 | World Cup, Q | 90 |
| 10 | 18.11.92 | Malta | Berne | 3-0 | 1 | World Cup, Q | 90 |
| 11 | 23.1.93 | Japan | Hong Kong | 1-1 | 0 | Friendly | 90 |
| 12 | 26.1.93 | Hong Kong | Hong Kong | 3-2 | 1 | Friendly | 90 |
| 13 | 17.3.93 | Tunisia | Tunis | 1-0 | 0 | Friendly | 90 |
| 14 | 31.3.93 | Portugal | Berne | 1-0 | 0 | World Cup, Q | 90 |
| 15 | 17.4.93 | Malta | Valletta | 2-0 | 0 | World Cup, Q | 90 |
| 16 | 1.5.93 | Italy | Berne | 1-0 | 0 | World Cup, Q | 90 |
| 17 | 11.8.93 | Sweden | Boras | 2-1 | 0 | Friendly | 90 |
| 18 | 8.9.93 | Scotland | Aberdeen | 1-1 | 0 | World Cup, Q | 90 |
| 19 | 13.10.93 | Portugal | Oporto | 0-1 | 0 | World Cup, Q | 90 |
| 20 | 9.3.94 | Hungary | Budapest | 2-1 | 1 | Friendly | Subbed 46 |
| 21 | 20.4.94 | Czech Republic | Zurich | 3-0 | 0 | Friendly | Subbed 46 |
| 22 | 27.5.94 | Liechtenstein | Basel | 2-0 | 0 | Friendly | 90 |
| 23 | 3.6.94 | Italy | Rome | 0-1 | 0 | Friendly | 90 |
| 24 | 11.6.94 | Bolivia | Montreal | 0-0 | 0 | Friendly | Subbed 77 |
| 25 | 18.6.94 | USA | Detroit | 1-1 | 0 | WC finals | Subbed 77 |
| 26 | 22.6.94 | Romania | Detroit | 4-1 | 0 | WC finals | 90 |
| 27 | 26.6.94 | Colombia | San Francisco | 0-2 | 0 | WC finals | 90 |
| 28 | 2.7.94 | Spain | Washington | 0-3 | 0 | WC finals | 90 |
| 29 | 12.10.94 | Sweden | Berne | 4-2 | 1 | E Nations, Q | 90 |
| 30 | 16.11.94 | Iceland | Lausanne | 1-0 | 0 | E Nations, Q | 90 |
| 31 | 14.12.94 | Turkey | Istanbul | 2-1 | 0 | E Nations, Q | 90 |
| 32 | 29.3.95 | Hungary | Budapest | 2-2 | 0 | E Nations, Q | 90 |
| 33 | 26.4.95 | Turkey | Berne | 1-2 | 0 | E Nations, Q | 90 |
| 34 | 19.6.95 | Italy | Lausanne | 0-1 | 0 | E Nations, Q | 90 |
| 35 | 23.6.95 | Germany | Berne | 1-2 | 0 | Berne | 90 |
| 36 | 16.8.95 | Iceland | Reykjavik | 2-0 | 0 | E Nations, Q | 90 |
| 37 | 6.9.95 | Sweden | Gothenburg | 0-0 | 0 | E Nations, Q | 90 |
| 38 | 11.10.95 | Hungary | Zurich | 3-0 | 1 | E Nations, Q | 90 |
| 39 | 15.11.95 | England | Wembley | 1-3 | 0 | Friendly | 90 |
| 40 | 13.3.96 | Luxembourg | Luxembourg | 1-1 | 0 | Friendly | 90 |

# HOLLAND

By Jan Buitenga

For many people, Holland are the big and hot favourites for Euro 96. But the Dutch themselves, however, are not that optimistic. Their performance against the Republic of Ireland in Liverpool in December 1995 may have been very impressive, but if you can play football like that, why do you need a play-off to reach the final tournament?

Because that's typical of the Dutch national team: one game brilliant, the next struggling. The backbone of the team now consists of Ajax players, because coach Guus Hiddink decided to copy the famous and successful Ajax system. How fit (physically and mentally) will all those Ajax players be, after another long and exhausting season at national and international level? How hungry for success will they be after winning every trophy at club level?

Hopefully they learned from their lesson in June 1995. With seven of new European Champions Ajax in the starting line-up, the Dutch were humiliated in Minsk by Belarus. It was a game they needed to win, because the previous match, away to the Czechs, also ended in defeat (1-3). On that dark night in Minsk, everything seemed to be over and out for the Dutch. Captain Danny Blind even said that it was his last match for the national team. When somebody told him that Luxembourg had beaten the Czechs with a sensational last-minute goal, Blind answered this was not the kind of humour he liked. Lucky for him, it was true and Blind decided to change his mind. For him, it's the last opportunity to play in a big tournament and he deserves this. All those youngsters already know they can get another chance in Euro 2000, when Holland and Belgium are the hosts.

Another mystery for many people (including the insiders) is the difference of form the players show when they wear the jersey of the Dutch national team instead of their club jersey. Even the players themselves don't understand this.

But one thing is sure, the Dutch always go out to play football! They never go on the pitch just to get a result. Their performances in the 1992 competition were more highly appreciated by the fans than those of 1988, when they won it. Although Holland went out on penalties against those likeable Danes, nobody blamed them. In all their matches, the Dutch showed their great skill, technique, tactical knowhow and added this to the right fighting spirit. Of course, everybody was disappointed to go out on penalties, but we reached the semi-finals and did this with very good football.

# HOLLAND

*Formation:* 3-3-3-1
*Coach:* Guus Hiddink

<table>
<tr><td></td><td>Van der Sar</td><td></td></tr>
<tr><td>Reiziger</td><td>Blind</td><td>F. de Boer</td></tr>
<tr><td>Davids</td><td>Seedorf</td><td>Winter</td></tr>
<tr><td>R. de Boer</td><td>Bergkamp</td><td>Overmars</td></tr>
<tr><td></td><td>Kluivert</td><td></td></tr>
</table>

| Player | Position | Club | Date | Caps | Goals |
|--------|----------|------|------|------|-------|
| Edwin van der Sar | G | Ajax | 29.10.70 | 5 | – |
| Eddie de Goey | G | Feyenoord | 20.12.66 | 27 | – |
| Frank de Boer | D | Ajax | 15.5.70 | 38 | 1 |
| Artur Numan | D | PSV | 14.12.69 | 13 | – |
| Danny Blind | D | Ajax | 1.8.61 | 36 | 1 |
| Michael Reiziger | D | Ajax | 3.5.73 | 6 | – |
| Johan de Kock | D | Roda JC | 25.10.64 | 6 | – |
| Aron Winter | M | Lazio (Ita) | 1.3.67 | 52 | 4 |
| Ronald de Boer | M | Ajax | 15.5.70 | 22 | 6 |
| Winston Bogarde | M | Ajax | 22.10.70 | 1 | – |
| Edgar Davids | M | Ajax | 13.3.73 | 5 | – |
| Glenn Helder | M | Arsenal (Eng) | 28.10.68 | 3 | – |
| Richard Witschge | M | Bordeaux (Fra) | 20.9.69 | 22 | 1 |
| Clarence Seedorf | M | Sampdoria (Ita) | 1.4.76 | 8 | 4 |
| Orlando Trustfull | M | Feyenoord | 4.8.70 | 2 | – |
| Eric van der Luer | M | Roda JC | 18.8.65 | 2 | – |
| Arnold Scholten | M | Ajax | 5.12.62 | – | – |
| Stan Valckx | D | PSV | 20.10.63 | 19 | – |
| Dennis Bergkamp | F | Arsenal (Eng) | 10.5.69 | 42 | 24 |
| Marc Overmars | F | Ajax | 29.3.72 | 29 | 6 |
| Patrick Kluivert | F | Ajax | 1.7.76 | 6 | 3 |
| Yuri Mulder | F | Schalke (Ger) | 23.3.69 | 5 | 3 |
| Bryan Roy | F | Nott'm Forest (Eng) | 12.2.70 | 32 | 9 |
| Gaston Taument | F | Feyenoord | 1.10.70 | 10 | 2 |

# HOLLAND A-Z

**DENNIS BERGKAMP** (Arsenal, England)
*Born:* 10.5.69   *Caps:* 42   *Goals:* 24
Cost Arsenal £7.5 million in summer 1995 from Inter of Milan after a couple of
unhappy seasons in Serie A. He was top scorer in the Dutch League in his last three
seasons (first season tied with Romario) scoring 75 goals in 91 league games – found
scoring a bit more difficult in Italy though. Starting out at the Ajax youth academy
where he was encouraged by Johan Cruyff, and an admirer of Glenn Hoddle, Bergkamp (who was named after Denis Law) was in the side that won the 1990 League and
1992 UEFA Cup. Was the 1992 Dutch Footballer of the Year.

**DANNY BLIND** (Ajax)
*Born:* 1.8.61   *Caps:* 36   *Goals:* 1
Just when it seemed that his days were numbered, he has come back to secure a national
place and is the club captain at Ajax, who have won the 1994 and 1995 Championship
and 1995 European Champions Cup and World Club Cup – he was man of the match
and scored the winning penalty in the World Club Cup shoot-out against Gremio last
November. One of the longest-serving defenders in Dutch football with Sparta Rotterdam and latterly with Ajax, he is way past 400 League games. Made his first-team debut
in 1979 for Sparta, and joined Ajax in 1985. First three caps in 1987, his fourth came
only in 1989. Missed the 1994 World Cup, but has been first choice again since. Will
miss the first game through suspension.

**WINSTON BOGARDE** (Ajax)
*Born:* 22.10.70   *Caps:* 1   *Goals:* –
Gained his first cap against Ireland in the Euro 96 play-off and was the last of the
Ajax-accredited first team to win a cap. Former Under-21 international with a solid
grounding in Premier Division football with Sparta Rotterdam, he was signed as the
ultimate utility midfielder in summer 1994 and has gone on to Championship, European Champions Cup and World Club Cup honours in 1995. Prefers to play up front.

**EDGAR DAVIDS** (Ajax)
*Born:* 13.3.73   *Caps:* 5   *Goals:* –
Another of the Ajax tribe – and from the youth team. He has had serious injury
problems in the last 18 months, but is so young that it shouldn't affect him. Now back to
fitness and form. First capped just before the 1994 World Cup, and first played for Ajax
in 1991. Born in that football hotbed of Paramaribo, Surinam. Former Under-21 star.

**FRANK DE BOER** (Ajax)
*Born:* 15.5.70   *Caps:* 38   *Goals:* 1
Twin brother of Ronald de Boer, and Holland's key central defender. Has always been
with Ajax since schooldays and was an important defender in the current treble of
European Champions Cup, Super Cup and World Club Cup. First played for Ajax in
1988 at the age of 18 and was an international a couple of years later.

**RONALD DE BOER** (Ajax)

*Born:* 15.5.70   *Caps:* 22   *Goals:* 6

Twin brother of Frank, he had an identical run through the Ajax youth system, until 1991 when he was loaned (then sold) to Twente Enschede. A year, and several goals later, he came back to Ajax and went into the national team. First cap in 1992 for Holland – Frank had reached 12 caps when Ronald gained his first cap. Key member – now more of a midfielder – of the 1994 and 1995 champions, and 1995 European Champions Cup and World Club Cup holders.

**EDDIE DE GOEY** (Feyenoord)

*Born:* 20.12.66   *Caps:* 27   *Goals:* –

Was the first-choice keeper since taking over from Ajax's Stanley Menzo in 1992 and played 27 consecutive internationals until being replaced by van der Sar in June 1995. He plays for the 1993 champions Feyenoord having joined them in 1989 from Sparta, another Rotterdam club, where he had been since making his first-team debut in 1985. He has worked his way through from the national Under-21 side and also won Cup medals in 1991, 1992, 1994 and 1995. His junior club was Olympia Gouda – where they make the cheese.

**JOHAN DE KOCK** (Roda JC Kerkrade)

*Born:* 25.10.64   *Caps:* 6   *Goals:* –

Was in the Roda team which commendably finished runners-up in the 1994-95 season and gained a national squad place off the back of Roda's achievement. Has been a Premier Division player for 11 seasons with Groningen and Utrecht and now Roda. International caps are reward for solid work every weekend for over a decade.

**GLENN HELDER** (Arsenal, England)

*Born:* 28.10.68   *Caps:* 3   *Goals:* –

Signed by Arsenal in January/February 1995 for around £2.5 million from the Dutch Premier Division club Vitesse Arnhem, after having started his senior career with Sparta Rotterdam. He was once rejected by Ajax as a youth. First cap in friendly against France in 1994.

**PATRICK KLUIVERT** (Ajax)

*Born:* 1.7.76   *Caps:* 6   *Goals:* 3

Remarkable first season in 1994-95 when he was club top scorer with 18 goals in the 1995 Championship win (in just 26 games), then scored the winning goal in the European Champions Cup final, and also gained his first cap. His form continued through the start of the 1995-96 season with a World Club Cup medal and then another career highlight – the two goals against Ireland that put Holland into the Euro 96 finals. Joined the Ajax youth set-up at the age of eight.

**YURI MULDER** (Schalke 04, Germany)

*Born:* 23.3.69   *Caps:* 5   *Goals:* 3

Has been gaining experience outside the country – he plays in the Bundesliga for Schalke and has been there since signing from Twente Enschede in summer 1993. Guess where he started his career – in the Ajax youth and first team before being sold to Twente as surplus to requirements in the Bergkamp days.

**ARTUR NUMAN** (PSV Eindhoven)

*Born:* 14.12.69    *Caps:* 13    *Goals:* –

This was the player who nearly came to Manchester City in 1992 for £1 million but was offered a better deal by PSV, where he now plays. He is the former Under-21 captain and was previously until 1992 with Twente Enschede before moving to PSV. His first cap was against Poland in the World Cup qualifying home leg. Numan is the former club top scorer in 1993-94 who is now played at left-back (reluctantly but resignedly) where his skills have earned him a permanent place in the side. He is now the club captain at PSV.

**MARC OVERMARS** (Ajax)

*Born:* 29.3.72    *Caps:* 29    *Goals:* 6

The 1992-93 term with Ajax was really his first full senior season and he went straight through the Under-21 side into the full national team. He played for Go Ahead Eagles when they were in Division 2 in 1990-91, then moved to Division 1 club Willem II Tilburg in 1991-92, before joining Ajax when in the Under-21 national side. His brother was a top-flight player with Go Ahead Eagles. Now really beginning to make a name for himself – as creator (and more than occasional scorer) for Ajax, the 1994 and 1995 champions and 1995 European Champions Cup and World Club Cup champions. Seriously damaged his knee ligaments in league game against De Graafschap just before Christmas and is almost certainly out of Euro 96.

**MICHAEL REIZIGER** (Ajax)

*Born:* 3.5.73    *Caps:* 6    *Goals:* –

Another from the Ajax youth set-up, he returned to the club after the 1994 Championship win after being out on loan for a season at Volendam and Groningen. Within two months he was in the national team. Shores up the right side of defence and has been an integral part of the all-conquering Ajax side.

**BRYAN ROY** (Nottingham Forest)

*Born:* 12.2.70    *Caps:* 32    *Goals:* 9

Signed from the Serie A club Foggia in August 1994 for £2.5 million, he is another of the Ajax products and played from youth team through to first team with Ajax. He played in the Ajax first team at 17, and also had two seasons in Serie A. Played in 1994 World Cup, since when he has been hugely popular in Nottingham.

**ARNOLD SCHOLTEN** (Ajax)

*Born:* 5.12.63    *Caps:* –    *Goals:* –

Combines with Bogarde in the role of Ajax utility man, mainly in midfield and defence. He has returned in summer 1995 to Ajax after spending seven seasons (1988-95) at the rivals Feyenoord with whom he won a league title and four Dutch Cups. First club was Den Bosch from 1983-86, and first spell at Ajax was from 1986-89 which included a European Cup-Winners' Cup medal in 1987.

**CLARENCE SEEDORF** (Sampdoria, Italy)

*Born:* 1.4.76    *Caps:* 8    *Goals:* 4

Signed by Sampdoria in summer 1995 for a comparatively cheap £3.2 million considering his potential – of all the Ajax youngsters who have gone into the first team, this one is the youngest at just 16 (in 1992) to have played at the top level. An international at 18, and in 1995 was a first choice. Born in Amsterdam.

**GASTON TAUMENT** (Feyenoord)
*Born:* 1.10.70   *Caps:* 10   *Goals:* 2
May well vie with Roy for the position that the injured Overmars may vacate. He was signed by Feyenoord in 1989 from an amateur side in his home town of Den Haag, and won a league medal and four Dutch Cups with the club.

**OLANDO TRUSTFULL** (Feyenoord)
*Born:* 4.8.70   *Caps:* 2   *Goals:* –
Came into the national squad in autumn 1995 to win his first caps. Former Ajax junior, he was released to join Haarlem, Dordrecht and Twente Enschede before moving to Feyenoord in 1992. One of the few to escape the Ajax net.

**STAN VALCKX** (PSV Eindhoven)
*Born:* 20.10.63   *Caps:* 19   *Goals:* –
Was a key member of Bobby Robson's PSV side that won the 1991 and 1992 titles and then went with Robson to Sporting Lisbon in 1992. Returned after three seasons in Portugal to his old club. He played before, during and after the 1994 World Cup which added to three caps gained some four years earlier.

**ERIC VAN DER LUER** (Roda JC)
*Born:* 18.8.65   *Caps:* 2   *Goals:* –
Plays his football down in the bottom corner of Holland, first for MVV Maastricht and since 1988 for Roda JC Kerkrade. His recent caps are reward for sterling efforts in the top flight since 1982.

**EDWIN VAN DER SAR** (Ajax)
*Born:* 29.10.70   *Caps:* 5   *Goals:* –
His performances at club level, where he has played in the Ajax team since taking over three seasons ago from Stanley Menzo, have forced him past de Goey for Holland's last four internationals. He was part of the team that won the 1994 and 1995 Championship, the 1995 European Champions Cup and World Club Cup, so would find it hard to be ignored. Originally from the famous Ajax youth academy.

**ARON WINTER** (Lazio, Italy)
*Born:* 1.3.67   *Caps:* 52   *Goals:* 4
Plays in midfield for Lazio, where he is a far more consistent performer than his former partner – Paul Gascoigne. Cost Lazio £4 million from Ajax in 1992 after the Ajax League win in 1990 and the UEFA Cup win in 1992. Originally from Surinam, like Gullit and Rijkaard, he moved to Holland as a child. Is certain of his place in the national side. Another product of the Ajax youth system.

**RICHARD WITSCHGE** (Bordeaux, France)
*Born:* 20.9.69   *Caps:* 22   *Goals:* 1
Now playing well for Bordeaux after a £2 million move from Barcelona in 1994 after not quite fitting in with Cruyff's plans. He returned to the national team in 1995 and has come full circle because an injury just before the World Cup forced him to drop out and be replaced in the national squad by brother Rob. Yet another of the Ajax youngsters, he became a full international – like his brother – with Ajax before moving to Barcelona.

**Coach: GUUS HIDDINK**

*Born:* 8.11.46

A player in the 1960s and 1970s with a host of Dutch clubs including De Graafschap, PSV and NEC Nijmegen, he also moved into the North American Soccer League with the Washington Diplomats and San Jose Earthquakes. After a spell as youth team coach with De Graafschap he joined PSV, first as assistant, then as coach in 1986. In 1988 he guided PSV to European Cup success before moving to Spain with Valencia. He succeeded Dick Advocaat as national coach in the autumn of 1994.

# KEY PLAYER

## DENNIS BERGKAMP

*Date of Birth:* 10.5.69
*Current club:* Arsenal
*Position:* Forward
*Height:* 1.85 m
*Weight:* 80 kg

### CAREER RECORD

| | | League | | Int | |
|---|---|---|---|---|---|
| Year | Club | Apps | Goals | Apps | Goals |
| 1986-87 | Ajax | 14 | 2 | | |
| 1987-88 | | 25 | 5 | | |
| 1988-89 | | 30 | 13 | | |
| 1989-90 | | 25 | 8 | | |
| 1990-91 | | 33 | 25 | 6 | 3 |
| 1991-92 | | 30 | 24 | 11 | 7 |
| 1992-93 | | 27 | 26 | 6 | 4 |
| 1993-94 | Inter | 31 | 8 | 13 | 9 |
| 1994-95 | | 21 | 3 | 3 | 1 |
| 1995-96 | Arsenal | | | 3 | |

### HONOURS

Dutch champion – 1990
Dutch Cup winner – 1987, 1993
Dutch top scorer – 1991, 1992, 1993
UEFA Cup winner – 1992 [Ajax], 1994 [Inter]
Cup-Winners' Cup winner – 1987

| No | Date | Opponents | Venue | Score | Goals | Competition | Subbed Sub |
|---|---|---|---|---|---|---|---|
| 1 | 26.9.90 | Italy | Palermo | 0-1 | 0 | Friendly | Sub pl 25 |
| 2 | 17.10.90 | Portugal | Porto | 0-1 | 0 | E Nations, Q | 90 |
| 3 | 21.11.90 | Greece | Rotterdam | 2-0 | 1 | E Nations, Q | Subbed 85 |
| 4 | 19.12.90 | Malta | Valletta | 8-0 | 2 | E Nations, Q | 90 |
| 5 | 13.3.91 | Malta | Rotterdam | 1-0 | 0 | E Nations, Q | 90 |
| 6 | 17.4.91 | Finland | Rotterdam | 2-0 | 0 | E Nations, Q | Subbed 73 |
| 7 | 11.9.91 | Poland | Eindhoven | 1-1 | 1 | Friendly | 90 |
| 8 | 16.10.91 | Portugal | Rotterdam | 1-0 | 0 | E Nations, Q | 90 |

| No | Date | Opponents | Venue | Score | Goals | Competition | Subbed Sub |
|----|------|-----------|-------|-------|-------|-------------|------------|
| 9 | 4.12.91 | Greece | Salonika | 2-0 | 1 | E Nations, Q | 90 |
| 10 | 12.2.92 | Portugal | Faro | 0-2 | 0 | Friendly | Subbed 46 |
| 11 | 27.5.92 | Austria | Sittard | 3-2 | 1 | Friendly | Subbed 46 |
| 12 | 30.5.92 | Wales | Utrecht | 4-0 | 0 | Friendly | Subbed 64 |
| 13 | 5.6.92 | France | Lens | 1-1 | 0 | Friendly | Subbed 46 |
| 14 | 12.6.92 | Scotland | Gothenburg | 1-0 | 1 | EN finals | Subbed 86 |
| 15 | 15.6.92 | CIS | Gothenburg | 0-0 | 0 | EN finals | Subbed 80 |
| 16 | 18.6.92 | Germany | Gothenburg | 3-1 | 1 | EN finals | Subbed 88 |
| 17 | 22.6.92 | Denmark | Gothenburg | 2-2 | 2 | EN finals | 120 |
| 18 | 9.9.92 | Italy | Eindhoven | 2-3 | 2 | Friendly | Subbed 68 |
| 19 | 23.9.92 | Norway | Oslo | 1-2 | 1 | World Cup, Q | 90 |
| 20 | 14.10.92 | Poland | Rotterdam | 2-2 | 0 | World Cup, Q | 90 |
| 21 | 24.2.93 | Turkey | Utrecht | 3-1 | 0 | World Cup, Q | 90 |
| 22 | 28.4.93 | England | Wembley | 2-2 | 1 | World Cup, Q | 90 |
| 23 | 9.6.93 | Norway | Rotterdam | 0-0 | 0 | World Cup, Q | 90 |
| 24 | 22.9.93 | San Marino | Bologna | 7-0 | 0 | World Cup, Q | 90 |
| 25 | 13.10.93 | England | Rotterdam | 2-0 | 1 | World Cup, Q | 90 |
| 26 | 17.11.93 | Poland | Poznan | 3-1 | 2 | World Cup, Q | 90 |
| 27 | 19.1.94 | Tunisia | Tunis | 2-2 | 0 | Friendly | Subbed 82 |
| 28 | 23.3.94 | Scotland | Glasgow | 1-0 | 0 | Friendly | Subbed 46 |
| 29 | 20.4.94 | Rep of Ireland | Tilburg | 0-1 | 0 | Friendly | Subbed 46 |
| 30 | 1.6.94 | Hungary | Eindhoven | 7-1 | 2 | Friendly | 90 |
| 31 | 12.6.94 | Canada | Toronto | 3-0 | 1 | Friendly | 90 |
| 32 | 21.6.94 | Saudi Arabia | Washington | 2-1 | 0 | WC finals | 90 |
| 33 | 25.6.94 | Belgium | Orlando | 0-1 | 0 | WC finals | 90 |
| 34 | 29.6.94 | Morocco | Orlando | 2-1 | 1 | WC finals | 90 |
| 35 | 4.7.94 | Rep of Ireland | Orlando | 2-0 | 1 | WC finals | 90 |
| 36 | 9.7.94 | Brazil | Dallas | 2-3 | 1 | WC finals | 90 |
| 37 | 12.10.94 | Norway | Oslo | 1-1 | 0 | E Nations, Q | Subbed 68 |
| 38 | 22.5.95 | Portugal | Eindhoven | 0-1 | 0 | Friendly | 90 |
| 39 | 29.3.95 | Malta | Rotterdam | 4-0 | 1 | E Nations, Q | 90 |
| 40 | 6.9.95 | Belarus | Rotterdam | 1-0 | 0 | E Nations, Q | 90 |
| 41 | 15.11.95 | Norway | Rotterdam | 3-0 | 0 | E Nations, Q | Subbed 79 |
| 42 | 13.12.95 | Rep of Ireland | Liverpool | 2-0 | 0 | E Nations, Q | Subbed 57 |

# SCOTLAND

Scotland play their European Championship Cup final on 15 June at Wembley. Delighted as they were to qualify for the Euro finals for the first time, common sense and everything else flew out of the window the moment they were drawn to face the auld enemy. Win that one and the Tartan Army will not worry or care if they fail to make it into the hat for the last eight.

Mind you, a win against the English and anything is possible as their last game is against one of the tournament outsiders, Switzerland. Two wins will be enough to reach the knockout stage with something to spare. But, before that, Scotland must play their opening game against the Championship favourites Holland in Birmingham on 10 June. A serious defeat and heads could drop as they prepare to face Terry Venables' England.

That is where coach Craig Brown comes in. A sensible, down-to-earth man is Mr Brown, a former educationalist who knows a thing or two about how to keep naughty boys under control.

Unlike some of his predecessors, Craig is aware of his team's deficiencies as well as their strengths and he is always careful not to promise those one-eyed fans too much in the way of expectation. Like most sensible Scots, he will never forget the embarrassment of Peru and Iran in 1978 in the Argentina World Cup. Brown would much rather remember the next game that side played – a win against the odds against the Dutch!

The coach will be looking to be solid and organised, to play the percentages and take advantage of any mistakes by the opposition. In this respect Colin Hendry is absolutely crucial, a rock in defence and an inspiration to the entire team.

In midfield a blend of Celtic's John Collins and Paul McStay, Rangers' Stuart McCall, Billy McKinlay of Blackburn Rovers and their jewel in the crown, Leeds United skipper Gary McAllister. Possibly the outstanding midfield player in British football, McAllister creates goals and scores them. His free kicks are Brazilian in style and he has an astute tactical brain.

But if Scotland are to hit the high spots then Craig Brown may have to swallow his pride and go for Duncan Ferguson, whom he studiously ignored while the Everton player had his problems on and off the pitch. He has little Pat Nevin for width if he wants him and a choice between Eoin Jess, John McGinlay, Ally McCoist, John Spencer and Duncan Shearer to join him up front.

NB: Figures in the Scotland section are provided up to and including 24 April.

# SCOTLAND

*Formation:* 5-3-2
*Coach:* Craig Brown

```
                        Goram

McKimmie     McLaren      Hendry       Boyd      T McKinlay

            McStay     McAllister    Collins

         Jess              Booth
```

| Player | Position | Club | Date | Caps | Goals |
|--------|----------|------|------|------|-------|
| Andy Goram | G | Rangers | 13.4.64 | 35 | – |
| Jim Leighton | G | Hibernian | 24.7.58 | 73 | – |
| Nicky Walker | G | Partick Thistle | 29.9.62 | 1 | – |
| Tommy Boyd | D | Celtic | 24.11.65 | 33 | – |
| Colin Calderwood | D | Tottenham H (Eng) | 20.1.65 | 9 | 1 |
| Colin Hendry | D | Blackburn R (Eng) | 7.12.65 | 16 | 1 |
| Stewart McKimmie | D | Aberdeen | 27.10.62 | 37 | 1 |
| Tosh McKinlay | D | Celtic | 3.12.64 | 3 | – |
| Alan McLaren | D | Rangers | 4.1.71 | 24 | – |
| Craig Burley | D | Chelsea (Eng) | 24.9.71 | 7 | – |
| John Collins | M | Celtic | 31.1.68 | 31 | 8 |
| Scot Gemmill | M | Nott'm Forest (Eng) | 2.1.71 | 5 | – |
| Gary McAllister | M | Leeds U (Eng) | 25.12.64 | 39 | 4 |
| Stuart McCall | M | Rangers | 10.6.64 | 32 | 1 |
| Billy McKinlay | M | Blackburn R (Eng) | 22.4.69 | 17 | 4 |
| Paul McStay | M | Celtic | 22.10.64 | 73 | 9 |
| Pat Nevin | M | Tranmere R (Eng) | 6.9.63 | 28 | 5 |
| John Robertson | F | Hearts | 2.10.64 | 16 | 3 |
| Ally McCoist | F | Rangers | 24.9.62 | 51 | 18 |
| John McGinlay | F | Bolton W (Eng) | 8.4.64 | 9 | 3 |
| Eoin Jess | F | Coventry C (Eng) | 13.12.70 | 10 | 1 |
| Darren Jackson | F | Hibernian | 25.7.66 | 11 | – |
| Scott Booth | F | Aberdeen | 16.12.71 | 10 | 5 |
| Duncan Shearer | F | Aberdeen | 28.8.62 | 7 | 2 |
| John Spencer | F | Chelsea (Eng) | 11.9.70 | 10 | – |

# SCOTLAND A-Z

### SCOTT BOOTH (Aberdeen)
*Born:* 16.12.71  *Caps:* 10  *Goals:* 5
Born in Aberdeen and signed by his home-town club as a 16-year-old in July 1988, he made his first-team debut the following year. Has come through the national Under-21 set up.

### TOMMY BOYD (Celtic)
*Born:* 24.11.65  *Caps:* 33  *Goals:* –
Played for Motherwell from schooldays to 1985 First Division title and 1991 captain of Scottish FA Cup win. Moved to Chelsea in 1991 but returned to Scotland in 1992 with Celtic in a swap deal with Tony Cascarino. Played in 1992 European Championship, and was in Celtic's 1995 Scottish Cup winning team.

### CRAIG BURLEY (Chelsea, England)
*Born:* 24.9.71  *Caps:* 7  *Goals:* –
Joined Chelsea as a trainee in September 1989, and played for the Scottish Schools, Youth and Under-21 teams before gaining his first senior caps. Nephew of former Ipswich and Scotland full back George Burley, the current Ipswich manager. First-team debut for Chelsea in April 1991.

### COLIN CALDERWOOD (Tottenham Hotspur, England)
*Born:* 20.1.65  *Caps:* 9  *Goals:* 1
Swindon captain in 1993 promotion to the Premiership, then immediately became Ossie Ardiles' first signing at Tottenham for £1.25 million. Benefited from Gerry Francis' coaching at Tottenham, and has become a key defender in 1995-96. Says he owes his initial caps to the media following Klinsmann at Tottenham.

### JOHN COLLINS (Celtic)
*Born:* 31.1.68  *Caps:* 31  *Goals:* 8
Like Tosh McKinlay, he began his career with the Celtic Boys Club team and is now back with the Celtic club. Moved from Celtic Boys Club after his father broke his leg and couldn't drive him from Galashiels to Glasgow – he eventually finished up at Hibernian in 1984. Moved back to Celtic for a then club record of £925,000 in summer 1990. Member of 1990 World Cup squad. Has been interesting Middlesbrough.

### SCOT GEMMILL (Nottingham Forest, England)
*Born:* 2.1.71  *Caps:* 5  *Goals:* –
Son of Archie Gemmill, the former Derby, Forest and Birmingham midfielder who gained 43 caps for Scotland, and who played well in the 1978 World Cup finals. Scot signed for Forest when his father was coach at the club.

### ANDY GORAM (Rangers)
*Born:* 13.4.64  *Caps:* 35  *Goals:* –
Born at Bury, and first-choice keeper for the national side until a series of injuries. Played in 1986 and 1990 World Cups and 1992 European Championships. Began his career with West Bromwich Albion as an apprentice, then moved to Oldham from 1981-87. Moved to Scotland with Hibernian for £325,000 and on to Rangers in 1991 for

£1 million, where he won three League titles, two Cup medals and a League Cup medal. Also Scotland cricket international.

**COLIN HENDRY** (Blackburn Rovers, England)
*Born:* 7.12.65    *Caps:* 16    *Goals:* 1
Second spell with the 1995 Premiership champions, he joined originally in 1987 from Dundee for £30,000 and scored winning goal in Full Members Cup final v Charlton. Moved on to Manchester City in November 1989 for £700,000 before returning for the same fee to Blackburn in November 1991. With Blackburn through promotion to elite and Premiership title. Contracted until 1998. Sent off v Spartak Moscow in 1995-96 Champions League.

**DARREN JACKSON** (Hibernian)
*Born:* 25.7.66    *Caps:* 11    *Goals:* –
Born in Edinburgh, he began his career with the local Meadowbank Thistle (Livingston) club and signed for Newcastle in 1986. Returned north of the border with Dundee United in early 1989 and moved to his present club Hibs in 1992. Has just signed a contract to bind him to Hibs until the year 2000.

**EOIN JESS** (Coventry City)
*Born:* 13.12.70    *Caps:* 10    *Goals:* 1
Comes from Portsoy on the north-east coast and signed from the Portsoy club by Aberdeen in 1987. Won two League Cup medals with Aberdeen including 1995-96. Former Under-21 international, he joined Coventry in February for £1.75 million.

**JIM LEIGHTON** (Hibernian)
*Born:* 24.7.58    *Caps:* 73    *Goals:* –
Began career at Aberdeen under Alex Ferguson, where he won two League titles, four Cup medals, a League Cup medal and a 1983 European Cup-Winners' Cup medal. Ferguson then signed him again for Manchester United in 1988 for a then British record fee for a goalkeeper of £750,000, but he never really played to his best and was dropped for the 1990 FA Cup final replay. Loaned to Arsenal and Reading, and then returned to Scotland with Dundee for £200,000 in February 1992. His move to Hibernian a year later resurrected his career and he won his way back into the national team.

**GARY McALLISTER** (Leeds United, England)
*Born:* 25.12.64    *Caps:* 39    *Goals:* 4
Captain of club and country. Consistently one of the best midfielders in the Premiership in the 1990s. Joined Leeds in June 1990 from Leicester City. Signed an extention to his contract in October 1994 that will keep him at Elland Road until summer 1999.

**STUART McCALL** (Rangers)
*Born:* 10.6.64    *Caps:* 32    *Goals:* 1
Born in Leeds and first played for Bradford City where he was picked for the England and Scotland Under-21 sides in the same week – followed the Scotland path, and says he'd like to finish his days with Bradford City. Moved to Everton in 1988 and scored both their goals as a sub in the 1989 FA Cup final v Liverpool (2-3). Joined Rangers for £1.2 million in August 1991 and has won League titles in all four seasons, plus two Cup and two League Cup medals. Played in 1990 World Cup and 1992 European Championships.

**ALLY McCOIST (Rangers)**
*Born:* 24.9.62   *Caps:* 51   *Goals:* 18
Is the ongoing Scottish Premier Division leading scorer with over 230 league goals and over 300 for the club. Began senior career with St Johnstone in 1978 then had two seasons with Sunderland (just eight goals in total) before a £185,000 move to Rangers in June 1983. Has won eight League titles, one Cup and a record eight League Cup medals with Rangers. Played in 1990 World Cup and 1992 European Championships and has been a 1996 *Question of Sport* captain.

**JOHN McGINLAY (Bolton Wanderers, England)**
*Born:* 8.4.64   *Caps:* 9   *Goals:* 3
Joined Bolton from Millwall in September 1992 for £125,000. Bolton's top scorer in last two seasons including 22 in 1994-95 (16 in League). Signed twice by Bruce Rioch in his career – from Bury to Millwall for £80,000 in January 1991 and then by Bolton.

**STEWART McKIMMIE (Aberdeen)**
*Born:* 27.10.62   *Caps:* 37   *Goals:* 1
Played in 1990 World Cup and 1992 European Championships. Aberdeen born, but his first club was Dundee from 1980-83. Has since played for Aberdeen where he has won two League titles, three Cup medals, and three League Cup medals.

**BILLY McKINLAY (Blackburn Rovers, England)**
*Born:* 22.4.69   *Caps:* 17   *Goals:* 4
Signed from Dundee United in October 1995 for £1.75 million as Blackburn rebuilt their team after the disastrous start to the 1995-96 Premiership and Champions League campaigns. Spent over eight seasons with Dundee United and nearly joined Celtic a week before Blackburn, but could not agree terms. Yet to gain a regular place in Blackburn's line-up.

**TOSH McKINLAY (Celtic)**
*Born:* 3.12.64   *Caps:* 3   *Goals:* –
Another to have come full-circle. Began his career with Celtic Boys Club then moved to Dundee in 1981 and to Hearts in 1988 for £300,000. After 205 League games for Hearts he returned to Celtic for £350,000 in summer 1994 and helped them to win the 1995 Scottish Cup, his first major honour.

**ALAN McLAREN (Rangers)**
*Born:* 4.1.71   *Caps:* 24   *Goals:* –
Edinburgh born, he joined the local Hearts club and stayed there for seven seasons before moving to Rangers for £2 million in September 1994. Won 1995 Championship medal in first season with Rangers. In squad for 1992 European Championship finals but did not play – has become a key player since.

**PAUL McSTAY (Celtic)**
*Born:* 22.10.64   *Caps:* 73   *Goals:* 9
Graduated from Celtic Boys Club in 1981 and made first-team debut in January 1982. Is now third in the Scottish all-time caps list after Dalglish and McLeish. Has won three League titles, four Cup medals and one League Cup, and has hit the heights with the 1988 double and lows with rivals Rangers' recent domination. Club captain since 1990

and won 1995 Scottish Cup medal – his first as captain. Played in 1986 and 1990 World Cups and 1992 European Championships.

## PAT NEVIN (Tranmere Rovers, England)
*Born:* 6.9.63  *Caps:* 28  *Goals:* 5
Began his League career with Clyde, and then moved to Chelsea from 1983-88. Joined Everton for £925,000 in 1988 and played in 1989 FA Cup final loss to Liverpool. Joined fellow Merseyside club Tranmere in August 1992 for £300,000 and has been in the team that has had several close attempts to reach the Premiership.

## JOHN ROBERTSON (Hearts)
*Born:* 2.10.64  *Caps:* 16  *Goals:* 3
Has been at Hearts since leaving school except for nine months with Newcastle in 1988. Has been top scorer at Hearts every season since 1982 and is second in the all-time Premier Division scoring lists behind McCoist, and is only the second player to 200 goals.

## DUNCAN SHEARER (Aberdeen)
*Born:* 28.8.62  *Caps:* 7  *Goals:* 2
He is a product of the Inverness Clachnacuddin club and then spent several seasons in England with Chelsea, Huddersfield, Swindon and Blackburn (where he was signed by Kenny Dalglish) before joining Aberdeen for £500,000 in July 1992. Aberdeen top scorer in 1993-94 and 1994-95. Scored 118 League goals in exactly 250 League games in England.

## JOHN SPENCER (Chelsea, England)
*Born:* 11.9.70  *Caps:* 10  *Goals:* –
He is 5ft 5in tall and has been with Chelsea since a £450,000 move from Rangers in August 1992. His bustling style has impressed Craig Brown from national Under-21 days. Played for Chelsea in 1994 FA Cup final.

## NICKY WALKER (Partick Thistle)
*Born:* 29.9.62  *Caps:* 1  *Goals:* –
Played early in his career for Leicester and Motherwell then was understudy to Chris Woods at Rangers, where he won a 1988 League Cup medal and 1989 Championship medal. Moved to Hearts from 1989 to 1994 and then to Partick Thistle in December 1994. First international cap against Germany in 1993.

## Coach: CRAIG BROWN
*Born:* 1.7.40
A schoolboy, youth and junior international, he played his club football with Rangers, Dundee – winning the League title in 1962 – and Falkirk. After his playing career was cut short through injury, he became a primary school head teacher and then lecturer before returning to football in 1974 as Motherwell's assistant manager. Between 1977 and 1986 he managed Clyde, winning the Second Division title in 1978 and 1982, before becoming assistant national and Under-21 coach. In November 1993 he succeeded Andy Roxburgh as national coach.

## SCOTLAND v BULGARIA

| Date | Venue | Score | Competition |
|---|---|---|---|
| 22-02-1978 | Glasgow | 2-1 | Friendly |
| 10-09-1986 | Glasgow | 0-0 | ENC qualifiers |
| 11-11-1987 | Sofia | 1-0 | ENC qualifiers |
| 14-11-1990 | Sofia | 1-1 | ENC qualifiers |
| 27-03-1991 | Glasgow | 1-1 | ENC qualifiers |

| | P | W | D | L | F | A |
|---|---|---|---|---|---|---|
| Home | 3 | 1 | 2 | 0 | 3 | 2 |
| Away | 2 | 1 | 1 | 0 | 2 | 1 |
| Total | 5 | 2 | 3 | 0 | 5 | 3 |

* Although the two sides have met four times in this competition, only once has there been a clear-cut result when Mackay of Hearts scored in Sofia. This result enabled the Republic of Ireland to qualify for the 1988 finals.

## SCOTLAND v CROATIA

The two sides have never met.

## SCOTLAND v CZECH REPUBLIC

*As Czechoslovakia*

| Date | Venue | Score | Competition |
|---|---|---|---|
| 22-05-1937 | Prague | 3-1 | Friendly |
| 08-12-1937 | Glasgow | 5-0 | Friendly |
| 14-05-1961 | Bratislava | 0-4 | WC qualifiers |
| 26-09-1961 | Glasgow | 3-2 | WC qualifiers |
| 29-11-1961 | Brussels (Belgium) | 2-4 | WC qualifiers |
| 02-07-1972 | Porto Alegre (Brazil) | 0-0 | Friendly |
| 26-09-1973 | Glasgow | 2-1 | WC qualifiers |
| 17-10-1973 | Prague | 0-1 | WC qualifiers |
| 13-10-1976 | Prague | 0-1 | WC qualifiers |
| 21-09-1977 | Glasgow | 3-1 | WC qualifiers |

| | P | W | D | L | F | A |
|---|---|---|---|---|---|---|
| Home | 4 | 4 | 0 | 0 | 13 | 4 |
| Away | 4 | 1 | 0 | 3 | 3 | 7 |
| Neutral | 2 | 0 | 1 | 1 | 2 | 4 |
| Total | 10 | 5 | 1 | 4 | 18 | 15 |

* Scotland knocked the then European Champions Czechoslovakia out of the 1978 World Cup finals in Argentina. The two sides have never met in this competition.

## SCOTLAND v DENMARK

| Date | Venue | Score | Competition |
|------|-------|-------|-------------|
| 12-05-1951 | Glasgow | 3-1 | Friendly |
| 25-05-1952 | Copenhagen | 2-1 | Friendly |
| 16-10-1968 | Copenhagen | 1-0 | Friendly |
| 11-11-1970 | Glasgow | 1-0 | ENC qualifiers |
| 09-06-1971 | Copenhagen | 0-1 | ENC qualifiers |
| 18-10-1972 | Copenhagen | 4-1 | WC qualifiers |
| 15-11-1972 | Glasgow | 2-0 | WC qualifiers |
| 03-09-1975 | Copenhagen | 1-0 | ENC qualifiers |
| 29-10-1975 | Glasgow | 3-1 | ENC qualifiers |
| 04-06-1986 | Neza (Mexico) | 0-1 | WC finals |
| 24-04-1996 | Copenhagen | 0-2 | Friendly |

|  | P | W | D | L | F | A |
|------|---|---|---|---|---|---|
| Home | 4 | 4 | 0 | 0 | 9 | 2 |
| Away | 6 | 4 | 0 | 2 | 8 | 5 |
| Neutral | 1 | 0 | 0 | 1 | 0 | 1 |
| Total | 11 | 8 | 0 | 3 | 17 | 8 |

* Finn Laudrup scored the winning goal against Scotland in 1971 in the only time Denmark have beaten the Scots in this competition. His sons Michael and Brian will figure strongly in the 1996 European Championships.

## SCOTLAND v ENGLAND

| Date | Venue | Score | Competition |
|------|-------|-------|-------------|
| 30-11-1872 | Glasgow | 0-0 | Friendly |
| 08-03-1873 | Kennington Oval | 2-4 | Friendly |
| 07-03-1874 | Glasgow | 2-1 | Friendly |
| 06-03-1875 | Kennington Oval | 2-2 | Friendly |
| 04-03-1876 | Glasgow | 3-0 | Friendly |
| 03-03-1877 | Kennington Oval | 3-1 | Friendly |
| 02-03-1878 | Glasgow | 7-2 | Friendly |
| 05-04-1879 | Kennington Oval | 4-5 | Friendly |
| 13-03-1880 | Glasgow | 5-4 | Friendly |
| 12-03-1881 | Kennington Oval | 6-1 | Friendly |
| 11-03-1882 | Glasgow | 5-1 |  |
| 10-03-1883 | Sheffield | 3-2 |  |
| 15-03-1884 | Glasgow | 1-0 |  |
| 21-03-1885 | Kennington Oval | 1-1 |  |
| 31-03-1886 | Glasgow | 1-1 |  |
| 19-03-1887 | Blackburn | 3-2 |  |
| 17-03-1888 | Glasgow | 0-5 |  |
| 13-04-1889 | Kennington Oval | 3-2 |  |
| 05-04-1890 | Glasgow | 1-1 |  |
| 06-04-1891 | Blackburn | 1-2 |  |
| 02-04-1892 | Glasgow | 1-4 |  |
| 01-04-1893 | Richmond | 2-5 |  |

| Date | Venue | Score | Competition |
|------|-------|-------|-------------|
| 07-04-1894 | Glasgow | 2-2 | |
| 06-04-1895 | Everton | 0-3 | |
| 04-04-1896 | Glasgow | 2-1 | |
| 03-04-1897 | Crystal Palace | 2-1 | |
| 02-04-1898 | Glasgow | 1-3 | |
| 08-04-1899 | Birmingham | 1-2 | |
| 07-04-1900 | Glasgow | 4-1 | |
| 30-03-1901 | Crystal Palace | 2-2 | |
| 03-03-1902 | Birmingham | 2-2 | |
| 04-04-1903 | Sheffield | 2-1 | |
| 09-04-1904 | Glasgow | 0-1 | |
| 01-04-1905 | Crystal Palace | 1-0 | |
| 07-04-1906 | Glasgow | 2-1 | |
| 06-04-1907 | Newcastle | 1-1 | |
| 04-04-1908 | Glasgow | 1-1 | |
| 03-04-1909 | Crystal Palace | 0-2 | |
| 02-04-1910 | Glasgow | 2-0 | |
| 01-04-1911 | Everton | 1-1 | |
| 23-03-1912 | Glasgow | 1-1 | |
| 05-04-1913 | Chelsea | 0-1 | |
| 14-04-1914 | Glasgow | 3-1 | |
| 10-04-1920 | Sheffield | 4-5 | |
| 09-04-1921 | Glasgow | 3-0 | |
| 08-04-1922 | Aston Villa | 1-0 | |
| 14-04-1923 | Glasgow | 2-2 | |
| 12-04-1924 | Wembley | 1-1 | |
| 04-04-1925 | Glasgow | 2-0 | |
| 17-04-1926 | Manchester | 1-0 | |
| 02-04-1927 | Glasgow | 1-2 | |
| 31-03-1928 | Wembley | 5-1 | |
| 13-04-1929 | Glasgow | 1-0 | |
| 05-04-1930 | Wembley | 2-5 | |
| 28-03-1931 | Glasgow | 2-0 | |
| 09-04-1932 | Wembley | 0-3 | |
| 01-04-1933 | Glasgow | 2-1 | |
| 14-04-1934 | Wembley | 0-3 | |
| 06-04-1935 | Glasgow | 2-0 | |
| 04-04-1936 | Wembley | 1-1 | |
| 17-04-1937 | Glasgow | 1-1 | |
| 09-04-1938 | Wembley | 1-0 | |
| 15-04-1939 | Glasgow | 1-2 | |
| 12-04-1947 | Wembley | 1-1 | |
| 10-04-1948 | Glasgow | 0-2 | |
| 09-04-1949 | Wembley | 3-1 | |
| 15-04-1950 | Glasgow | 0-1 | WC qualifiers |
| 14-04-1951 | Wembley | 3-2 | |
| 05-04-1952 | Glasgow | 1-2 | |
| 18-04-1953 | Wembley | 2-2 | |

| Date | Venue | Score | Competition |
|------|-------|-------|-------------|
| 03-04-1954 | Glasgow | 2-4 | WC qualifiers |
| 02-04-1955 | Wembley | 2-7 | |
| 14-04-1956 | Glasgow | 1-1 | |
| 06-04-1957 | Wembley | 1-2 | |
| 19-04-1958 | Glasgow | 0-4 | |
| 11-04-1959 | Wembley | 0-1 | |
| 19-04-1960 | Glasgow | 0-4 | |
| 15-04-1961 | Wembley | 3-9 | |
| 14-04-1962 | Glasgow | 2-0 | |
| 06-04-1963 | Wembley | 2-1 | |
| 11-04-1964 | Glasgow | 1-0 | |
| 10-04-1965 | Wembley | 2-2 | |
| 02-04-1966 | Glasgow | 4-3 | |
| 15-04-1967 | Wembley | 3-2 | ENC qualifiers |
| 24-01-1968 | Glasgow | 1-1 | ENC qualifiers |
| 10-05-1969 | Wembley | 1-4 | |
| 25-04-1970 | Glasgow | 0-0 | |
| 22-05-1971 | Wembley | 1-3 | |
| 27-05-1972 | Glasgow | 0-1 | |
| 14-02-1973 | Glasgow | 0-5 | |
| 19-05-1973 | Wembley | 0-1 | |
| 18-05-1974 | Wembley | 2-0 | |
| 24-05-1975 | Wembley | 1-5 | |
| 15-05-1976 | Glasgow | 2-1 | |
| 04-06-1977 | Wembley | 2-1 | |
| 20-05-1978 | Glasgow | 0-1 | |
| 26-05-1979 | Wembley | 1-3 | |
| 24-05-1980 | Glasgow | 0-2 | |
| 23-05-1981 | Wembley | 1-0 | |
| 29-05-1982 | Glasgow | 0-1 | |
| 01-06-1983 | Wembley | 0-2 | |
| 26-05-1984 | Glasgow | 1-1 | |
| 25-05-1985 | Glasgow | 0-1 | Friendly |
| 23-04-1986 | Wembley | 1-2 | Friendly |
| 23-05-1987 | Glasgow | 0-0 | Friendly |
| 21-05-1988 | Wembley | 0-1 | Friendly |
| 27-05-1989 | Glasgow | 0-2 | Friendly |

Matches where there is no indication of competition are British Home International games.

| | P | W | D | L | F | A |
|------|-----|-----|-----|-----|-----|-----|
| Home | 53 | 22 | 13 | 18 | 79 | 73 |
| Away | 54 | 18 | 11 | 25 | 89 | 115 |
| Total | 107 | 40 | 24 | 43 | 168 | 188 |

* Scotland became the first team to beat England after the 1966 World Cup final, when they won in a European Nations Cup qualifier. Law, Lennox and McCalliog were the scorers.

* Scotland have won only once in their last five visits to Wembley.

# SCOTLAND v FRANCE

| Date | Venue | Score | Competition |
|------|-------|-------|-------------|
| 18-05-1930 | Paris | 2-0 | Friendly |
| 08-05-1932 | Paris | 3-1 | Friendly |
| 23-05-1948 | Paris | 0-3 | Friendly |
| 27-04-1949 | Glasgow | 2-0 | Friendly |
| 27-05-1950 | Paris | 1-0 | Friendly |
| 16-05-1951 | Glasgow | 1-0 | Friendly |
| 15-06-1958 | Orebro (Sweden) | 1-2 | WC finals |
| 01-06-1984 | Marseille | 0-2 | Friendly |
| 08-03-1989 | Glasgow | 2-0 | WC qualifiers |
| 11-10-1989 | Paris | 0-3 | WC qualifiers |

|  | P | W | D | L | F | A |
|------|---|---|---|---|---|---|
| Home | 3 | 3 | 0 | 0 | 5 | 0 |
| Away | 6 | 3 | 0 | 3 | 6 | 9 |
| Neutral | 1 | 0 | 0 | 1 | 1 | 2 |
| Total | 10 | 6 | 0 | 4 | 12 | 11 |

* Scotland and France have never met in this competition. Despite losing 3-0 to France (including conceding an Eric Cantona goal) the last time they met, it was Scotland not France who qualified for Italia 90.

# SCOTLAND v GERMANY

| Date | Venue | Score | Competition |
|------|-------|-------|-------------|
| 01-06-1929 | Berlin | 1-1 | Friendly |
| 14-10-1936 | Glasgow | 2-0 | Friendly |

*As West Germany*

| Date | Venue | Score | Competition |
|------|-------|-------|-------------|
| 22-05-1957 | Stuttgart | 3-1 | Friendly |
| 06-05-1959 | Glasgow | 3-2 | Friendly |
| 12-05-1964 | Hannover | 2-2 | Friendly |
| 16-04-1969 | Glasgow | 1-1 | WC qualifiers |
| 22-10-1969 | Hamburg | 2-3 | WC qualifiers |
| 14-11-1973 | Glasgow | 1-1 | Friendly |
| 27-03-1974 | Frankfurt | 1-2 | Friendly |
| 08-06-1986 | Queretaro (Mexico) | 1-2 | Friendly |

*As Germany*

| Date | Venue | Score | Competition |
|------|-------|-------|-------------|
| 15-06-1992 | Norrkoping (Sweden) | 0-2 | ENC finals |
| 24-03-1993 | Glasgow | 0-1 | Friendly |

|  | P | W | D | L | F | A |
|--|---|---|---|---|---|---|
| Home | 5 | 2 | 2 | 1 | 7 | 5 |
| Away | 5 | 1 | 2 | 2 | 9 | 9 |
| Neutral | 2 | 0 | 0 | 2 | 1 | 4 |
| Total | 12 | 3 | 4 | 5 | 17 | 18 |

* Scotland haven't beaten Germany since 1959. In their one meeting in this competition, Riedle and Effenberg scored to knock Scotland out.

## SCOTLAND v HOLLAND

| Date | Venue | Score | Competition |
|------|-------|-------|-------------|
| 04-06-1929 | Amsterdam | 2-0 | Friendly |
| 21-05-1938 | Amsterdam | 3-1 | Friendly |
| 27-05-1959 | Amsterdam | 2-1 | Friendly |
| 11-05-1966 | Glasgow | 0-3 | Friendly |
| 30-05-1968 | Amsterdam | 0-0 | Friendly |
| 01-12-1971 | Rotterdam | 1-2 | Friendly |
| 11-06-1978 | Mendoza (Argentina) | 3-2 | WC finals |
| 23-03-1982 | Glasgow | 2-1 | Friendly |
| 29-04-1986 | Eindhoven | 0-0 | Friendly |
| 12-06-1992 | Gothenburg (Sweden) | 0-1 | ENC finals |
| 23-03-1994 | Glasgow | 0-1 | Friendly |
| 27-05-1994 | Utrecht | 1-3 | Friendly |

|  | P | W | D | L | F | A |
|--|---|---|---|---|---|---|
| Home | 3 | 1 | 0 | 2 | 2 | 5 |
| Away | 7 | 3 | 2 | 2 | 9 | 7 |
| Neutral | 2 | 1 | 0 | 1 | 3 | 3 |
| Total | 12 | 5 | 2 | 5 | 14 | 15 |

* Scotland have met Holland in competitive matches only twice, both times in the finals of a tournament. Scotland have never yet progressed from a group in which Holland are rivals. Dennis Bergkamp was the scorer in Gothenburg.

# SCOTLAND v ITALY

| Date | Venue | Score | Competition |
|------|-------|-------|-------------|
| 20-05-1931 | Rome | 0-3 | Friendly |
| 09-11-1965 | Glasgow | 1-0 | WC qualifiers |
| 07-12-1965 | Naples | 0-3 | WC qualifiers |
| 22-12-1988 | Perugia | 0-2 | Friendly |
| 18-11-1992 | Glasgow | 0-0 | WC qualifiers |
| 13-10-1993 | Rome | 1-3 | WC qualifiers |

| | P | W | D | L | F | A |
|------|---|---|---|---|---|---|
| Home | 2 | 1 | 1 | 0 | 1 | 0 |
| Away | 4 | 0 | 0 | 4 | 1 | 11 |
| Total | 6 | 1 | 1 | 4 | 2 | 11 |

* Scotland's only victory over Italy came in the qualifying competition for the 1966 World Cup.

# SCOTLAND v PORTUGAL

| Date | Venue | Score | Competition |
|------|-------|-------|-------------|
| 21-05-1950 | Lisbon | 2-2 | Friendly |
| 04-05-1955 | Glasgow | 3-0 | Friendly |
| 03-06-1959 | Lisbon | 0-1 | Friendly |
| 18-06-1966 | Glasgow | 0-1 | Friendly |
| 21-04-1971 | Lisbon | 0-2 | ENC qualifiers |
| 13-10-1971 | Glasgow | 2-1 | ENC qualifiers |
| 13-05-1975 | Glasgow | 1-0 | Friendly |
| 29-11-1978 | Lisbon | 0-1 | ENC qualifiers |
| 26-03-1980 | Glasgow | 4-1 | ENC qualifiers |
| 15-10-1980 | Glasgow | 0-0 | WC qualifiers |
| 18-11-1981 | Lisbon | 1-2 | WC qualifiers |
| 14-10-1992 | Glasgow | 0-0 | WC qualifiers |
| 28-04-1993 | Lisbon | 0-5 | WC qualifiers |

| | P | W | D | L | F | A |
|------|----|---|---|---|----|----|
| Home | 7 | 4 | 2 | 1 | 10 | 3 |
| Away | 6 | 0 | 1 | 5 | 3 | 13 |
| Total | 13 | 4 | 3 | 6 | 13 | 16 |

* Portugal and Scotland have a 50/50 record against each other in the European Nations Cup. However, Scotland's 4-1 victory in 1980 was their last against the Portuguese.

## SCOTLAND v ROMANIA

| Date | Venue | Score | Competition |
|------|-------|-------|-------------|
| 01-06-1975 | Bucharest | 1-1 | ENC qualifiers |
| 17-12-1975 | Glasgow | 1-1 | ENC qualifiers |
| 26-03-1986 | Glasgow | 3-0 | Friendly |
| 12-09-1990 | Glasgow | 2-1 | ENC qualifiers |
| 16-10-1991 | Bucharest | 0-1 | ENC qualifiers |

| | P | W | D | L | F | A |
|------|---|---|---|---|---|---|
| Home | 3 | 2 | 1 | 0 | 6 | 2 |
| Away | 2 | 0 | 1 | 1 | 1 | 2 |
| Total | 5 | 2 | 2 | 1 | 7 | 4 |

\* All Scotland's competitive matches against Romania have been in the European Nations Cup. Despite losing to a Hagi penalty in 1991, it was Scotland not Romania, Bulgaria, or the Swiss, who qualified from their group. All four sides are involved in the finals this time.

## SCOTLAND v RUSSIA

*As USSR*

| Date | Venue | Score | Competition |
|------|-------|-------|-------------|
| 10-05-1967 | Glasgow | 0-2 | Friendly |
| 14-06-1971 | Moscow | 0-1 | Friendly |
| 22-06-1982 | Malaga (Spain) | 2-2 | WC finals |
| 06-02-1991 | Glasgow | 0-1 | Friendly |

*As CIS*

| Date | Venue | Score | Competition |
|------|-------|-------|-------------|
| 18-06-1992 | Norrkoping (Sweden) | 3-0 | ENC finals |

*As Russia*

| Date | Venue | Score | Competition |
|------|-------|-------|-------------|
| 16-11-1994 | Glasgow | 1-1 | ENC qualifiers |
| 29-03-1995 | Moscow | 0-0 | ENC qualifiers |

|         | P | W | D | L | F | A |
|---------|---|---|---|---|---|---|
| Home    | 3 | 0 | 1 | 2 | 1 | 4 |
| Away    | 2 | 0 | 1 | 1 | 0 | 1 |
| Neutral | 2 | 1 | 1 | 0 | 5 | 2 |
| Total   | 7 | 1 | 3 | 3 | 6 | 7 |

* Scotland played Russia in their qualifying group for this year's Championships. A good performance in Russia gave them the confidence to get through.
* Scotland beat the CIS in the finals in Sweden in 1992. It was Scotland's best game of the tournament, and it meant that they could go back to Scotland with their heads held high, even after being eliminated in the first stage. McStay, McClair and McAllister were the scorers.

## SCOTLAND v SPAIN

| Date | Venue | Score | Competition |
|------|-------|-------|-------------|
| 08-05-1957 | Glasgow | 4-2 | WC qualifiers |
| 26-05-1957 | Madrid | 1-4 | WC qualifiers |
| 13-06-1963 | Madrid | 6-2 | Friendly |
| 08-05-1965 | Glasgow | 0-0 | Friendly |
| 20-11-1974 | Glasgow | 1-2 | ENC qualifiers |
| 05-02-1975 | Valencia | 1-1 | ENC qualifiers |
| 24-02-1982 | Valencia | 0-3 | Friendly |
| 14-11-1984 | Glasgow | 3-1 | WC qualifiers |
| 27-02-1985 | Seville | 0-1 | WC qualifiers |
| 27-04-1988 | Madrid | 0-0 | Friendly |

|       | P  | W | D | L | F  | A  |
|-------|----|---|---|---|----|----|
| Home  | 4  | 2 | 1 | 1 | 8  | 5  |
| Away  | 6  | 1 | 2 | 3 | 8  | 11 |
| Total | 10 | 3 | 3 | 4 | 16 | 16 |

* Scotland have never beaten Spain in a European Nations Cup match, though they have taken equal honours in the World Cup.

## SCOTLAND v SWITZERLAND

| Date | Venue | Score | Competition |
|------|-------|-------|-------------|
| 24-05-1931 | Geneva | 3-2 | Friendly |
| 17-05-1948 | Berne | 1-2 | Friendly |
| 26-04-1950 | Glasgow | 3-1 | Friendly |
| 19-05-1957 | Basle | 2-1 | WC qualifiers |
| 06-11-1957 | Glasgow | 3-2 | WC qualifiers |
| 22-06-1973 | Berne | 0-1 | Friendly |
| 07-04-1976 | Glasgow | 1-0 | Friendly |
| 17-11-1982 | Berne | 0-2 | ENC qualifiers |

| Date | Venue | | Score | | Competition | |
|------|-------|---|-------|---|-------------|---|
| 30-05-1983 | Glasgow | | 2-2 | | ENC qualifiers | |
| 17-10-1990 | Glasgow | | 2-1 | | ENC qualifiers | |
| 11-09-1991 | Berne | | 2-2 | | ENC qualifiers | |
| 09-09-1992 | Berne | | 1-3 | | WC qualifiers | |
| 08-09-1993 | Aberdeen | | 1-1 | | WC qualifiers | |

| | P | W | D | L | F | A |
|------|----|---|---|---|----|----|
| Home | 6 | 4 | 2 | 0 | 12 | 7 |
| Away | 7 | 2 | 1 | 4 | 9 | 13 |
| Total | 13 | 6 | 3 | 4 | 21 | 20 |

* They have met four times in the European Nations Cup. In the qualifiers for the 1992 competition, Scotland's home win and away draw enabled them to go through to Sweden ahead of the Swiss.

## SCOTLAND v TURKEY

| Date | Venue | | Score | | Competition | |
|------|-------|---|-------|---|-------------|---|
| 08-06-1960 | Ankara | | 2-4 | | Friendly | |

| | P | W | D | L | F | A |
|------|---|---|---|---|---|---|
| Away | 1 | 0 | 0 | 1 | 2 | 4 |
| Total | 1 | 0 | 0 | 1 | 2 | 4 |

* When the sides met for the only time, Young and Caldow were Scotland's scorers. It was Caldow's first goal for his country.

## KEY PLAYER

### GARY McALLISTER
*Date of Birth:* 25.12.64
*Current club:* Leeds United
*Position:* Midfield
*Height:* 1.86 m
*Weight:* 78 kg

#### CAREER RECORD

| | | League | | Int | |
|------|------|------|-------|------|-------|
| Year | Club | Apps | Goals | Apps | Goals |
| 1981-82 | Motherwell | 1 | | | |
| 1982-83 | | 1 | | | |
| 1983-84 | | 21 | | | |
| 1984-85 | | 35 | 6 | | |
| 1985-86 | | 1 | | | |
| 1985-86 | Leicester | 31 | 7 | | |
| 1986-87 | | 39 | 10 | | |

109

| Year | Club | League Apps | Goals | Int Apps | Goals |
|------|------|-------------|-------|----------|-------|
| 1987-88 | | 42 | 9 | | |
| 1988-89 | | 46 | 11 | | |
| 1989-90 | | 43 | 10 | 3 | 0 |
| 1990-91 | Leeds United | 38 | 2 | 5 | 1 |
| 1991-92 | | 42 | 5 | 10 | 3 |
| 1992-93 | | 32 | 5 | 4 | 0 |
| 1993-94 | | 42 | 8 | 6 | 0 |
| 1994-95 | | 41 | 6 | 5 | 0 |
| 1995-96 | | | | 5 | 0 |

## HONOURS
English champions – 1992

| No | Date | Opponents | Venue | Score | Goals | Competition | Subbed Sub |
|----|------|-----------|-------|-------|-------|-------------|------------|
| 1 | 25.4.90 | East Germany | Glasgow | 0-1 | 0 | Friendly | 90 |
| 2 | 19.5.90 | Poland | Glasgow | 1-1 | 0 | Friendly | Subbed 83 |
| 3 | 28.5.90 | Malta | Valletta | 2-1 | 0 | Friendly | Sub pl 45 |
| 4 | 12.9.90 | Romania | Glasgow | 2-1 | 0 | E Nations, Q | Subbed 73 |
| 5 | 17.10.90 | Switzerland | Glasgow | 2-1 | 1 | E Nations, Q | Subbed 79 |
| 6 | 14.11.90 | Bulgaria | Sofia | 1-1 | 0 | E Nations, Q | 90 |
| 7 | 26.2.91 | USSR | Glasgow | 0-1 | 0 | Friendly | Sub pl 21 |
| 8 | 1.5.91 | San Marino | Serraville | 2-0 | 0 | E Nations, Q | 90 |
| 9 | 11.9.91 | Switzerland | Berne | 2-2 | 0 | E Nations, Q | Sub pl 47 |
| 10 | 13.11.91 | San Marino | Glasgow | 4-0 | 0 | E Nations, Q | 90 |
| 11 | 19.2.92 | Northern Ireland | Glasgow | 1-0 | 0 | Friendly | 90 |
| 12 | 25.3.92 | Finland | Glasgow | 1-1 | 0 | Friendly | Sub pl 25 |
| 13 | 17.5.92 | USA | Colorado | 1-0 | 0 | Friendly | 90 |
| 14 | 21.5.92 | Canada | Toronto | 3-1 | 2 | Friendly | Subbed 78 |
| 15 | 3.6.92 | Norway | Oslo | 0-0 | 0 | Friendly | Subbed 78 |
| 16 | 12.6.92 | Holland | Gothenburg | 0-1 | 0 | EN finals | 90 |
| 17 | 15.6.92 | Germany | Norrkoping | 0-2 | 0 | EN finals | 90 |
| 18 | 18.6.92 | CIS | Norrkoping | 3-0 | 1 | EN finals | 90 |
| 19 | 9.9.92 | Switzerland | Berne | 1-3 | 0 | World Cup, Q | 90 |
| 20 | 14.10.92 | Portugal | Glasgow | 0-0 | 0 | World Cup, Q | 90 |
| 21 | 18.11.92 | Italy | Glasgow | 0-0 | 0 | World Cup, Q | 90 |
| 22 | 17.2.93 | Malta | Glasgow | 3-0 | 0 | World Cup, Q | Subbed 71 |
| 23 | 8.9.93 | Switzerland | Aberdeen | 1-1 | 0 | World Cup, Q | 90 |
| 24 | 13.10.93 | Italy | Rome | 1-3 | 0 | World Cup, Q | 90 |
| 25 | 17.11.93 | Malta | Valletta | 2-0 | 0 | World Cup, Q | 90 |
| 26 | 23.3.94 | Holland | Glasgow | 0-1 | 0 | Friendly | 90 |
| 27 | 20.4.94 | Austria | Vienna | 2-1 | 0 | Friendly | 90 |
| 28 | 27.5.94 | Holland | Utrecht | 1-3 | 0 | Friendly | 90 |
| 29 | 7.9.94 | Finland | Helsinki | 2-0 | 0 | E Nations, Q | 90 |
| 30 | 16.11.94 | Russia | Glasgow | 1-1 | 0 | E Nations, Q | 90 |
| 31 | 18.12.94 | Greece | Athens | 0-1 | 0 | E Nations, Q | 90 |
| 32 | 29.3.95 | Russia | Moscow | 0-0 | 0 | E Nations, Q | 90 |
| 33 | 26.4.95 | San Marino | Serraville | 2-0 | 0 | E Nations, Q | 90 |
| 34 | 16.8.95 | Greece | Glasgow | 1-0 | 0 | E Nations, Q | 90 |
| 35 | 6.9.95 | Finland | Glasgow | 1-0 | 0 | E Nations, Q | 90 |
| 36 | 11.10.95 | Sweden | Stockholm | 0-2 | 0 | Friendly | Subbed 60 |
| 37 | 15.11.95 | San Marino | Glasgow | 5-0 | 0 | E Nations, Q | Subbed 47 |
| 38 | 27.3.96 | Australia | Glasgow | 1-0 | 0 | Friendly | 90 |
| 39 | 24.4.96 | Denmark | Copenhagen | 0-2 | 0 | Friendly | 90 |

# GROUP B

## FIXTURES

| | | | |
|---|---|---|---|
| 9 June | Spain v Bulgaria | Elland Road | 14.30 |
| 10 June | Romania v France | St James' Park | 19.30 |
| 13 June | Bulgaria v Romania | St James' Park | 16.30 |
| 15 June | France v Spain | Elland Road | 18.00 |
| 18 June | France v Bulgaria | St James' Park | 16.30 |
| 18 June | Romania v Spain | Elland Road | 16.30 |

## CONTENTS

# GROUP B PREVIEW

There is no tougher group from which to pick two for the quarter-finals than Group B, where seeded Spain vie with France, Bulgaria and Romania. So finely balanced are these four teams that the odds are that they will all take points out of each other, leaving a desperate scramble for the tape.

Spain will, rightly, start as the narrow favourites, for there is no shrewder coach than Javier Clemente, who has had six months to prepare his thoughts and his tactics for the games at Leeds and Newcastle. Clemente, a manager who does not suffer stars or fools gladly, is noted not only for the way he dissects the opposition, probing for their weaknesses and their faults, but he is also adept at shuffling his own pack to such an extent that opponents rarely know what to expect.

They were good in the USA two years ago and desperately unlucky to lose out to finalists Italy after outplaying them. They are even better now and, in Real Madrid's teenage wonder-boy Raul, they will soon have a potential match-winner and a new star in years to come, even if he plays no part in Euro 96.

Clemente's biggest problem is to cover for the absence of Miguel Angel Nadal, who will be suspended for the first two games against Bulgaria and France. The strength will lie in midfield with Fernando Hierro, the temperamental Jose Luis Caminero, South American-born Donato and Josep Guardiola among those vying for the places.

France, seemingly, have even greater riches, judging by the reluctance of coach Aime Jacquet to nominate either his former captain Eric Cantona or Newcastle's elegant David Ginola. Jacquet is a law unto himself, down-to-earth and openly despondent about the draw, having said that he wanted to avoid both Romania and Spain. Why he should be so concerned about the Romanians, having already beaten them in Bucharest in the qualifying tournament, only he knows. His strength also lies in his midfield, with Milan's impressive Marcel Desailly, PSG's Yuri Djorkaeff and Zinedine Zidane of Bordeaux.

Bulgaria, it is suggested, may be past their sell by date, but I wouldn't bet on it. If they reached their peak when they ousted the Germans in the USA two years ago, how come they managed to do it all over again in the qualifying tournament?

If anything, they should be a stronger team for their World Cup experience and in Hristo Stoichkov they have an undisputed match winner. The Parma man can sulk and moan – but can he play. He is not on his own with forwards of the talent of Emil Kostadinov, Lubo Penev and Ilian Iliev, all of whom can live with the very best on their day.

Romania, who finished above France in their group despite that home defeat, are also said to be below the force that they were in the last World Cup and, indeed, some of their key players are reaching the autumn of their careers.

They will rely more heavily on Espanol's Florin Raducioiu than the ageing Gheorghe Hagi, who is more likely to flit in and out of things than to dominate as he has done in the past. His creative role should be taken on by Ilie Dumitrescu, now that he is back playing regular football again with West Ham United.

# SPAIN

Spain's success has been built around their defensive set-up and their ability to break down opposition sides. They have no outstanding forward which means that Clemente must use the best at his disposal. Keeper and captain Andoni Zubizarreta is in the 100 club – the Valencia keeper has 105 caps. Defensively the Barcelona contingent are favoured – Ferrer, Nadal, Abelardo and Sergi.

The scorers from midfield are Luis Enrique and Real Madrid clubmate Fernando Hierro and Atletico Madrid midfielder Juan Luis Caminero. Bilbao's 21-year-old star Julen Guerrero has 21 caps already and seven goals – he could make it at Euro 96.

The best current striker is the Argentinian-born Juan Pizzi, who plays for Tenerife, and has come into the side since Alfonso (Betis) was injured. Pizzi has 10 caps and four goals for Spain. Sadly the experienced Julio Salinas has left a void in attack and players like Quico (Atletico Madrid), Manjarin (Deportivo) and Goicoechea (Bilbao) are all around and about but don't hint at any permanency. At least they all play in Spain!

*Formation:* 4-5-1
*Coach:* Javier Clemente

|  |  |  |  |  |
|---|---|---|---|---|
| | | Zubizarreta | | |
| Ferrer | Alcorta | Abelardo | | Sergi |
| Luis Enrique | Nadal | Caminero | Hierro | Amavisca |
| | | Pizzi | | |

| Player | Position | Club | Date | Caps | Goals |
|---|---|---|---|---|---|
| Andoni Zubizarreta | G | Valencia | 23.10.61 | 105 | – |
| Jose Santiago Canizares | G | Real Madrid | 18.12.69 | 9 | – |
| Alberto Belsue | D | Zaragoza | 2.3.68 | 11 | – |
| Rafael Alcorta | D | Real Madrid | 11.9.68 | 35 | – |
| Abelardo | D | Barcelona | 19.3.70 | 24 | 2 |
| Sergi | D | Barcelona | 28.12.71 | 18 | 1 |
| Albert Ferrer | D | Barcelona | 6.6.70 | 27 | – |
| Fransisco Camarasa | D | Valencia | 27.9.67 | 14 | – |
| Aitor Karanka | D | Athletic Bilbao | 18.9.73 | 1 | – |
| Miguel Angel Nadal | M | Barcelona | 28.7.66 | 29 | 2 |
| Fernando Hierro | M | Real Madrid | 23.3.68 | 40 | 11 |
| Luis Enrique | M | Real Madrid | 8.5.70 | 20 | 3 |
| Jose Luis Caminero | M | Atletico Madrid | 8.11.67 | 18 | 7 |
| Donato | M | Deportivo La Coruna | 30.12.62 | 10 | 3 |
| Juan Andoni Goicoechea | M | Athletic Bilbao | 21.10.65 | 35 | 4 |
| Javier Fransisco Fran | M | Deportivo La Coruna | 14.7.69 | 7 | – |
| Josep Guardiola | M | Barcelona | 18.1.71 | 14 | 2 |
| Julen Guerrero | F | Athletic Bilbao | 7.1.74 | 21 | 7 |
| Alfonso | F | Betis Seville | 26.9.72 | 10 | 2 |
| Jose Amavisca | F | Real Madrid | 19.6.71 | 10 | 1 |
| Juan Antonio Pizzi | F | Tenerife | 7.6.68 | 10 | 4 |
| Javier Manjarin | F | Deportivo La Coruna | 31.12.69 | 5 | 1 |
| Quico | F | Atletico Madrid | 26.4.72 | 7 | 1 |
| Julio Salinas | F | Sporting Gijon | 11.9.62 | 54 | 22 |

# SPAIN A-Z

**ABELARDO** (Barcelona)
*Born:* 19.3.70   *Caps:* 24   *Goals:* 2
Brought up and developed via the Sporting Gijon youth network, he was one of the heroes of the Olympic gold medal team, scoring the first goal in the final. He moved from Sporting to Barcelona in the summer of 1994 for £2.2 million after playing in all Spain's five games at the 1994 World Cup, and has become the pivotal figure in the Barcelona defence.

**RAFAEL ALCORTA** (Real Madrid)
*Born:* 16.9.68   *Caps:* 35   *Goals:* –
Moved in the summer of 1993 from Athletic Bilbao to Real Madrid for £2.2 million and had a tricky start in a Real side which had its worst start to a season in 1993-94 since 1952. He came through internationally in the 1990 World Cup and played again in the 1994 finals. He was one of only three Real players in the World Cup 22 and the Euro 96 quota may not be much higher.

**ALFONSO** (Betis Seville)
*Born:* 26.9.72   *Caps:* 10   *Goals:* 2
Signed from Real Madrid in summer 1995, he was a Bernabeu favourite who needed to move on to get regular first team football. He is another graduate from the Olympic gold medal-winning team from Barcelona's games and is originally from Real's famous nursery at Castilla.

**JOSE AMAVISCA** (Real Madrid)
*Born:* 19.6.71   *Caps:* 10   *Goals:* 1
Another from the Olympic gold medal-winning squad of 1992, he wasted a couple of years with struggling Division 1 club Valladolid, but signed for Real Madrid in summer 1994 and his career took off in the Championship win of 1994-95.

**ALBERTO BELSUE** (Zaragoza)
*Born:* 2.3.68   *Caps:* 11   *Goals:* –
Has come into the squad since the 1994 World Cup off the back of Zaragoza's 1994 Spanish Cup win and 1995 European Cup-Winners' Cup success. He is the club's sole representative at present in the national squad. He was born in Zaragoza, and joined the club in 1988 from a club in the principality of Andorra. He has been a Spanish Under-21 international so has been in the eyes of national selectors.

**FRANSISCO CAMARASA** (Valencia)
*Born:* 27.9.67   *Caps:* 14   *Goals:* –
Was born in the city of Valencia and moved into the first-team squad in 1988, and into the first team virtually straight away. Very much a local lad. Maintains excellent and steady club form. Played in the 1994 World Cup finals in USA.

**JOSE LUIS CAMINERO** (Atletico Madrid)
*Born:* 8.11.67    *Caps:* 18    *Goals:* 7
Had a major break after joining Atletico Madrid from Valladolid in 1993. He was then in a shambles of a club side, but made the national team and played really well. He scored three goals in four games at the 1994 World Cup and created a fine impression. Continues to excel at club level in a side that are favourites for the 1996 title.

**JOSE SANTIAGO CANIZARES** (Real Madrid)
*Born:* 18.12.68    *Caps:* 9    *Goals:* –
Once rejected by Real Madrid, he went to Celta Vigo to help shore up their defence and played so well that Real had to buy him back in summer 1994 as their keeper of the future. Was the reserve keeper in the 1992 Olympic Games win, and played in the first match of the 1994 World Cup finals when Zubizarreta was suspended. Second choice at his club behind Paco Buyo.

**DONATO** (Deportivo La Coruna)
*Born:* 30.12.62    *Caps:* 10    *Goals:* 3
Made dream debut for Spain with a goal in the 3-1 win in the European Championship qualifiers against the holders Denmark, just when it seemed that his international days would never come. He is a Brazilian who played for the famous Vasco da Gama club but was never capped by Brazil, and came to Atletico Madrid from 1988 to 1993 to play well in the Spanish First Division. He moved to Deportivo in 1993 and continued to perform well, and, as his Spanish papers had come through, became available to play for Spain at the age of 31.

**LUIS ENRIQUE** (Real Madrid)
*Born:* 8.5.70    *Caps:* 20    *Goals:* 3
Left Sporting Gijon, where he had developed through their youth set-up, for £1 million and went to Real Madrid in 1991 as the star of the Under-21 national side and also Gijon's top scorer with 15 goals. He is another from the 1992 Olympic gold medal-winning side. But his career at Real has seen him as an attacking full back in the general technical confusion. He had an excellent World Cup, playing four games and scoring a goal against Switzerland, but was the victim of a horrible tackle by Mauro Tassotti in the match against Italy.

**ALBERT FERRER** (Barcelona)
*Born:* 6.6.70    *Caps:* 27    *Goals:* –
Has played for Barcelona since 1990-91. A tough, right-sided wing-back, he is likely to be a regular in the side during Euro 96. He was in Spain's Olympic-winning team in 1992 and played in all their games in the 1994 World Cup finals.

**JAVIER FRANSISCO FRAN** (Deportivo La Coruna)
*Born:* 14.7.69    *Caps:* 7    *Goals:* –
Has come through to the national squad from Deportivo's back-to-back runners-up places in the Championship in 1994 and 1995. He was developed by Deportivo's youth and reserve set-up, and made the first-team squad in 1988. Is the club's playmaker and number 10.

**JUAN ANDONI GOICOECHEA** (Athletic Bilbao)

*Born:* 21.10.65    *Caps:* 35    *Goals:* 4

A Basque, he joined Athletic Bilbao in summer 1994, from Barcelona, where he played in their four recent title wins. He had moved in 1990 to Barca from Real Sociedad where he played alongside John Aldridge. Won a European Cup medal in 1992. Had not scored for Spain until the first two games of the 1994 World Cup when he found the net against Korea and Germany.

**JOSEP GUARDIOLA** (Barcelona)

*Born:* 18.1.71    *Caps:* 14    *Goals:* 2

Was in the Barcelona team for three of their four Championship wins of the 1990s, and the European Cup success. Was developed in the club's youth and reserve teams. He was often the first name pencilled in by Johan Cruyff. His recent times have been blighted by injuries and suspensions. Another of the 1992 Olympic gold medal team.

**JULEN GUERRERO** (Athletic Bilbao)

*Born:* 7.1.74    *Caps:* 21    *Goals:* 7

The hot property of Spanish football at present and, at 19 years 20 days, was Spain's second youngest international behind Zubieta in 1936 who was 17 years 10 months. He was developed under the German Jupp Heynckes, coming through the Athletic Bilbao junior system and owes much to Heynckes' coaching. Made two appearances in USA 94.

**FERNANDO HIERRO** (Real Madrid)

*Born:* 23.3.68    *Caps:* 40    *Goals:* 11

Real Madrid midfielder who was moved up by the club from central defence to striker and now appears to be on the way back through the team again. With 21 goals he was runner-up in the League scoring charts back in 1991-92. He joined Real in 1990 from Valladolid; his brother was also a pro at that club. Played in all five games for Spain at the 1994 World Cup.

**AITOR KARANKA** (Athletic Bilbao)

*Born:* 18.9.73    *Caps:* 1    *Goals:* –

From the famous youth nursery at Bilbao, he has been a star in the national set-up, but needs his club side to be more consistent if he is to progress internationally. Came into the Bilbao first team in 1993.

**JAVIER MANJARIN** (Deportivo La Coruna)

*Born:* 31.12.69    *Caps:* 5    *Goals:* 1

Another of the Olympic Games gold medal squad, he has had a couple of fine seasons, 1993-95, with Deportivo's successive runners-up spots in the League. Is a winger, who joined the Coruna club from Sporting Gijon in 1993.

**MIGUEL ANGEL NADAL** (Barcelona)

*Born:* 28.7.66    *Caps:* 29    *Goals:* 2

Barcelona defender or defensive midfielder who joined the club from Mallorca in 1991 and was in the 1992, 1993, and 1994 championship sides. Has played in every position on the field for Johan Cruyff except goalkeeper. Played in three of the five games in the 1994 World Cup but was sent off in his first game, against Korea. He will be suspended for the first two matches of Euro 96. His name means 'Christmas' in Spanish.

**JUAN ANTONIO PIZZI** (Tenerife)
*Born:* 7.6.68    *Caps:* 10    *Goals:* 4
Like Donato, this forward has now opted for Spain – he is an Argentine who played for
Santa Fe and Rosario Central, then moved to Toluca in the Mexican First Division. He
came to Tenerife in 1991, and played well for the club 1991-93. He then had an unsuccess-
ful 1993-94 season with Valencia and is now scoring goals again for Tenerife. International
squad member from autumn 1994, making his debut in a friendly against Finland.

**QUICO** (Atletico Madrid)
*Born:* 26.4.72    *Caps:* 7    *Goals:* 1
Also spelt 'Kiko', he was the hero of the 1992 Olympic Games win after he scored two
goals against Poland in the final. He was then playing for his hometown club Cadiz, and
was transferred to Atletico Madrid when Cadiz were relegated in 1993. After a couple of
patchy years, he has had a fine 1995-96 season under new Atletico trainer Raddy Antic.

**JULIO SALINAS** (Sporting Gijon)
*Born:* 11.9.62    *Caps:* 54    *Goals:* 22
Emphasises the plight of Spanish football at the moment – he couldn't get regularly
into the first team at Barcelona and Deportivo and is now at Sporting this season – but
was recalled to answer a real problem of goalscoring against countries other than the
minnows in the last World Cup qualifiers. Well past the proverbial sell-by date, he was
with Barcelona 1988-94, and his previous clubs were Athletic Bilbao (where he was
born) and Atletico Madrid. European Cup medal 1992 and bit-part role in Barcelona's
four consecutive title wins as a squad member.

**SERGI** (Barcelona)
*Born:* 28.12.71    *Caps:* 18    *Goals:* 1
Made his debut for Barcelona in the 1993-94 Champions League against Galatasaray
and by the end of the season was at the World Cup. Plucked out of Barcelona's reserve
team by Cruyff, whose judgement has proved right. Played all five games in USA and is
a fixture in the attacking left back role.

**ANDONI ZUBIZARRETA** (Valencia)
*Born:* 23.10.61    *Caps:* 105    *Goals:* –
First Spaniard to play in 100 internationals, and was the only member of the Barcelona
team to be an ever-present in all their first three consecutive title wins (1991-93) – and
missed only four games (dropped) in 1993-94, when they kept their title. He came to
Valencia in summer 1994 when he was out of contract with Barcelona and upset by
Johan Cruyff's criticism of him. He had moved to Barcelona from Bilbao in 1986 and
was bought by Terry Venables for what was then a world record fee for a keeper of £1.2
million. Has won two titles with Bilbao as well as the four titles with Barcelona.

**Coach: JAVIER CLEMENTE**
*Born:* 12.3.50
A Basque who played for Athletic Bilbao before serious injury ended his career at the
age of 24. He immediately turned to coaching and later returned to Bilbao as youth
coach. In 1981 he was appointed first-team trainer and guided them to three league
titles and one cup, including a league-and-cup double. Later he led Espanol to the 1988
UEFA Cup final before joining Atletico Madrid. He was appointed national coach in
July 1992, succeeding Vicente Miera.

# KEY PLAYER

## FERNANDO HIERRO
*Date of Birth:* 23.3.68
*Current club:* Real Madrid
*Position:* Midfield/Defender
*Height:* 1.87 m
*Weight:* 84 kg

### CAREER RECORD

| Year | Club | League Apps | Goals | Int Apps | Goals |
|------|------|-------------|-------|----------|-------|
| 1987-88 | Real Valladolid | 29 | 1 | | |
| 1988-89 | | 29 | 2 | | |
| 1989-90 | Real Madrid | 37 | 7 | 2 | |
| 1990-91 | | 35 | 6 | 2 | 1 |
| 1991-92 | | 37 | 21 | 7 | 3 |
| 1992-93 | | 33 | 13 | 4 | 1 |
| 1993-94 | | 34 | 10 | 13 | 2 |
| 1994-95 | | 33 | 7 | 8 | 2 |
| 1995-96 | | | | 3 | 2 |

### HONOURS
Spanish champions – 1990, 1995
Spanish Cup winner – 1993

| No | Date | Opponents | Venue | Score | Goals | Competition | Subbed Sub |
|----|------|-----------|-------|-------|-------|-------------|-----|
| 1 | 20.9.89 | Poland | La Coruna | 1-0 | 0 | Friendly | Sub pl 67 |
| 2 | 11.10.89 | Hungary | Budapest | 2-2 | 0 | World Cup, Q | Sub pl 9 |
| 3 | 19.12.90 | Albania | Seville | 9-0 | 1 | E Nations, Q | 90 |
| 4 | 16.1.91 | Portugal | Castellon | 1-1 | 0 | Friendly | 90 |
| 5 | 25.9.91 | Iceland | Reykjavik | 0-2 | 0 | E Nations, Q | Sub pl 23 |
| 6 | 12.10.91 | France | Seville | 1-2 | 0 | E Nations, Q | 90 |
| 7 | 13.11.91 | Czechoslovakia | Seville | 2-1 | 0 | E Nations, Q | 90 |
| 8 | 15.1.92 | Portugal | Torres N | 0-0 | 0 | Friendly | 90 |
| 9 | 19.2.92 | CIS | Valencia | 1-1 | 1 | Friendly | 90 |
| 10 | 11.3.92 | USA | Valladolid | 2-0 | 1 | Friendly | 90 |
| 11 | 22.4.92 | Albania | Seville | 3-0 | 1 | World Cup, Q | 90 |
| 12 | 14.10.92 | Northern Ireland | Belfast | 0-0 | 0 | World Cup, Q | 90 |
| 13 | 18.11.92 | Rep of Ireland | Seville | 0-0 | 0 | World Cup, Q | 90 |
| 14 | 28.4.93 | Northern Ireland | Seville | 3-1 | 1 | World Cup, Q | 90 |
| 15 | 2.6.93 | Lithuania | Vilnius | 2-0 | 0 | World Cup, Q | 90 |
| 16 | 8.9.93 | Chile | Alicante | 2-0 | 0 | Friendly | 90 |
| 17 | 22.9.93 | Albania | Tirana | 5-1 | 0 | World Cup, Q | 90 |
| 18 | 13.10.93 | Rep of Ireland | Dublin | 3-1 | 0 | World Cup, Q | 90 |
| 19 | 17.11.93 | Denmark | Seville | 1-0 | 1 | World Cup, Q | 90 |
| 20 | 19.1.94 | Portugal | Vigo | 2-2 | 0 | Friendly | Sub pl 45 |
| 21 | 9.2.94 | Poland | Tenerife | 1-1 | 0 | Friendly | Subbed 46 |
| 22 | 23.3.94 | Croatia | Valencia | 0-2 | 0 | Friendly | Subbed 46 |
| 23 | 2.6.94 | Finland | Tampere | 2-1 | 0 | Friendly | 90 |
| 24 | 17.6.94 | South Korea | Dallas | 2-2 | 0 | WC finals | 90 |

118

| No | Date | Opponents | Venue | Score | Goals | Competition | Subbed Sub |
|----|------|-----------|-------|-------|-------|-------------|------------|
| 25 | 21.6.94 | Germany | Chicago | 1-1 | 0 | WC finals | 90 |
| 26 | 27.6.94 | Bolivia | Chicago | 3-1 | 0 | WC finals | Sub pl 45 |
| 27 | 2.7.94 | Switzerland | Washington | 3-0 | 1 | WC finals | Subbed 76 |
| 28 | 9.7.94 | Italy | Boston | 1-2 | 0 | WC finals | Sub pl 25 |
| 29 | 7.9.94 | Cyprus | Limassol | 2-1 | 0 | E Nations, Q | 90 |
| 30 | 12.10.94 | Macedonia | Skopje | 2-0 | 0 | E Nations, Q | 90 |
| 31 | 30.11.94 | Finland | Malaga | 2-0 | 0 | Friendly | 90 |
| 32 | 17.12.94 | Belgium | Brussels | 4-1 | 1 | E Nations, Q | 90 |
| 33 | 18.1.95 | Uruguay | La Coruna | 2-2 | 0 | Friendly | 90 |
| 34 | 22.2.95 | Germany | Jerez | 0-0 | 0 | Friendly | 90 |
| 35 | 29.3.95 | Belgium | Seville | 1-1 | 0 | E Nations, Q | 90 |
| 36 | 7.6.95 | Armenia | Seville | 1-0 | 0 | E Nations, Q | 90 |
| 37 | 6.9.95 | Cyprus | Granada | 6-0 | 1 | E Nations, Q | 90 |
| 38 | 20.9.95 | Argentina | Madrid | 2-2 | 0 | Friendly | Sub pl 45 |
| 39 | 11.10.95 | Denmark | Copenhagen | 1-1 | 1 | E Nations, Q | 90 |
| 40 | 7.2.96 | Norway | Las Palmas | 1-0 | 0 | Friendly | Subbed 46 |

# BULGARIA

Virtually the entire team now play abroad – many in the very top leagues like the Bundesliga and Serie A. Most of the players who were in the 1994 World Cup semi-finals are back to maintain the challenge for European honours – the likes of Stoichkov, Kostadinov, Balakov, Letchkov and Co. will make them dangerous floaters in their group.

The defence is also very much the same as the World Cup squad. Will there be British interest in the form of Reading's wig-wearing keeper Boris Mikhailov, or Boncho Guentchev of Luton?

*Formation:* 1-3-3-3
*Coach:* Dimitar Penev

                    Mikhailov

                    Houbchev

    Kiriakov        Ivanov          Tsvetanov

    Lechkov         Yankov          Balakov

    Kostadinov      Penev           Stoichkov


| Player | Position | Club | Date | Caps | Goals |
|--------|----------|------|------|------|-------|
| Boris Mikhailov | G | Reading (Eng) | 12.3.62 | 91 | – |
| Dimitar Popov | G | CSKA Sofia | 27.2.70 | 13 | – |
| Plamen Nikolov | G | Levski Sofia | 20.8.61 | 6 | – |
| Emil Kremenliev | D | Olympiakos (Gre) | 13.6.69 | 24 | – |
| Trifon Ivanov | D | Rapid Vienna (Aus) | 27.7.65 | 58 | 5 |
| Petar Houbchev | D | SV Hamburg (Ger) | 26.2.64 | 30 | – |
| Ilian Kiriakov | D | Anorthosis (Cyp) | 4.8.67 | 52 | – |
| Zlatko Yankov | D | Uerdingen (Ger) | 7.8.66 | 48 | 4 |
| Tsanko Tsvetanov | D | Wald. Mannheim (Ger) | 6.1.70 | 33 | – |
| Gosho Ginchev | D | Denizlispor (Tur) | 11.12.69 | 3 | – |
| Daniel Borimirov | M | 1860 Munich (Ger) | 16.1.70 | 20 | 2 |
| Krasimir Balakov | M | Stuttgart (Ger) | 28.4.66 | 50 | 7 |
| Yordan Lechkov | M | SV Hamburg (Ger) | 9.7.67 | 32 | 4 |
| Ivailo Iordanov | M | Sporting Lisbon (Por) | 26.6.66 | 21 | – |
| Vladko Shalamanov | M | Slavia Sofia | 25.4.67 | 5 | – |
| Emil Kostadinov | F | Bayern Munich (Ger) | 12.8.67 | 49 | 16 |
| Hristo Stoichkov | F | Parma (Ita) | 8.2.66 | 59 | 29 |
| Luboslav Penev | F | Atletico Madrid (Spa) | 31.8.66 | 49 | 11 |
| Nasko Sirakov | F | Slavia Sofia | 26.4.62 | 78 | 22 |
| Petar Alexandrov | F | Luzern (Swi) | 7.12.62 | 27 | 5 |
| Petar Mikhtarski | F | Campomaiorense (Por) | 15.7.66 | 8 | – |
| Boncho Guentchev | F | Luton Town (Eng) | 7.7.64 | 9 | – |
| Ilian Iliev | F | Benfica (Por) | 2.7.68 | 5 | – |

# BULGARIA A-Z

### PETAR ALEXANDROV (Luzern, Switzerland)
*Born:* 7.12.62    *Caps:* 27    *Goals:* 5
Has been in Switzerland in recent seasons, first with the 1993 champions Aarau, then in 1994-95 was Swiss League top scorer with 24 goals, and is now with Luzern. Was in the 1994 World Cup squad but didn't play and looks as though he is standby in case of injury to any of the more well-known names. Formerly with the many times champions Levski Sofia.

### KRASIMIR BALAKOV (VfB Stuttgart, Germany)
*Born:* 29.3.66    *Caps:* 50    *Goals:* 7
The 1995 Bulgarian Footballer of the Year and a summer 1995 signing by Stuttgart of the Bundesliga from Sporting Lisbon. He had a fine World Cup in which he played all seven games – he was in many people's team of the tournament on the left side of midfield. Made his name when his local provincial club Etur of Tranavo won the 1991 Championship, and he went through to the national squad. He left halfway through Etur's Championship season and joined Sporting.

### DANIEL BORIMIROV (1860 Munich, Germany)
*Born:* 16.1.70    *Caps:* 20    *Goals:* 2
He cost 1860 Munich (the side West Ham beat in the 1965 European Cup-Winners' Cup) some £900,000 from Levski Sofia in summer 1994, and has done well in the Bundesliga. Joined Levski from Division 2 club Bodin Vidin in 1989, and won his first cap in 1993. He was a valued part of the Levski side who won the 1993 title and the 1994 double of League and Cup. Also scored a first-leg goal when Rangers were beaten by Levski in the first round of the 1993-94 European Cup.

### GOSHO GINCHEV (Denizlispor, Turkey)
*Born:* 11.12.69    *Caps:* 2    *Goals:* –
Has been part of Levski's last three titles on the trot from 1993-95 and is a defender who played against Germany in the final game of the Euro 96 qualifiers. New to the squad. Recently moved to play his club football in Turkey.

### BONCHO GUENTCHEV (Luton Town, England)
*Born:* 7.7.64    *Caps:* 9    *Goals:* –
Moved in summer 1995 from Ipswich to Luton on a free transfer and is making a considerable improvement under Lennie Lawrence after failing to get on with Terry Westley's methods. Three substitute appearances at the 1994 World Cup. Is another from the little provincial side Etur Tranavo, finishing top scorer for the club in their Championship-winning season of 1991 with 15 goals. That earned him a move to Sporting Lisbon with Balakov, but he did not stay long and came to Ipswich in 1993.

### PETAR HOUBCHEV (SV Hamburg, Germany)
*Born:* 26.2.64    *Caps:* 30    *Goals:* –
Played all seven games at the 1994 World Cup. Moved during the 1993-94 season from the champions Levski Sofia to the Bundesliga club SV Hamburg for £400,000. He joined Levski in 1989 from Osaam Lovech, a Second Division club. Has another year of his contract to go at Hamburg, who are well pleased with him, but has been injured for much of 1995-96.

**ILIAN ILIEV** (Benfica, Portugal)
*Born:* 2.7.68    *Caps:* 5    *Goals:* –
Joined Benfica in 1995 from Levski Sofia, but Benfica are currently right off the rails and he has suffered as a misfit overseas player. He was with Levski from 1991-95 where he was in the side that won three successive doubles. Midfield/forward.

**IVAILO IORDANOV** (Sporting Lisbon, Portugal)
*Born:* 26.6.66    *Caps:* 21    *Goals:* –
He has just returned to the Sporting line-up in 1996 after long-term injuries from a car crash. He played for Lokomotiv Gorna Orahovitsa in the Bulgarian First Division and moved to Portugal in 1992 with Sporting. He was not initially in the front line of overseas players at the club and tends to get his first-team games only when injuries prevail, but life is better than at home! He played in five of the seven World Cup games in 1994 and performed particularly well in the squad situation.

**TRIFON IVANOV** (Rapid Vienna, Austria)
*Born:* 27.7.65    *Caps:* 58    *Goals:* 5
Regular central defender at the 1994 World Cup, he moved in summer 1994 from the promoted Spanish club Betis Seville to the Swiss Division 1 club Neuchatel Xamax and on again in summer 1995 to Rapid. Has been punted around several English clubs by various agents, but no one has yet taken him on. First capped in 1988 he was with CSKA Sofia from 1988-91 and was originally with Etur of Tranavo.

**ILIAN KIRIAKOV** (Anorthosis, Cyprus)
*Born:* 4.8.67    *Caps:* 52    *Goals:* –
Chunky little reddish-haired player who had to double as full back in the 1994 World Cup, and seemed to find a new role in his career, though only 5ft 3in tall. Subsequently played really well in the 1995-96 European Champions League prelims v Rangers shortly after his move from Deportivo La Coruna. At Deportivo he was the fourth overseas player behind Bebeto, Mauro Silva and Djukic, the Yugoslav who missed the penalty that would have won the 1994 Championship. First capped in 1988, he began his career in Etur's Championship team of 1991 with Balakov, Guentchev and Tsvetanov.

**EMIL KOSTADINOV** (Bayern Munich, Germany)
*Born:* 12.8.67    *Caps:* 49    *Goals:* 16
Moved to Bayern in summer 1995 for a fee of £1 million after a loan spell, signed from FC Porto, who had also loaned him to Deportivo La Coruna to sub for the injured Mauro Silva. Played all seven games at the World Cup, but surprisingly failed to score. Another who started his career with the army side CSKA Sofia, and moved to Portugal in 1990 with FC Porto after he and Stoichkov had won back-to-back titles in 1989 and 1990. Was in Porto's 1992 and 1993 Championship wins. Scored the two goals in Paris that scuppered French hopes of reaching the 1994 World Cup finals in the last of the qualifiers.

**EMIL KREMENLIEV** (Olympiakos Piraeus, Greece)
*Born:* 13.6.69    *Caps:* 24    *Goals:* –
Played in five of the games at the 1994 World Cup but was victim of a sending-off in the Mexico match by a very poor referee, who was sent home. His Greek club signed the full

back in 1995 from Levski Sofia. Came through to the national team off the back of Levski's double-winning season, and made a major breakthrough in 1993-94. Levski retained the title in 1995 so it was time to move on.

### YORDAN LECHKOV (SV Hamburg, Germany)
*Born:* 9.7.67   *Caps:* 32   *Goals:* 4
Is in his fourth season in Germany with SV Hamburg and they are delighted with him. Originally from the provincial Sliven club, he moved to CSKA for a couple of seasons then on to Hamburg. Recommended his national team-mate Houbchev to Hamburg. Easily recognisable with his balding head, Lechkov played all seven games at the World Cup and was one of the stars of the tournament, scoring the winner against holders Germany.

### BORIS MIKHAILOV (Reading, England)
*Born:* 12.2.62   *Caps:* 91   *Goals:* –
Played his football in the French Division 2 for modest Mulhouse until, after an excellent 1994 World Cup, he put himself around. But no one was interested in him (or his wig) and he returned home to Bulgaria. Joined Reading in September 1995 for £300,000 but was one of six keepers used by Reading and had a long-term Achilles injury. First capped 12 years ago v Wales in November 1983. Played all four World Cup games in 1986 and all seven in their 1994 run to the semi-final. Was one of the players banned a few years ago when the Levski v CSKA Cup final erupted so went West to Belenenses in Portugal before going to Mulhouse in 1991. Captain of Bulgaria through 1994 World Cup, and approaching Hristo Bonev's national cap record of 96.

### PETAR MIKHTARSKI (Campomaiorense, Portugal)
*Born:* 15.7.66   *Caps:* 8   *Goals:* –
He was in Portugal from 1991 to 1994 with FC Porto, but was surplus to requirements, despite efforts to marry him off with a local girl to gain home nationality! He was loaned out a couple of times. Went back to CSKA in 1994-95 and was Bulgarian League top scorer with 24 goals, and has now settled for Portuguese club Campomaiorense, a side promoted for 1995-96 who may return whence they came. His first major club was Levski Sofia, and he played part of the 1994-95 season with Pirin Blagoevgrad. In the 1994 World Cup squad but did not play.

### PLAMEN NIKOLOV (Levski Sofia)
*Born:* 20.8.61   *Caps:* 6   *Goals:* –
Keeper with the champions Levski Sofia, he has been with the club since 1991 when he joined from Lokomotiv Sofia. Levski won the 1992-93 and 1994-95 Championships and in 1993-94 completed the double. Played as sub in the World Cup of 1994 against Sweden in the third-place match. Probable third choice.

### LUBOSLAV PENEV (Atletico Madrid, Spain)
*Born:* 31.8.66   *Caps:* 49   *Goals:* 11
Signed by Atletico, who are dominating the title race in 1995-96, in summer 1995 for around £800,000, and is having his best season in Spain. The nephew of the coach, he missed the 1994 World Cup after being diagnosed as having cancer of the testicles, but happily he has recovered after making slow but steady progress through the club and national sides. Was at Valencia from 1990-95, and was top scorer in each of his five seasons. His Bulgarian club was CSKA Sofia.

**DIMITAR POPOV** (CSKA Sofia)

*Born:* 27.2.70    *Caps:* 13    *Goals:* –

Is the best young keeper in the country, and moved across from Spartak Plovdiv to CSKA Sofia in 1994. Not in the World Cup squad but played in the first of the 1994-95 European Championship qualifiers in Mikhailov's place (v Georgia), also played against Germany in the final qualifying game.

**VLADKO SHALAMANOV** (Slavia Sofia)

*Born:* 25.4.67    *Caps:* 5    *Goals:* –

Has been part of his club's revival in fortunes in the last couple of seasons. Has been with the club for a decade.

**NASKO SIRAKOV** (Slavia Sofia)

*Born:* 26.4.62    *Caps:* 78    *Goals:* 22

A wily and experienced campaigner who arrived back in Bulgaria at the end of the 1992-93 season from RC Lens, of the French First Division, to play for Levski and has since switched to reviving the fortunes of Slavia. He began his career with Levski and then moved to Spain to play for Espanol and Valladolid before going to Lens. Attacking midfielder who is a good goalscorer, now a little past his peak but still a useful squad member. One of the best of the domestic scorers – despite his absence abroad, he has five times been Bulgarian League top scorer, the last time being in 1994.

**HRISTO STOICHKOV** (Parma, Italy)

*Born:* 8.2.66    *Caps:* 59    *Goals:* 29

Moved in summer 1995 from Barcelona to Parma for about £4.8 million. Equal top scorer at the World Cup with six goals, he has scored eight in his last eight internationals and 14 in the last 18 internationals after a slow start. Made his name with CSKA Sofia and then, after sharing the European Golden Boot award with 38 goals with Hugo Sanchez, he signed in 1990 for Barcelona for £1.5 million. He was five times Bulgaria's Footballer of the Year and was 1994 European Footballer of the Year. He won League medals with CSKA in 1989 and 1990 and then four in a row with Barcelona, so it looks as though 1995-96 may be the first season in his last six that he hasn't won a League title!

**TSANKO TSVETANOV** (Waldhof Mannheim, Germany)

*Born:* 6.1.70    *Caps:* 33    *Goals:* –

Played in six of the seven games at the 1994 World Cup but missed the Mexico match after being sent off v Argentina. He is a 1994 signing from Levski Sofia and was originally with Etur Tranavo, with whom he won the Championship in 1991 at the age of 21. He then won his second title with Levski's double win in 1993-94. Improving defender, now in a Division 2 side in Germany.

**ZLATKO YANKOV** (Uerdingen, Germany)

*Born:* 7.8.66    *Caps:* 48    *Goals:* 4

Cost the Bundesliga club $350,000 from Spanish club Valladolid in 1994, the year in which he played in six of the seven 1994 World Cup games and 15 of 16 internationals. First capped in 1990 and now considered by trainer Penev as one of his more regular midfielders. Is being courted by his old club Levski after playing for two struggling clubs outside Bulgaria.

**Coach: DIMITAR PENEV**

*Born:* 12.7.45

Penev began his career with Lokomotiv Sofia where he won seven League titles and five cups. Capped 90 times by Bulgaria, he played in three World Cup finals (1966, 1970 and 1974). He began his coaching career with CSKA, spent two years in Kuwait then returned to CSKA, winning five League titles and five cups. He was appointed national coach in July 1991, succeeding Ivan Vutsov.

## KEY PLAYER

### HRISTO STOICHKOV

*Date of Birth:* 8.2.66
*Current club:* Parma
*Position:* Forward
*Height:* 1.78 m
*Weight:* 73 kg

### CAREER RECORD

| Year | Club | League Apps | Goals | Int Apps | Goals |
|------|------|------|-------|------|-------|
| 1984-85 | CSKA Sofia | 11 | | | |
| 1985-86 | | 0 | | | |
| 1986-87 | | 25 | 6 | | |
| 1987-88 | | 27 | 14 | 7 | 1 |
| 1988-89 | | 26 | 23 | 12 | 3 |
| 1989-90 | | 30 | 38 | 5 | 1 |
| 1990-91 | Barcelona | 24 | 14 | 3 | |
| 1991-92 | | 32 | 17 | 5 | 2 |
| 1992-93 | | 34 | 20 | 6 | 4 |
| 1993-94 | | 34 | 16 | 11 | 8 |
| 1994-95 | | 27 | 9 | 6 | 7 |
| 1995-96 | Parma | | | 4 | 3 |

### HONOURS

Bulgarian Footballer of the Year – 1989, 1990, 1991, 1992, 1994
Bulgarian champion – 1987, 1989, 1990
Bulgarian Cup winner – 1987, 1988, 1989
Bulgarian top scorer – 1989, 1990
Spanish champion – 1991, 1992, 1993, 1994
European Cup winner – 1992
European Footballer of the Year – 1994
Top scorer in the 1989 European Cup-Winners' Cup competition
Joint top scorer 1994 World Cup finals – 6 goals

| No | Date | Opponents | Venue | Score | Goals | Competition | Subbed Sub |
|----|------|-----------|-------|-------|-------|-------------|------------|
| 1 | 23.9.87 | Belgium | Sofia | 2-0 | 0 | E Nations, Q | Subbed 68 |
| 2 | 14.10.87 | Rep of Ireland | Dublin | 0-2 | 0 | E Nations, Q | 90 |
| 3 | 11.11.87 | Scotland | Sofia | 0-1 | 0 | E Nations, Q | 90 |
| 4 | 21.1.88 | Qatar | Doha | 3-2 | 1 | Friendly | Sub pl 45 |

| No | Date | Opponents | Venue | Score | Goals | Competition | Subbed Sub |
|----|------|-----------|-------|-------|-------|-------------|------------|
| 5 | 3.2.88 | Egypt | Cairo | 0-1 | 0 | Friendly | 90 |
| 6 | 23.3.88 | Czechoslovakia | Sofia | 2-0 | 0 | Friendly | 90 |
| 7 | 13.4.88 | East Germany | Burgas | 1-1 | 0 | Friendly | 90 |
| 8 | 4.5.88 | Finland | Vaasa | 1-1 | 0 | Friendly | Subbed 46 |
| 9 | 7.8.88 | Iceland | Reykjavik | 3-2 | 0 | Friendly | Subbed 85 |
| 10 | 9.8.88 | Norway | Oslo | 1-1 | 1 | Friendly | Sub pl 72 |
| 11 | 24.8.88 | Poland | Bialystok | 2-3 | 1 | Friendly | Sub pl 45 |
| 12 | 21.9.88 | [USSR 'B'] | Sofia | 2-2 | 1 | Friendly | 90 |
| 13 | 19.10.88 | Romania | Sofia | 1-3 | 0 | World Cup, Q | 90 |
| 14 | 2.11.88 | Denmark | Copenhagen | 1-1 | 0 | World Cup, Q | Subbed 88 |
| 15 | 24.12.88 | UAE | Surjah | 1-0 | 0 | Friendly | 90 |
| 16 | 21.2.89 | USSR | Sofia | 1-2 | 0 | Friendly | 90 |
| 17 | 22.3.89 | West Germany | Sofia | 1-2 | 0 | Friendly | 90 |
| 18 | 26.4.89 | Denmark | Sofia | 0-2 | 0 | World Cup, Q | 90 |
| 19 | 17.5.89 | Romania | Bucharest | 0-1 | 0 | World Cup, Q | 90 |
| 20 | 23.8.89 | East Germany | Erfurt | 1-1 | 0 | Friendly | Subbed 75 |
| 21 | 20.9.89 | Italy | Cesena | 0-4 | 0 | Friendly | 90 |
| 22 | 11.10.89 | Greece | Varna | 4-0 | 1 | World Cup, Q | 90 |
| 23 | 15.11.89 | Greece | Athens | 0-1 | 0 | World Cup, Q | 90 |
| 24 | 5.5.90 | Brazil | Campinas | 1-2 | 0 | Friendly | Subbed 85 |
| 25 | 12.9.90 | Switzerland | Geneva | 0-2 | 0 | E Nations, Q | 90 |
| 26 | 17.10.90 | Romania | Bucharest | 3-0 | 0 | E Nations, Q | 90 |
| 27 | 14.11.90 | Scotland | Sofia | 1-1 | 0 | E Nations, Q | 90 |
| 28 | 25.9.91 | Italy | Sofia | 2-1 | 1 | Friendly | 90 |
| 29 | 16.10.91 | San Marino | Sofia | 4-0 | 1 | E Nations, Q | Subbed 69 |
| 30 | 20.11.91 | Romania | Sofia | 1-1 | 0 | E Nations, Q | 90 |
| 31 | 28.4.92 | Switzerland | Berne | 2-0 | 0 | Friendly | Subbed 75 |
| 32 | 14.5.92 | Finland | Helsinki | 3-0 | 0 | World Cup, Q | Subbed 69 |
| 33 | 19.8.92 | Mexico | Sofia | 1-1 | 1 | Friendly | Subbed 70 |
| 34 | 9.9.92 | France | Sofia | 2-0 | 1 | World Cup, Q | 90 |
| 35 | 2.12.92 | Israel | Tel Aviv | 2-0 | 0 | World Cup, Q | 90 |
| 36 | 14.4.93 | Austria | Vienna | 1-3 | 0 | World Cup, Q | 90 |
| 37 | 28.4.93 | Finland | Sofia | 2-0 | 1 | World Cup, Q | 90 |
| 38 | 12.5.93 | Israel | Sofia | 2-2 | 1 | World Cup, Q | 90 |
| 39 | 8.9.93 | Sweden | Sofia | 1-1 | 1 | World Cup, Q | 90 |
| 40 | 13.10.93 | Austria | Sofia | 4-1 | 1 | World Cup, Q | 90 |
| 41 | 17.11.93 | France | Paris | 2-1 | 0 | World Cup, Q | 90 |
| 42 | 3.6.94 | Ukraine | Sofia | 1-0 | 0 | Friendly | Subbed 67 |
| 43 | 22.6.94 | Nigeria | Dallas | 0-4 | 0 | WC finals | 90 |
| 44 | 26.6.94 | Greece | Chicago | 4-0 | 2 | WC finals | 90 |
| 45 | 30.6.94 | Argentina | Dallas | 2-0 | 0 | WC finals | 90 |
| 46 | 5.7.94 | Mexico | New York | 1-1 | 1 | WC finals | 90 |
| 47 | 10.7.94 | Germany | New York | 2-1 | 1 | WC finals | 90 |
| 48 | 13.7.94 | Italy | New York | 1-2 | 1 | WC finals | Subbed 85 |
| 49 | 16.7.94 | Sweden | Los Angeles | 0-4 | 0 | WC finals | Subbed 79 |
| 50 | 12.10.94 | Georgia | Sofia | 2-0 | 0 | E Nations, Q | 90 |
| 51 | 16.11.94 | Moldova | Sofia | 4-1 | 2 | E Nations, Q | 90 |
| 52 | 14.12.94 | Wales | Cardiff | 3-0 | 1 | E Nations, Q | 90 |
| 53 | 29.3.95 | Wales | Sofia | 3-1 | 0 | E Nations, Q | 90 |
| 54 | 26.4.95 | Moldova | Chisinau | 3-2 | 2 | E Nations, Q | Subbed 79 |
| 55 | 7.6.95 | Germany | Sofia | 3-2 | 2 | E Nations, Q | 90 |
| 56 | 6.9.95 | Albania | Tirana | 1-1 | 1 | E Nations, Q | 90 |
| 57 | 7.10.95 | Albania | Sofia | 3-0 | 0 | E Nations, Q | 90 |
| 58 | 11.10.95 | Georgia | Tbilisi | 1-2 | 1 | E Nations, Q | 90 |
| 59 | 15.11.95 | Germany | Berlin | 1-3 | 1 | E Nations, Q | 90 |

# ROMANIA

If nothing else, this side deserve some luck – they were bounced out of both of the last two World Cups only on penalties so are due some luck. The usual team remains intact, and a skilful one which bemused England for much of a friendly at Wembley over 18 months ago. Many of the names are familiar internationals – Hagi, Petrescu, Popescu, Raducioiu, Lacatus and Co. have been around for ages.

The team is dispersed all over Europe, which is often the drawback, while the home-based players are built around the Steaua Bucharest team, a Champions League side in 1995-96. There will be British interest in Chelsea's Petrescu, Spurs old boy Popescu, and West Ham's ex-spur Dumitrescu (whose international record is superb).

*Formation:* 5-4-1
*Coach:* Angel Iordanescu

Stelea

Petrescu   Mihali   Lupescu   Prodan   Selymes

Sabau   Popescu   Hagi   Munteanu

Raducioiu

| Player | Position | Club | Date | Caps | Goals |
|---|---|---|---|---|---|
| Bogdan Stelea | G | Steaua Bucharest | 5.12.67 | 33 | – |
| Florin Prunea | G | Dinamo Bucharest | 8.8.68 | 29 | – |
| Dan Petrescu | D | Chelsea (Eng) | 22.12.67 | 50 | 5 |
| Daniel Prodan | D | Steaua Bucharest | 23.3.72 | 34 | 2 |
| Georghe Mihali | D | Guingamp (Fra) | 9.12.65 | 29 | – |
| Gica Popescu | D | Barcelona (Spa) | 9.10.67 | 60 | 3 |
| Tibor Selymes | D | Cercle Bruges (Bel) | 14.6.70 | 26 | – |
| Mirodrag Belodedici | D | Villareal (Spa) | 20.5.64 | 45 | 5 |
| Ioan Lupescu | M | B. Leverkusen (Ger) | 9.12.68 | 46 | 5 |
| Ovidiu Sabau | M | Brescia (Ita) | 12.2.68 | 46 | 8 |
| Dorinel Munteanu | M | Cologne (Ger) | 25.6.68 | 44 | 4 |
| Basarab Panduru | M | Benfica (Por) | 11.7.70 | 21 | 1 |
| Gheorghe Hagi | M | Barcelona (Spa) | 5.2.65 | 95 | 27 |
| Daniel Timofte | M | Samsunspor (Tur) | 1.10.67 | 22 | 2 |
| Dorin Mateut | M | Dinamo Bucharest | 5.8.65 | 56 | 10 |
| Constantin Galca | M | Steaua Bucharest | 8.3.72 | 18 | – |
| Marius Lacatus | F | Steaua Bucharest | 5.4.64 | 81 | 14 |
| Ioan Vladoiu | F | Steaua Bucharest | 5.11.68 | 21 | 1 |
| Ilie Dumitrescu | F | West Ham (Eng) | 6.1.69 | 54 | 19 |
| Florin Raducioiu | F | Espanol (Spa) | 13.3.70 | 36 | 20 |
| Adrian Ilie | F | Steaua Bucharest | 20.4.74 | 6 | 3 |
| Danut Lupu | F | Dinamo Bucharest | 27.2.67 | 11 | – |

# ROMANIA A-Z

### MIRODRAG BELODEDICI (Villareal, Spain)
*Born:* 20.5.64    *Caps:* 45    *Goals:* 5

Played all five World Cup games in the USA in 1994, and scored his fifth international goal against Azerbaijan. Moved from Valencia to Valladolid in the summer of 1994 for around £450,000. Is in the record books as the first player to win the European Cup with two different clubs – Steaua Bucharest (1986) and Red Star Belgrade (1991), an honour subsequently won by Ronald Koeman, Dejan Savicevic and Marcel Desailly. Was to have played for Yugoslavia in the 1990 World Cup finals, but in the end he turned down their invitation – he is from Romanian Serb stock. Missed nearly four years' international football when in Yugoslavia. Based in Spain since 1992, currently with Villareal in Division 2 but has had contractual arguments with the club, and hardly played.

### ILIE DUMITRESCU (West Ham United, England)
*Born:* 6.1.69    *Caps:* 54    *Goals:* 19

Played all five games at the 1994 World Cup and scored twice in the win which eliminated Argentina. Moved in August 1994 from Steaua Bucharest to Spurs for £2.6 million. With Steaua he was an attacking midfielder in the Platini role. He had been with Steaua since a teenager in 1988, and has improved with every season. Very much a key player in the last two Championship wins in 1993 (Romanian League top scorer with 23 goals) and 1994 (second in Romanian League scorers' list with 17 goals). He played twice in the 1990 finals, and went into the 1994 World Cup with 14 goals in his previous 18 internationals. Was going to be transferred to Seville from Tottenham but would have lost £500,000 in bonuses, so went on loan instead at the end of 1994. Returned to Tottenham in summer 1995, but old doubts of acclimatisation existed. After a lengthy transfer wrangle involving the Home Office he finally moved from Tottenham to West Ham in March 1996 for £1.65 million. Good player struggling for identity at club level.

### COSTANTIN GALCA (Steaua Bucharest)
*Born:* 8.3.72    *Caps:* 18    *Goals:* –

Played twice in the 1994 World Cup as a sub for a total of just ten minutes, but announced himself in 1994-95 with all five goals in Steaua's 5-0 win against Brasov in September 1994. Another of the fine young squad being developed by Steaua, the 1986 European Cup winners. Originally with the provincial Division 1 side Arges Pitesti, he moved to Steaua in 1991 and has been a key member of their 1993, 1994 and 1995 Championship-winning teams. First cap in September 1993.

### GHEORGHE HAGI (Barcelona, Spain)
*Born:* 5.2.65    *Caps:* 95    *Goals:* 27

At the 1994 World Cup he at last made his mark on the international stage with goals against Colombia, Switzerland and Argentina, and a fine all-round performance in all five games. That earned a transfer from Serie B with Brescia back into the limelight with Barcelona – moving in August 1994 for £2.1 million. Former boy wonder who has been nearly 13 years in the national side since 1983, he was one of the first to take advantage of the breakdown of the old Iron Curtain, though his form for Real Madrid – he cost £2 million in 1990 – was not that earth-shattering. In 1992 he moved to the Romanian enclave at Brescia. He began his career at Farul Constanta, then to Sportul, and on to a Steaua side that won the double in 1987, 1988 and 1989 with Ceausescu's son as president of the club! Wears size five boots and took a pay cut to leave Real Madrid so that he could play in Italy. For Barcelona his form is much improved from the start to the 1995-96 season.


### ADRIAN ILIE (Steaua Bucharest)
*Born:* 20.4.74    *Caps:* 6    *Goals:* 3
Capped in 1994 against Israel, he was formerly with Electroputere Craiova, whose arrival in Division 1 was down to Ilie's scoring talents. A useful member of the Steaua squad since signing for them in 1993, though is being played wide on the wing rather than as an authentic striker these days. Helped them to their titles in 1994 and 1995, and their Champions League campaigns.


### MARIUS LACATUS (Steaua Bucharest)
*Born:* 5.4.64    *Caps:* 81    *Goals:* 14
Not in 1994 World Cup squad but recalled in September 1994 against Azerbaijan for his first international for 16 months. Talented but indisciplined player who returned to Steaua in 1993 after three years with Fiorentina in Serie A and Oviedo in the Spanish First Division. He was with Steaua from 1983-90, winning five League titles and scoring in the shoot-out to give Steaua the 1986 European Cup against Venables' Barcelona. He is the only player who played in the 1986 European Cup win for Steaua who is still playing for the club. Showing useful domestic form again and deservedly recalled.


### IOAN LUPESCU (Bayer Leverkusen, Germany)
*Born:* 9.12.68    *Caps:* 46    *Goals:* 5
Played in all five games at the 1994 World Cup and has been in outstanding Bundesliga form. Went from Dinamo Bucharest's double team of 1990 to the World Cup, where he played in three of the four games. Transferred to Bayer Leverkusen for £1 million and now very highly rated in the Bundesliga. Can play as midfield marker or in defence.


### DANUT LUPU (Dinamo Bucharest)
*Born:* 27.2.67    *Caps:* 11    *Goals:* –
Is on a rehabilitation course – he played in the 1990 World Cup when with Dinamo, and was in their League and Cup double-winning side of 1990, but went to Panathinaikos in Greece after the World Cup for £1 million. Unfortunately he failed to heed the saying of beware of Greeks bearing gifts and served a prison sentence after being caught for drugs and procuring women. Returned to Dinamo and is rebuilding his career – the talent is still there.


### DORIN MATEUT (Dinamo Bucharest)
*Born:* 5.8.65    *Caps:* 56    *Goals:* 10
Midfielder who was the surprise European Golden Boot winner in 1989 with 43 goals, but under suspicious circumstances involving the previous political regime. None the less a useful midfielder, he had two seasons in Spain with Zaragoza in the early 1990s, but is much happier back with his Dinamo colleagues.

**GEORGHE MIHALI** (Guingamp, France)

*Born: 9.12.65    Caps: 29    Goals: –*

Played at the 1994 World Cup in four of the five matches, missing the quarter-final game with Sweden. First capped in 1991, after the defections of many of the 1990 World Cup defenders to the West, he continued to play in the Romanian League and formerly played for Dinamo Bucharest, champions in 1990 and 1992 and runners-up in 1993-94 to Steaua. Signed for Guingamp, newly promoted into the French First Division, in summer 1995 and is an integral part of a watertight defence so far in the 1995-96 season.

**DORINEL MUNTEANU** (Cologne, Germany)

*Born: 25.6.68    Caps: 44    Goals: 4*

First capped in 1991, he played all five games at the 1994 World Cup, many experts considering him to be a key player – the workhorse around whom all the other talents flowed. Started his career with the provincial club FC Olt, and Inter Sibiu, before a worthwhile move to Dinamo Bucharest in 1991. He played in Dinamo's Championship win of 1992 and he was third in the national scoring lists in 1992-93; now in his first season at Cologne after having two years in Belgium with Cercle Bruges. Cologne spotted him in the Belgian League and paid £1.2 million for him.

**BASARAB PANDURU** (Benfica, Portugal)

*Born: 11.7.70    Caps: 21    Goals: 1*

Two substitute appearances at the 1994 World Cup including the penalty shoot-out in the quarter-final against Sweden. Joined Steaua after his first club, Second Division CSM Resita, had a one-year flirtation with Division 1; he has made excellent progress in the 1993, 1994 and 1995 Championship teams. First capped in 1993, he moved in summer 1995 to Benfica where he is currently struggling to find a way into their side. Benfica are in turmoil and sacked their trainer.

**DAN PETRESCU** (Chelsea, England)

*Born: 22.12.67    Caps: 50    Goals: 5*

Moved from Sheffield Wednesday to Chelsea in late 1995 for £2.3 million. Played all five games in the 1994 World Cup, and scored against the USA, also a scorer against Azerbaijan in September 1994. Arrived in Sheffield from Genoa in Serie A in August 1994 for £1.3 million. Had a knee injury and missed the 1990 World Cup finals. He was the captain of the Steaua Bucharest team (unbeaten for three years!) who won the double in both 1988 and 1989, and then moved to Serie A, first with Foggia in 1991 and then Genoa in 1993. Some coaches prefer him in midfield, others in defence – it depends who is in charge.

**GEORGHE (GICA) POPESCU** (Barcelona, Spain)

*Born: 9.10.67    Caps: 60    Goals: 3*

The 1995 Romanian Footballer of the Year, he played all five games in the 1994 World Cup, winning his 50th cap v Sweden in the quarter-finals. Signed by Tottenham in September 1994 for £2.9 million from PSV Eindhoven. Sold to Barcelona in summer 1995 for £2.2 million. Bought a week before Bobby Robson's arrival at PSV from Universitatea Craiova for £1 million, Popescu became one of the best of his PSV squad that won the 1991 and 1992 Dutch Championships. Always a bit of a rebel, he was a brave man in the Ceausescu days when he moved from Universitatea Craiova to Steaua

Bucharest (the army side) and promptly decided to go back home – against the Ceausescus' wishes! First capped in 1988 at the age of 20, he played well in the 1990 World Cup in all four games in the finals.


**DANIEL PRODAN** (Steaua Bucharest)

*Born:* 25.3.72   *Caps:* 34   *Goals:* 2

A fine prospect who is certain for higher honours, he first made the grade in Steaua's 1993 Championship-winning team and went straight through to the national side. He gained his first cap in a 5-2 World Cup qualifying loss to the RCS, but has hardly missed a game since (playing 28 of the last 32) and appeared in all five games at the 1994 World Cup. Has played three seasons of Division 1 football, champions on each occasion in 1993, 1994 and 1995. Will miss the first game through suspension.


**FLORIN PRUNEA** (Dinamo Bucharest)

*Born:* 8.8.68   *Caps:* 29   *Goals:* –

Played in the last three games at the 1994 World Cup after Stelea was dropped following the 1-4 loss to the Swiss. However, Stelea has subsequently regained the number one spot. Played initially for Dinamo in 1988, then went to the two Universitatea clubs in the First Division at Cluj and then Craiova (who won the double in 1991), before rejoining Dinamo in 1992.


**FLORIN RADUCIOIU** (Espanol, Spain)

*Born:* 13.3.70   *Caps:* 36   *Goals:* 20

Superb record at international level, he scored twice in the 1994 World Cup against both Colombia and in the quarter-final against Sweden in his four games at the finals. Scored the winner at Cardiff to put Romania in the World Cup finals in November 1993. He moved from AC Milan to Espanol of Barcelona in July 1994 for £2.2 million and quickly added quality to the improving Catalan side. He had played in Italy since the 1990 World Cup when he played all four games. In fact, 1990 was a key year for him as he gained his first cap early that year and was part of the Dinamo Bucharest double-winning side. His Italian clubs have since been Bari (with Platt), Verona, Brescia and Milan, who were doubtless impressed by his 13 Serie A goals for Brescia in a relegated side. Sent off v Israel in a Euro 96 qualifier, which earned him a suspension.


**OVIDIU SABAU** (Brescia, Italy)

*Born:* 12.2.68   *Caps:* 46   *Goals:* 8

Is a key player in the Romanian set-up, for he is the midfield workhorse and ball-winner. Highly thought of after a fine 1990 World Cup which took him to Feyenoord for the two seasons 1990-92, and thence on to Brescia from July 1992. He was a member of Dinamo Bucharest's double-winning team in 1990 having previously been with Universitatea Cluj and Targu Mures learning his trade. Has gained wide respect in Italy for staying in a side that is now playing in Serie B, though he is worth a place in Serie A. Brescia has been an enclave for Romanians with former national coach Mircea Lucescu at the helm, and Hagi playing there until August 1994.

**TIBOR SELYMES** (Cercle Bruges, Belgium)
*Born:* 14.6.70  *Caps:* 26  *Goals:* –
Forced his way into the World Cup team after being a sub in the first game, and has been there or thereabouts in most internationals since. Promising player who began his career with FCM Brasov before moving to Dinamo Bucharest from 1990-93. He then signed a five-year contract with his current club which expires in 1998. Is from the Hungarian enclave in Romania. One of three Romanians signed by Cercle Bruges in 1993 along with Dorinel Munteanu (now Cologne) and Marius Cheregi, he is a credit to their League.

**BOGDAN STELEA** (Steaua Bucharest)
*Born:* 5.12.67  *Caps:* 33  *Goals:* –
Played in the 1994 World Cup against Colombia and Switzerland, but was dropped after the 1-4 loss to the Swiss – he returned for the European Championship qualifier v Azerbaijan in September 1994. Also moved from Dinamo Bucharest to the Turkish Division 1 club Samsunspor in summer 1994, but returned in summer 1995 to Steaua. Formerly with Dinamo Bucharest, he has also had spells with Mallorca in 1991 (who were relegated despite his fine efforts) and the Belgian club Standard Liege (when first choice Gilbert Bodart was injured). Non-playing member of 1990 World Cup squad, he made his international debut in 1988 and was a member of the Dinamo side that won the double in 1990.

**DANIEL TIMOFTE** (Samsunspor, Turkey)
*Born:* 1.10.67  *Caps:* 22  *Goals:* 2
This was the player who missed the crucial penalty in the 1990 World Cup shoot-out against Ireland. Formerly with the 1990 double winners Dinamo Bucharest, he moved to the Bundesliga with Bayer Uerdingen and thence to Samsunspor in 1994.

**IOAN VLADOIU** (Steaua Bucharest)
*Born:* 5.11.68  *Caps:* 21  *Goals:* 1
Sent home from the 1994 World Cup after being sent off inside four minutes against the Swiss, and then fell out with the coach. At club level he is in his third spell with Steaua, after previous skirmishes with the management. Played in the interim for Arges Pitesti and Rapid Bucharest. Returned to Steaua in summer 1995 for the Champions League – and so far has kept himself under control. He was the Romanian League's leading scorer going into the spring in 1996.

**Coach: ANGHEL IORDANESCU**
*Born:* 4.3.50
Having scored 26 goals in 64 games for the national team, he spent most of his club career with Steaua Bucharest where he won four League titles and the 1986 European Cup when he was both assistant coach and substitute player. After a two-year spell with Cypriot team Anorthosis Famagusta he returned to Steaua in 1992 and was appointed national coach in 1993, succeeding Cornel Dinu. Claims his team were unlucky in USA 94; now he has expressed concerns that many of his squad changed clubs in January 1995 and may not have bedded down yet.

# KEY PLAYER

## GHEORGHE HAGI

*Date of Birth:* 5.2.65
*Current club:* Barcelona
*Position:* Forward
*Height:* 1.74 m
*Weight:* 74 kg

### CAREER RECORD

| Year | Club | League Apps | Goals | Int Apps | Goals |
|---|---|---|---|---|---|
| 1982-83 | Farul Constanta | 18 | 7 | | |
| 1983-84 | Sportul Studentesc | 31 | 2 | 12 | 0 |
| 1984-85 | | 30 | 20 | 8 | 4 |
| 1985-86 | | 31 | 31 | 9 | 2 |
| 1986-87 | | 16 | 5 | | |
| | Steaua Bucharest | 14 | 10 | 8 | 4 |
| 1987-88 | | 31 | 25 | 5 | 0 |
| 1988-89 | | 30 | 31 | 7 | 2 |
| 1989-90 | | 22 | 10 | 13 | 2 |
| 1990-91 | Real Madrid | 29 | 3 | 5 | 1 |
| 1991-92 | | 35 | 12 | 5 | 4 |
| 1992-93 | Brescia | 31 | 5 | 5 | 1 |
| 1993-94 | | 30 | 9 | 10 | 5 |
| 1994-95 | Barcelona | 16 | 4 | 5 | 1 |
| 1995-96 | | | | 3 | 1 |

### HONOURS

Romanian top scorer – 1985, 1986
Romanian champion – 1987, 1988, 1989
Romanian Cup winner – 1987, 1988, 1989

| No | Date | Opponents | Venue | Score | Goals | Competition | Subbed Sub |
|---|---|---|---|---|---|---|---|
| 1 | 10.8.83 | Norway | Oslo | 0-0 | 0 | Friendly | 90 |
| 2 | 24.8.83 | East Germany | Budapest | 1-0 | 0 | Friendly | Subbed 80 |
| 3 | 7.9.83 | Poland | Krakow | 2-2 | 0 | Friendly | Subbed 67 |
| 4 | 8.11.83 | Israel | Tel Aviv | 1-1 | 0 | Friendly | Subbed 46 |
| 5 | 12.11.83 | Cyprus | Limassol | 1-0 | 0 | E Nations, Q | Sub pl 45 |
| 6 | 22.1.84 | Ecuador | Guayaquil | 3-1 | 0 | Friendly | Sub pl 27 |
| 7 | 7.2.84 | Algeria | Algiers | 1-1 | 0 | Friendly | 90 |
| 8 | 7.3.84 | Greece | Criaova | 2-0 | 0 | Friendly | 90 |
| 9 | 11.4.84 | Israel | Oradea | 0-0 | 0 | Friendly | 90 |
| 10 | 14.6.84 | Spain | St Etienne | 1-1 | 0 | EN finals | Sub pl 14 |
| 11 | 17.6.84 | West Germany | Lens | 1-2 | 0 | EN finals | Subbed 46 |
| 12 | 31.7.84 | China | Buziu | 1-0 | 0 | Friendly | Subbed 46 |
| 13 | 29.8.84 | East Germany | Gera | 1-2 | 0 | Friendly | Subbed 78 |
| 14 | 12.9.84 | Northern Ireland | Belfast | 2-3 | 1 | World Cup, Q | 90 |
| 15 | 21.11.84 | Israel | Tel Aviv | 1-1 | 0 | Friendly | 90 |
| 16 | 30.1.85 | Portugal | Lisbon | 3-2 | 1 | Friendly | Sub pl 8 |
| 17 | 27.3.85 | Poland | Sibiu | 0-0 | 0 | Friendly | 90 |

| No | Date | Opponents | Venue | Score | Goals | Competition | Subbed Sub |
|---|---|---|---|---|---|---|---|
| 18 | 3.4.85 | Turkey | Craiova | 3-0 | 1 | World Cup, Q | 90 |
| 19 | 1.5.85 | England | Bucharest | 0-0 | 0 | World Cup, Q | 90 |
| 20 | 6.6.85 | Finland | Helsinki | 1-1 | 1 | World Cup, Q | 90 |
| 21 | 7.8.85 | USSR | Moscow | 0-2 | 0 | Friendly | 90 |
| 22 | 28.8.85 | Finland | Timisoara | 2-0 | 1 | World Cup, Q | 90 |
| 23 | 11.9.85 | England | Wembley | 1-1 | 0 | World Cup, Q | 90 |
| 24 | 16.10.85 | Northern Ireland | Bucharest | 0-1 | 0 | World Cup, Q | 90 |
| 25 | 13.11.85 | Turkey | Izmir | 3-1 | 0 | World Cup, Q | 90 |
| 26 | 28.2.86 | Egypt | Alexandria | 2-2 | 0 | Friendly | 90 |
| 27 | 2.3.86 | Egypt | Alexandria | 1-0 | 0 | Friendly | 90 |
| 28 | 26.3.86 | Scotland | Glasgow | 0-3 | 0 | Friendly | 90 |
| 29 | 23.4.86 | USSR | Timisoara | 2-1 | 1 | Friendly | 90 |
| 30 | 20.8.86 | Norway | Oslo | 2-2 | 1 | Friendly | 90 |
| 31 | 10.9.86 | Austria | Bucharest | 3-0 | 1 | E Nations, Q | 90 |
| 32 | 8.10.86 | Israel | Tel Aviv | 4-2 | 0 | Friendly | Subbed 80 |
| 33 | 12.11.86 | Spain | Seville | 0-1 | 0 | E Nations, Q | 90 |
| 34 | 4.3.87 | Turkey | Ankara | 3-1 | 0 | Friendly | Subbed 61 |
| 35 | 11.3.87 | Greece | Athens | 1-1 | 1 | Friendly | 90 |
| 36 | 25.3.87 | Albania | Bucharest | 5-1 | 1 | E Nations, Q | Subbed 67 |
| 37 | 29.4.87 | Spain | Bucharest | 3-1 | 0 | E Nations, Q | 90 |
| 38 | 2.9.87 | Poland | Bydgoszcz | 1-3 | 0 | Friendly | Subbed 46 |
| 39 | 7.10.87 | Greece | Bucharest | 2-2 | 0 | Friendly | 90 |
| 40 | 28.10.87 | Albania | Vlore | 1-0 | 0 | E Nations, Q | Subbed 84 |
| 41 | 18.11.87 | Austria | Vienna | 0-0 | 0 | E Nations, Q | 90 |
| 42 | 1.6.88 | Holland | Amsterdam | 0-2 | 0 | Friendly | Subbed 76 |
| 43 | 21.9.88 | Albania | Constanta | 3-0 | 1 | Friendly | 90 |
| 44 | 19.10.88 | Bulgaria | Sofia | 3-1 | 0 | World Cup, Q | 90 |
| 45 | 2.11.88 | Greece | Bucharest | 3-0 | 1 | World Cup, Q | 90 |
| 46 | 29.3.89 | Italy | Sibiu | 1-0 | 0 | Friendly | Subbed 86 |
| 47 | 12.4.89 | Poland | Warsaw | 1-2 | 0 | Friendly | 90 |
| 48 | 26.4.89 | Greece | Athens | 0-0 | 0 | World Cup, Q | 90 |
| 49 | 17.5.89 | Bulgaria | Bucharest | 1-0 | 0 | World Cup, Q | 90 |
| 50 | 31.8.89 | Portugal | Setubal | 0-0 | 0 | Friendly | Subbed 76 |
| 51 | 5.9.89 | Czechoslovakia | Nitra | 0-2 | 0 | Friendly | 90 |
| 52 | 11.10.89 | Denmark | Copenhagen | 0-3 | 0 | World Cup, Q | 90 |
| 53 | 15.11.89 | Denmark | Bucharest | 3-1 | 0 | World Cup, Q | 90 |
| 54 | 4.2.90 | Algeria | Algiers | 0-0 | 0 | Friendly | 90 |
| 55 | 28.3.90 | Egypt | Cairo | 3-1 | 0 | Friendly | Subbed 71 |
| 56 | 3.4.90 | Switzerland | Lucerne | 1-2 | 1 | Friendly | 90 |
| 57 | 25.4.90 | Israel | Haifa | 4-1 | 1 | Friendly | Subbed 46 |
| 58 | 21.5.90 | Egypt | Bucharest | 1-0 | 0 | Friendly | Subbed 46 |
| 59 | 26.5.90 | Belgium | Brussels | 2-2 | 0 | Friendly | Subbed 46 |
| 60 | 14.6.90 | Cameroon | Bari | 1-2 | 0 | WC finals | Subbed 55 |
| 61 | 18.6.90 | Argentina | Naples | 1-1 | 0 | WC finals | 90 |
| 62 | 25.6.90 | Rep of Ireland | Genoa | 0-0 | 0 | WC finals | 90 |
| 63 | 12.9.90 | Scotland | Glasgow | 1-2 | 0 | E Nations, Q | 90 |
| 64 | 17.10.90 | Bulgaria | Bucharest | 0-3 | 0 | E Nations, Q | 90 |
| 65 | 27.3.91 | San Marino | Serraville | 3-1 | 1 | E Nations, Q | 90 |
| 66 | 3.4.91 | Switzerland | Neuchatel | 0-0 | 0 | E Nations, Q | Subbed 85 |
| 67 | 17.4.91 | Spain | Caceres | 2-0 | 0 | Friendly | Subbed 61 |
| 68 | 16.10.91 | Scotland | Bucharest | 1-0 | 1 | E Nations, Q | 90 |
| 69 | 13.11.91 | Switzerland | Bucharest | 1-0 | 0 | E Nations, Q | 90 |
| 70 | 20.11.91 | Bulgaria | Sofia | 1-1 | 0 | E Nations, Q | 90 |
| 71 | 6.5.92 | Faroe Isles | Bucharest | 7-0 | 1 | World Cup, Q | 90 |
| 72 | 20.5.92 | Wales | Bucharest | 5-1 | 2 | World Cup, Q | Subbed 70 |

| No | Date | Opponents | Venue | Score | Goals | Competition | Subbed Sub |
|----|------|-----------|-------|-------|-------|-------------|-----|
| 73 | 14.10.92 | Belgium | Brussels | 0-1 | 0 | World Cup, Q | 90 |
| 74 | 14.11.92 | Czechoslovakia | Bucharest | 1-1 | 0 | World Cup, Q | 90 |
| 75 | 29.11.92 | Cyprus | Larnaca | 4-1 | 1 | World Cup, Q | 90 |
| 76 | 14.4.93 | Cyprus | Bucharest | 2-1 | 0 | World Cup, Q | 90 |
| 77 | 2.6.93 | Czechoslovakia | Kosice | 2-5 | 0 | World Cup, Q | 90 |
| 78 | 8.9.93 | Faroe Isles | Toftir | 4-0 | 0 | World Cup, Q | 90 |
| 79 | 13.10.93 | Belgium | Bucharest | 2-1 | 0 | World Cup, Q | Subbed 87 |
| 80 | 17.11.93 | Wales | Cardiff | 2-1 | 1 | World Cup, Q | 90 |
| 81 | 23.3.94 | Northern Ireland | Belfast | 0-2 | 0 | Friendly | Sent off |
| 82 | 12.6.94 | Sweden | Mission Viejo | 1-1 | 1 | Friendly | Subbed 84 |
| 83 | 18.6.94 | Colombia | Los Angeles | 3-1 | 1 | WC finals | 90 |
| 84 | 22.6.94 | Switzerland | Detroit | 1-4 | 1 | WC finals | 90 |
| 85 | 26.6.94 | USA | Los Angeles | 1-0 | 0 | WC finals | 90 |
| 86 | 3.7.94 | Argentina | Los Angeles | 3-2 | 1 | WC finals | Subbed 86 |
| 87 | 10.7.94 | Sweden | San Francisco | 2-2 | 0 | WC finals | 120 |
| 88 | 8.10.94 | France | St Etienne | 0-0 | 0 | E Nations, Q | 90 |
| 89 | 12.10.94 | England | Wembley | 1-1 | 0 | Friendly | Subbed 46 |
| 90 | 12.11.94 | Slovakia | Bucharest | 3-2 | 1 | E Nations, Q | 90 |
| 91 | 14.12.94 | Israel | Ramat Gan | 1-1 | 0 | E Nations, Q | 90 |
| 92 | 29.3.95 | Poland | Bucharest | 2-1 | 0 | E Nations, Q | Subbed 87 |
| 93 | 11.10.95 | France | Bucharest | 1-3 | 0 | E Nations, Q | Subbed 62 |
| 94 | 15.11.95 | Slovakia | Kosice | 2-0 | 1 | E Nations, Q | Subbed 84 |
| 95 | 27.3.96 | Yugoslavia | Belgrade | 0-1 | 0 | Friendly | Subbed 50 |

# FRANCE

The French have improved of late – and lack only a proven striker, though Yuri Djorkaeff is making a fine job of a Platini-type role. This is more a solid than a typically flamboyant French team, with a useful group of players from Paris St Germain and considerable help from those in Serie A – Angloma, Deschamps, Karembeu and Desailly all play for top clubs.

Bordeaux provide some very promising youngsters despite their alarming League position. Loko has lived up to his name – he was League top scorer with the champions Nantes in 1994-95 but after his first outing for Paris St Germain he had an altercation with a group of policemen and medical staff at a hospital and was only quietly brought back.

The sad thing from a British standpoint was that the French qualified without Ginola and Cantona in their final push towards Euro 96. Ginola would probably return, but what of Eric? Jacquet has left the door ajar for him, but has clashed with the Manchester United man in the past. Euro 96 in England without these two stars of the Premiership seems unthinkable, especially as France will play at Ginola's adopted home of St James' Park.

# FRANCE

*Formation:* 4-4-2
*Coach:* Aime Jacquet

Lama

Angloma        Leboeuf        Desailly        Di Meco

Karembeu        Deschamps        Guerin        Zidane

Djorkaeff        Dugarry

| Player | Position | Club | Date | Caps | Goals |
|--------|----------|------|------|------|-------|
| Bernard Lama | G | Paris SG | 17.4.63 | 26 | – |
| Fabien Barthez | G | Monaco | 28.6.71 | 2 | – |
| Bruno Martini | G | Montpellier | 25.1.62 | 30 | – |
| Jocelyn Angloma | D | Torino (Ita) | 7.8.65 | 32 | 1 |
| Lilian Thuram | D | Monaco | 1.1.72 | 8 | – |
| Frank Leboeuf | D | Strasbourg | 22.1.68 | 7 | 2 |
| Bixente Lizarazu | D | Bordeaux | 9.12.69 | 17 | 1 |
| Marcel Desailly | D | AC Milan (Ita) | 7.9.68 | 20 | 1 |
| Eric Di Meco | D | Monaco | 7.9.63 | 20 | – |
| Laurent Blanc | D | Auxerre | 19.11.65 | 47 | 8 |
| Didier Deschamps | M | Juventus (Ita) | 15.10.68 | 48 | 3 |
| Zinedine Zidane | M | Bordeaux | 23.6.72 | 10 | 5 |
| Vincent Guerin | M | Paris SG | 22.11.65 | 10 | 2 |
| Christian Karembeu | M | Sampdoria (Ita) | 3.12.70 | 14 | 1 |
| Reynald Pedros | M | Nantes | 10.10.71 | 17 | 2 |
| Jean-Michel Ferri | M | Nantes | 7.2.69 | 4 | – |
| Paul Le Guen | M | Paris SG | 1.3.64 | 17 | – |
| Corentin Martins | M | Auxerre | 11.7.69 | 12 | 1 |
| Robert Pires | M | Metz | 29.1.73 | – | – |
| Sabri Lamouchi | M | Auxerre | 9.11.71 | 3 | 1 |
| Christophe Dugarry | F | Bordeaux | 17.3.72 | 9 | 1 |
| David Ginola | F | Newcastle U (Eng) | 25.1.67 | 17 | 3 |
| Yuri Djorkaeff | F | Paris SG | 9.3.68 | 15 | 10 |
| Patrice Loko | F | Paris SG | 6.2.70 | 11 | 4 |
| Eric Cantona | F | Manchester U (Eng) | 24.5.66 | 45 | 20 |
| Christophe Cocard | F | Auxerre | 23.11.67 | 9 | 1 |
| Marc Keller | F | Strasbourg | 14.1.68 | 1 | – |
| Nicolas Ouedec | F | Nantes | 28.10.71 | 5 | – |
| Jean-Pierre Papin | F | Bayern Munich (Ger) | 5.11.63 | 54 | 30 |
| Michael Madar | F | Monaco | 8.5.68 | 2 | – |
| Cyrille Pouget | F | Metz | 6.12.72 | 3 | – |

# FRANCE A-Z

**JOCELYN ANGLOMA** (Torino, Italy)
*Born:* 7.8.65    *Caps:* 32    *Goals:* 1
Another of the former Marseille team – and another from the 1993 European Cup win – he joined Torino in Serie A in summer 1994. He began his career with Division 1 clubs Rennes and Lille before Paris SG took him for the 1990-91 season, and thence to Marseille from 1991-94. The national selectors always had their eyes on him after he was in the national Under-21 team that won the 1988 European Championship. First capped in November 1990 v Czechoslovakia.

**FABIEN BARTHEZ** (Monaco)
*Born:* 28.6.71    *Caps:* 2    *Goals:* –
Like fellow squad member Eric Di Meco, he now plays for Monaco after the disbanding of the Marseille team that won the 1993 European Cup. Barthez was virtually the last of the 1993 European Cup winners to leave, but a further disciplinary sentence to stay in Division 2 meant that he had to leave Marseille to save his career. Joined Monaco in summer 1995, and has made the national squad after breaking a finger early in his Monaco career. Originally with Toulouse (1988-92) and gained first cap v Australia in May 1994. Returned in March 1996 after being banned for two months for drug-taking.

**LAURENT BLANC** (Auxerre)
*Born:* 19.11.65    *Caps:* 47    *Goals:* 8
Sweeper with a fine scoring record, an instinct for goal which was left over from his midfield days, but has scored over 100 career goals. Was with Montpellier from 1983-91 then went to Serie A with Napoli for 1991-92 before returning to Nimes and St Etienne and on to Auxerre as an old head among the younger element in summer 1995. Former Footballer of the Year.

**ERIC CANTONA** (Manchester United, England)
*Born:* 24.5.66    *Caps:* 45    *Goals:* 20
Manchester United's cult hero has not impressed trainer Aime Jacquet enough in spring 1996 to recall him to the squad. Began his career with the fine Auxerre youth system but after leaving Auxerre in 1989, he embarked on a seeming trail of self destruction via Marseille, Bordeaux, Montpellier and Nimes. Rescued by Leeds in 1992 for their Championship win, he moved in November 1992 to Old Trafford for further League and Cup success, including the double in 1994, when he was PFA Player of the Year. In 1996 he was voted FWA Footballer of the Year.

**CHRISTOPHE COCARD** (Auxerre)
*Born:* 23.11.67    *Caps:* 9    *Goals:* 1
A winger who returned to fitness with his club and has been on the fringe of selection through 1995-96; scored the record tenth goal against Azerbaijan. A typical Auxerre product, he has come from their youth team through to full international honours.

**MARCEL DESAILLY** (AC Milan, Italy)
*Born:* 7.9.68   *Caps:* 20   *Goals:* 1
Is one of four players to have won the European Cup with two different clubs – but the
only one to do so in successive seasons (1993 Marseille, 1994 AC Milan). Played in the
last three European Cup finals with Milan's 1995 defeat by Ajax. Born in Ghana, he has
come on into world class while with Milan, and is the most consistent of their foreign
players since the days of the Dutchmen. His French career encompassed Nantes
(1986-92) and Marseille (1992-94). First capped in August 1993 v Sweden and missed
only one game since.

**DIDIER DESCHAMPS** (Juventus, Italy)
*Born:* 15.10.68   *Caps:* 48   *Goals:* 3
Won 1994-95 Championship medal and Cup medal in his first season in Serie A but his
appearances were limited by an early-season knee ligament problem, though he played
the crucial end-of-season games. Fine midfielder who was a star in the Marseille team
that won the 1993 European Cup and the 1990 and 1992 French titles. First club was
Nantes from 1985-90, then Marseille from 1989-94 except for a season at Bordeaux in
1990-91. Former national captain, but the honour affected his play. First capped in
April 1989 v Yugoslavia.

**ERIC DI MECO** (Monaco)
*Born:* 7.9.63   *Caps:* 20   *Goals:* –
Has moved along the coast to captain Monaco since 1994 after being a key member of
the famous Marseille team that won the 1993 European Cup. He won four Championship medals in a career that spanned 1981-94 with Marseille. A temperamental player,
with a below average disciplinary record in club football and has been sent off for
France, but now is reformed and will be captain. First capped in August 1989 v Sweden.

**YURI DJORKAEFF** (Paris St Germain)
*Born:* 9.3.68   *Caps:* 15   *Goals:* 10
Summer 1995 signing after increasingly productive seasons with Monaco from November 1990. He was club top scorer in his last three seasons at Monaco and was French
League top scorer in 1993-94 with 20 goals from an attacking midfield role. Early career
with Grenoble and Strasbourg was unconvincing until 21 goals in Division 2 in 1989-90
made the bigger clubs look at him. Father Jean was capped 48 times by France as a full
back in a rare father-son international double for the French. First capped in October
1993 v Israel, and has developed a good international scoring record.

**CHRISTOPHE DUGARRY** (Bordeaux)
*Born:* 17.3.72   *Caps:* 8   *Goals:* 1
Born in Bordeaux, he has gravitated through the club's junior teams to full national
honours. Has played for France at junior, Under-21 and now full level. Played in the
Bordeaux first team at the age of 17, and has been earmarked for higher honours. First
capped in August 1994 v Czech Republic.

**JEAN-MICHEL FERRI** (Nantes)
*Born:* 7.2.69   *Caps:* 4   *Goals:* –
Joined Nantes at 16, made the first team at 19, and captained the club to 1995
Championship. Plays in central midfield, but has been injured for part of 1995-96.

**DAVID GINOLA** (Newcastle United, England)
*Born:* 25.1.67   *Caps:* 17   *Goals:* 3
Ginola's form on the left wing for Newcastle this season has made him one of the bargain buys of the summer of 1995. However, the former French Footballer of the Year has not been a regular in the national team for the last couple of years.

**VINCENT GUERIN** (Paris St Germain)
*Born:* 22.11.65   *Caps:* 10   *Goals:* 2
Key midfielder in PSG's recent success, he has won a 1994 Championship medal and the 1993 and 1995 FFA Cups in the last three seasons. Paris born but played for Brest (1984-88), Racing Paris (1988-89) and Montpellier (1989-92 – won Cup medal 1990) before joining PSG in 1992. First capped in September 1993 v Finland, and one of four players to captain his country in the 1995-96 season.

**CHRISTIAN KAREMBEU** (Sampdoria, Italy)
*Born:* 3.12.70   *Caps:* 14   *Goals:* 1
Summer 1995 signing by Sampdoria for £3.4 million after being in the Nantes 1995 Championship-winning team. He was spotted by Nantes after his arrival from the Pacific island of New Caledonia, and is now the first from that country to play in Serie A. Played for Nantes from 1990-95 with increasing authority before setting out for Serie A. First capped in November 1992 v Finland.

**MARC KELLER** (Strasbourg)
*Born:* 14.1.68   *Caps:* 1   *Goals:* –
Another who has come through after a fine start to 1995-96, and has earned his ticket from the France A team through to the full national squad. From the Alsace region of France, he played for Mulhouse in Division 2 from 1987-91, before their bigger neighbours Strasbourg spotted his potential in summer 1991. First capped as sub v Israel in the last of the Euro 96 group qualifiers.

**BERNARD LAMA** (Paris St Germain)
*Born:* 17.4.63   *Caps:* 26   *Goals:* –
National keeper who replaced Bruno Martini as France's first choice. Has done the rounds of the French League with Lille, Metz, Brest, Lens and has been at PSG since 1992. Was captain of 1994 Championship team and has captained France.

**SABRI LAMOUCHI** (Auxerre)
*Born:* 9.11.71   *Caps:* 3   *Goals:* 1
Joined the national squad in 1996 after a fine first half of the season with his club, who challenge PSG for the title. Played well against Nottingham Forest in the UEFA Cup. One of the few not from the Auxerre youth set-up, he came from Ales in summer 1994.

**FRANK LEBOEUF** (Strasbourg)
*Born:* 22.1.68   *Caps:* 7   *Goals:* 2
Goalscoring central defender from Strasbourg, who is a recent addition to the national squad after 45 goals for Strasbourg from November 1991 to the start of the 1995-96 season. He played for Laval in their Division 1 days from 1988-91, and has made fine progress at Strasbourg. First capped in August 1995 v Norway, and his first goals came in the 10-0 win v Azerbaijan.

**PAUL LE GUEN** (Paris St Germain)

*Born:* 1.3.64   *Caps:* 17   *Goals:* –

Part of the PSG success story in the 1990s, he arrived in the capital in 1991 after spells with Brest and Nantes and has won a League title in 1994 and French Cup medals in 1993 and 1995. Has played First Division football for 14 seasons now.

**BIXENTE LIZARAZU** (Bordeaux)

*Born:* 9.12.69   *Caps:* 17   *Goals:* 1

A Basque from the rugby stronghold of St Jean de Luz near the Spanish border, he was spotted by the Bordeaux club and made his debut for them in 1988. Club captain at Bordeaux and cover for Di Meco in current national set-up. First capped in November 1992 v Finland.

**PATRICE LOKO** (Paris St Germain)

*Born:* 6.2.70   *Caps:* 11   *Goals:* 4

Was League top scorer in 1994-95 with 22 goals in Nantes' Championship win and then transferred to PSG in summer 1995 only to hit problems off the field. Now restored to the club and country teams. Developed by Nantes in their youth system.

**MICHAEL MADAR** (Monaco)

*Born:* 8.5.68   *Caps:* 2   *Goals:* –

A run of goals in the French League has propelled Madar into the national squad for the first time, after not being a first choice at the start of the 1995-96 season. His first club was Sochaux from 1986-92, then played for Cannes from 1992-94 before leaving one famous seaside resort for another in summer 1994 with Monaco. His squad selection is reward for hard work in the darker days with lesser clubs – and his wife gave birth almost at the same time he won his first cap.

**BRUNO MARTINI** (Montpellier)

*Born:* 25.1.62   *Caps:* 30   *Goals:* –

France's first-choice keeper until 1994 when a serious knee ligament injury for his then club Auxerre forced him out for several months. When he recovered he found that his replacement had played so well that Martini was allowed to go to Montpellier in summer 1995. But his form is good and he is still in national contention. Spent 13 years at Auxerre, though made his Division 1 debut on loan at Nancy-Lorraine. Was in the side that won the European Under-21 Championship and took over from Joel Bats in the national team. Is well past 400 Division 1 games and gained first cap against the old West Germany in August 1987.

**CORENTIN MARTINS** (Auxerre)

*Born:* 11.7.69   *Caps:* 12   *Goals:* 1

Playmaker for Auxerre, where he is club captain. Joined Auxerre in 1991 when Brest, his previous club, went into liquidation. Has been eyed by some of Europe's bigger clubs.

**NICOLAS OUEDEC** (Nantes)

*Born:* 28.10.71   *Caps:* 5   *Goals:* –

Was runner-up in the 1994-95 League scoring charts to former team-mate Patrice Loko in Nantes' Championship win, but has suffered injuries since. Came from Divsion 2 club Lorient but has been at Nantes for 10 years already.

**JEAN-PIERRE PAPIN** (Bayern Munich, Germany)

*Born:* 5.11.63   *Caps:* 54   *Goals:* 30

Now making a tentative recovery from an ankle operation, he had not settled away from France with AC Milan and Bayern, though he was in Milan's team that won the 1993 and 1994 titles. Been at Bayern since 1994. His French form was exemplary with four League titles with Marseille and five consecutive seasons on top of the league scoring charts. Was elected the 1991 European Footballer of the Year.

**REYNALD PEDROS** (Nantes)

*Born:* 10.10.71   *Caps:* 17   *Caps:* 2

Now a consistent member of his club's and the French international eleven's left side of midfield, he is a Nantes youth team product who has gone through from schooldays to full national honours via the Under-21 team. Can be a little undisciplined. Won a 1995 Championship medal.

**ROBERT PIRES** (Metz)

*Born:* 29.1.73   *Caps:* –   *Goals:* –

Was called into the squad for the first time after a fine 1995-96 season so far with Metz. He is from the national Under-21 set-up, and is another player who was developed in the Metz youth team.

**CYRILLE POUGET** (Metz)

*Born:* 6.12.72   *Caps:* 3   *Goals:* –

Brought into the squad for the first time after first choice Reynald Pedros (Nantes) withdrew with bronchitis. Metz-born Pouget played well in Metz's unbeaten run to the top of the French League in 1995-96. Made his first-team debut only in February 1994 and after 11 goals in 1994-95, and a good start to 1995-96, he is in the national squad. First cap v Portugal in January 1996.

**LILIAN THURAM** (Monaco)

*Born:* 1.1.72   *Caps:* 8   *Goals:* –

Young defender who is making progress in the squad, and has played for his only club Monaco since 1991. Born on the French West Indian island of Guadeloupe, he has quietly worked his passage through the Monaco youth set-up. Former Under-21 international captain. First capped in August 1994 v Czech Republic.

**ZINEDINE ZIDANE** (Bordeaux)

*Born:* 23.6.72   *Caps:* 10   *Goals:* 5

Played in the First Division for Cannes at the age of 17, and moved to the bigger Bordeaux club in 1992. He is another junior and Under-21 international, who has gone on to full honours. First capped in August 1994 v Czech Republic, scoring twice on debut after coming on as a substitute.

**Coach: AIME JACQUET**

*Born:* 27.11.41

Capped twice by France, he completed his playing career with St Etienne and Lyon before moving into coaching. Among the clubs he led were Lyon, Bordeaux, Montpellier and Nancy before being appointed assistant to Gerard Houllier, whom he succeeded in December 1993 when France failed to qualify for the World Cup finals in the USA.

# KEY PLAYER

## ERIC CANTONA

*Date of Birth:* 24.5.66
*Current club:* Manchester United
*Position:* Forward
*Height:* 1.80 m
*Weight:* 78 kg

### CAREER RECORD

| Year | Club | League Apps | Goals | Int Apps | Goals |
|------|------|------|-------|------|-------|
| 1983-84 | Auxerre | 2 | | | |
| 1984-85 | | 4 | 2 | | |
| 1985-86 | | 7 | | | |
| | Martigues | 0 | | | |
| 1986-87 | Auxerre | 36 | 13 | | |
| 1987-88 | | 32 | 8 | 5 | 1 |
| 1988-89 | Marseille | 22 | 5 | | |
| | Bordeaux | 11 | 6 | | |
| 1989-90 | Montpellier | 33 | 10 | 8 | 8 |
| 1990-91 | Marseille | 18 | 8 | 5 | 1 |
| 1991-92 | Nimes | 17 | 2 | | |
| | Leeds United | 15 | 3 | 9 | 2 |
| 1992-93 | | 13 | 6 | | |
| | Manchester United | 22 | 9 | 4 | 5 |
| 1993-94 | | 34 | 18 | 8 | 3 |
| 1994-95 | | 21 | 12 | 6 | 0 |
| 1995-96 | | | | | |

### HONOURS

French champion – 1991
French Cup winner – 1992
English League champion – 1992 [Leeds United], 1993, 1994 [Man Utd]
English FA Cup winner – 1994
PFA Player of the Year – 1994
FWA Footballer of the Year – 1996

| No | Date | Opponents | Venue | Score | Goals | Competition | Subbed Sub |
|----|------|-----------|-------|-------|-------|-------------|------------|
| 1 | 12.8.87 | West Germany | Berlin | 1-2 | 1 | Friendly | 90 |
| 2 | 14.10.87 | Norway | Paris | 1-1 | 0 | E Nations, Q | 90 |
| 3 | 18.11.87 | East Germany | Paris | 0-1 | 0 | E Nations, Q | 90 |
| 4 | 21.1.88 | Israel | Tel Aviv | 1-1 | 0 | Friendly | 90 |
| 5 | 23.3.88 | Spain | Bordeaux | 2-1 | 0 | Friendly | 90 |
| 6 | 16.8.89 | Sweden | Malmo | 4-2 | 2 | Friendly | 90 |
| 7 | 5.9.89 | Norway | Oslo | 1-1 | 0 | World Cup, Q | 90 |
| 8 | 11.10.89 | Scotland | Paris | 3-0 | 1 | World Cup, Q | 90 |
| 9 | 18.11.89 | Cyprus | Toulouse | 2-0 | 0 | World Cup, Q | 90 |
| 10 | 21.1.90 | Kuwait | Kuwait City | 1-0 | 0 | Friendly | Subbed 46 |
| 11 | 24.1.90 | East Germany | Kuwait City | 3-0 | 2 | Friendly | 90 |

| No | Date | Opponents | Venue | Score | Goals | Competition | Subbed Sub |
|----|------|-----------|-------|-------|-------|-------------|------------|
| 12 | 28.2.90 | West Germany | Montpellier | 2-1 | 1 | Friendly | 90 |
| 13 | 28.3.90 | Hungary | Budapest | 3-1 | 2 | Friendly | 90 |
| 14 | 15.8.90 | Poland | Paris | 0-0 | 0 | Friendly | 90 |
| 15 | 5.9.90 | Iceland | Reykjavik | 2-1 | 1 | E Nations, Q | Subbed 84 |
| 16 | 13.10.90 | Czechoslovakia | Paris | 2-0 | 0 | E Nations, Q | 90 |
| 17 | 20.2.91 | Spain | Paris | 3-1 | 0 | Friendly | 90 |
| 18 | 30.3.91 | Albania | Paris | 5-0 | 0 | E Nations, Q | 90 |
| 19 | 12.10.91 | Spain | Seville | 2-1 | 0 | E Nations, Q | 90 |
| 20 | 20.11.91 | Iceland | Paris | 3-1 | 2 | E Nations, Q | 90 |
| 21 | 19.2.92 | England | Wembley | 0-2 | 0 | Friendly | 90 |
| 22 | 25.3.92 | Belgium | Paris | 3-3 | 0 | Friendly | 90 |
| 23 | 27.5.92 | Switzerland | Lausanne | 1-2 | 0 | Friendly | Subbed 46 |
| 24 | 5.6.92 | Holland | Lens | 1-1 | 0 | Friendly | 90 |
| 25 | 10.6.92 | Sweden | Stockholm | 1-1 | 0 | EN finals | 90 |
| 26 | 14.6.92 | England | Malmo | 0-0 | 0 | EN finals | 90 |
| 27 | 17.6.92 | Denmark | Malmo | 1-2 | 0 | EN finals | 90 |
| 28 | 14.10.92 | Austria | Paris | 2-0 | 1 | World Cup, Q | 90 |
| 29 | 14.11.92 | Finland | Paris | 2-1 | 1 | World Cup, Q | 90 |
| 30 | 17.2.93 | Israel | Tel Aviv | 4-0 | 1 | World Cup, Q | 90 |
| 31 | 28.4.93 | Sweden | Paris | 2-1 | 2 | World Cup, Q | 90 |
| 32 | 28.7.93 | Russia | Caen | 3-1 | 1 | Friendly | 90 |
| 33 | 22.8.93 | Sweden | Stockholm | 1-1 | 0 | World Cup, Q | 90 |
| 34 | 8.9.93 | Finland | Tampere | 2-0 | 0 | World Cup, Q | 90 |
| 35 | 13.10.93 | Israel | Paris | 2-3 | 0 | World Cup, Q | 90 |
| 36 | 17.11.93 | Bulgaria | Paris | 1-2 | 1 | World Cup, Q | 90 |
| 37 | 16.2.94 | Italy | Naples | 1-0 | 0 | Friendly | 90 |
| 38 | 26.5.94 | Australia | Kobe | 1-0 | 1 | Friendly | 90 |
| 39 | 29.5.94 | Japan | Tokyo | 4-1 | 0 | Friendly | 90 |
| 40 | 17.8.94 | Czech Republic | Bordeaux | 2-2 | 0 | Friendly | 90 |
| 41 | 7.9.94 | Slovakia | Bratislava | 0-0 | 0 | E Nations, Q | 90 |
| 42 | 8.10.94 | Romania | St Etienne | 0-0 | 0 | E Nations, Q | 90 |
| 43 | 16.11.94 | Poland | Zabrze | 0-0 | 0 | E Nations, Q | 90 |
| 44 | 13.12.94 | Azerbaijan | Trabzon | 2-0 | 0 | E Nations, Q | 90 |
| 45 | 18.1.95 | Holland | Utrecht | 1-0 | 0 | Friendly | 90 |

# GROUP C

## FIXTURES

| | | | |
|---|---|---|---|
| 9 June | Germany v Czech Republic | Old Trafford | 17.00 |
| 11 June | Italy v Russia | Anfield | 16.30 |
| 14 June | Czech Republic v Italy | Anfield | 19.30 |
| 16 June | Russia v Germany | Old Trafford | 15.00 |
| 19 June | Russia v Czech Republic | Anfield | 19.30 |
| 19 June | Italy v Germany | Old Trafford | 19.30 |

## CONTENTS

# GERMANY

For once it is the all-powerful Germans who go into a major tournament unsure of themselves and concerned that they might not even qualify for the second phase of Euro 96.

Apart from Italy – whom coach Berti Vogts nominated as one of the favourites – they also face the consistent Russians and the underdogs from the Czech Republic who have nothing to lose.

It seems inconceivable that the Germans, with six World Cup finals and four European Championship finals, might not make the quarter-finals this time. But that is the real fear in Germany as Vogts tries to make his mark as an international coach. A defender with 96 caps and just about every honour, Vogts is desperately trying to find that crucial blend between his youngsters and his veterans, with half the squad aged over 30!

To make matters worse, he must begin the tournament without Jurgen Klinsmann who faces a suspension from the opening game against the Czechs. The former Spurs striker is critical of Vogts' plans, as is 35-year-old sweeper Lothar Matthaus and Stefan Kuntz (33). The athletic former East German international Matthias Sammer of Borussia Dortmund carries a lot of weight on his shoulders. How Vogts must wish the flamboyant Andreas Moller could produce his best as frequently.

Failure – and that means anything short of the last four – will mean the end for Vogts. He is the only German coach never to have won either the European Championship or the World Cup.

The key players include Jurgen Klinsmann (Bayern Munich), who is now back home after his season with Spurs, and is the top striker in the national team with 34 goals in 79 internationals. The German problem is who plays alongside him – the highly promising young Dortmund striker Heiko Herrlich is the most likely candidate. His team-mate Andy Moller is still a bit of an enigma but now has 22 goals in 58 internationals, while the experienced Thomas Hassler (Karlsruhe) is back in form and well respected.

The defence is sound with Jurgen Kohler and Matthias Sammer (both Dortmund) and Thomas Helmer (Bayern) adding experience, with the younger element of Christian Ziege and Markus Babbel (both Bayern) being highly promising.

Lothar Matthaus has regained fitness, but will he be selected? He has been playing at sweeper for Bayern, but Vogts has been playing three central defenders and two wing-backs pushing up, and it is not certain that German's talisman Matthaus still has the pace for central midfield.

# GERMANY

*Formation:* 5-3-2
*Coach:* Berti Vogts

                          Kopke

    Reuter      Babbel       Sammer      Helmer       Ziege

        Moller              Eilts                Hassler

        Klinsmann                    Herrlich


| Player | Position | Club | Date | Caps | Goals |
|---|---|---|---|---|---|
| Andreas Kopke | G | Eintracht | 12.3.62 | 31 | – |
| Olivier Kahn | G | Bayern Munich | 15.6.69 | 3 | – |
| Stefan Klos | G | Borussia Dortmund | 16.8.71 | – | – |
| Thomas Helmer | D | Bayern Munich | 21.4.65 | 44 | 2 |
| Jurgen Kohler | D | Borussia Dortmund | 6.10.65 | 80 | – |
| Markus Babbel | D | Bayern Munich | 8.9.72 | 12 | 1 |
| Matthias Sammer | D | Borussia Dortmund | 5.9.67 | 38 | 5* |
| Stefan Reuter | D | Borussia Dortmund | 16.10.66 | 50 | 2 |
| Thomas Strunz | M | Bayern Munich | 25.4.68 | 25 | 1 |
| Steffan Freund | M | Borussia Dortmund | 19.1.70 | 12 | – |
| Andreas Moller | M | Borussia Dortmund | 2.9.67 | 58 | 22 |
| Mario Basler | M | Werder Bremen | 18.12.68 | 16 | 1 |
| Dieter Eilts | M | Werder Bremen | 13.12.64 | 13 | – |
| Christian Ziege | M | Bayern Munich | 1.2.72 | 15 | 1 |
| Thomas Hassler | M | Karlsruhe | 30.5.66 | 71 | 8 |
| Jorg Heinrich | M | Borussia Dortmund | 6.12.69 | 2 | – |
| Fredi Bobic | F | Stuttgart | 30.10.71 | 6 | 1 |
| Mehmet Scholl | F | Bayern Munich | 16.10.70 | 5 | – |
| Jurgen Klinsmann | F | Bayern Munich | 30.7.64 | 81 | 34 |
| Ulf Kirsten | F | Bayer Leverkusen | 4.12.65 | 17 | 6* |
| Stefan Kuntz | F | Besiktas (Tur) | 30.10.62 | 15 | 2 |
| Karlheinz Riedle | F | Borussia Dortmund | 16.9.65 | 42 | 16 |
| Jorg Albertz | F | SV Hamburg | 29.1.71 | 2 | – |
| Oliver Bierhoff | F | Udinese (Ita) | 1.5.68 | 2 | 2 |

*\* GDR caps – Sammer 23 (6 goals); Kirsten 49 (14 goals)*

# GERMANY A-Z

**JORG ALBERTZ** (SV Hamburg)
*Born:* 29.1.71  *Caps:* 2  *Goals:* –
The brightest of the current crop of developing players from Hamburg, who are coming out of a slump. Formerly with Borussia Monchengladbach and Fortuna Dusseldorf, he has been at Hamburg since summer 1993.

**MARKUS BABBEL** (Bayern Munich)
*Born:* 8.9.72  *Caps:* 12  *Goals:* 1
Almost a fixture in the team since his first cap in the 1994-95 season and a highly promising young defender who plays alongside the experienced Kohler and Helmer at the back. Signed by Bayern from a junior club, he also had a season with SV Hamburg in 1993-94 only to return home.

**MARIO BASLER** (Werder Bremen)
*Born:* 18.12.68  *Caps:* 16  *Goals:* 1
Has a bit of a bad-boy image: he made a Christmas song with a porn star, and fell out with Bremen coach Rehhagel because he thought a move to Juventus was being blocked. When focused he is a fine midfielder who settled well at Bremen initially after spells with Kaiserslautern, Hertha Berlin and Rot Weiss Essen. Went home early from the 1994 World Cup.

**OLIVER BIERHOFF** (Udinese, Italy)
*Born:* 1.5.68  *Caps:* 2  *Goals:* –
Former Uerdingen, SV Hamburg and Borussia Monchengladbach forward, he has been abroad since 1990. He went first to Austria Salzburg where his 23 goals in 1990-91 caught the attention of Serie A club Ascoli. When Ascoli dipped into Serie B he went with them, but Udinese spotted his goals and bought him back to Serie A in 1995. He is scoring regularly in 1995-96 Serie A, and national selection was a natural progression.

**FREDI BOBIC** (Stuttgart)
*Born:* 30.10.71  *Caps:* 6  *Goals:* 1
Of Yugoslav extraction, and already snapped up by the Germans – his parents worked in the Stuttgart car factories (Porsche, Mercedes, etc.) – Bobic followed the same Jurgen Klinsmann career path from Stuttgart Kickers to VfB Stuttgart. He joined Stuttgart in 1994, and was their top scorer in the 1994-95 season with 12 goals. He gained his first cap in the friendly against Hungary in September 1994.

**DIETER EILTS** (Werder Bremen)
*Born:* 13.12.64  *Caps:* 13  *Goals:* –
Late developer in international terms after a slog of some 200 Bundesliga games. He joined Bremen in 1984 and was part of their 1988 and 1993 Bundesliga successes and 1992 European Cup-Winners' Cup win. Steady and reliable midfielder.

**STEFFAN FREUND** (Borussia Dortmund)
*Born:* 19.1.70   *Caps:* 12   *Goals:* –
Another from the 1995 champions Borussia Dortmund, and one who has come through the national Under-21 and Olympic teams. Originally from the old GDR, having played in their Oberliga with Stahl Brandenburg before joining Schalke, then moving to Dortmund in 1993. Consistent member of national team in 1995-96. Will miss the first game through suspension.

**THOMAS HASSLER** (Karlsruhe)
*Born:* 30.5.66   *Caps:* 71   *Goals:* 8
Returned to Germany in summer 1994 for £2.2 million from AS Roma and now plays for Karlsruhe. He was the 1989 Footballer of the Year and played his early football for Cologne before a £5.5 million move to Juventus after his 1990 World Cup final medal. He stayed at Juve for a year and had been at Roma from 1991-94. Only 5ft 5in tall, he played all five games in the 1994 World Cup, and was one of the better players in their disappointing tournament. Has sometimes replaced Jurgen Klinsmann as national captain.

**JORG HEINRICH** (Borussia Dortmund)
*Born:* 6.12.69   *Caps:* 2   *Goals:* –
Midfielder who joined Dortmund in the midwinter break in January 1996 from Freiburg, where he had gained his caps in a remarkable first season with them in which Freiburg finished third in the 1994-95 Bundesliga. He has been cup-tied for the Champions League though. 1994-95 was his first Bundesliga season, having previously played lower league football in the old East Germany.

**THOMAS HELMER** (Bayern Munich)
*Born:* 21.4.65   *Caps:* 44   *Goals:* 2
He joined Bayern for £2.8 million after the 1992 European Championships when his previous club Borussia Dortmund had lost the 1992 title on goal difference – and suffered exactly the same fate with another last-day loss in 1993 with Bayern. So it was third time lucky when Bayern won the 1994 title. First club was Armenia Bielefeld, he moved to Dortmund in 1986 and progressed via the Under-21 side and the club captaincy into the national side. Was one of Berti Vogts' first introductions after the 1990 World Cup win when he made his international debut v Sweden in October. Is useful to Vogts in that he can play either sweeper or stopper.

**OLIVIER KAHN** (Bayern Munich)
*Born:* 15.6.69   *Caps:* 3   *Goals:* –
Was signed by Bayern for £2.2 million around the time of the 1994 World Cup from Karlsruhe, after having an outstanding 1993-94 season. Early 1994-95 injury and loss of confidence at Bayern hindered his progress but he was recalled to the national squad for the Swiss Centenary games in June 1995. Has been given the chance to succeed Kopke but only when he achieves more consistency.

**ULF KIRSTEN** (Bayer Leverkusen)
*Born:* 4.12.65   *Caps:* 17   *Goals:* 6
Played 49 times for the old GDR with 14 goals before coming to Leverkusen in 1990 from Dynamo Dresden, often the GDR champions. Was twice GDR Footballer of the Year. He has suffered the indignity of being sent off for Germany, v Austria in

November 1992. Back in the squad since Leverkusen led the Bundesliga in the 1993 winter break. He was in the squad for the 1994 World Cup but did not play in the finals.

## JURGEN KLINSMANN (Bayern Munich)
*Born:* 30.7.64    *Caps:* 81    *Goals:* 34

National captain; returned to Germany from Tottenham on his 'get-out' clause of £1 million after spending the 1994-95 season at White Hart Lane. Previously played for Stuttgart, Inter Milan and Monaco in a glittering career, and was the 1995 English Footballer of the Year after 29 goals (20 in Premiership) in his spell at Tottenham. Returned to Bayern where he is top scorer in the 1995-96 UEFA Cup. Will miss the first game through suspension.

## STEFAN KLOS (Borussia Dortmund)
*Born:* 16.8.71    *Caps:* –    *Goals:* –

Third-choice keeper in the squad who may gain higher elevation, he is from the 1995 champions and has been with them since joining from a junior side, Eintracht Dortmund in 1990. Has come through the national Under-21 system.

## JURGEN KOHLER (Borussia Dortmund)
*Born:* 6.10.65    *Caps:* 80    *Goals:* –

Key defender in the national side since debut in 1986 against Denmark, immediately after the World Cup final loss. Was Beckenbauer's first choice each time. Moved from Waldhof Mannheim (where he made his first-team debut at 16) to Cologne and on to Bayern in 1989 – both transfers were Bundesliga internal records at £1.2 million (he was the reigning Footballer of the Year). He was in the 1990 World Cup final side. Joined Juventus in 1991 for £4 million – he was in the team that won the 1993 UEFA Cup. Rated by the Italians as the best centre half in the world. Recently returned to play his club football in Germany.

## ANDREAS KOPKE (Eintracht Frankfurt)
*Born:* 12.3.62    *Caps:* 31    *Goals:* –

Took over from Illgner as the number one choice after the 1992 European Championships, but lost his place to Illgner for the 1994 World Cup finals in the USA. He joined Eintracht in 1994 for £1 million from Nurnberg, who were relegated at the end of 1993-94 despite his captaincy and all-round performance. He had joined Nurnberg in 1986 after his former club, Hertha Berlin, were also relegated. He made his way into the national squad via the Olympic team and was Nurnberg's captain for three seasons.

## STEFAN KUNTZ (Besiktas, Turkey)
*Born:* 30.10.62    *Caps:* 15    *Goals:* 2

One of those players who thought their day would never come, he gained his first cap at the age of 31; he was an outstanding Bundesliga player for several seasons, yet the only time he managed to crack the national squad before 1994, he fell off the team bus! He was top scorer in the Bundesliga in 1986 with 22 goals when at unfashionable Bochum, then moved to Bayer Uerdingen and from 1989 he was with Kaiserslautern. He captained the team that won the 1991 Bundesliga and was 1991 Footballer of the Year, the year he made his untimely exit from the German national team bus. Top scorer in the 1994 Bundesliga for the second time along with Tony Yeboah of Eintracht on 18 goals. Joined Besiktas, the then Turkish champions, for £1.5 million in June 1995.

**ANDREAS MOLLER** (Borussia Dortmund)

*Born:* 2.9.67    *Caps:* 58    *Goals:* 22

Began his career with his local team Eintracht Frankfurt in 1985 and moved to Borussia Dortmund (1988-90), before returning to Eintracht (1990-92) and then on to Juventus. He cost the Italians the usual £4 million. Returned to Borussia Dortmund in summer 1994 from Juventus (Italy) for a fee of £5 million which included Julio Cesar, the Brazilian international, as part of the combined package – the move turned out to be an inspired one as Dortmund won the 1995 Championship. Bit of a playboy image, but when motivated and concentrating (not often enough), is a class act. Had two seasons with the 1993 UEFA Cup winners Juventus. Was given a sharp reminder when not picked for 1990 World Cup final. Very quick.

**STEFAN REUTER** (Borussia Dortmund)

*Born:* 16.10.66    *Caps:* 50    *Goals:* 2

Another of the 1990 World Cup winners to return to the fold – he was brought back into the squad in autumn 1994 after not having played since October 1992. Began his career with Nurnberg, where he made the national team, and then earned a transfer to Bayern Munich. He then moved for a season to Juventus in Serie A and has been back with the new 1995 champions Borussia Dortmund since 1992, and playing with increasing authority again.

**KARLHEINZ RIEDLE** (Borussia Dortmund)

*Born:* 16.9.65    *Caps:* 42    *Goals:* 16

Returned to the Dortmund team in late 1995 after being a long-term injury casualty. He joined Dortmund for £5.5 million in 1993 from Lazio – the same fee as Lazio had bought him for three seasons earlier from Werder Bremen. Won Championship medal with Bremen. Fine header of the ball.

**MATTHIAS SAMMER** (Borussia Dortmund)

*Born:* 5.9.67    *Caps:* 38    *Goals:* 5

The 1995 German Footballer of the Year, and is the son of Klaus Sammer, a former GDR international (and later Bundesliga trainer) who played in Peter Shilton's first international in 1970. Matthias is back in Germany now after a spell with Inter of Milan which didn't really work out. He played 23 times for the old GDR, scoring their last two goals in international football (six goals in all GDR games), and was then the first GDR player to be selected for the united Germany in December 1990. He played for Dynamo Dresden and Stuttgart before his move to Italy. Had a quite outstanding season in 1994-95 in a new role of sweeper, winning a Championship medal with Dortmund, and helped marshall their defence in their Champions League campaign.

**MEHMET SCHOLL** (Bayern Munich)

*Born:* 16.10.70    *Caps:* 5    *Goals:* –

Son of a Turkish immigrant worker, he joined Bayern for £2.1 million in 1992 after having been at his previous club Karlsruhe since the age of 13. Was equal top scorer in Bayern's 1994 Bundesliga win with 11 goals. First capped v Wales in April 1995 (sub). Former Under-21 international, and left-sided forward/winger.

151

**THOMAS STRUNZ** (Bayern Munich)
*Born:* 25.4.68    *Caps:* 25    *Goals:* 1
Returned to Bayern in 1995 for a second spell with the club after having been with
Stuttgart between 1992 and 1995. It was with Stuttgart that he made his international
name, and Bayern were keen to make up for having moved him on. Originally with
MSV Duisburg.

**CHRISTIAN ZIEGE** (Bayern Munich)
*Born:* 1.2.72    *Caps:* 15    *Goals:* 1
Welcome return for the young international who was a star of the Bayern win in the
1994 Bundesliga, but who missed the World Cup through injury and is only now
beginning to regain form. He is a left-sided midfielder/defender who has been with
Bayern since the age of 18 in 1990, when he signed from Hertha Zehlendorf of Berlin,
the first club of Pierre Littbarski, the famous former international. Ziege has come
through the junior system at Bayern and will give teams some balance with his
left-footed priority. He is a former Under-21 international and has already logged in
over 100 Bundesliga games. First capped in the 1993 USA Cup.

**Coach: BERTI VOGTS**
*Born:* 30.12.46
A World Cup winner with West Germany in 1974, he won 96 caps at full back for his
country. At club level he spent 14 years at Borussia Monchengladbach, winning five
League titles, one cup and two UEFA Cups. After retiring in 1979 he was appointed
national youth coach and in 1982 he took charge of the Under-16s and Under-21s and
later became assistant to Franz Beckenbauer, whom he succeeded after the 1990 World
Cup. After his 11-year apprenticeship in the top job, expectations were high that he
would be a winner. Yet in the 1992 European Championship final his German side lost
to the unsung Danes, while in the 1994 World Cup Bulgaria proved Germany's
downfall.

# KEY PLAYER

# JURGEN KLINSMANN

*Date of Birth:* 30.7.64
*Current club:* Bayern Munich
*Position:* Forward
*Height:* 1.85 m
*Weight:* 75 kg

**CAREER RECORD**

| | | League | | Int | |
|---|---|---|---|---|---|
| *Year* | *Club* | *Apps* | *Goals* | *Apps* | *Goals* |
| 1981-82 | Stuttgart Kickers | 6 | 1 | | |
| 1982-83 | | 20 | 2 | | |
| 1983-84 | | 35 | 19 | | |
| 1984-85 | VfB Stuttgart | 32 | 15 | | |
| 1985-86 | | 33 | 16 | | |

| Year | Club | League Apps | Goals | Int Apps | Goals |
|------|------|-------------|-------|----------|-------|
| 1986-87 | | 32 | 16 | | |
| 1987-88 | | 34 | 19 | 9 | 2 |
| 1988-89 | | 25 | 13 | 3 | 0 |
| 1989-90 | Inter Milan | 31 | 13 | 13 | 5 |
| 1990-91 | | 33 | 14 | 7 | 2 |
| 1991-92 | | 31 | 7 | 9 | 1 |
| 1992-93 | Monaco | 35 | 19 | 10 | 7 |
| 1993-94 | | 30 | 10 | 14 | 8 |
| 1994-95 | Tottenham H | 41 | 21 | 9 | 6 |
| 1995-96 | Bayern Munich | | | 7 | 3 |

## HONOURS

World Cup winner – 1991
UEFA Cup winner – 1991
FWA Footballer of the Year – 1995

| No | Date | Opponents | Venue | Score | Goals | Competition | Subbed Sub |
|----|------|-----------|-------|-------|-------|-------------|------------|
| 1 | 12.12.87 | Brazil | Brasilia | 1-1 | 0 | Friendly | 90 |
| 2 | 16.12.87 | Argentina | Buenos Aires | 0-1 | 0 | Friendly | 90 |
| 3 | 2.4.88 | Argentina | Berlin | 1-0 | 0 | Friendly | 90 |
| 4 | 27.4.88 | Switzerland | Kaiserslautern | 1-0 | 1 | Friendly | 90 |
| 5 | 4.6.88 | Yugoslavia | Bremen | 1-1 | 0 | Friendly | 90 |
| 6 | 10.6.88 | Italy | Dusseldorf | 1-1 | 0 | EN finals | 90 |
| 7 | 14.6.88 | Denmark | Gelsenkirchen | 2-0 | 1 | EN finals | 90 |
| 8 | 17.6.88 | Spain | Munich | 2-0 | 0 | EN finals | Subbed 85 |
| 9 | 21.6.88 | Holland | Hamburg | 1-2 | 0 | EN finals | 90 |
| 10 | 19.10.88 | Holland | Munich | 0-0 | 0 | World Cup, Q | Subbed 68 |
| 11 | 26.4.89 | Holland | Rotterdam | 1-1 | 0 | World Cup, Q | Sub pl 56 |
| 12 | 31.5.89 | Wales | Cardiff | 0-0 | 0 | World Cup, Q | Sub pl 12 |
| 13 | 4.10.89 | Finland | Dortmund | 6-1 | 1 | World Cup, Q | 90 |
| 14 | 15.11.89 | Wales | Koln | 2-1 | 0 | World Cup, Q | 90 |
| 15 | 28.2.90 | France | Montpellier | 1-2 | 0 | Friendly | 90 |
| 16 | 24.5.90 | Uruguay | Stuttgart | 3-3 | 1 | Friendly | 90 |
| 17 | 26.5.90 | Czechoslovakia | Dusseldorf | 1-0 | 0 | Friendly | Subbed 75 |
| 18 | 30.5.90 | Denmark | Gelsenkirchen | 1-0 | 0 | Friendly | Subbed 67 |
| 19 | 10.6.90 | Yugoslavia | Milan | 4-1 | 1 | WC finals | 90 |
| 20 | 15.6.90 | UAE | Milan | 5-1 | 0 | WC finals | Subbed 72 |
| 21 | 19.6.90 | Colombia | Milan | 1-1 | 0 | WC finals | 90 |
| 22 | 24.6.90 | Holland | Milan | 2-1 | 1 | WC finals | Subbed 79 |
| 23 | 1.7.90 | Czechoslovakia | Milan | 1-0 | 0 | WC finals | 90 |
| 24 | 4.7.90 | England | Turin | 1-1 | 0 | WC finals | 90 |
| 25 | 8.7.90 | Argentina | Rome | 1-0 | 0 | WC finals | 90 |
| 26 | 29.8.90 | Portugal | Lisbon | 1-1 | 0 | Friendly | Sub pl 45 |
| 27 | 10.10.90 | Sweden | Stockholm | 3-1 | 1 | Friendly | 90 |
| 28 | 31.10.90 | Luxembourg | Luxembourg | 3-2 | 1 | E Nations, Q | 90 |
| 29 | 19.12.90 | Switzerland | Stuttgart | 4-0 | 0 | Friendly | 90 |
| 30 | 27.3.91 | USSR | Frankfurt | 2-1 | 0 | Friendly | 90 |
| 31 | 1.5.91 | Belgium | Hannover | 1-0 | 0 | E Nations, Q | 90 |
| 32 | 5.6.91 | Wales | Cardiff | 0-1 | 0 | E Nations, Q | 90 |
| 33 | 11.9.91 | England | Wembley | 1-0 | 0 | Friendly | Sub pl 8 |
| 34 | 25.3.92 | Italy | Turin | 0-1 | 0 | Friendly | Sub pl 45 |
| 35 | 22.4.92 | Czechoslovakia | Prague | 1-1 | 0 | Friendly | 90 |

| No | Date | Opponents | Venue | Score | Goals | Competition | Subbed Sub |
|----|------|-----------|-------|-------|-------|-------------|------------|
| 36 | 30.5.92 | Turkey | Gelsenkirchen | 1-0 | 0 | Friendly | Subbed 55 |
| 37 | 12.6.92 | CIS | Norrkoping | 1-1 | 0 | EN finals | Sub pl 27 |
| 38 | 15.6.92 | Scotland | Norrkoping | 2-0 | 0 | EN finals | 90 |
| 39 | 18.6.92 | Holland | Gothenburg | 1-3 | 1 | EN finals | 90 |
| 40 | 21.6.92 | Sweden | Stockholm | 3-2 | 0 | EN finals | 90 |
| 41 | 26.6.92 | Denmark | Gothenburg | 0-2 | 0 | EN finals | 90 |
| 42 | 9.9.92 | Denmark | Copenhagen | 2-1 | 0 | Friendly | Subbed 87 |
| 43 | 14.10.92 | Mexico | Dresden | 1-1 | 0 | Friendly | Sub pl 45 |
| 44 | 18.11.92 | Austria | Nurnberg | 0-0 | 0 | Friendly | 90 |
| 45 | 16.12.92 | Brazil | Porto Alegre | 1-3 | 0 | Friendly | 90 |
| 46 | 20.12.92 | Uruguay | Montevideo | 4-1 | 1 | Friendly | Subbed 78 |
| 47 | 24.3.93 | Scotland | Glasgow | 1-0 | 0 | Friendly | 90 |
| 48 | 14.4.93 | Ghana | Bochum | 6-1 | 2 | Friendly | 90 |
| 49 | 10.6.93 | Brazil | Washington | 3-3 | 2 | Friendly | 90 |
| 50 | 13.6.93 | USA | Chicago | 4-3 | 1 | Friendly | Subbed 69 |
| 51 | 19.6.93 | England | Detroit | 2-1 | 1 | Friendly | 90 |
| 52 | 13.10.93 | Uruguay | Karlsruhe | 5-0 | 0 | Friendly | 90 |
| 53 | 17.11.93 | Brazil | Koln | 2-1 | 0 | Friendly | Subbed 84 |
| 54 | 15.12.93 | Argentina | Miami | 1-2 | 0 | Friendly | Subbed 68 |
| 55 | 18.12.93 | USA | San Francisco | 3-0 | 0 | Friendly | Subbed 63 |
| 56 | 22.12.93 | Mexico | Mexico City | 0-0 | 0 | Friendly | Subbed 71 |
| 57 | 23.3.94 | Italy | Stuttgart | 2-1 | 2 | Friendly | 90 |
| 58 | 29.5.94 | Rep of Ireland | Dublin | 0-2 | 0 | Friendly | 90 |
| 59 | 2.6.94 | Austria | Vienna | 5-1 | 1 | Friendly | Subbed 62 |
| 60 | 8.6.94 | Canada | Toronto | 2-0 | 0 | Friendly | Subbed 46 |
| 61 | 17.6.94 | Bolivia | Chicago | 1-0 | 1 | WC finals | 90 |
| 62 | 21.6.94 | Spain | Chicago | 1-1 | 1 | WC finals | 90 |
| 63 | 27.6.94 | South Korea | Dallas | 3-2 | 2 | WC finals | 90 |
| 64 | 2.7.94 | Belgium | Chicago | 3-2 | 1 | WC finals | Subbed 86 |
| 65 | 10.7.94 | Bulgaria | New York | 1-2 | 0 | WC finals | 90 |
| 66 | 7.9.94 | Russia | Moscow | 1-0 | 0 | Friendly | 90 |
| 67 | 12.10.94 | Hungary | Budapest | 0-0 | 0 | Friendly | 90 |
| 68 | 16.11.94 | Albania | Tirana | 2-1 | 1 | E Nations, Q | 90 |
| 69 | 14.12.94 | Moldova | Chisinau | 3-0 | 1 | E Nations, Q | 90 |
| 70 | 18.12.94 | Albania | Kaiserslautern | 2-1 | 1 | E Nations, Q | 90 |
| 71 | 22.2.95 | Spain | Jerez | 0-0 | 0 | Friendly | 90 |
| 72 | 29.3.95 | Georgia | Tbilisi | 2-0 | 2 | E Nations, Q | 90 |
| 73 | 26.4.95 | Wales | Dusseldorf | 1-1 | 0 | E Nations, Q | 90 |
| 74 | 7.6.95 | Bulgaria | Sofia | 2-3 | 1 | E Nations, Q | 90 |
| 75 | 6.9.95 | Georgia | Nurnberg | 4-1 | 0 | E Nations, Q | 90 |
| 76 | 8.10.95 | Moldova | Leverkusen | 6-1 | 0 | E Nations, Q | 90 |
| 77 | 11.10.95 | Wales | Cardiff | 2-1 | 1 | E Nations, Q | 90 |
| 78 | 15.11.95 | Bulgaria | Berlin | 3-1 | 2 | E Nations, Q | 90 |
| 79 | 15.12.95 | South Africa | Johannesburg | 0-0 | 0 | Friendly | 90 |
| 80 | 21.2.96 | Portugal | Porto | 2-1 | 0 | Friendly | 90 |
| 81 | 27.3.96 | Denmark | Munich | 2-0 | 0 | Friendly | 90 |

# CZECH REPUBLIC

The Czech Republic are Euro 96's biggest outsiders – and they don't give a damn! They weren't given much of a chance before the draw, but when they came out of the hat in Birmingham with Germany, Russia and Italy they were promptly pushed out to 50–1 and written off. But they, and their Eastern European neighbours, Russia, fancy their chances of causing one of the biggest upsets for years in ousting the two joint-second favourites to win the trophy.

No one needs to tell the Germans and Italians of the dangers of the Russians, four times Championship finalists and the most comfortable of all the 16 qualifiers. But no one fancies the Czechs.

'That suits us,' says coach Dusan Uhrin. 'They didn't fancy us in our qualifying group, either.'

Yet the newly formed team, playing in their first tournament, finished above favourites Holland and knocked World Cup finalists Norway out of the competition.

Playing the best won't frighten them either, for their worst results were against the minnows, losing to Luxembourg and drawing with Malta, but taking four points off Holland and the same from Norway.

Like most of the eastern bloc teams, their top players are scattered far and wide, with more than half the squad expected to come from their foreign legions. Most important of the lot is the Genoa striker Thomas Skuhravy, currently on loan to Sporting Lisbon. When he plays, the Czechs play.

It is a solid mix of the old Czechoslovakian national team, who were developing nicely when the country was divided, and some talented youngsters.

The side is based around a contingent of top-flight Bundesliga players – Latal, Nemec, Kuka, Kadlec, Berger – while others play in Spain and Italy. The experienced group from the 1990 Czech World Cup team are available – Skuhravy, Kadlec, Nemecek, Hapal, Kuka – while there are some very promising youngsters, especially Berger.

The two Prague clubs, Slavia and Sparta, are having good seasons; Slavia reached the semi-finals of the UEFA Cup, losing to Bordeaux, while Milan put out Sparta only after a close tie.

# CZECH REPUBLIC

*Formation:* 5-3-2
*Coach:* Dusan Uhrin

|   |   | Kouba |   |   |
|---|---|---|---|---|
| Hapal | Repka | Kadlec | Suchoparek | Nedved |
|   | Fydek |   | Nemecek | Berger |
|   | Kuka |   |   | Skuhravy |

| Player | Position | Club | Date | Caps | Goals |
|---|---|---|---|---|---|
| Peter Kouba | G | Sparta Prague | 28.1.69 | 28 | – |
| Pavel Srnicek | G | Newcastle U (Eng) | 10.3.68 | 3 | – |
| Ludek Miklosko | G | West Ham U (Eng) | 9.12.61 | 40 | – |
| Radoslav Latal | D | Schalke (Ger) | 6.1.70 | 25 | 3 |
| Jan Suchoparek | D | Slavia Prague | 25.9.69 | 29 | 3 |
| Miroslav Kadlec | D | Kaiserslautern (Ger) | 22.6.64 | 50 | 2 |
| Tomas Repka | D | Sparta Prague | 2.1.74 | 13 | – |
| Vaclav Nemecek | D | Servette (Swi) | 25.1.67 | 54 | 6 |
| Michal Hornak | D | Sparta Prague | 28.4.70 | 3 | – |
| Jiri Lerch | D | Slavia Prague | 17.10.71 | 1 | – |
| Pavel Hapal | M | Tenerife (Spa) | 27.7.69 | 30 | 1 |
| Jiri Nemec | M | Schalke (Ger) | 16.5.66 | 33 | – |
| Patrick Berger | M | Bor. Dortmund (Ger) | 10.11.73 | 12 | 8 |
| Martin Frydek | M | Sparta Prague | 9.3.69 | 21 | 2 |
| Pavel Nedved | M | Sparta Prague | 30.8.72 | 6 | – |
| Karel Poborsky | M | Slavia Prague | 30.3.72 | 12 | – |
| Pavel Kuka | F | Kaiserslautern (Ger) | 19.7.68 | 40 | 14 |
| Radek Drulak | F | Drnovice | 12.1.62 | 11 | 4 |
| Thomas Skuhravy | F | Sporting Lisbon (loan) | 7.9.65 | 49 | 17 |
| Vratislav Lokvenc | F | Sparta Prague | 27.9.73 | 2 | – |
| Petr Samec | F | Hradec Kralove | 14.2.64 | 9 | 2 |
| Vladimir Smicer | F | Slavia Prague | 24.5.73 | 2 | – |

*Statistics include caps with the old Czechoslovakia international team.*

# CZECH REPUBLIC A-Z

Please note statistics include appearances for former Czechoslovakia.

**PATRICK BERGER** (Borussia Dortmund, Germany)
*Born:* 10.11.73  *Caps:* 12  *Goals:* 8
Registered by Dortmund as an amateur, he is a very talented midfielder who is making progress with the 1995 champions, and forcing the other overseas players like Ruben Sosa, Julio Cesar, and Stephane Chapuisat not to slacken. He has played for both leading Prague clubs, Sparta and Slavia. Cost Dortmund just £250,000.

**RADEK DRULAK** (Drnovice)
*Born:* 12.1.62  *Caps:* 11  *Goals:* 4
At 34 he is in the form of his life – he is the 1995 Czech Footballer of the Year and top scorer in the 1995-96 Czech League. All this after being released to play for the provincial club Drnovice. First capped back in 1983 when with the army club Union Cheb, recalled in 1995 to national colours.

**MARTIN FRYDEK** (Sparta Prague)
*Born:* 9.3.69  *Caps:* 21  *Goals:* 2
The midfield motor for the champions Sparta Prague, who have won five of the six titles since he arrived in 1990 from a Fourth Division club. Key midfielder for club and country.

**PAVEL HAPAL** (Tenerife, Spain)
*Born:* 27.7.69  *Caps:* 30  *Goals:* 1
Now plays for Tenerife in Spain where he was a summer 1995 signing for Jupp Heynckes' team from Bayer Leverkusen of the Bundesliga. Made his name in 1991 with an outstanding display when Sigma Olomouc, his home town club, knocked Hamburg out of the UEFA Cup thanks to his brilliance. Everyone in Germany rated him.

**MICHAL HORNAK** (Sparta Prague)
*Born:* 28.4.70  *Caps:* 3  *Goals:* –
First played for Sparta in 1988, then went to Union Cheb for his national service and has been back with Sparta since 1990. Has been involved in their five out of six championship wins.

**MIROSLAV KADLEC** (Kauserslautern, Germany)
*Born:* 22.6.64  *Caps:* 50  *Goals:* 2
Outstanding key defender who now plays in the Bundesliga for Kaiserslautern, whom he joined from provincial Czech club Vitkovice after an excellent 1990 World Cup. Was in the Kaiserslautern team that won the 1991 Bundesliga but was injured in the final run-in.

**PETR KOUBA** (Sparta Prague)
*Born:* 28.1.69  *Caps:* 28  *Goals:* –
Goalkeeper who plays for Sparta Prague and has been first choice for four seasons in the national team. Kouba's father played for Czechoslovakia in the 1960s. Moved to Sparta Prague from Bohemians during the 1990-91 season at the midwinter break. Four League title wins with Sparta.

**PAVEL KUKA** (Kaiserslautern, Germany)
*Born:* 19.7.68   *Caps:* 40   *Goals:* 14
Former Slavia Prague striker and top scorer in the old Czech League, he moved to Kaiserslautern in the Bundesliga in 1993 after four seasons with Slavia. Plays club football alongside Kadlec. Good scoring record with clubs and country.

**RADOSLAV LATAL** (Schalke, Germany)
*Born:* 6.1.70   *Caps:* 25   *Goals:* 3
Former Under-21 international who played for the provincial club Sigma Olomouc in the UEFA Cup before Schalke came in for him in 1994. First club was Dukla Prague, now faded from sight.

**JIRI LERCH** (Slavia Prague)
*Born:* 17.10.71   *Caps:* 1   *Goals:* –
New to the squad in 1995. His club, Slavia Prague, are currently league leaders and reached the semi-finals of the UEFA Cup.

**VRATISLAV LOKVENC** (Sparta Prague)
*Born:* 27.9.73   *Caps:* 2   *Goals:* –
New to the squad for 1995-96. From the national Under-21 team. Came on as a late substitute in the Czechs' last game in the qualifiers against Luxembourg, having made his debut against Norway in Prague.

**LUDEK MIKLOSKO** (West Ham United, England)
*Born:* 9.12.61   *Caps:* 40   *Goals:* –
Oldest and longest-serving of West Ham's League of Nations team. He arrived at Upton Park in 1990, from Banik Ostrava (who also provided Pavel Srnicek) and for a fee of £300,000. Has played 250 League games for West Ham, and is back in the squad after fine Premiership performances. Before 1996, he had not played for his country since the England game in 1992.

**PAVEL NEDVED** (Sparta Prague)
*Born:* 30.8.72   *Caps:* 6   *Goals:* –
Recent addition to the Sparta ranks and has come through to the national team from the 1995 Championship win.

**JIRI NEMEC** (Schalke, Germany)
*Born:* 16.5.66   *Caps:* 33   *Goals:* –
First capped in 1988 and in the 1990 World Cup squad, he began with the famous old Dukla Prague side and then moved to the champions Sparta Prague. Moved to Germany in 1993 after Champions League performances.

**VACLAV NEMECEK** (Servette, Switzerland)
*Born:* 25.1.67   *Caps:* 54   *Goals:* 6
Previous experience in the French First Division for FC Toulouse and was formerly with Sparta Prague until 1992. Experienced international, he was first capped in 1987. Played in 1990 World Cup. Joined Servette in summer 1995.

**KAREL POBORSKY** (Slavia Prague)
*Born:* 30.3.72   *Caps:* 12   *Goals:* –
A summer 1995 signing by Slavia from Viktoria Zizkov, the 1994 European Cup-Winners' Cup representatives who lost to Chelsea in that competition. Former Under-21 star and highly thought of.


**TOMAS REPKA** (Sparta Prague)
*Born:* 2.1.74   *Caps:* 13   *Goals:* –
Left-sided defender who moved from Banik Ostrava to Sparta Prague in 1994. First capped at the age of 19, and very promising.


**PETR SAMEC** (Hradec Kralóve)
*Born:* 14.2.64   *Caps:* 9   *Goals:* 2
Also played for Union Cheb, the army team which, like Dukla Prague, is now defunct. Capped late on in career, a reward for steady plodding in the First Division.


**THOMAS SKUHRAVY** (Sporting Lisbon, Portugal)
*Born:* 7.9.65   *Caps:* 49   *Goals:* 17
In 1996 he moved from Genoa on loan to Sporting Lisbon. Played in Serie A and B for Genoa, where he signed on from Sparta Prague after the 1990 World Cup. Had an impressive Italia 90 which included two goals against the USA and a hat-trick against Costa Rica. Averages 12-15 goals a season in Italy which is better than people thought he would achieve. Old fashioned centre forward and a bit of a rebel – was injured in 1993 over-celebrating a League goal!


**VLADIMIR SMICER** (Slavia Prague)
*Born:* 24.5.73   *Caps:* 2   *Goals:* –
New to the squad in 1995. From the national Under-21 squad, and another late substitute in the game against Luxembourg. He made his debut against Slovakia in May 1995.


**PAVEL SRNICEK** (Newcastle United, England)
*Born:* 10.3.68   *Caps:* 3   *Goals:* –
Newcastle keeper, and is the club's second choice this season, though he got an extended run in the team after injury to Shaka Hislop. The international keeper cost £350,000 from Banik Ostrava back in 1991 and is approaching 150 league games for the Premiership side.


**JAN SUCHOPAREK** (Slavia Prague)
*Born:* 25.9.69   *Caps:* 29   *Goals:* 3
Highly rated defender who began his career with the famous army team Dukla Prague. He hit the skids in 1991 when Iron Curtain countries disbanded after the Cold War. He moved to Slavia Prague in 1992 and has come through the national Under-21 system.

**Trainer: DUSAN UHRIN**

*Born:* 5.2.45

Former Third Division footballer, he coached Red Star Cheb and then took Sparta Prague to two titles. Also looked after the national Under-21 side. The Czechs failed to reach the 1990 World Cup finals and after the split with Slovakia, the Republic coach Vaclav Jezek retired and Uhrin took over.


# KEY PLAYER


## PAVEL KUKA

*Date of Birth:* 19.7.68
*Current club:* Kaiserslautern
*Position:* Forward
*Height:* 1.80 m
*Weight:* 80 kg

### CAREER RECORD

| Year | Club | League Apps | Goals | Int Apps | Goals |
|------|------|------|-------|------|-------|
| 1988-89 | Ruda H. Cheb | 22 | 6 | | |
| 1989-90 | Slavia Prague | 29 | 2 | | |
| 1990-91 | | 27 | 14 | 7 | 3 |
| 1991-92 | | 27 | 19 | 7 | 1 |
| 1992-93 | | 30 | 23 | 7 | 2 |
| 1993-94 | | 12 | 5 | 7 | 5 |
| | Kaiserslautern | 10 | 8 | | |
| 1994-95 | | 34 | 16 | 7 | 1 |
| 1995-96 | | | | 5 | 2 |

| No | Date | Opponents | Venue | Score | Goals | Competition | Subbed Sub |
|----|------|-----------|-------|-------|-------|-------------|-----|
| 1 | 29.8.90 | Finland | Kuusankoski | 1-1 | 1 | Friendly | Sub pl 45 |
| 2 | 14.11.90 | Spain | Prague | 3-2 | 0 | E Nations, Q | Sub pl 2 |
| 3 | 30.1.91 | Australia | Melbourne | 1-0 | 0 | Friendly | Subbed 78 |
| 4 | 6.2.92 | Australia | Sydney | 2-0 | 0 | Friendly | Sub pl 25 |
| 5 | 27.3.91 | Poland | Olomouc | 4-0 | 1 | Friendly | Subbed 73 |
| 6 | 1.5.91 | Albania | Tirana | 2-0 | 1 | E Nations, Q | 90 |
| 7 | 5.6.91 | Iceland | Reykjavik | 1-0 | 0 | E Nations, Q | Sub pl 49 |
| 8 | 21.8.91 | Switzerland | Prague | 1-1 | 0 | Friendly | Sub pl 40 |
| 9 | 4.9.91 | France | Bratislava | 1-2 | 0 | E Nations, Q | 90 |
| 10 | 25.9.91 | Norway | Oslo | 3-2 | 1 | Friendly | Sub pl 45 |
| 11 | 16.10.91 | Albania | Olomouc | 2-1 | 0 | E Nations, Q | 90 |
| 12 | 4.1.92 | Egypt | Cairo | 0-2 | 0 | Friendly | 90 |
| 13 | 22.4.92 | Germany | Prague | 1-1 | 0 | Friendly | 90 |
| 14 | 27.5.92 | Poland | Jastrzebie | 0-1 | 0 | Friendly | Subbed 74 |
| 15 | 19.8.92 | Austria | Bratislava | 2-2 | 0 | Friendly | Sub pl 28 |
| 16 | 23.9.92 | Faroe Isles | Kosice | 4-0 | 2 | World Cup, Q | 90 |
| 17 | 14.11.92 | Romania | Bucharest | 1-1 | 0 | World Cup, Q | Sub pl 53 |
| 18 | 24.3.93 | Cyprus | Limassol | 1-1 | 0 | World Cup, Q | 90 |
| 19 | 28.4.93 | Wales | Ostrava | 1-1 | 0 | World Cup, Q | 90 |
| 20 | 2.6.93 | Romania | Kosice | 5-2 | 0 | World Cup, Q | Subbed 80 |

| No | Date | Opponents | Venue | Score | Goals | Competition | Subbed Sub |
|----|------|-----------|-------|-------|-------|-------------|------------|
| 21 | 16.6.93 | Faroe Isles | Tofir | 3-0 | 0 | World Cup, Q | Subbed 53 |
| 22 | 8.9.93 | Wales | Cardiff | 2-2 | 1 | World Cup, Q | 90 |
| 23 | 27.10.93 | Cyprus | Kosice | 3-0 | 0 | World Cup, Q | Subbed 82 |
| 24 | 17.11.93 | Belgium | Brussels | 0-0 | 0 | World Cup, Q | 90 |
| 25 | 23.2.94 | Turkey | Istanbul | 4-1 | 0 | Friendly | 90 |
| 26 | 20.4.94 | Switzerland | Zurich | 0-3 | 0 | Friendly | Subbed 46 |
| 27 | 25.5.94 | Lithuania | Ostrava | 5-3 | 2 | Friendly | Subbed 66 |
| 28 | 5.6.94 | Rep of Ireland | Dublin | 3-1 | 2 | Friendly | 90 |
| 29 | 17.8.94 | France | Bordeaux | 2-2 | 0 | Friendly | Sub pl 45 |
| 30 | 6.9.94 | Malta | Ostrava | 6-1 | 0 | E Nations, Q | 90 |
| 31 | 12.10.94 | Malta | Valletta | 0-0 | 0 | E Nations, Q | 90 |
| 32 | 16.11.94 | Holland | Rotterdam | 0-0 | 0 | E Nations, Q | Subbed 89 |
| 33 | 29.3.95 | Belarus | Ostrava | 4-2 | 1 | E Nations, Q | 90 |
| 34 | 26.4.95 | Holland | Prague | 3-1 | 0 | E Nations, Q | Subbed 89 |
| 35 | 7.6.95 | Luxembourg | Luxembourg | 0-1 | 0 | E Nations, Q | 90 |
| 36 | 16.8.95 | Norway | Oslo | 1-1 | 0 | E Nations, Q | 90 |
| 37 | 6.9.95 | Norway | Prague | 2-0 | 0 | E Nations, Q | Subbed 17 |
| 38 | 7.10.95 | Belarus | Minsk | 2-0 | 0 | E Nations, Q | 90 |
| 39 | 15.11.95 | Luxembourg | Prague | 3-0 | 0 | E Nations, Q | Subbed 87 |
| 40 | 26.3.96 | Turkey | Ostrava | 3-0 | 2 | Friendly | 90 |

# ITALY

By Jurrian van Wessem

It is 28 long years since the Italian fans have seen the Azzurri triumphant in the European Championships. They have to go back to the summer of 1968 when, two years after being humiliated by North Korea in the World Cup, they took the title on their own turf, beating Russia and Yugoslavia with more luck than class. They could only get past the Russians with the toss of a coin after 120 goalless minutes and then needed two games to beat the talented Yugoslavs. They drew 1-1 after extra time in the first game and then, two days later with a much changed, fresher team, won 2-0 with goals from Riva and Anastasi.

Since then they have hosted the Championships again in 1980 but could only reach the semi-final, a feat they also achieved in 1988. Italy's reputation as big tournament players has really been built up over the World Cup and three finals rather than their exploits in the European Championships which have often left something to be desired.

They come to England on the back of reaching the World Cup final in the USA two years ago but it was not a performance which thrilled the Tifosi because they did so without playing the outstanding football they had hoped for. National coach Arrigo Sacchi had promised a more attractive way of playing football but his players couldn't deliver the goods and they struggled in almost every game. No one in Italy was really surprised when they lost to Brazil on penalties in the final and Sacchi returned home to discover that he was not a popular man.

It became much worse after the European Championship qualifying defeat at home to Croatia and he was almost fired, saved only by the Federation President Antonio Matarrese who kept confidence in him but asked that he should listen a little more to his critics!

There were a lot of questions to be asked, especially as to why he chose to ignore Vialli. After months of negotiations Vialli couldn't be persuaded to come back and Sacchi began to build a new team around league champions Juventus, and Peruzzi, Ferrara, Di Livio, Del Piero and Ravanelli in particular. They were asked to blend in with the Milan players Costacurta, Maldini, Albertini and the other two key players Di Matteo of Lazio and Zola from Parma. Since then the team began to improve steadily and now they seem to be a side with which the fans can identify.

Sacchi admits: 'This team may be less gifted but they have more determination than the World Cup team. I have changed the team and adjusted the tactics and now they are showing confidence in the system we have adopted.

'They now play with a natural instinct and we have every hope that they will be at their best in England, well prepared physically by their clubs.'

Sacchi does not now always favour the 4-3-3 style of the past, changing it to more of a 4-4-2, using Ravanelli and Zola in attack.

His biggest problem would seem to be how to keep all his star players satisfied. There are some stirrings of discontent with whispers that Roberto Baggio and Signori would rather not go to England if it means sitting on the substitutes' bench. It seems likely as Ravenelli, Zola and the talented young Del Piero are all ahead of them while the outstanding Sampdoria forward Chiesa may also be seen as an alternative. Chiesa is a rising star of the Italian game, looking more and more like Paolo Rossi before he exploded on to the world scene in the 1978 World Cup.

The defence and midfield look happy and settled as Sacchi blends together the players from Milan, Parma and Juventus. This could be the moment for captain Paolo Maldini to come good eight years on since his debut. In between he has played in two World Cups and has hung his head in despair at both of them as Italy have been on the wrong end of penalty shoot-outs.

He says: 'This time we want to win the cup. I think that, this time, we deserve a bit more luck.'

The rivals, particularly Germany, can be warned.

The return of Roberto Baggio, injured for some of the early part of 1995-96, hasn't happened after a breakdown between him and Sacchi, who feels that the little Milan maestro is too injury-prone – but the coach may yet relent. If Baggio returns, he would replace Di Livio. Attilio Lombardo (now Juventus) was a regular when injured, breaking a leg pre-season, but is now back in contention.

The Italians are also having to do without the formidable talents of Gianluca Vialli, who has distanced himself from Sacchi and the international set-up. The new strike force which helped the Italians through to the finals comprised Gianfranco Zola (Parma) and Fabrizio Ravanelli, the Juventus striker. Zola scored a hat-trick in the final round against Lithuania. Italy still await some international goals from Guiseppe Signori – who has dried up and been dropped after a frustrating run in Serie A.

The exciting young Alessandro Del Piero from Juventus and Milan's Demetrio Albertini are key midfielders, while Lazio's Roberto Di Matteo is the workhorse.

Defensively Italy are always strong – Milan's Paolo Maldini is the class act with 67 caps already, while Juventus keeper Angelo Peruzzi is currently number one choice. Team-mate Ciro Ferrara is back in defence, alongside Milan's Alessandro Costacurta, but they will have to excel to fill the gap vacated by the great Franco Baresi.

# ITALY

*Formation:* 4-4-2
*Coach:* Arrigo Sacchi

|  | Peruzzi |  |  |
|---|---|---|---|
| Benarrivo | Ferrara | Costacurta | Maldini |
| Di Livio | Di Matteo | Albertini | Del Piero |
| Zola |  | Ravanelli |  |

| Player | Position | Club | Date | Caps | Goals |
|---|---|---|---|---|---|
| Angelo Peruzzi | G | Juventus | 16.2.70 | 6 | – |
| Francesco Toldo | G | Fiorentina | 2.12.71 | 2 | – |
| Ciro Ferrara | D | Juventus | 11.2.67 | 31 | – |
| Alessandro Costacurta | D | AC Milan | 24.4.66 | 35 | 2 |
| Luigi Apolloni | D | Parma | 2.5.67 | 10 | 1 |
| Paolo Maldini | D | AC Milan | 26.6.68 | 67 | 3 |
| Antonio Benarrivo | D | Parma | 21.8.68 | 20 | – |
| Roberto Mussi | D | Parma | 25.8.63 | 8 | – |
| Amedeo Carboni | D | Roma | 6.4.65 | 10 | – |
| Paolo Negro | D | Lazio | 16.4.72 | 3 | – |
| Roberto Di Matteo | M | Lazio | 29.5.70 | 11 | – |
| Demetrio Albertini | M | AC Milan | 23.8.71 | 34 | 2 |
| Angelo Di Livio | M | Juventus | 26.7.66 | 3 | – |
| Alessandro Del Piero | M | Juventus | 9.11.74 | 8 | 2 |
| Massimo Crippa | M | Parma | 17.5.65 | 16 | 1 |
| Dino Baggio | M | Parma | 24.7.71 | 29 | 7 |
| Francesco Statuto | M | Roma | 13.7.71 | 3 | – |
| Gianfranco Zola | F | Parma | 5.7.66 | 19 | 7 |
| Fabrizio Ravanelli | F | Juventus | 11.12.68 | 8 | 5 |
| Marco Simone | F | AC Milan | 7.1.69 | 3 | – |
| Pierluigi Casiraghi | F | Lazio | 4.3.69 | 29 | 7 |
| Attilio Lombardo | F | Juventus | 6.1.66 | 14 | 3 |

# ITALY A-Z

### DEMETRIO ALBERTINI (AC Milan)
*Born:* 23.8.71    *Caps:* 34    *Goals:* 2
One of the few at Milan who have come through the system – he made his debut for them in January 1989 and has been in the first team ever since, winning three Serie A titles and two European Cup medals. He was in trainer Sacchi's Milan team and was then commandeered by the same Sacchi for the national side. Played in every game at the 1994 World Cup.

### LUIGI APOLLONI (Parma)
*Born:* 2.5.67    *Caps:* 10    *Goals:* 1
Parma's central defender who arrived at the club in 1987 from Reggiana. He has been a solid first choice ever since, and has been with the club through Serie B and on to 1992 Italian Cup and 1993 European Super Cup and European Cup-Winners' Cup success and 1995 UEFA Cup win. He came on as a sub in the 1994 World Cup final.

### DINO BAGGIO (Parma)
*Born:* 24.7.71    *Caps:* 29    *Goals:* 7
Has had a few clubs since his Serie A debut in 1990 with Torino – he moved to Inter of Milan in 1991, then to Juventus in 1992, and on to Parma for £4 million after the 1994 World Cup final. International career on hold at the moment. UEFA Cup medals in 1993 and 1995.

### ANTONIO BENARRIVO (Parma)
*Born:* 21.8.68    *Caps:* 20    *Goals:* -
Full back from Parma who has been injured for parts of the 1994-96 seasons and has not played regularly in the national team since a highly impressive 1994 World Cup tournament – where he played all the games after the loss to the Irish. He arrived at Parma in 1991 from Padova, then in Serie B. He was in Parma's 1992 Italian Cup and 1993 European Cup-Winners' Cup and European Super Cup wins and 1995 UEFA Cup success.

### AMEDEO CARBONI (Roma)
*Born:* 6.4.65    *Caps:* 10    *Goals:* -
Is the reserve full-back to Maldini in the national squad but has played internationally in Maldini's absence and when he plays central defence. Carboni has been with Roma since 1990, when he signed from Sampdoria. Earlier in his career he played for Bari and Empoli in Serie A and Parma when they were down in Serie B.

### PIERLUIGI CASIRAGHI (Lazio)
*Born:* 4.3.69    *Caps:* 29    *Goals:* 7
He began his career with Monza, then moved in 1989 to Juventus where he was the junior partner alongside Salvatore Schillaci (remember him), and was signed by Lazio in 1993 where he now plays. Has improved his scoring rate for both Lazio and Italy since 1994, he is now far more worth his place in the squad.

**ALESSANDRO COSTACURTA** (AC Milan)

*Born:* 24.4.66   *Caps:* 35   *Goals:* 2

This central defender managed the double of being suspended for both the 1994 World Cup final and 1994 European Cup final. Few reach those heights, even fewer throw away opportunities like those. Has always been with Milan, joining in 1986 and winning four Serie A titles, two World Club Cups and two European Cups.


**MASSIMO CRIPPA** (Parma)

*Born:* 17.5.65   *Caps:* 16   *Goals:* 1

Vital midfield cog for Torino, then Napoli, and Parma since 1993. Was in the Maradona team in 1990 Serie A success and 1989 UEFA win in a successful five-season stint at that club. UEFA success again in 1995 with Parma, and in his tenth season of Serie A football.


**ALESSANDRO DEL PIERO** (Juventus)

*Born:* 9.11.74   *Caps:* 8   *Goals:* 2

The brightest of all young Italian hopes for their future, he won a Championship medal with Juve in his first full season, having made his debut the previous season. His first club was Padova, then in Serie B from 1991-93. Was second top scorer in the 1995-96 Champions League section behind Litmanen (Ajax). Into national squad after 1994 World Cup. His 1995 emergence allowed Juve to sell Roberto Baggio to Milan.


**ANGELO DI LIVIO** (Juventus)

*Born:* 26.7.66   *Caps:* 3   *Goals:* –

Latish developer who was released by Roma to go into the lower leagues and was rescued by Juventus in 1993 from Padova, who were then in Serie B. He was a key right-sided player in the 1995 championship win for Juve and made it into the national team. He was expected to be replaced by Lombardo in 1995-96, but the newcomer broke his leg.


**ROBERTO DI MATTEO** (Lazio)

*Born:* 29.5.70   *Caps:* 11   *Goals:* –

Midfielder who was a shrewd buy by Lazio in 1993 from the then Swiss champions Aarau. He was born in Switzerland of Italian parentage and came into Italian football from a career in Switzerland with home-town club Schaffhausen (Division 2), FC Zurich and Aarau. He has shown fine progress after coming into the squad after the World Cup.


**CIRO FERRARA** (Juventus)

*Born:* 11.2.67   *Caps:* 31   *Goals:* –

His departure from Napoli in 1994 brought a 1994-95 Serie A medal. He was born in Naples and played for them from 1984; he was an integral part of the two Championship wins in 1987 (including the double) and 1990, and 1989 UEFA Cup success. Internal strife at Napoli post-Maradona left them struggling, and Ferrara came to Juve with immediate success and regained his national place. Full back or central defence.

**ATTILIO LOMBARDO** (Juventus)

*Born:* 6.1.66   *Caps:* 14   *Goals:* 3

Has just come back into contention in spring 1996 after missing the first half of the 1995-96 season with a broken leg – he had been signed by Juventus in summer 1995. He arrived at Samp in 1989 and was in their 1991 Serie A title win and 1990 European Cup-Winners' Cup win, plus 1992 European Cup final. His first major club was Cremonese. Missed out on World Cup selection so will welcome a chance at Euro 96. Moved to Juventus from Sampdoria along with veteran defender Pietro Vierchowod and Vladimir Jugovic.

**PAOLO MALDINI** (AC Milan)

*Born:* 26.6.68   *Caps:* 67   *Goals:* 3

Probably the best player in the world at the moment – winning FIFA and *World Soccer* awards, and increasingly adept at filling in as central defender as well as his own left-back role. He is the son of Cesare Maldini, the current Under-21 coach, who was the captain of Milan when they won the 1963 European Cup and played internationally. Paolo has always played for Milan, and made his first-team debut at the age of 16; was an international at 19 and was the youngest Italian player at both the 1988 European Championships and the 1990 World Cup. Has celebrated 11 full seasons already in the Milan first team. He has won four Serie A titles, three European Cup medals and two World Club Cup medals.

**ROBERTO MUSSI** (Parma)

*Born:* 25.8.63   *Caps:* 8   *Goals:* –

Infrequent appearances in the national team but did play in the 1994 World Cup final. Now in his second spell at Parma, he played for them in 1984-86 when they were in C1! But he missed Parma's climb from the depths as he went on to Milan and Torino. Returned to Parma in 1994-95 and won UEFA Cup medal.

**PAOLO NEGRO** (Lazio)

*Born:* 16.4.72   *Caps:* 3   *Goals:* –

Played for Bologna and Brescia in Serie A before his move to Lazio in 1993 where he has developed rapidly, and joined the national squad after the 1994 World Cup when Italy were looking for the next generation. Squad member rather than first choice.

**ANGELO PERUZZI** (Juventus)

*Born:* 16.2.70   *Caps:* 6   *Goals:* –

Came into the side in 1995 and gained his first cap in the 4-1 win against Estonia. He is the first-choice keeper for the 1995 Serie A champions Juventus, and has been at the club since 1991 when he moved from his first club Roma. He is the former national Under-21 keeper and played in the side that won the 1992 European Under-21 Championship.

**FABRIZIO RAVANELLI** (Juventus)

*Born:* 11.12.68   *Caps:* 8   *Goals:* 5

Prematurely greying forward, who has done well in his international career so far, after only really establishing himself in Juve's first team halfway through their 1995 Championship win. Was very much the super-sub before then. Useful scorer in Serie B and C1 before joining Juve in 1993 from Padova at the same time as Del Piero.

**MARCO SIMONE** (AC Milan)
*Born:* 7.1.69    *Caps:* 3    *Goals:* –
Never certain of his club place over the seasons with the host of foreign stars in his forward positions, and badly hampered by injuries for the last three seasons, he has added 1995-96 caps to a single 1992 international cap. He began in Serie A with Como, then first played in the Milan first team in 1989. His 17 League goals in 1994-95 represented a major breakthrough.

**FRANCESCO STATUTO** (Roma)
*Born:* 13.7.71    *Caps:* 3    *Goals:* –
First joined the national team for the June 1995 matches in the Swiss Centenary tournament and has held his place in the squad. He was born in Rome and played for the home club in 1989. He then went on loan to three clubs, the third of which – Udinese – played him with success in Serie A in 1993-94, so back home he came.

**FRANCESCO TOLDO** (Fiorentina)
*Born:* 2.12.71    *Caps:* 2    *Goals:* –
Has come through to claim the number two keeper's jersey in 1995-96 after Fiorentina's fine early-season form. He made Fiorentina's first team when they were in Serie B in 1993-94, and has developed with the improvement shown in the standards at the club. Toldo's progression at national level has come via the European Under-21 Championship-winning side of 1994.

**GIANFRANCO ZOLA** (Parma)
*Born:* 5.7.66    *Caps:* 19    *Goals:* 7
Remembered as the player who was sent off against Nigeria in the World Cup just after coming on as a sub. Since then he has scored seven goals in 12 internationals and become an integral cog in the team. He is the playmaker and top scorer for Parma, and collected 18 goals in his first season there in 1993-94. He went one better in 1994-95 with 19 goals. Zola made his name with Napoli, where he took over the number 10 shirt from a certain D. Maradona Esq, and became as much a hero at Napoli as the Argentine.

**Coach: ARRIGO SACCHI**
*Born:* 1.4.46
Never a top league player, he began his coaching career with the Cesena youth team in 1977. In 1982 he joined Third Division Rimini as their manager before joining Parma in 1985, bringing them out of Serie C. In 1987 he joined Milan and enjoyed huge success in his five years there, winning two European Cups, two League titles and two World Club Championships. He succeeded Azeglio Vicini as national coach in the autumn of 1991.

# KEY PLAYER

## PAOLO MALDINI

*Date of Birth:* 26.6.68
*Current club:* Milan
*Position:* Defender
*Height:* 1.85 m
*Weight:* 77 kg

### CAREER RECORD

| Year | Club | League Apps | Goals | Int Apps | Goals |
|------|------|------|-------|------|-------|
| 1984-85 | Milan | 1 | 0 | | |
| 1985-86 | | 27 | 0 | | |
| 1986-87 | | 29 | 1 | | |
| 1987-88 | | 26 | 2 | 7 | 0 |
| 1988-89 | | 26 | 0 | 7 | 0 |
| 1989-90 | | 30 | 1 | 12 | 0 |
| 1990-91 | | 26 | 4 | 6 | 0 |
| 1991-92 | | 31 | 3 | 8 | 0 |
| 1992-93 | | 31 | 2 | 7 | 2 |
| 1993-94 | | 30 | 1 | 11 | 0 |
| 1994-95 | | 29 | 2 | 6 | 0 |
| 1995-96 | | | | 3 | 1 |

### HONOURS

Italian champion – 1988, 1992, 1993, 1994
European Cup winner – 1989, 1990, 1994
Intercontinental Cup winner – 1989, 1990
European Super Cup winner – 1989, 1990, 1995
Italian Super Cup winner – 1988, 1992, 1993, 1994
World Footballer of the Year – 1994

| No | Date | Opponents | Venue | Score | Goals | Competition | Subbed Sub |
|----|------|-----------|-------|-------|-------|-------------|------------|
| 1 | 31.3.88 | Yugoslavia | Split | 1-1 | 0 | Friendly | Sub pl 37 |
| 2 | 27.4.88 | Luxembourg | Luxembourg | 3-0 | 0 | Friendly | 90 |
| 3 | 4.6.88 | Wales | Brescia | 0-1 | 0 | Friendly | 90 |
| 4 | 10.6.88 | West Germany | Dusseldorf | 1-1 | 0 | EN finals | 90 |
| 5 | 14.6.88 | Spain | Frankfurt | 1-0 | 0 | EN finals | 90 |
| 6 | 17.6.88 | Denmark | Koln | 2-0 | 0 | EN finals | 90 |
| 7 | 22.6.88 | USSR | Stuttgart | 0-2 | 0 | EN finals | Subbed 64 |
| 8 | 19.10.88 | Norway | Pescara | 2-1 | 0 | Friendly | 90 |
| 9 | 16.11.88 | Holland | Rome | 1-0 | 0 | Friendly | 90 |
| 10 | 22.12.88 | Scotland | Perugia | 2-0 | 0 | Friendly | 90 |
| 11 | 22.2.89 | Denmark | Pisa | 1-0 | 0 | Friendly | 90 |
| 12 | 25.3.89 | Austria | Vienna | 1-0 | 0 | Friendly | Subbed 46 |
| 13 | 29.3.89 | Romania | Sibiu | 0-1 | 0 | Friendly | Sub pl 52 |
| 14 | 26.4.89 | Hungary | Taranto | 4-0 | 0 | Friendly | Subbed 78 |
| 15 | 20.9.89 | Bulgaria | Cesena | 4-0 | 0 | Friendly | Subbed 61 |
| 16 | 15.11.89 | England | Wembley | 0-0 | 0 | Friendly | 90 |

| No | Date | Opponents | Venue | Score | Goals | Competition | Subbed Sub |
|----|------|-----------|-------|-------|-------|-------------|-----|
| 17 | 21.12.89 | Argentina | Cagliari | 0-0 | 0 | Friendly | Subbed 46 |
| 18 | 21.2.90 | Holland | Rotterdam | 0-0 | 0 | Friendly | 90 |
| 19 | 31.3.90 | Switzerland | Basle | 1-0 | 0 | Friendly | Subbed 46 |
| 20 | 9.6.90 | Austria | Rome | 1-0 | 0 | WC finals | 90 |
| 21 | 14.6.90 | USA | Rome | 1-0 | 0 | WC finals | 90 |
| 22 | 19.6.90 | Czechoslovakia | Rome | 2-0 | 0 | WC finals | 90 |
| 23 | 25.6.90 | Uruguay | Rome | 2-0 | 0 | WC finals | 90 |
| 24 | 30.6.90 | Rep of Ireland | Rome | 1-0 | 0 | WC finals | 90 |
| 25 | 3.7.90 | Argentina | Naples | 1-1 | 0 | WC finals | 120 |
| 26 | 7.7.90 | England | Bari | 2-1 | 0 | WC finals | 90 |
| 27 | 26.9.90 | Holland | Palermo | 1-0 | 0 | Friendly | 90 |
| 28 | 3.11.90 | USSR | Rome | 0-0 | 0 | E Nations, Q | 90 |
| 29 | 1.5.91 | Hungary | Salerno | 3-1 | 0 | E Nations, Q | 90 |
| 30 | 5.6.91 | Norway | Oslo | 1-2 | 0 | E Nations, Q | 90 |
| 31 | 12.6.91 | Denmark | Malmo | 2-0 | 0 | Friendly | 90 |
| 32 | 16.6.91 | USSR | Stockholm | 1-1 | 0 | Friendly | 90 |
| 33 | 25.9.91 | Bulgaria | Sofia | 1-2 | 0 | Friendly | Subbed 57 |
| 34 | 12.10.91 | USSR | Moscow | 0-0 | 0 | E Nations, Q | 90 |
| 35 | 13.11.91 | Norway | Genoa | 1-1 | 0 | E Nations, Q | 90 |
| 36 | 21.12.91 | Cyprus | Foggia | 2-0 | 0 | E Nations, Q | 90 |
| 37 | 19.2.92 | San Marino | Cesena | 4-0 | 0 | Friendly | 90 |
| 38 | 31.5.92 | Portugal | New Haven | 0-0 | 0 | Friendly | 90 |
| 39 | 4.6.92 | Rep of Ireland | Boston | 2-0 | 0 | Friendly | 90 |
| 40 | 6.6.92 | USA | Chicago | 1-1 | 0 | Friendly | 90 |
| 41 | 9.9.92 | Holland | Eindhoven | 3-2 | 0 | Friendly | 90 |
| 42 | 18.11.92 | Scotland | Glasgow | 0-0 | 0 | World Cup, Q | 90 |
| 43 | 16.12.92 | Malta | Valletta | 2-1 | 0 | World Cup, Q | 90 |
| 44 | 20.1.93 | Mexico | Florence | 2-0 | 1 | Friendly | 90 |
| 45 | 24.2.93 | Portugal | Oporto | 3-1 | 0 | World Cup, Q | 90 |
| 46 | 24.3.93 | Malta | Palermo | 6-1 | 1 | World Cup, Q | 90 |
| 47 | 1.5.93 | Switzerland | Berne | 0-1 | 0 | World Cup, Q | 90 |
| 48 | 17.11.93 | Portugal | Milan | 1-0 | 0 | World Cup, Q | 90 |
| 49 | 16.2.94 | France | Naples | 0-1 | 0 | Friendly | 90 |
| 50 | 23.3.94 | Germany | Stuttgart | 1-2 | 0 | Friendly | 90 |
| 51 | 3.6.94 | Switzerland | Rome | 1-0 | 0 | Friendly | Subbed 46 |
| 52 | 18.6.94 | Rep of Ireland | New York | 0-1 | 0 | WC finals | 90 |
| 53 | 23.6.94 | Norway | New York | 1-0 | 0 | WC finals | 90 |
| 54 | 28.6.94 | Mexico | Washington | 1-1 | 0 | WC finals | 90 |
| 55 | 5.7.94 | Nigeria | Boston | 2-1 | 0 | WC finals | 120 |
| 56 | 9.7.94 | Spain | Boston | 2-1 | 0 | WC finals | 90 |
| 57 | 13.7.94 | Bulgaria | New York | 2-1 | 0 | WC finals | 90 |
| 58 | 17.7.94 | Brazil | Los Angeles | 0-0 | 0 | WC final | 120 |
| 59 | 8.10.94 | Estonia | Tallinn | 2-0 | 0 | E Nations, Q | 90 |
| 60 | 16.11.94 | Croatia | Palermo | 1-2 | 0 | E Nations, Q | 90 |
| 61 | 25.3.95 | Estonia | Salerno | 4-1 | 0 | E Nations, Q | 90 |
| 62 | 29.3.95 | Ukraine | Kiev | 2-0 | 0 | E Nations, Q | 90 |
| 63 | 26.4.95 | Lithuania | Vilnius | 1-0 | 0 | E Nations, Q | 90 |
| 64 | 21.6.95 | Germany | Zurich | 0-2 | 0 | Friendly | 90 |
| 65 | 8.10.95 | Croatia | Split | 1-1 | 0 | E Nations, Q | 90 |
| 66 | 11.11.95 | Ukraine | Bari | 3-1 | 1 | E Nations, Q | 90 |
| 67 | 15.11.95 | Lithuania | Reggio Emilia | 4-0 | 0 | E Nations, Q | Subbed 72 |

# RUSSIA

The Russians are no one-man band, although they rely heavily for their backbone on European Champions League quarter-finalists Spartak Moscow. Coach Oleg Romantsev was coach to the great Moscow team as well, winning a hat-trick of titles with them before taking over the national team from Pavel Sadyrin. Apart from his home-based players, Romantsev has top players picking up experience in all the major European leagues.

There is nothing he won't know about the Germans from Vladimir Beschastnykh of Werder Bremen and Sergei Kiriakov from Karlsruhe. Nor will he be short of information on the Italians with Igor Shalimov of Udinese and Igor Kolivanov of Foggia. Then there is Dmitri Kharine of Chelsea, Valeri Karpin of Real Sociedad, Andrei Kanchelskis of Everton, Nicolai Pissarev of Merida in Spain, Alexander Mostovoi of Strasbourg and Dmitri Radchenko of Deportivo La Coruna.

Not all the foreign moves work out to Romantsev's benefit, however, and he will be cursing the day that Vassili Kulkov and Sergei Yuran opted out of Spartak Moscow's European Champions League bid to join Millwall in the English First Division. It has been a disastrous move and has put their places in the squad very much at doubt as they have struggled to settle, not even managing to play regularly for the Londoners.

Even without them, though, Russia would have a formidable team, and the Germans and Italians will have sleepless nights before playing them.

Coach Oleg Romantsev, who doubled as trainer of Spartak and the national team for a while, has temporarily given up the club job in order to concentrate on Euro 96. His assistant will look after Spartak -. and few national problems are anticipated because he would know all the players well.

Watch out for the Spartak contingent (especially Nikiforov and Tsymbalar) and the others with teams abroad are well known. Premiership players Kanchelskis (especially) and Kharine should have roles to play.

# RUSSIA

*Formation:* 5-3-2
*Coach:* Oleg Romantsev

Cherchesov

Tetradze     Khlestov     Nikiforov     Kovtun     Tsymbalar

Kanchelskis          Onopko          Shalimov

Kolivanov          Radchenko

| Player | Position | Club | Date | Caps | Goals |
|--------|----------|------|------|------|-------|
| Dmitri Kharine | G | Chelsea (Eng) | 16.8.68 | 32 | – |
| Stanislav Cherchesov | G | Tirol Innsbruck (Aust) | 2.9.63 | 31 | – |
| Sergei Ovchinnikov | G | Lokomotiv Moscow | 11.10.70 | 2 | – |
| Yuri Kovtun | D | Dynamo Moscow | 5.1.70 | 13 | – |
| Yuri Nikiforov | D | Spartak Moscow | 16.9.70 | 28 | 4 |
| Ilia Tsymbalar | D | Spartak Moscow | 17.2.69 | 14 | 3 |
| Dimitri Khlestov | D | Spartak Moscow | 21.1.71 | 22 | – |
| Ramiz Mamedov | D | Spartak Moscow | 21.6.72 | 11 | – |
| Omar Tetradze | D | Alania Vladikavkaz | 13.10.69 | 20 | – |
| Vladislav Radimov | D | CSKA Moscow | 26.11.75 | 6 | – |
| Valeri Karpin | M | Real Sociedad (Spa) | 2.2.69 | 26 | 7 |
| Victor Onopko | M | Oviedo (Spa) | 14.10.69 | 43 | 2 |
| Vassili Kulkov | M | Millwall (Eng) | 11.6.66 | 41 | 5 |
| Andrei Kanchelskis | M | Everton (Eng) | 23.1.69 | 40 | 5 |
| Andrei Piatnitski | M | Spartak Moscow | 27.9.67 | 18 | 4 |
| Igor Shalimov | M | Udinese (Ita) | 2.2.69 | 43 | 5 |
| Valeri Ketchinov | M | Spartak Moscow | 5.8.74 | 3 | 1 |
| Andrei Afanasiev | M | Spartak Moscow | 15.5.64 | 4 | 1 |
| Nicholai Pissarev | M | Merida (Spa) | 23.11.68 | 3 | 1 |
| Alexander Mostovoi | F | Strasbourg (Fra) | 22.8.68 | 30 | 7 |
| Dimitri Radchenko | F | Deportivo (Spa) | 2.12.70 | 31 | 9 |
| Igor Kolivanov | F | Foggia (Ita) | 6.3.68 | 38 | 10 |
| Sergei Kiriakov | F | Karlsruhe (Ger) | 1.1.70 | 31 | 13 |
| Vladimir Beschastnykh | F | Werder Bremen (Ger) | 1.4.74 | 16 | 1 |
| Oleg Veritennikov | F | Rotor Volgograd | 5.1.70 | 1 | – |

*Please note that statistics include matches played for the old USSR and CIS.*

# RUSSIA A-Z

Please note statistics include appearances for USSR and CIS.

## ANDREI AFANASIEV (Spartak Moscow)
*Born:* 15.5.64   *Caps:* 4   *Goals:* 1
Formerly played for two other Moscow clubs Torpedo and CSKA (1991 champions), before moving to Spartak in summer 1995 to boost the Spartak bid for the European Cup (subsequently scuppered by six players leaving before the knockout stage).

## VLADIMIR BESCHASTNYKH (Werder Bremen, Germany)
*Born:* 1.4.74   *Caps:* 16   *Goals:* 1
He is a young winger (no April Fool is this one!) who joined Bremen for £2 million in summer 1994 from Spartak Moscow. He was ill just before the 1994 World Cup, and played only one game as sub; has often been unavailable because of club commitments.

## STANISLAV CHERCHESOV (Tirol Innsbruck, Austria)
*Born:* 2.9.63   *Caps:* 28   *Goals:* –
Had played for both Spartak Moscow (reserve to the great Rinat Dassaev) and for Lokomotiv Moscow before going to the Bundesliga with Dynamo Dresden in 1993. He returned to Spartak Moscow for the 1995-96 Champions League, then amazingly was one of six players to jump ship after the qualifying group success. He now plays in the Austrian First Division, so financial security clearly outweighed medal hopes.

## ANDREI KANCHELSKIS (Everton, England)
*Born:* 23.1.69   *Caps:* 40   *Goals:* 5
Well known enough! Joined Manchester United from Shakhtjor Donetsk in 1991 and has opted to play for Russia rather than Ukraine, though he was among the 1994 World Cup troublemakers and didn't go to the finals. Also played for Dynamo Kiev. Moved to Everton in late summer 1995 for around £5 million in a long drawn-out transfer deal. Won the Premiership with United in 1993 and the double in 1994.

## VALERI KARPIN (Real Sociedad, Spain)
*Born:* 2.2.69   *Caps:* 26   *Goals:* 7
Could have played for his native Estonia but chose better! Scorer of the first ever goal for Russia in August 1992 against Mexico in a 2-0 win after 60 minutes. Part of Spartak's 1992, 1993 and 1994 Championship successes. He was originally with Sport FC of Tallinn in Estonia before coming to Moscow where his first club was CSKA. Joined Spartak in 1990. In June 1994 he signed a three-year contract to play for Real Sociedad for a fee of £350,000. He was one of the first to come back into the fold after the player power revolt and finished up by playing in all three games in the 1994 World Cup. He is in outstanding form for Real Sociedad in 1996, under new trainer Salva Irureta, who has brought the best out of him.

## VALERI KETCHINOV (Spartak Moscow)
*Born:* 5.8.74   *Caps:* 3   *Goals:* 1
One of the dark horses for full selection, he is one of the young group of players from Spartak Moscow who was born in Uzbekistan and came to Spartak from the old USSR Division 1 club Pakhtakor of Tashkent in 1994. Has made his way through the national Under-21 set-up.

**DMITRI KHARINE** (Chelsea, England)
*Born:* 16.8.68   *Caps:* 32   *Goals:* –
Has played for three Moscow clubs – Torpedo (where he made his debut at 17), Dynamo and then CSKA with whom he won the 1992 league title before moving to Chelsea. Is one of that rare breed – an Olympic gold medallist, from the 1988 Games at Seoul. He played under coach Sadyrin at CSKA in their first Championship win for 21 years. Younger brother Mikhail has kept goal against England at Under-21 level. Played in 1994 FA Cup final, but in 1995-96 lost his place in Chelsea's first team.

**DIMITRI KHLESTOV** (Spartak Moscow)
*Born:* 21.1.71   *Caps:* 22   *Goals:* –
Has come through the youth system at Spartak and was a youth international. An integral part of the team that has won the 1992, 1993 and 1994 Russian Championship. Capped for the old CIS on three occasions, he played three games at the World Cup in 1994 and was a solid member of the 1995-96 Champions League success. Broke leg early in 1996 and faces fitness fightback.

**SERGEI KIRIAKOV** (Karlsruhe, Germany)
*Born:* 1.1.70   *Caps:* 31   *Goals:* 13
Fine performances in the Bundesliga for Karlsruhe, whom he joined in 1992 from his Russian club Dynamo Moscow. Highly thought of at international level with an improving record. Didn't go to the World Cup as he was one of the dissidents – he apologised at the last minute, then wasn't taken!

**IGOR KOLIVANOV** (Foggia, Italy)
*Born:* 6.3.68   *Caps:* 38   *Goals:* 7
Forward with Foggia who are now in Serie B, he has been a frequent member of the squad for the 1992 European Championship and 1994 World Cup. He joined Foggia in November 1991 after being Russian league top scorer in 1991 with his home-based club Dynamo Moscow. Member of the team that won the European Under-21 Championship.

**YURI KOVTUN** (Dynamo Moscow)
*Born:* 5.1.70   *Caps:* 13   *Goals:* –
Has done well with Dynamo after leaving his first club Rostel (Division 1) for the capital in 1994. Former youth and Under-21 international and has come through the national system.

**VASSILI KULKOV** (Millwall, England)
*Born:* 11.6.66   *Caps:* 41   *Goals:* 5
Current international who was one of the abstainers from the 1994 World Cup. Joined Benfica from Spartak Moscow in 1992 and was in Benfica's 1994 Championship winning team. He then moved on loan to Porto and played in their 1995 Championship success. After that he went back to Spartak Moscow for the 1995-96 Champions League and thence to Millwall. Returned to the international team after World Cup apology. He has moved everywhere in tandem with Sergei Yuran – Millwall is their fifth move together.

**RAMIZ MAMEDOV** (Spartak Moscow)
*Born:* 21.6.72    *Caps:* 11    *Goals:* –
Came from the Spartak youth team and made it into the first team in time for a 1992 Championship medal, and has subsequently been involved in the 1993 and 1994 Championship wins and 1995-96 Champions League success.

**ALEXANDER MOSTOVOI** (Strasbourg, France)
*Born:* 22.8.68    *Caps:* 30    *Goals:* 7
Moved around Europe at bewildering speed in 1994 – he was at Benfica, then moved on to the French League with Caen, and was then involved in a late-1994 swap deal with Strasbourg, for whom he now plays. Former Under-21 star, and a fine talent who appears now to have settled. His first home club was Spartak Moscow, with whom he won two titles before a 1991 move to Portugal.

**YURI NIKIFOROV** (Spartak Moscow)
*Born:* 16.9.70    *Caps:* 28    *Goals:* 4
Originally thought he would play for the Ukraine, having been brought up in the old USSR Division 1 club Chernomorets Odessa, but has opted to play for Russia. Member of the Spartak side that won the 1993 and 1994 Russian leagues. The interesting point is that he has actually played three times for the new Ukraine, starting in a friendly v Hungary on 26 August 1992; Ukraine were not in FIFA then and awaiting their entry. Current international and first-choice defender who has had a fine 1995-96 Champions League season. Will miss the first game through suspension.

**VICTOR ONOPKO** (Oviedo, Spain)
*Born:* 14.10.69    *Caps:* 43    *Goals:* 2
Former team-mate of Kanchelskis at Shakhtjor Donetsk, he moved to Spartak and opted to play for Russia rather than his native Ukraine after being picked for the Russian 1992 European Championship team. Has made enormous strides and was the key player in Moscow Spartak's 1992, 1993 and 1994 Championship wins. He was club captain in their 1995-96 Champions League success before leaving in January 1996 to join Oviedo. Delayed playing in Spain because his mother-in-law couldn't get a visa! Twice Russian Footballer of the Year.

**SERGEI OVCHINNIKOV** (Lokomotiv Moscow)
*Born:* 11.10.70    *Caps:* 2    *Goals:* –
Goalkeeper with the Lokomotiv Moscow club who is third choice behind Kharine and Cherchasov, and the best home-based keeper of 1994 and 1995. He has been first choice with Lokomotiv since 1991, and his first cap was awarded against El Salvador in a February 1993 friendly on tour in Los Angeles.

**ANDREI PIATNITSKI** (Spartak Moscow)
*Born:* 27.9.67    *Caps:* 18    *Goals:* 4
Midfield motor in the Spartak Moscow side who won the 1993 and 1994 Championship, and one of the workhorses in the national team. He is originally from Uzbekistan and was first capped with the local side Pakhtakor of Tashkent in the old USSR league. He has prefered to go to the capital rather than the West. Was also a star in the USSR European Under-21 Championship-winning team in 1990, and has been in the national selectorial eye ever since.

175

**NICOLAI PISSAREV** (Merida, Spain)
*Born:* 23.11.68   *Caps:* 3   *Goals:* 1
Has come through the old USSR system and was in the team that won the 1990 European Under-21 Championship. He was then at Torpedo Moscow but wandered off to the Swiss Division 2 with Winterthur from 1990-92 and lost impetus. Returned to Russia with Spartak and earned his first cap against Slovakia after fine performances in the 1993 and 1994 Championship wins. Career is now back on hold as he is unable to command a first-team place on a regular basis in a side at the basement of the Spanish League.

**DIMITRI RADCHENKO** (Deportivo La Coruna, Spain)
*Born:* 2.12.70   *Caps:* 31   *Goals:* 9
Left Spartak Moscow during the 1993-94 season to play in the Spanish First Division for Racing Santander. He had been top scorer in the last three seasons for Spartak Moscow, champions in 1992 and 1993. His first club was Zenit Leningrad and he joined Spartak in 1991. Scored the other goal in the 1994 World Cup when Oleg Salenko scored his record five in a match against Cameroon (6-1). Moved from Racing to Deportivo in summer 1995 to play alongside Bebeto, but it has not worked well yet.

**VLADISLAV RADIMOV** (CSKA Moscow)
*Born:* 26.11.75   *Caps:* 6   *Goals:* –
Had his first season in the national squad in 1994-95, this young midfielder/forward from the CSKA club shows immense promise.

**IGOR SHALIMOV** (Udinese, Italy)
*Born:* 2.2.69   *Caps:* 43   *Goals:* 5
Reputed ringleader of the 1994 World Cup dissidents, his club career has also come off the rails a little. He is a fine player who argued with Inter of Milan and went on loan to bottom-of-the-Bundesliga team MSV Duisburg, before rejoining Serie A in 1995 with Udinese. Began with Spartak Moscow then went to Foggia in 1991, and then on to Inter in 1992 for £6.5 million. Came through the national Under-21 side who were European champions at that level and the 1988 Olympic gold medal team and needs to improve his self-discipline.

**OMAR TETRADZE** (Alania Vladikavkaz)
*Born:* 13.10.69   *Caps:* 20   *Goals:* –
Georgian by birth, and originally from the famous Dynamo Tbilisi club, popular European Cup-Winners' Cup winners in 1982, he opted to play for Russia and has come via their Under-21 system into the national side. Gained three caps for the old CIS in early 1992. Played in the 1994 World Cup in the final game against Cameroon (6-1). Moved from Tbilisi to Dynamo Moscow and thence on to Vladikavkaz back near his home, the club that were the surprise winners of the 1995 Russian Championship, in which he was outstanding.

**ILIA TSYMBALAR** (Spartak Moscow)
*Born:* 17.2.69   *Caps:* 14   *Goals:* 3
Joined Spartak at the same time as Nikiforov (also from Chernomorets Odessa) in 1992 and played in the 1993 and 1994 Championship successes. Had a fine 1995-96 Champions League season. Like Nikiforov, he also played for the Ukraine since the break-up of the Soviet Union, but before Ukraine was admitted to FIFA/UEFA.

**OLEG VERETENNIKOV** (Rotor Volgograd)
*Born:* 5.1.70    *Caps:* 1    *Goals:* –
Top scorer from the club which knocked Manchester United out of the 1995-96 UEFA
Cup with a goal at Old Trafford. Top scorer in the 1995 Russian League with 24 goals.

**Coach: OLEG ROMANTSEV**
*Born:* 4.1.54
Capped 10 times for the Soviet Union, he was Spartak Moscow's left-back in the late
1970s and early 1980s and was a member of the Soviet team who finished third at the
1980 Moscow Olympics. After spells coaching Third Division clubs Krasnaya Presniya
and Orzhonkhidze Spartak he was appointed manager of Spartak Moscow in 1989. He
proved a success, leading them to three consecutive League titles in 1992, 1993 and
1994. He was appointed national coach, in conjunction with his Spartak appointment,
in August 1994, succeeding Pavel Sadyrin. He will reassess his position after the end of
Euro 96, deciding whether to return to Spartak or to continue with the national job or
do both.

# KEY PLAYER

## IGOR KOLIVANOV
*Date of Birth:* 6.3.68
*Current club:* Foggia
*Position:* Forward
*Height:* 1.78 m
*Weight:* 70 kg

### CAREER RECORD

| Year | Club | League Apps | Goals | Int Apps | Goals |
|------|------|------|-------|------|-------|
| 1985 | FSM Moscow | 2 | | | |
| 1986 | Dynamo Moscow | 17 | 4 | | |
| 1987 | | 26 | 2 | | |
| 1988 | | 26 | 2 | | |
| 1989 | | 25 | 11 | 1 | 0 |
| 1990 | | 19 | 5 | 8 | 1 |
| 1991 | | 27 | 18 | 9 | 1 |
| 1991-92 | Foggia | 15 | 3 | 6 | 1 |
| 1992-93 | | 26 | 5 | 5 | 1 |
| 1993-94 | | 25 | 6 | 2 | 0 |
| 1994-95 | | 11 | 4 | 3 | 2 |
| 1995-96 | | | | 4 | 4 |

### HONOURS
Russian top scorer – 1991

*For USSR/CIS*

| No | Date | Opponents | Venue | Score | Goals | Competition | Subbed/Sub |
|----|------|-----------|-------|-------|-------|-------------|------------|
| 1 | 23.8.89 | Poland | Lubin | 1-1 | 0 | Friendly | Sub pl 45 |
| 2 | 20.2.90 | Colombia | Los Angeles | 0-0 | 0 | Friendly | Sub pl 46 |
| 3 | 22.2.90 | Costa Rica | Los Angeles | 1-2 | 0 | Friendly | Sub pl 38 |
| 4 | 24.2.90 | USA | Palo Alto | 3-1 | 0 | Friendly | Subbed 46 |
| 5 | 29.8.90 | Romania | Moscow | 1-2 | 0 | Friendly | Sub pl 34 |
| 6 | 12.9.90 | Norway | Moscow | 2-0 | 0 | E Nations, Q | Sub pl 20 |
| 7 | 21.11.90 | USA | Port of Spain | 0-0 | 0 | Friendly | Subbed 46 |
| 8 | 23.11.90 | Trinidad & Tobago | Port of Spain | 2-0 | 0 | Friendly | Subbed 46 |
| 9 | 30.11.90 | Guatemala | Guatemala City | 3-0 | 1 | Friendly | Sub pl 61 |
| 10 | 6.2.91 | Scotland | Glasgow | 1-0 | 0 | Friendly | Sub pl 28 |
| 11 | 27.3.91 | Germany | Frankfurt | 1-2 | 0 | Friendly | Subbed 69 |
| 12 | 17.4.91 | Hungary | Budapest | 1-0 | 0 | E Nations, Q | 90 |
| 13 | 21.5.91 | England | Wembley | 1-3 | 0 | Friendly | 90 |
| 14 | 23.5.91 | Argentina | Manchester | 1-1 | 1 | Friendly | 90 |
| 15 | 30.5.91 | Cyprus | Moscow | 4-0 | 0 | E Nations, Q | 90 |
| 16 | 28.8.91 | Norway | Oslo | 1-0 | 0 | E Nations, Q | 90 |
| 17 | 25.9.91 | Hungary | Moscow | 2-2 | 0 | E Nations, Q | 90 |
| 18 | 12.10.91 | Italy | Moscow | 0-0 | 0 | E Nations, Q | 90 |
| 19 | 13.11.91 | Cyprus | Larnaca | 3-0 | 0 | E Nations, Q | Subbed 46 |
| 20 | 19.2.92 | Spain | Valencia | 1-1 | 0 | Friendly | 90 |
| 21 | 29.4.92 | England | Moscow | 2-2 | 0 | Friendly | Subbed 46 |
| 22 | 3.6.92 | Denmark | Brondby | 1-1 | 1 | Friendly | Subbed 65 |
| 23 | 12.6.92 | Germany | Norrkoping | 1-1 | 0 | EN finals | 90 |
| 24 | 15.6.92 | Holland | Gothenburg | 0-0 | 0 | EN finals | 90 |

*For Russia*

| No | Date | Opponents | Venue | Score | Goals | Competition | Subbed/Sub |
|----|------|-----------|-------|-------|-------|-------------|------------|
| 1 | 14.10.92 | Iceland | Moscow | 1-0 | 0 | World Cup, Q | Sub pl 13 |
| 2 | 14.4.93 | Luxembourg | Luxembourg | 4-0 | 0 | World Cup, Q | 90 |
| 3 | 28.4.93 | Hungary | Moscow | 3-0 | 1 | World Cup, Q | 90 |
| 4 | 23.5.93 | Greece | Moscow | 1-1 | 0 | World Cup, Q | 90 |
| 5 | 2.6.93 | Iceland | Reykjavik | 1-1 | 0 | World Cup, Q | 90 |
| 6 | 8.9.93 | Hungary | Budapest | 3-1 | 0 | World Cup, Q | 90 |
| 7 | 17.11.93 | Greece | Athens | 0-1 | 0 | World Cup, Q | 90 |
| 8 | 7.9.94 | Germany | Moscow | 0-1 | 0 | Friendly | Subbed 46 |
| 9 | 12.10.94 | San Marino | Moscow | 4-0 | 1 | E Nations, Q | Sub pl 34 |
| 10 | 7.6.95 | San Marino | Serraville | 7-0 | 1 | E Nations, Q | 90 |
| 11 | 16.8.95 | Finland | Helsinki | 6-0 | 2 | E Nations, Q | 90 |
| 12 | 6.9.95 | Faroe Isles | Toftir | 5-2 | 1 | E Nations, Q | 90 |
| 13 | 11.10.95 | Greece | Moscow | 2-1 | 0 | E Nations, Q | 90 |
| 14 | 27.3.96 | Rep of Ireland | Dublin | 2-0 | 1 | Friendly | Subbed 70 |

# GROUP D

## FIXTURES

| | | | |
|---|---|---|---|
| 9 June | Denmark v Portugal | Hillsborough | 19.30 |
| 11 June | Turkey v Croatia | City Ground | 19.30 |
| 14 June | Portugal v Turkey | City Ground | 16.30 |
| 16 June | Croatia v Denmark | Hillsborough | 18.00 |
| 19 June | Croatia v Portugal | City Ground | 16.30 |
| 19 June | Turkey v Denmark | Hillsborough | 16.30 |

## CONTENTS

# GROUP D PREVIEW

If you are looking for an outsider to win the tournament, then look no further than Group D – and I am not talking about defending champions Denmark. The Danes, the experts feel, had their day four years ago, when Yugoslavia's sudden exclusion gave Denmark a wild-card entry after they had failed to qualify. They brought the players back from vacations all over the world to upset the odds and beat favourites Germany in the final.

But, despite the presence of the world's best goalkeeper, Peter Schmeichel, and those talented Laudrup brothers, Brian and Michael, they don't look like doing it again – and coach Richard Moller Nielsen has already announced that he is off to try to change the fortunes of Finland after the Championships.

Long before the draw, in fact way before the qualifications had even been completed, England coach Terry Venables nominated Croatia as his dark horses, and nothing that has happened since has changed his mind. But coming up on the rails are Portugal, who have impressed everyone with their slick football, their teamwork and their talent. The meeting between the two at Nottingham's City Ground on 19 June promises to be one of the highlights of the entire competition.

The Portuguese have banked on continuity, with most of their squad having come through Youth, Under-21 and Olympic teams. They lost just one of their qualifying games – away to the Republic of Ireland – and had everyone singing their praises with the way they demolished Jack Charlton's team in the return game.

Coach Antonio Luis Alves Ribeiro de Oliveira has developed a pleasing-to-the-eye passing game with his midfield of Rui Costa, Paulo Sousa and Luis Figo. They are solid in defence, travel better than they have in years and genuinely believe that they can win the title. The one doubt is over their ability to score enough goals, and they will be looking to Paulo Alves and Domingos to provide the cutting edge that has sometimes been lacking.

No such problems with Croatia, who have the lethal Davor Suker, on his way to Real Madrid, who scored in every round of the qualifying tournament, including two in the win against Italy. Coach Miroslav Blazevic has no doubts, saying: 'We have the best players. We will win the Championship.'

There is no doubting the quality of the players at Blazevic's beck and call, but an even stronger card is the awesome team spirit, engendered by the trials and tribulations of the new country as they have fought a bloody war for their independence. The Croatian players may be scattered across the length and breadth of Europe, but every one of them has enormous pride in his country and a desperate urge to write the headlines for something other than a sad civil war.

But don't run away with the idea they do it only for love and pride. They fought their own bitter battle to ensure their bonus payments, and they have learned the value of the pound, lira, franc or peseta in their pocket with their top players earning fortunes abroad. Slaven Bilic (West Ham), Robert Jarni (Betis Seville), Nicola Jurcevic (Freiburg), Nikola Jerkan (Oviedo), Igor Stimac (Derby County), Zvonimir Boban (Milan), Robert Prosinecki (Barcelona), Alen Boksic (Lazio), Robert Spehar (FC Bruges), Goran Vlaovic (Padova) and Suker are the foreign legion who threaten the rest of Europe.

As if all this isn't enough, there is Turkey to add a little eastern promise – Europe's emergent nation followed by the world's most fanatical fans. Turkey may not be ready to take the Championships by storm just yet, but the big Hakan Sukur leads a team from the front, determined to show that the Turks have arrived on the international front.

# DENMARK

The holders will parade many of the team from the 1992 European Championship success – Brian Laudrup, Vilfort, Schmeichel, Piechnik, Jensen and the returning Michael Laudrup, who missed the last Euros after falling out with Moller Nielsen. New faces include Risager, Beck, Rieper, Hogh, Andersson, and Rasmussen from Danish champions Aalborg. There is plenty of British interest here – Brian Laudrup, Schmeichel, Jensen, Andersson, Kjeldbjerg, Thomsen and Rieper are playing or have played in Scotland and England, while others like Wieghorst at Celtic may come into contention. The team is still sound – but may lack goal flair.

*Formation:* 5-4-1
*Coach:* Richard Moller Nielsen

<table>
<tr><td></td><td></td><td>Schmeichel</td><td></td><td></td></tr>
<tr><td>Helveg</td><td>Rieper</td><td>J. Hogh</td><td>Piechnik</td><td>Risager</td></tr>
<tr><td>B. Laudrup</td><td>Vilfort</td><td>Steen-Nielsen</td><td></td><td>M. Laudrup</td></tr>
<tr><td></td><td></td><td>Beck</td><td></td><td></td></tr>
</table>

| Player | Position | Club | Date | Caps | Goals |
|--------|----------|------|------|------|-------|
| Peter Schmeichel | G | Manchester U (Eng) | 18.11.63 | 82 | – |
| Morgens Krogh | G | Brondby | 31.10.63 | 6 | – |
| Lars Hogh | G | Odense | 14.1.59 | 10 | – |
| Jakob Laursen | D | Silkeborg | 6.10.71 | 12 | 1 |
| Marc Rieper | D | West Ham U (Eng) | 5.6.68 | 36 | – |
| Jes Hogh | D | Fenerbahce (Tur) | 7.5.66 | 21 | 1 |
| Jens Risager | D | Brondby | 9.4.71 | 10 | – |
| Torben Piechnik | D | Aarhus | 21.5.63 | 16 | – |
| Thomas Helveg | D | Udinese (Ita) | 24.6.71 | 11 | 1 |
| Jakob Kjeldbjerg | D | Chelsea (Eng) | 21.10.69 | 14 | – |
| Lars Olsen | D | Brondby | 2.2.61 | 87 | 4 |
| Jacob Friis-Hansen | D | Bordeaux (Fra) | 6.3.67 | 15 | – |
| Claus Thomsen | M | Ipswich T (Eng) | 31.5.70 | 4 | – |
| John Jensen | M | Bronby | 3.5.65 | 69 | 4 |
| Brian Steen-Nielsen | M | Odense | 28.12.68 | 37 | – |
| Michael Laudrup | M | Real Madrid (Spa) | 15.6.64 | 86 | 34 |
| Kim Vilfort | M | Brondby | 15.11.62 | 74 | 14 |
| Michael Schjonberg | M | Odense | 19.1.67 | 15 | 2 |
| Allan Nielsen | M | Brondby | 13.3.71 | 5 | 1 |
| Morten Wieghorst | M | Celtic (Sco) | 25.2.71 | 5 | 2 |
| Mikkel Beck | F | Fortuna Cologne (Ger) | 12.5.73 | 7 | 3 |
| Brian Laudrup | F | Rangers (Sco) | 22.2.69 | 61 | 10 |
| Peter Rasmussen | F | Aalborg | 16.5.67 | 16 | 3 |
| Erik Bo Andersson | F | Rangers (Sco) | 14.11.70 | 9 | 2 |
| Bent Christensen | F | Compostela (Spa) | 4.1.67 | 26 | 8 |
| Mark Strudal | F | Naestved | 29.4.68 | 9 | 3 |
| Henrik Larson | F | Lyngby | 17.5.66 | 42 | 6 |

# DENMARK A-Z

**ERIK BO ANDERSSON** (Rangers, Scotland)
*Born:* 14.11.70  *Caps:* 9  *Goals:* 2
The 1994-95 Danish League top scorer with 24 goals for first-time champions Aalborg, he joined Rangers for £1.5 million after four seasons of steady improvement with Aalborg.

**MIKKEL BECK** (Fortuna Cologne)
*Born:* 12.5.73  *Caps:* 7  *Goals:* 3
Lively young forward who played in the later stages of the Euro 96 qualifiers. He plays in the Bundesliga Division 2 and has been with the club since 1993. Previously with Kolding, then Odense.

**BENT CHRISTENSEN** (Compostela, Spain)
*Born:* 4.1.67  *Caps:* 26  *Goals:* 8
Has been recalled to the squad after the enforced retirement of Flemming Povlsen. He is one of the 'abroad' players, who gained experience in the Bundesliga with Schalke and the Swiss Division 1 side Young Boys, before joining the Greek club Olympiakos of Pireus in 1993 and subsequently moving to Spain in 1994. He had a fine track record in Denmark while at Brondby, being Danish League top scorer in 1988, 1989 (shared), 1990 and 1991.

**JACOB FRIIS-HANSEN** (Bordeaux, France)
*Born:* 6.3.67  *Caps:* 15  *Goals:* –
Originally with Fram of Copenhagen, he has been playing in the French League since 1990, first for Lille and, since the start of 1995-96, with Bordeaux. One of the newer elements in the national squad, he has impressed in France.

**THOMAS HELVEG** (Udinese, Italy)
*Born:* 24.6.71  *Caps:* 11  *Goals:* 1
His Serie A experience with Udinese stands him in good stead. He played for Odense, the 1993 Danish Cup winners from 1989 to 1994 and made his way into the full squad via the Under-21 set-up.

**JES HOGH** (Fenerbahce, Turkey)
*Born:* 7.5.66  *Caps:* 21  *Goals:* 1
Formerly playing for Brondby, he has now replaced Steen-Nielsen as the Dane at Fenerbahce. A good utility man who can play in midfield or in defensive situations, he was first capped in 1991.

**LARS HOGH** (Odense)
*Born:* 14.1.59  *Caps:* 10  *Goals:* –
Mr Odense, he has been with the club all his life and is approaching 650 League games in a small league, aiming for the Danish record of 709 games by A.B. Jensen. A long-time squad member, who tends to get caps when Schmeichel is unavailable.

**JOHN JENSEN** (Brondby)

*Born:* 3.5.65    *Caps:* 69    *Goals:* 4

Returned to his former club Brondby on loan from Arsenal for the rest of the season in March 1996, after scoring just one goal for the Gunners since he joined Arsenal in 1992 after the European finals for £1 million from Brondby. It had been his great strike in the 1992 European Championship final in the 2-0 win against Germany that had helped secure the transfer. He is a former Footballer of the Year in Denmark and also had a spell with SV Hamburg from 1988-90.


**JAKOB KJELDBJERG** (Chelsea, England)

*Born:* 21.10.69    *Caps:* 14    *Goals:* –

Joined Chelsea in August 1993 for £400,000 from Silkeborg, who are in the Premier Division of the Danish League, but finds it difficult to get into the Chelsea side these days. Made two recent appearances at Wembley in the match against England and the 1994 FA Cup final.


**MORGENS KROGH** (Brondby)

*Born:* 31.10.63    *Caps:* 6    *Goals:* –

Another long-serving keeper, he has vied with Hogh for the number two spot in the national team when Schmeichel is unavailable. He has been at Brondby since 1991, when he signed from Ikast.


**HENRIK LARSON** (Lyngby)

*Born:* 17.5.66    *Caps:* 42    *Goals:* 6

Top scorer for the Danes in the 1992 European Championships, he has been quiet since then and has returned to Denmark after failing to settle in European football. He went to Serie A club Pisa, Bundesliga Division 2 club Waldhof Mannheim and on loan to Aston Villa. Now more settled back in Denmark.


**BRIAN LAUDRUP** (Rangers, Scotland)

*Born:* 22.2.69    *Caps:* 61    *Goals:* 10

Voted the 1995 Scottish Footballer of the Year after a fine season in Rangers' Championship win. Unlike his brother, he ended his exile with the national side in time to win a 1992 European Championship medal. A bit of a wanderer at club level, he moved from Brondby to Bayer Uerdingen, Bayern Munich, Fiorentina and then AC Milan – where he couldn't get a regular place (just 11 league games played) because Milan had seven overseas players – before joining Rangers in 1994. His brother Michael and father Finn also played for Denmark and all three have been Footballer of the Year.


**MICHAEL LAUDRUP** (Real Madrid, Spain)

*Born:* 15.6.64    *Caps:* 86    *Goals:* 34

Returned to play for Denmark in 1993-94, having missed 29 internationals – including the 1992 European Championship win – after falling out with Richard Moller Nielsen over team tactics when the Danes lost a qualifier in that compttetition to Yugoslavia in November 1990. He was with Barcelona from 1990 and consoled himself with four consecutive titles, before moving to Real in 1994 for a fifth in a row. Intelligent and skilled, he was formerly at Brondby, Lazio and Juventus, and was the Danish Footballer of the Year at 18. Sadly, old wounds are resurfacing with the team management.

**JACOB LAURSEN** (Silkeborg)
*Born:* 6.10.71   *Caps:* 12   *Goals:* 1
Plays in Denmark for the 1994 champions Silkeborg and came into the national squad around the same time. Has been a permanent fixture in the squad since.

**ALLAN NIELSEN** (Brondby)
*Born:* 13.3.71   *Caps:* 5   *Goals:* 1
New to the squad in 1995, he scored on his international debut against Armenia in August in the European qualifiers.

**LARS OLSEN** (Brondby)
*Born:* 2.2.61   *Caps:* 87   *Goals:* 4
Recalled in early 1996 after four years in the international wilderness, he is still fit and capable and could well stay in the squad for Euro 96. One of the strong men in defence in the 1992 European Championship win, he was about to be put out to grass when the Danes originally failed to qualify for those European finals, but was reinstated when the Danes were asked to the finals in place of Yugoslavia. He started with Brondby, before moving to the Turkish club Trabzonspor, Belgian club Seraing, and Swiss club FC Basle. Now back at Brondby.

**TORBEN PIECHNIK** (Aarhus)
*Born:* 21.5.63   *Caps:* 16   *Goals:* –
Came into the Danish national team at the end of 1991 and quickly formed a good partnership alongside Kent Nielsen and Lars Olsen. His form in the 1992 finals earned him a transfer to Liverpool, but he didn't settle. Recently recalled to the squad, having found his old form at Aarhus.

**PETER RASMUSSEN** (Aalborg)
*Born:* 16.5.67   *Caps:* 16   *Goals:* 3
Erik Bo Andersson's forward partner in the 1995 Championship win. He made a breakthrough as an untested youngster with the Bundesliga club Stuttgart and returned home to play a further 200 games for Aalborg.

**MARC RIEPER** (West Ham United, England)
*Born:* 5.6.68   *Caps:* 36   *Goals:* –
Took over from Aston Villa's Kent Nielsen in the national team. Originally from AGF Aarhus, he joined West Ham from Brondby in 1994-95 for £1 million and has enjoyed a consistently good season with improving West Ham in 1995-96.

**JENS RISAGER** (Brondby)
*Born:* 9.4.71   *Caps:* 10   *Goals:* –
Defender who has come through the famous Brondby system of the Laudrups, Schmeichel, Jensen and Co., and has made the national squad via the Under-21 team.

**MICHAEL SCHJOENBERG** (Odense)
*Born:* 19.1.67   *Caps:* 15   *Goals:* 2
Has made the left side of midfield/defence his own in the last 18 months since joining the national squad. Joined Odense in 1994 and immediately went into the national squad.

**PETER SCHMEICHEL** (Manchester United, England)
*Born:* 18.11.63   *Caps:* 82   *Goals:* –
Possibly the world's best goalkeeper, his form in 1995-96 was a vital factor in Manchester United's latest title bid. In Sweden four years ago, he was a key figure in Denmark's success, dominating his own defenders and opposition forwards alike, screaming abuse and taking complete control of the penalty area. He is extremely agile for such a big man. Joined United from Brondby in the summer of 1991 for £750,000 and has won two Championships (1993 and 1994) and the FA Cup (1994).

**BRIAN STEEN-NIELSEN** (Odense)
*Born:* 28.12.68   *Caps:* 37   *Goals:* –
Has returned to Odense after a short spell with the Turkish club Fenerbahce and is more settled back in Denmark. A defensive midfield/defender, he is one of the few home-based players in the starting line-up.

**MARK STRUDAL** (Naestved)
*Born:* 29.4.68   *Caps:* 9   *Goals:* 3
Although he first played for Denmark back in 1988, he has played only two full games for them – the rest of his appearances have been as substitute or he has been substituted. Used to play for Brondby.

**CLAUS THOMSEN** (Ipswich Town, England)
*Born:* 31.5.70   *Caps:* 4   *Goals:* –
Bought by Ipswich from Aarhus for £250,000 in June 1994, he experienced relegation from the Premiership in his first season, despite being club top scorer. He is hoping to regain Premiership status in 1996.

**KIM VILFORT** (Brondby)
*Born:* 15.11.62   *Caps:* 74   *Goals:* 14
Scorer in 1992 European Championship final against Germany. He has always played for Brondby except for a short spell in the mid 1980s with Lille in the French First Division. Is the ball-winner in midfield and has been a good steady international for more than a decade.

**MORTEN WIEGHORST** (Celtic, Scotland)
*Born:* 25.2.71   *Caps:* 5   *Goals:* 2
Part of the Celtic squad who are having an improved season, he moved there from Dundee in December 1995 for £600,000, but initially failed to make the first team. Joined Dundee in 1992 from Lyngby.

**Coach: RICHARD MOLLER NIELSEN**
*Born:* 19.8.37
Capped twice by Denmark, an injury ended his playing career prematurely. As a coach, he began with Odense, guiding them to two League titles in 1977 and 1982. He also coached the national Olympic and Under-21 teams. He succeeded Sepp Piontek as national coach in 1990, having previously been his assistant. In 1992 he guided Denmark to their first European Championship success and in January 1995 took them to victory in the Intercontinental Cup.

# KEY PLAYER

## BRIAN LAUDRUP
*Date of Birth:* 22.2.69
*Current club:* Rangers
*Position:* Forward/Midfield
*Height:* 1.86 m
*Weight:* 78 kg

### CAREER RECORD

| Year | Club | League Apps | Goals | Int Apps | Goals |
|------|------|------|------|------|------|
| 1986 | Brondby | 2 | | | |
| 1987 | | 24 | 11 | 1 | 0 |
| 1988 | | 12 | | 3 | 1 |
| 1989 | | 11 | 2 | 10 | 2 |
| 1989-90 | Bayer Uerdingen | 34 | 6 | 4 | 1 |
| 1990-91 | Bayern Munich | 33 | 9 | 4 | 1 |
| 1991-92 | | 20 | 2 | 8 | 0 |
| 1992-93 | Fiorentina | 31 | 5 | 10 | 0 |
| 1993-94 | Milan | 9 | 1 | 8 | 2 |
| 1994-95 | Rangers | 33 | 10 | 11 | 3 |
| 1995-96 | | | | 2 | 0 |

### HONOURS
Danish champions – 1987, 1988
Danish Cup winner – 1989
Italian champions – 1994
Scottish champions – 1995
European Nations Cup winner – 1992
Scottish Footballer of the Year – 1995

| No | Date | Opponents | Venue | Score | Goals | Competition | Subbed Sub |
|----|------|-----------|-------|-------|-------|-------------|------------|
| 1 | 18.11.87 | West Germany | Aarhus | 0-1 | 0 | Olympic, Q | Subbed 76 |
| 2 | 30.3.88 | West Germany | Osnabruck | 1-1 | 0 | Olympic, Q | 90 |
| 3 | 20.4.88 | Greece | Aalborg | 4-0 | 1 | Olympic, Q | 90 |
| 4 | 27.4.88 | Austria | Vienna | 0-1 | 0 | Friendly | Sub pl 28 |
| 5 | 8.2.89 | Malta | Valletta | 2-0 | 0 | Friendly | Subbed 81 |
| 6 | 10.2.89 | Finland | Valletta | 0-0 | 0 | Friendly | 90 |
| 7 | 12.2.89 | Algeria | Valletta | 0-0 | 0 | Friendly | 90 |
| 8 | 22.2.89 | Italy | Pisa | 0-1 | 0 | Friendly | 90 |
| 9 | 12.4.89 | Canada | Aalborg | 2-0 | 0 | Friendly | Subbed 75 |
| 10 | 26.4.89 | Bulgaria | Sofia | 2-0 | 1 | World Cup, Q | 90 |
| 11 | 17.5.89 | Greece | Copenhagen | 7-1 | 1 | World Cup, Q | 90 |
| 12 | 7.6.89 | England | Copenhagen | 1-1 | 0 | Friendly | Subbed 87 |
| 13 | 14.6.89 | Sweden | Copenhagen | 6-0 | 0 | Friendly | Sub pl 10 |
| 14 | 18.6.89 | Brazil | Copenhagen | 4-0 | 0 | Friendly | Subbed 46 |
| 15 | 6.9.89 | Holland | Amsterdam | 2-2 | 0 | Friendly | 90 |
| 16 | 11.10.89 | Romania | Copenhagen | 3-1 | 1 | World Cup, Q | 90 |
| 17 | 15.11.89 | Romania | Bucharest | 1-3 | 0 | World Cup, Q | 90 |

| No | Date | Opponents | Venue | Score | Goals | Competition | Subbed Sub |
|----|------|-----------|-------|-------|-------|-------------|-----|
| 18 | 15.5.90 | England | Wembley | 0-1 | 0 | Friendly | 90 |
| 19 | 11.9.90 | Wales | Copenhagen | 1-0 | 1 | E Nations, Q | 90 |
| 20 | 10.10.90 | Faroe Isles | Copenhagen | 4-1 | 0 | E Nations, Q | 90 |
| 21 | 17.10.90 | Northern Ireland | Belfast | 1-1 | 0 | E Nations, Q | Subbed 70 |
| 22 | 14.11.90 | Yugoslavia | Copenhagen | 0-2 | 0 | E Nations, Q | 90 |
| 23 | 8.4.92 | Turkey | Ankara | 1-2 | 0 | Friendly | 90 |
| 24 | 29.4.92 | Norway | Aarhus | 1-0 | 0 | Friendly | Subbed 78 |
| 25 | 3.6.92 | CIS | Brondby | 1-1 | 0 | Friendly | Subbed 73 |
| 26 | 11.6.92 | England | Malmo | 0-0 | 0 | EN finals | 90 |
| 27 | 14.6.92 | Sweden | Stockholm | 0-1 | 0 | EN finals | 90 |
| 28 | 17.6.92 | France | Malmo | 2-1 | 0 | EN finals | Subbed 69 |
| 29 | 22.6.92 | Holland | Gothenburg | 2-2 | 0 | EN finals | Subbed 57 |
| 30 | 26.6.92 | Germany | Gothenburg | 2-0 | 0 | EN finals | 90 |
| 31 | 26.8.92 | Latvia | Riga | 0-0 | 0 | World Cup, Q | 90 |
| 32 | 9.9.92 | Germany | Copenhagen | 1-2 | 0 | Friendly | 90 |
| 33 | 23.9.92 | Lithuania | Vilnius | 0-0 | 0 | World Cup, Q | 90 |
| 34 | 14.10.92 | Rep of Ireland | Copenhagen | 0-0 | 0 | World Cup, Q | 90 |
| 35 | 18.11.92 | Northern Ireland | Belfast | 1-0 | 0 | World Cup, Q | 90 |
| 36 | 24.2.93 | Argentina | Buenos Aires | 1-1 | 0 | Friendly | 90 |
| 37 | 31.3.93 | Spain | Copenhagen | 1-0 | 0 | World Cup, Q | Subbed 87 |
| 38 | 14.4.93 | Latvia | Copenhagen | 2-0 | 0 | World Cup, Q | 90 |
| 39 | 28.4.93 | Rep of Ireland | Dublin | 1-1 | 0 | World Cup, Q | 90 |
| 40 | 2.6.93 | Albania | Copenhagen | 4-0 | 0 | World Cup, Q | 90 |
| 41 | 25.8.93 | Lithuania | Copenhagen | 4-0 | 1 | World Cup, Q | 90 |
| 42 | 8.9.93 | Albania | Tirana | 1-0 | 0 | World Cup, Q | 90 |
| 43 | 13.10.93 | Northern Ireland | Copenhagen | 1-0 | 1 | World Cup, Q | 90 |
| 44 | 17.11.93 | Spain | Seville | 0-1 | 0 | World Cup, Q | 90 |
| 45 | 9.4.94 | England | Wembley | 0-1 | 0 | Friendly | 90 |
| 46 | 20.4.94 | Hungary | Copenhagen | 3-1 | 0 | Friendly | Subbed 71 |
| 47 | 26.5.94 | Sweden | Copenhagen | 1-0 | 0 | Friendly | 90 |
| 48 | 1.6.94 | Norway | Oslo | 1-2 | 0 | Friendly | 90 |
| 49 | 17.8.94 | Finland | Copenhagen | 2-1 | 1 | Friendly | 90 |
| 50 | 7.9.94 | Macedonia | Skopje | 1-1 | 0 | E Nations, Q | 90 |
| 51 | 12.10.94 | Belgium | Copenhagen | 3-1 | 0 | E Nations, Q | 90 |
| 52 | 16.11.94 | Spain | Seville | 0-3 | 0 | E Nations, Q | 90 |
| 53 | 8.5.95 | Saudi Arabia | Riyadh | 2-0 | 1 | Friendly | 90 |
| 54 | 10.1.95 | Mexico | Riyadh | 1-1 | 0 | Friendly | 90 |
| 55 | 13.1.95 | Argentina | Riyadh | 2-0 | 0 | Friendly | 90 |
| 56 | 29.3.95 | Cyprus | Limassol | 1-1 | 0 | E Nations, Q | 90 |
| 57 | 26.4.95 | Macedonia | Copenhagen | 1-0 | 0 | E Nations, Q | 90 |
| 58 | 31.5.95 | Finland | Helsinki | 1-0 | 0 | Friendly | 90 |
| 59 | 7.6.95 | Cyprus | Copenhagen | 4-0 | 1 | E Nations, Q | 90 |
| 60 | 6.9.95 | Belgium | Brussels | 3-1 | 0 | E Nations, Q | Subbed 80 |
| 61 | 27.3.96 | Germany | Munich | 0-2 | 0 | Friendly | 90 |

# PORTUGAL

The Portuguese squad has been built around those players who won the Junior World Cup in 1989 and retained it in 1991. Although some have fallen away, the basis of the two squads remains and the problem is how to graduate that talent.

Those who have gone to Italian and Spanish clubs form the basis of the team – you can't play for many better clubs than Barcelona (Figo), Parma (Fernando Couto) and Juventus (Paulo Sousa). Otherwise the big three at home dominate, with players from Porto, Benfica and a crop of excellent youngsters from Sporting Lisbon. The Porto defensive block is very solid, having conceded just 13 League goals in 28 games to 1 April.

If there is a fault – and a serious one – it is the lack of proven goalscoring against top opposition. The group tables have been inflated with 15 goals against Liechtenstein. Domingos is a useful domestic scorer but has yet to prove himself in international terms.

# PORTUGAL

*Formation:* 4-5-1
*Coach:* Antonio Luis Alves Ribeiro de Oliveira

Vitor Baia

Secretario     Fernando Couto     Jorge Costa     Paulinho Santos

Figo     Joao Pinto II     Paulo Sousa     Oceano     Rui Costa

Domingos

| Player | Position | Club | Date | Caps | Goals |
|--------|----------|------|------|------|-------|
| Vitor Baia | G | FC Porto | 15.10.69 | 40 | – |
| Rui Correa | G | Sporting Braga | 22.10.67 | 1 | – |
| Neno | G | Vitoria Guimaraes | 27.1.62 | 9 | – |
| Cristavao Helder | D | Benfica | 21.3.71 | 17 | 2 |
| Paulinho Santos | D | FC Porto | 21.11.70 | 11 | 2 |
| Dimas | D | Benfica | 16.2.69 | 5 | – |
| Fernando Couto | D | Parma (Ita) | 2.8.69 | 31 | 3 |
| Rui Jorge | D | FC Porto | 27.3.73 | – | – |
| Jorge Costa | D | FC Porto | 14.10.71 | 16 | – |
| Oceano | M | Sporting Lisbon | 29.7.62 | 39 | 8 |
| Paulo Sousa | M | Juventus (Ita) | 30.8.70 | 24 | – |
| Luis Figo | M | Barcelona (Spa) | 4.11.72 | 27 | 4 |
| Rui Costa | M | Fiorentina (Ita) | 29.3.72 | 21 | 7 |
| Carlos Secretario | M | FC Porto | 12.5.70 | 12 | 1 |
| Dani Carvalho | M | West Ham U (Eng) | 2.11.76 | 2 | – |
| Emilio Peixe | M | Sporting Lisbon | 16.1.73 | 12 | – |
| Paulo Alves | F | Sporting Lisbon | 10.12.69 | 11 | 7 |
| Antonio Folha | F | FC Porto | 21.5.71 | 18 | 4 |
| Domingos | F | FC Porto | 2.1.69 | 27 | 7 |
| Jose Dominguez | F | Sporting Lisbon | 16.2.74 | 3 | – |
| Ricardo Sa Pinto | F | Sporting Lisbon | 10.10.72 | 9 | – |
| Pedro Barbosa | F | Sporting Lisbon | 6.8.70 | 9 | 1 |
| Joao Pinto II | F | Benfica | 19.8.71 | 23 | 6 |
| Nuno Gomes | F | Boavista | 5.7.76 | 2 | – |

# PORTUGAL A-Z

**PAULO ALVES** (Sporting Lisbon)
*Born:* 10.12.69   *Caps:* 11   *Goals:* 7
After winning his first cap in Portugal's Euro 96 qualifier against Latvia on 12 October 1994 as a sub, he joined Sporting in summer 1995 from Maritimo, a First Division club in Madeira. Has also played for Gil Vicente, Tirsense, and Sporting Braga. He scored a hat-trick when coming on as sub in the international in Liechtenstein, was Maritimo's leading scorer for the 1994-95 seaon with 15 goals, and started the same way at Sporting.

**VITOR BAIA** (FC Porto)
*Born:* 15.10.69   *Caps:* 40   *Goals:* –
One of the best goalkeepers in Europe, he made his debut for the Porto club in 1988 and has missed just six games since. His family are Benfica fans and he only went to FC Porto for a trial to keep another player company. He was in the Porto teams that won the 1990, 1992, 1993 and 1995 Championships and he was the 1992 Portuguese Footballer of the Year. His first international cap was against the USA on 19 December 1990. Conceded only 15 goals in 34 League games in winning the 1995 title, and has conceded 22 goals in his first 40 internationals.

**PEDRO BARBOSA** (Sporting Lisbon)
*Born:* 6.8.70   *Caps:* 9   *Goals:* 1
Summer 1995 signing for Sporting from Vitoria Guimares, where he had already established himself in the national team in the 1994-95 season after four seasons of steady improvement. He has had less success internationally while at Sporting.

**DANIEL (DANI) CARVALHO** (West Ham United, England)
*Born:* 2.11.76   *Caps:* 2   *Goals:* –
Is currently on loan for the rest of the season at West Ham United. Another of the young Sporting Lisbon crop, he is also from the Under-21 side. He had made only three appearances for Sporting before 1995-96 and is now in the full national squad. Born in Lisbon and has come through the Sporting youth teams. Known as Dani.

**RUI CORREA** (Sporting Braga)
*Born:* 22.10.67   *Caps:* 1   *Goals:* –
Reserve keeper, who has come through from national number four choice to number two in a useful season with one of the smaller Division 1 clubs. He won his only cap in the Euro 96 qualifiers in September 1995 against Leichtenstein as a sub and never had a shot to save. Began his career with Sporting Lisbon, and played for Chaves and Setubal before settling at Braga in 1991.

**JORGE COSTA** (FC Porto)
*Born:* 14.10.71   *Caps:* 16   *Goals:* –
From the FC Porto defence, and another from the successful Junior World Cup team of 1991, he has also come through the Porto youth system to full national honours. Has been a first choice in the national side recently, although he's missed a couple of games through injury.

**RUI COSTA** (Fiorentina, Italy)

*Born:* 29.3.72   *Caps:* 21   *Goals:* 7

Having helped Portugal win the World Youth Cup in 1991 playing as a full back, he was recalled by Benfica from Fafe, where he was on loan, and transformed into a midfielder. Has developed into Portugal's key midfielder since his debut against Switzerland in March 1993. Having helped Benfica to the Championship in 1994, he was transferred to Fiorentina that summer in a big-money deal and has continued to improve since arriving in Serie A.

**FERNANDO COUTO** (Parma, Italy)

*Born:* 2.8.69   *Caps:* 31   *Goals:* 3

Part of the Parma success story, he joined the club in summer 1994 from Porto. He played 27 of 34 Serie A games for Parma in 1994-95 and was in the team that won the 1995 UEFA Cup but just lost the League and Cup to Juventus. Was probably the most secure of the Parma foreign players who include Brolin (now Leeds), Asprilla (now Newcastle), Stoichkov and Co. He played in the 1989 Junior World Cup success.

**DIMAS** (Benfica)

*Born:* 16.2.69   *Caps:* 5   *Goals:* –

One of increasingly few members of the Benfica club in the current squad, he was a new member of the national set-up in August 1995 and won his first cap that month against Liechtenstein. He had a solid grounding in the League with lesser clubs Academica, Estrella Amadora and Guimares before joining Benfica in summer 1994, and has subsequently gone through to the full national team. Plays for his club at right back.

**DOMINGOS** (FC Porto)

*Born:* 2.1.69   *Caps:* 27   *Goals:* 7

The 1995-96 Porto captain when the ageing right back Joao Pinto does not play, he has been with Porto from their youth and junior teams. He is way out in the lead in the 1995-96 League scoring charts and was League runner-up and club top scorer in 1990-91 with 24 goals, before suffering injury problems. He recovered well in 1994-95 and was runner-up again in the League lists and Porto's top scorer with 19 goals. Has been in Porto's 1990, 1992, 1993 and 1995 Championship teams and won his first cap on 19 December 1990 against USA – scoring on debut.

**JOSE DOMINGUEZ** (Sporting Lisbon)

*Born:* 16.2.74   *Caps:* 3   *Goals:* –

This was the youngster that Barry Fry took to Birmingham from Benfica reserves in 1994 paying £150,000, only to sell him back to Portugal and to Sporting for £1.4 million. Has come on in astonishing fashion back home and won his first cap as a sub against Austria on 11 October 1995. Played 30 League games for Birmingham in 1994-95 (18 as sub), scoring three goals.

**LUIS FIGO** (Barcelona, Spain)

*Born:* 4.11.72    *Caps:* 27    *Goals:* 4

Now plays for Barcelona after a move from Sporting Lisbon for some £4.2 million in summer 1995. Had always been with Sporting, making his debut for them in the 1989-90 season. He was first capped as a teenager v Luxembourg on 12 October 1991 and was in the 1991 Junior World Cup-winning side. He was the subject of a major transfer in early 1995, when he signed firstly for Juventus, then a more meaningful contract with Parma, but both transfers were deemed illegal by UEFA. He has had a superb start with Barcelona and was a revelation in the early part of the 1995-96 Spanish season.

**ANTONIO FOLHA** (FC Porto)

*Born:* 21.5.71    *Caps:* 18    *Goals:* 4

One of the Porto block, and another from the 1991 Junior World Cup-winning side to come through to major honours, he is often used internationally as a sub to give the team some width. His first club was Gil Vicente and he has been with Porto since 1991, becoming a regular in their 1995 Championship win.

**NUNO GOMES** (Boavista)

*Born:* 5.7.76    *Caps:* 2    *Goals:* –

Has been with the national Under-21 side from 1995 and made his international debut against France in January 1996 as sub. First-team debut for Boavista only in the 1994-95 season, from a local junior club.

**CRISTAVAO HELDER** (Benfica)

*Born:* 21.3.71    *Caps:* 17    *Goals:* 2

A key defender in Benfica's 1994 Championship success, he signed from fellow First Division club Estoril in 1992, having played for that club since his junior days. He is the linchpin of the Benfica defence, and one of the few to crack the Porto axis on a permanent basis in the national set-up.

**RUI JORGE** (FC Porto)

*Born:* 27.3.73    *Caps:* –    *Goals:* –

New to the squad in 1995, he shores up the left defence for Porto with Paulinho Santos and is a reluctant defender, having moved back from midfield. He has always been with Porto and started in their youth team. On loan to Rio Ave in 1991, he did so well that Porto called him straight back into their first-team squad, where he has been since a teenager.

**NENO** (Vitoria Guimaraes)

*Born:* 27.1.62    *Caps:* 9    *Goals:* –

Reserve keeper, who may return as favourite to be second choice to Vitor Baia. It is a problem position and experience may tell. He is in his third spell with Guimares, his first club, having spent 1985-87 and 1990-95 with Benfica and featured in their Championship wins of 1991 and 1994.

**OCEANO** (Sporting Lisbon)
*Born:* 29.7.62   *Caps:* 39   *Goals:* 8
He returned to his first club, Sporting Lisbon, in summer 1994, after three seasons in the Spanish First Division with Real Sociedad, where he was one of John Toshack's team and an overseas replacement for Kevin Richardson. A former midfield international who reads the game superbly, he is increasingly being used in a defensive capacity by Portugal. He made his first-team debut for Sporting in 1984 and won his first international cap against Romania on 30 January 1985.

**EMILIO PEIXE** (Sporting Lisbon)
*Born:* 16.1.73   *Caps:* 12   *Goals:* –
Returned in November 1995 to Sporting Lisbon after a sad spell with the Spanish First Division club Seville, who are racked with internal financial problems. He and Figo both made their international debuts as teenagers, but Peixe has recently been operating in the Under-21 team which qualified for their section of the European finals. However, he has not played in the full national side since October 1993 – a has-been at 20!

**JOAO PINTO II** (Benfica)
*Born:* 19.8.71   *Caps:* 23   *Goals:* 6
The future captain (if not already) of the national side, he played in the 1989 Junior World Cup-winning side and captained the team that retained the Cup in 1991. He now captains Benfica, though has been injured recently. He was discovered by Boavista and switched to Benfica in 1992, captaining their 1994 Championship side. A winger by inclination.

**RICARDO SA PINTO** (Sporting Lisbon)
*Born:* 10.10.72   *Caps:* 9   *Goals:* –
Midfielder who joined Sporting Lisbon in 1994 from the Porto-based Division 1 club Salgueiros. He came through to full national honours within a few months of the move, but as yet is more of a national squad member than a first choice.

**PAULINHO SANTOS** (FC Porto)
*Born:* 21.11.70   *Caps:* 11   *Goals:* 2
A relative newcomer to the international team, he gained his first cap as a sub against Spain on 19 January 1994. He joined FC Porto in 1991 from Division 2 club Rio Ave and has made sound progress, featuring in Porto's 1993 and 1995 Championship wins.

**CARLOS SECRETARIO** (FC Porto)
*Born:* 12.5.70   *Caps:* 12   *Goals:* 1
Another from the 1995 champions, FC Porto, he is a right-sided midfielder/winger who has played in all Portugal's last nine internationals. He joined Porto in 1993 and immediately fitted into the system after scrambling around with lowly Division 1 teams Penafiel, Famalicao and Sporting Braga. Can also play in the attacking right-back role, and is filling the position formerly held by Joao Pinto I.

**PAULO SOUSA** (Juventus, Italy)

*Born:* 30.8.70    *Caps:* 24    *Goals:* –

Having joined Juventus in Serie A in Italy after a £2.8 million move from Sporting Lisbon in summer 1994, he played 26 Serie A games in their 1994-95 Championship win. Originally with Benfica, he moved to Sporting in 1993 when a pay cheque from Benfica bounced. He is another who was in the 1989 Junior World Cup-winning team and was awarded his first cap against Spain on 19 January 1991.

**Coach: ANTONIO LUIS ALVES RIBEIRO DE OLIVEIRA**

*Born:* 10.6.52

A midfielder who played with FC Porto, Panafiel, Sporting Lisbon and in Spain for Real Betis of Seville. He began his coaching career in 1985 with Nacional and later managed Guimares, Academica Coimbra, Gil Vicente and Sporting Braga before being appointed technical director of the national team in December 1994.

# KEY PLAYER

## LUIS FIGO

*Date of Birth:* 4.11.72
*Current club:* Barcelona
*Position:* Midfield
*Height:* 1.80 m
*Weight:* 75 kg

**CAREER RECORD**

| Year | Club | League | | Int | |
|------|------|--------|-------|------|-------|
| | | Apps | Goals | Apps | Goals |
| 1989-90 | Sporting | 3 | | | |
| 1990-91 | | | | | |
| 1991-92 | | 34 | 1 | 7 | 0 |
| 1992-93 | | 32 | | 8 | 1 |
| 1993-94 | | 31 | 8 | 1 | 0 |
| 1994-95 | | 34 | 7 | 7 | 3 |
| 1995-96 | Barcelona | | | 4 | 0 |

**HONOURS**

Portugal Cup winner – 1995
World Youth Cup winner – 1991

| No | Date | Opponents | Venue | Score | Goals | Competition | Subbed/Sub |
|----|------|-----------|-------|-------|-------|-------------|------------|
| 1 | 12.10.91 | Luxembourg | Luxembourg | 1-1 | 0 | Friendly | Subbed 46 |
| 2 | 16.10.91 | Holland | Rotterdam | 0-1 | 0 | E Nations, Q | Sub pl 33 |
| 3 | 20.11.91 | Greece | Lisbon | 1-0 | 0 | E Nations, Q | Sub pl 75 |
| 4 | 12.2.92 | Holland | Faro | 2-0 | 0 | Friendly | 90 |
| 5 | 31.5.92 | Italy | New Haven | 0-0 | 0 | Friendly | Subbed 80 |
| 6 | 3.6.92 | USA | Chicago | 0-1 | 0 | Friendly | Subbed 82 |
| 7 | 7.6.92 | Rep of Ireland | Boston | 0-2 | 0 | Friendly | Subbed 46 |
| 8 | 2.9.92 | Austria | Linz | 1-1 | 0 | Friendly | Sub pl 22 |
| 9 | 14.10.92 | Scotland | Glasgow | 0-0 | 0 | World Cup, Q | Sub pl 38 |
| 10 | 11.11.92 | Bulgaria | Saint Ouen | 2-1 | 1 | Friendly | Subbed 89 |
| 11 | 24.1.93 | Malta | Valletta | 1-0 | 0 | World Cup, Q | 90 |
| 12 | 10.2.93 | Norway | Faro | 1-1 | 0 | Friendly | Subbed 61 |
| 13 | 24.2.93 | Italy | Oporto | 1-3 | 0 | World Cup, Q | 90 |
| 14 | 31.3.93 | Switzerland | Berne | 1-1 | 0 | World Cup, Q | Subbed 70 |
| 15 | 19.6.93 | Malta | Oporto | 4-0 | 0 | World Cup, Q | Sub pl 20 |
| 16 | 20.1.94 | Spain | Vigo | 2-2 | 0 | Friendly | Sub pl 36 |
| 17 | 7.9.94 | Northern Ireland | Belfast | 2-1 | 0 | E Nations, Q | 90 |
| 18 | 9.10.94 | Latvia | Riga | 3-1 | 1 | E Nations, Q | Subbed 81 |
| 19 | 13.11.94 | Austria | Lisbon | 1-0 | 1 | E Nations, Q | 90 |
| 20 | 18.12.94 | Liechtenstein | Lisbon | 8-0 | 0 | E Nations, Q | 90 |
| 21 | 22.2.95 | Holland | Eindhoven | 1-0 | 0 | Friendly | Subbed 89 |
| 22 | 26.4.95 | Rep of Ireland | Dublin | 0-1 | 0 | E Nations, Q | Subbed 76 |
| 23 | 3.6.95 | Latvia | Oporto | 3-2 | 1 | E Nations, Q | 90 |
| 24 | 3.9.95 | Northern Ireland | Oporto | 1-1 | 0 | E Nations, Q | 90 |
| 25 | 15.11.95 | Rep of Ireland | Lisbon | 3-1 | 0 | E Nations, Q | 90 |
| 26 | 12.12.95 | England | Wembley | 1-1 | 0 | Friendly | Subbed 46 |
| 27 | 21.2.96 | Germany | Oporto | 1-2 | 0 | Friendly | Subbed 46 |

# TURKEY

Turkey are through to the European finals for the first time ever. Their only other finals experience was in the 1954 World Cup, where they qualified after drawing lots against Spain – this after a two-leg game and a replay had finished all square.

The basis of the success comes from the junior and youth team who have won UEFA Championships recently and have moved through to the senior level. Turkey won the 1992 European Under-18 title, were runners up in 1994 and European Under-16 champions in 1994. It seems that – at last – discipline has been added to undoubted talent. The former coach Sepp Piontek, instilled the discipline, with the current coach, Fatih Terim (Turkey's most capped player until Oguz overtook him this year), adding the local knowledge and flair.

The team is based around the three Istanbul clubs – Besiktas, Fenerbahce and Galatasaray – as well as Trabzonspor, the League leaders from the provinces who knocked Villa out of Europe a couple of seasons ago. All the players are home based since Hakan returned from Torino in November 1995, suffering from homesickness.

# TURKEY

*Formation.* 5-3-2
*Coach:* Fatih Terim

Rustu

Recep    Alpay    Ogun    Osman    Abdullah

Tolounay    Oguz    Tugay

Hakan    Hami

| Player | Position | Club | Date | Caps | Goals |
|--------|----------|------|------|------|-------|
| Rustu Recber | G | Fenerbahce | 10.5.73 | 7 | – |
| Engin Ipekoglu | G | Fenerbahce | 7.6.71 | 28 | – |
| Nihat Tumkaya | G | Trabzonspor | 24.3.72 | – | – |
| Recep Cetin | D | Besiktas | 1.10.65 | 45 | 1 |
| Ogun Temizkanoglu | D | Trabzonspor | 6.10.69 | 35 | 4 |
| Osman Ozkoyiu | D | Trabzonspor | 26.8.71 | 11 | – |
| Alpay Ozalan | D | Besiktas | 29.5.73 | 17 | 1 |
| Bulent Korkmaz | D | Galatasaray | 24.11.68 | 44 | 1 |
| Gokhan Keskin | D | Besiktas | 1.3.66 | 41 | 1 |
| Emre Asik | D | Fenerbahce | 13.12.73 | 9 | 1 |
| Tugay Kerimoglu | M | Galatasaray | 24.8.70 | 36 | – |
| Abdullah Ercan | M | Trabzonspor | 8.12.71 | 24 | – |
| Sergen Yalcin | M | Besiktas | 5.10.72 | 12 | 3 |
| Oguz Cetin | M | Fenerbahce | 15.2.63 | 57 | 2 |
| Tolounay Kafkas | M | Trabzonspor | 31.3.68 | 17 | 2 |
| Halil Ibrahim Kara | M | Fenerbahce | 26.9.72 | 2 | – |
| Tayfun Korkut | M | Fenerbahce | 2.4.74 | 1 | – |
| Kemalettin Senturk | M | Fenerbahce | 9.2.70 | 4 | 1 |
| Bulent Uygun | M | Fenerbahce | 1.8.71 | 11 | 1 |
| Hakan Sukur | F | Galatasaray | 1.9.71 | 25 | 13 |
| Hami Mandirali | F | Trabzonspor | 20.7.68 | 37 | 7 |
| Ertugrul Saglam | F | Besiktas | 19.11.69 | 21 | 9 |
| Arif Erdem | F | Galatasaray | 2.1.72 | 9 | 1 |
| Oktay Derelioglu | F | Besiktas | 17.12.75 | 1 | – |
| Orhan Cikirikci | F | Trabzonspor | 15.4.67 | 25 | 2 |
| Aykut Kocaman | F | Fenerbahce | 5.4.65 | 12 | 1 |

*NB: Turkish players are known by their first names.*

# TURKEY A-Z

**ABDULLAH ERCAN** (Trabzonspor)
*Born:* 8.12.71   *Caps:* 24   *Goals:* –
Highly talented and versatile left-footed player who has been watched by several English and Italian clubs. A good performance in England could seal him a lucrative future. He has blossomed under coach Fatih Terim who promoted him after he had been ignored by previous coach Sepp Piontek. Played in all but one of Turkey's qualifying games.

**ALPAY OZALAN** (Besiktas)
*Born:* 29.5.73   *Caps:* 17   *Goals:* 1
Central defender from the 1995 champions Besiktas, for whom he has played since 1993 when he arrived from Division 1 club Altay of Izmir. He is now a first choice in the national side.

**ARIF ERDEM** (Galatasaray)
*Born:* 2.1.72   *Caps:* 9   *Goals:* 1
Remembered at Old Trafford as the player who scored a fine opening goal in the 3-3 Champions League game in 1993-94, he was also part of the Championship wins in 1991 and 1992. Prefers to be an old-fashioned right winger.

**AYKUT KOCAMAN** (Fenerbahce)
*Born:* 5.4.65   *Caps:* 12   *Goals:* 1
Has three times been top scorer in the Turkish League – in 1988 (24), 1992 (25) and again in 1995 with 27 in 34 games. However, he is similar to Hakan and not as good at international level, so is perhaps another case of a good domestic scorer struggling in the top flight.

**BULENT KORKMAZ** (Galatasaray)
*Born:* 24.11.68   *Caps:* 44   *Goals:* 1
Well known in England due to his recent Champions League matches against Manchester United, he has been with his club since schooldays and has come through the ranks to be a full international of considerable standing. Until recently had a virtually unchallenged run in the national side since May 1990 and featured in title wins in 1993 and 1994.

**BULENT UYGUN** (Fenerbahce)
*Born:* 1.8.71   *Caps:* 11   *Goals:* 1
No relation to the defender Bulent Korkmaz. Joined Fenerbahce in 1993 from Istanbul Division 1 club Kocaelispor and was an immediate success, his 21 goals making him top scorer in the Turkish League and contributing to the club's 1993-94 title win. He scored the winner against Poland on debut in 1993 but has not scored since.

**EMRE ASIK** (Fenerbahce)
*Born:* 13.12.73   *Caps:* 9   *Goals:* 1
He is having problems with the Fenerbahce coaching staff, especially Carlos Alberto Parreira, and this may hold him back in the national team.

**ENGIN IPEKOGLU** (Fenerbahce)
*Born:* 7.6.61   *Caps:* 28   *Goals:* –
Lost his place in the national team to club-mate Rustu, after breaking his leg in a club match in May 1995, and has been unable to regain his position for 1995-96, although he is still good enough for the squad. He signed for Fenerbahce to replace Harald Schumacher, costing the club £350,000, after a brief stay at Besiktas from 1989-91.

**ERTUGRUL SAGLAM** (Besiktas)
*Born:* 19.11.69   *Caps:* 21   *Goals:* 9
Has the second-best goal record of the current squad after Hakan. He was club top scorer for the 1995 champions Besiktas with 23 goals in 30 games, this after being signed in 1994 from Samsunspor where he had an even better record of 21 goals in 17 games. To the start of 1995-96 he had scored 44 goals in his last 47 games and is improving by the game.

**GOKHAN KESKIN** (Besiktas)
*Born:* 1.3.66   *Caps:* 41   *Goals:* 1
Has been with Besiktas for 11 years, since arriving as a 19-year-old, and has won five League titles, including the hat-trick from 1990-92. He plays on the left side of defence.

**HAKAN SUKUR** (Galatasaray)
*Born:* 1.9.71   *Caps:* 25   *Goals:* 13
Returned to Galatasaray after just five games in two months in Serie A with Torino (one goal) in 1995-96 and a failed marriage. He first joined Galatasaray from Bursaspor in 1992 and scored 54 goals in three seasons with the 1993 and 1994 champions, before moving to Torino for £2 million. An old-style English-type centre forward, he has an excellent scoring record with the national team.

**HALIL IBRAHIM KARA** (Fenerbahce)
*Born:* 26.9.72   *Caps:* 2   *Goals:* –
Joined Fenerbahce from another Istanbul Division 1 club, Kocaelispor, and has come through the national junior and Under-21 ranks. May be one for the next World Cup.

**HAMI MANDIRALI** (Trabzonspor)
*Born:* 20.7.68   *Caps:* 37   *Goals:* 7
Often takes second place to star striker Hakan Sukur but he is a quality player in his own right, with a good striking rate and a dazzling free-kick specialist. A useful domestic scorer who has been at Trabzonspor for eight seasons, he has netted some 120 League goals. He was outstanding in the UEFA Cup victory over Aston Villa and went on to score against Lazio in the next round in Rome's Olympic Stadium.

**KEMALETTIN SENTURK** (Fenerbahce)
*Born:* 9.2.70   *Caps:* 4   *Goals:* 1
As he is one of four or five from his club's midfield who are in the national squad, his club chances are restricted. He is a ball winner and a hard worker.

**NIHAT TUMKAYA** (Trabzonspor)
*Born:* 24.3.72   *Caps:* -   *Goals:* -
The keeper for the current League leaders Trabzonspor, he has had an excellent 1995-96 season in front of a miserly defence.

**OGUN TEMIZKANOGLU** (Trabzonspor)
*Born:* 6.10.69   *Caps:* 35   *Goals:* 4
An experienced international defender, who began his career in Germany and came to Trabzonspor in 1990, immediately making the national team.

**OGUZ CETIN** (Fenerbahce)
*Born:* 15.2.63   *Caps:* 57   *Goals:* 2
One of the finest talents produced by the country, he has just overtaken his coach Fatih Terim as their most capped player. Born and raised in Germany, he played for Sariyerspor when they won the Cup in 1984 and that immediately earned a ticket to Fenerbahce, where he has been ever since. Has been an international since 1988 and is the key figure in midfield for both club and country, pulling the strings and making the moves.

**OKTAY DERELIOGLU** (Besiktas)
*Born:* 17.12.75   *Caps:* 1   *Goals:* -
Very much one for the future, he has come through the national junior ranks and is an Under-21 star. After he joined Besiktas from Trabzonspor in summer 1993, their League title win in 1995 propelled him into the national team.

**ORHAN CIKIRIKCI** (Trabzonspor)
*Born:* 15.4.67   *Caps:* 25   *Goals:* 2
A left winger by trade, he has recently returned to full fitness after suffering a broken leg playing for his club side. Has been with Trabzonspor since 1989, when he was signed from a provincial Division 1 club Eskesehirspor.

**OSMAN OZKOYIU** (Trabzonspor)
*Born:* 26.8.71   *Caps:* 11   *Goals:* -
First-choice central defender for the national side, he is with the current League leaders Trabzonspor. Highly rated in his own League.

**RECEP CETIN** (Besiktas)
*Born:* 1.10.65   *Caps:* 45   *Goals:* 1
Another experienced international defender who plays down the right flank, he won his fourth league medal with Besiktas in 1995 after the hat-trick of titles from 1990-92. First capped in 1988, the same year in which he moved from provincial Division 1 club Boluspor. May now struggle to remain a first choice.

**RUSTU RECBER** (Fenerbahce)
*Born:* 10.5.73   *Caps:* 7   *Goals:* -
Took over from the injured Engin in the Fenerbahce goal in May 1995 and has held on ever since. Formerly with provincial Division 1 club Antalyaspor, he attracted Fenerbahce's attention when he got into the national Under-21 side.

**SERGEN YALCIN** (Besiktas)
*Born:* 5.10.72    *Caps:* 12    *Goals:* 3
Key midfielder in the Besiktas side which won the 1995 title, but often has to play
second fiddle to Tugay in the national side. From the club's youth set-up, he made his
first-team debut in 1991.

**TAYFUN KORKUT** (Fenerbahce)
*Born:* 2.4.74    *Caps:* 1    *Goals:* -
A summer 1995 signing by Fenerbahce from the Bundesliga Division 2 club Stuttgart
Kickers (with whom he played as a teenager in the Bundesliga), he immediately gained
international recognition in Recep's place down the right side.

**TOLOUNAY KAFKAS** (Trabzonspor)
*Born:* 31.3.68    *Caps:* 17    *Goals:* 2
Trabzonspor's ball winner and known as The Tank, he has been in fine form in the
qualifiers, especially in the key games against Sweden, where he was Man of the Match.

**TUGAY KERIMOGLU** (Galatasaray)
*Born:* 24.8.70    *Caps:* 36    *Goals:* -
Has always been with Galatasaray and was a key member of their side which won the
1993 and 1994 titles and played Champions League. He is a bit of a night owl, which
doesn't please coaches, but his talent has been evident in the national team since his
debut in 1992.

**Coach: FATIH TERIM**
*Born:* 14.9.53
Capped 51 times by Turkey, then a national record, he made his name with Adan-
ademirspor and then spent 13 years with Galatasaray. After retiring he coached
Ankaragucu and Goztepe Izmir and was appointed manager of the Turkish Under-21s
in 1990. He then became assistant to national coach Sepp Piontek, succeeding him in
July 1993.

# KEY PLAYER

# HAKAN SUKUR
*Date of Birth:* 1.9.71
*Current club:* Galatasaray
*Position:* Forward
*Height:* 1.88 m
*Weight:* 83 kg

## CAREER RECORD

| Year | Club | League Apps | Goals | Int Apps | Goals |
|------|------|------|-------|------|-------|
| 1988-89 | Sakaryaspor | 9 | 5 | | |
| 1989-90 | | 27 | 5 | | |
| 1990-91 | Bursaspor | 28 | 5 | | |
| 1991-92 | | 28 | 7 | 3 | 1 |
| 1992-93 | Galatasaray | 30 | 19 | 7 | 4 |
| 1993-94 | | 26 | 16 | 2 | 1 |
| 1994-95 | | 33 | 19 | 8 | 4 |
| 1995-96 | Torino | 5 | 1 | | |
| | Galatasaray | | | 5 | 3 |

## HONOURS

Turkish champion – 1993, 1994
Turkish Cup winner – 1993

| No | Date | Opponents | Venue | Score | Goals | Competition | Subbed Sub |
|----|------|-----------|-------|-------|-------|-------------|-----|
| 1 | 25.3.92 | Luxembourg | Luxembourg | 3-2 | 0 | Friendly | 90 |
| 2 | 8.4.92 | Denmark | Ankara | 2-1 | 1 | Friendly | 90 |
| 3 | 30.5.92 | Germany | Gelsenkirchen | 0-1 | 0 | Friendly | 90 |
| 4 | 26.8.92 | Bulgaria | Trabzon | 3-2 | 2 | Friendly | 90 |
| 5 | 23.9.92 | Poland | Poznan | 0-1 | 0 | World Cup, Q | 90 |
| 6 | 28.10.92 | San Marino | Ankara | 4-1 | 2 | World Cup, Q | 90 |
| 7 | 18.11.92 | England | Wembley | 0-4 | 0 | World Cup, Q | 90 |
| 8 | 16.12.92 | Holland | Istanbul | 1-3 | 0 | World Cup, Q | 90 |
| 9 | 24.2.93 | Holland | Utrecht | 1-3 | 0 | World Cup, Q | 90 |
| 10 | 28.4.93 | Norway | Oslo | 1-3 | 0 | World Cup, Q | Subbed 66 |
| 11 | 27.10.93 | Poland | Istanbul | 2-1 | 1 | World Cup, Q | 90 |
| 12 | 23.2.94 | Czech Republic | Istanbul | 1-4 | 0 | Friendly | 90 |
| 13 | 31.8.94 | Macedonia | Skopje | 2-0 | 0 | Friendly | 90 |
| 14 | 7.9.94 | Hungary | Budapest | 2-2 | 1 | E Nations, Q | 90 |
| 15 | 12.10.94 | Iceland | Istanbul | 5-0 | 2 | E Nations, Q | Subbed 61 |
| 16 | 14.12.94 | Switzerland | Istanbul | 1-2 | 0 | E Nations, Q | 90 |
| 17 | 15.2.95 | Romania | Izmir | 1-1 | 0 | Friendly | Subbed 55 |
| 18 | 8.3.95 | Israel | Istanbul | 2-1 | 0 | Friendly | 90 |
| 19 | 29.3.95 | Sweden | Istanbul | 2-1 | 0 | E Nations, Q | 90 |
| 20 | 26.4.95 | Switzerland | Berne | 2-1 | 1 | E Nations, Q | 90 |
| 21 | 6.9.95 | Hungary | Istanbul | 2-0 | 2 | E Nations, Q | Subbed 88 |
| 22 | 11.10.95 | Iceland | Reykjavik | 0-0 | 0 | E Nations, Q | 90 |
| 23 | 15.11.95 | Sweden | Stockholm | 2-2 | 1 | E Nations, Q | 90 |
| 24 | 14.2.96 | Belarus | Izmir | 3-2 | 0 | Friendly | Subbed 46 |
| 25 | 26.3.96 | Czech Republic | Ostrava | 0-3 | 0 | Friendly | Subbed 65 |

# CROATIA

This is the team that won 2-1 in Italy to top their group and have a host of quality players, the bulk of whom were in the triumphant 1987 Junior World Cup team for Yugoslavia and in the Yugoslav national team just as it broke up.

There is quality all over this side, whose forwards like Prosinecki, Boksic, Suker and Boban are among the top names in Europe. Then the younger element shines through in the shape of Stanic – currently top scorer in the Belgian League – plus a group of others who are with good sides in other lands. This region has always produced technically sound players, almost off a conveyor belt, and despite the political troubles, the system still works. There will be British interest in the form of Derby's recent signing, Igor Stimac, and West Ham's Slaven Bilic.

*Formation:* 5-3-2
*Coach:* Miroslav Blazevic

```
                        Ladic
   Jurcevic      Bilic        Jerkan        Stimac         Jarni
      Prosinecki              Boban               Asanovic
         Boksic                        Suker
```

| Player | Position | Club | Date | Caps | Goals |
|---|---|---|---|---|---|
| Drazen Ladic | G | Croatia Zagreb | 1.1.63 | 22 | – |
| Tonci Gabric | G | Hajduk Split | 11.3.61 | 7 | – |
| Marijan Mrmic | G | Varteks Varazdin | 6.5.65 | 3 | – |
| Robert Jarni | D | Betis Seville (Spa) | 26.10.68 | 18 | – |
| Igor Stimac | D | Derby County (Eng) | 6.9.67 | 15 | 1 |
| Nikola Jerkan | D | Oviedo (Spa) | 8.12.64 | 18 | 1 |
| Slaven Bilic | D | West Ham U (Eng) | 11.9.68 | 19 | – |
| Zvonimir Soldo | D | Croatia Zagreb | 2.11.67 | 9 | – |
| Nikola Jurcevic | D | Freiburg (Ger) | 14.9.66 | 13 | 2 |
| Elvis Brajkovic | D | 1860 Munich (Ger) | 12.6.69 | 7 | 2 |
| Dubravko Pavlicic | D | Hercules Alicante (Spa) | 28.11.67 | 14 | – |
| Niko Ceko | D | NK Zagreb | 13.2.69 | 2 | – |
| Dzevad Turkovic | D | Croatia Zagreb | 17.8.72 | 6 | – |
| Mirsad Hibic | D | Hajduk Split | 11.10.73 | – | – |
| Mladen Mladenovic | M | Osaka (Jap) | 13.9.64 | 15 | 3 |
| Robert Prosinecki | M | Barcelona (Spa) | 12.1.69 | 12 | 3 |
| Zvonimir Boban | M | AC Milan (Ita) | 8.10.68 | 15 | 2 |
| Nenad Pralija | M | Hajduk Split | 11.12.70 | 6 | – |
| Aljosa Asanovic | M | Hajduk Split | 14.12.65 | 17 | 1 |
| Mario Stanic | F | FC Bruges (Bel) | 10.4.72 | 6 | 1 |
| Davor Suker | F | Seville (Spa) | 1.1.68 | 17 | 17 |
| Alen Boksic | F | Lazio (Ita) | 31.1.70 | 11 | 1 |
| Goran Vlaovic | F | Padova (Ita) | 7.8.72 | 7 | 4 |
| Robert Spehar | F | FC Bruges (Bel) | 13.5.70 | 6 | – |
| Ardian Kozniku | F | Cannes (Fra) | 27.10.67 | 4 | 1 |

*NB: These figures do not include any caps gained for Yugoslavia.*

# CROATIA A-Z

**ALJOSA ASANOVIC** (Hajduk Split)
*Born:* 14.12.65   *Caps:* 17   *Goals:* 1
He played for Yugoslavia at all levels and gained three caps for the national team back in 1987-88. Has also played in the French First Division for Metz, Cannes and Montpellier, and spent the first three months of the 1995-96 season with Valladolid in the Spanish First Division before returning to Hajduk.

**SLAVEN BILIC** (West Ham United, England)
*Born:* 11.9.68   *Caps:* 19   *Goals:* –
A key defender, who joined the Hammers in February 1996 for £1.65 million from the Bundesliga club Karlsruhe, for whom he played from 1993-95. His home club was Hajduk Split, and he was part of their 1992 title win.

**ZVONIMIR BOBAN** (AC Milan, Italy)
*Born:* 8.10.68   *Caps:* 15   *Goals:* 2
Plays for one of the very top European sides and is a former Croatia Zagreb forward, who joined AC Milan in 1992 and played in the 1994 European Cup final (beating Barcelona) and 1995 (losing to Ajax). The national team's captain, he was another member of Yugoslavia's victorious 1987 Junior World Cup team and played eight times for the old Yugoslavia. He will welcome the chance of playing in Euro 96 as he was banned from the 1990 World Cup finals with Yugoslavia after a fracas with a Serb policeman in a League game.

**ALEN BOKSIC** (Lazio, Italy)
*Born:* 31.1.70   *Caps:* 11   *Goals:* 1
Was outstanding in his spell at Marseille from 1991 to 1993, winning a European Cup medal in 1993 and being French League top scorer with 23 goals. He cost Lazio £8 million after the Marseille financial problems. His first club was Hajduk Split and he was a non-playing squad member of the 1990 Yugoslavia team at the World Cup. Finding goals has proved a little more difficult in Serie A and at international level, but he remains a fine player.

**ELVIS BRAJKOVIC** (1860 Munich, Germany)
*Born:* 12.6.69   *Caps:* 7   *Goals:* 2
Was a mid season 1994-95 signing for 1860 Munich of the Bundesliga from his home club of Rijeka, with whom he played in the old Yugoslav First Division. Named after you know who.

**NIKO CEKO** (NK Zagreb)
*Born:* 13.2.69   *Caps:* 2   *Goals:* –
A fringe international who has spent all his senior career with the No. 2 club in Zagreb, playing in the old Yugoslav First Division.

204

**TONCI GABRIC** (Hajduk Split)

*Born:* 11.3.61   *Caps:* 7   *Goals:* –

Since playing in the first international for the new nation, he has been understudy to Ladic in the national team. He began his career with Hajduk, played five seasons with Rijeka in the old Yugoslav Division 1, and for PAOK Salonica in Greece before returning to Hajduk in July 1994 for the double win of 1994-95 season.


**MIRSAD HIBIC** (Hajduk Split)

*Born:* 11.10.73   *Caps:* –

A young central defender who has come through from the new Croatian Under-21 set-up. He joined Hajduk in 1993 from the former Yugoslav Division 1 club Zenica in Bosnia and was in the Hajduk team that won the double in 1995.


**ROBERT JARNI** (Betis Seville, Spain)

*Born:* 26.10.68   *Caps:* 18   *Goals:* –

A class defender who fills the left back/midfield role. He is a quality player who won a 1995 Italian Championship medal with Juventus before a £3 million move in summer 1995 to Betis, where he is having a fine season. He was a member of the Yugoslav team that won the Junior World Cup in 1987 and was in the 1990 World Cup squad for Yugoslavia, for whom he won seven caps. He left his home club, Hajduk Split, in 1991 for Serie A duty with Bari, Juventus and a loan spell at Torino.


**NIKOLA JERKAN** (Oviedo, Spain)

*Born:* 8.12.64   *Caps:* 18   *Goals:* 1

Has been playing for Oviedo since 1990 and is highly thought of in the Spanish League with an unfashionable club. Formerly with Hajduk Split, he is the sweeper in the national team and another who played for the old Yugoslavia (two caps).


**NIKOLA JURCEVIC** (Freiburg, Germany)

*Born:* 14.9.66   *Caps:* 13   *Goals:* 2

Moved in autumn 1995 from the 1994 and 1995 Austrian champions Austria Salzburg, who also reached the 1994 UEFA final. Played originally for both Zagreb sides, Croatia and NK Zagreb, moved to Salzburg in 1991 and now plays in the Bundesliga. An attacking right back, he is an excellent scorer for a midfield/defender, and was twice club top scorer.


**ARDIAN KOZNIKU** (Cannes, France)

*Born:* 27.10.67   *Caps:* 4   *Goals:* 1

Plays in the French First Division and has been Cannes top scorer since joining from Hajduk Split in 1994. Was at Hajduk from 1990-94 and prior to that with Pristina in the old Yugoslav Division 2.


**DRAZEN LADIC** (Croatia Zagreb)

*Born:* 1.1.63   *Caps:* 22   *Goals:* –

He is the fledgling country's most-capped player and has also won two caps for the old Yugoslavia in their final days in 1991. Has been with the Dynamo club for over a decade, winning the League title in 1993.

**MLADEN MLADENOVIC** (Osaka, Japan)
*Born:* 13.9.64    *Caps:* 15    *Goals:* 3
Was with the 1994 and 1995 Austrian champions, Austria Salzburg, until the end of 1995 when he set off for the J-League. He was a team-mate of Jurcevic at Salzburg. He formerly played in the old Yugoslav First Division for Croatia Zagreb and Rijeka. May have ruled himself out of contention with his move to Japan, though he did come on as a substitute against England.

**MARIJAN MRMIC** (Varteks Varazdin)
*Born:* 6.5.65    *Caps:* 3    *Goals:* –
Usually third-choice keeper, he plays in the Croatian First Division for one of the provincial clubs. Previously at Cibalia Vinkovci. He played in Croatia's 7-1 qualifying victory over Estonia, coming on as a substitute.

**DUBRAVKO PAVLICIC** (Hercules Alicante, Spain)
*Born:* 28.11.67    *Caps:* 14    *Goals:* –
Formerly played in the old Yugoslavia for Croatia Zagreb and Rijeka until summer 1994, before going to Hercules who play in the Spanish Second Division.

**NENAD PRALIJA** (Hajduk Split)
*Born:* 11.12.70    *Caps:* 6    *Goals:* –
Has made progress through the Hajduk Split team after signing in 1993 from the Division 2 club NK Split. Moved into the national squad after winning the League and Cup double with Hajduk in 1995.

**ROBERT PROSINECKI** (Barcelona, Spain)
*Born:* 12.1.69    *Caps:* 12    *Goals:* 3
Another player with one of Europe's top clubs, he was in Red Star Belgrade's European Cup winning team in 1991 and then moved for £3 million in 1992 to Real Madrid. After a 1994-95 season with Oviedo on loan, he switched to Barcelona in summer 1995. He also played in Yugoslavia's successful 1987 Junior World Cup team, going on to play in the 1990 World Cup finals, and gaining 15 Yugoslav caps in all. Born in Stuttgart, he was rejected by Croatia Zagreb and went to Red Star.

**ZVONIMIR SOLDO** (Croatia Zagreb)
*Born:* 2.11.67    *Caps:* 9    *Goals:* –
One of the home based players, he has been a solid defender in the Croatian League and played in the old Yugoslav First Division with Croatia since 1988, winning a League title medal in 1992.

**ROBERT SPEHAR** (FC Bruges, Belgium)
*Born:* 13.5.70    *Caps:* 6    *Goals:* –
Joined FC Bruges in summer 1995 with Mario Stanic, and was the Croatian League's top scorer in 1994-95 with 25 goals when with his previous club FK Osijek. He is having a fine season with the current Belgian League leaders.

**MARIO STANIC** (FC Bruges, Belgium)

*Born:* 10.4.72   *Caps:* 6   *Goals:* 1

Having an outstanding first season in Belgian football, he is currently the Belgian League's top scorer, this despite missing a few weeks with a knee injury. He was signed by Bruges in summer 1995 from Benfica's reserves, where he had been languishing as a promising prospect but not getting games because of a large foreign contingent at the club. His home club was Zeleznicar Sarajevo, a former Yugoslav Division 1 club.


**IGOR STIMAC** (Derby County, England)

*Born:* 6.9.67   *Caps:* 15   *Goals:* 1

A member of the Yugoslav team that won the 1987 Junior World Cup, he is a former Hajduk Split player, winning the double with them in 1995. He has also played in Spain for Cadiz and joined Derby County in October 1995, after a move to Vicenza of Serie A fell through.


**DAVOR SUKER** (Seville, Spain)

*Born:* 1.1.68   *Caps:* 17   *Goals:* 17

Has a phenomenal goalscoring record at national level – far better than his club form – and was the top scorer in all Euro 96 qualifying groups with 12 goals. He has earned a £3 million move for the 1996-97 season to Real Madrid on a four-year contract. Began his career with Osijek then played for Croatia Zagreb until his move to Spain in 1991. He was top scorer in the 1987 Yugoslav Junior World Cup-winning team and was in the squad for the 1990 World Cup, although he didn't play in the finals. Gained two caps for Yugoslavia (one goal) in 1991-92 before the war.


**DZEVAD TURKOVIC** (Croatia Zagreb)

*Born:* 17.8.72   *Caps:* 6   *Goals:* –

One of the promising younger players, he first played in the national team in 1994. He has been at Croatia since joining from OFK Titograd in 1988, played in the old Yugoslav Division 1 and won a League title medal in 1992.


**GORAN VLAOVIC** (Padova, Italy)

*Born:* 7.8.72   *Caps:* 7   *Goals:* 4

He is currently playing in Serie A – having joined Padova from Croatia Zagreb, where he was top scorer in 1993 in the Croatian League with 24 goals in Croatia's title win. Finding it a bit hard going in Serie A with a relegation-threatened team.


**Coach: MIROSLAV BLAZEVIC**

*Born:* 10.2.35

A midfielder or defender, he played for Sarajevo, Rijeka and Dinamo (now FC Croatia) of Zagreb. As a coach he moved abroad and managed in Switzerland (Lausanne, Grasshopper Club, Sion, Vevey and the Swiss national team) as well as in France with Nantes. He was appointed national coach in 1994, succeeding Vlatko Markovic.

# KEY PLAYER

## DAVOR SUKER
*Date of Birth:* 1.1.68
*Current club:* Seville
*Position:* Forward
*Height:* 1.88 m
*Weight:* 77 kg

### CAREER RECORD

| Year | Club | League Apps | Goals | Int Apps | Goals |
|------|------|------|------|------|------|
| 1987-88 | Osijek | 1 | | | |
| 1988-89 | | 26 | 18 | | |
| 1989-90 | Dinamo Zagreb | 28 | 12 | | |
| 1990-91 | | 32 | 22 | 2/1 | 1/0 |
| 1991-92 | Seville | 22 | 6 | | |
| 1992-93 | | 33 | 13 | 2 | 3 |
| 1993-94 | | 34 | 24 | 2 | 1 |
| 1994-95 | | 32 | 17 | 7 | 7 |
| 1995-96 | | | | 5 | 6 |

### HONOURS
World Youth Cup winner – 1987

*For Yugoslavia*

| No | Date | Opponents | Venue | Score | Goals | Competition | Subbed Sub |
|----|------|-----------|-------|-------|-------|-------------|------------|
| 1 | 27.2.91 | Turkey | Smyrna | 1-1 | 0 | Friendly | Sub pl 27 |
| 2 | 16.5.91 | Faroe Isles | Belgrade | 7-0 | 1 | E Nations, Q | Sub pl 23 |

*For Croatia*

| No | Date | Opponents | Venue | Score | Goals | Competition | Subbed Sub |
|----|------|-----------|-------|-------|-------|-------------|------------|
| 1 | 22.12.90 | Romania | Fiume | 2-0 | 0 | Friendly | 90 |
| 2 | 22.10.92 | Mexico | Zagreb | 3-0 | 2 | Friendly | 90 |
| 3 | 25.6.93 | Ukraine | Zagreb | 3-1 | 1 | Friendly | Subbed 82 |
| 4 | 23.3.94 | Spain | Valencia | 2-0 | 1 | Friendly | 90 |
| 5 | 4.6.94 | Argentina | Zagreb | 0-0 | 0 | Friendly | Subbed 76 |
| 6 | 4.9.94 | Estonia | Tallinn | 2-0 | 2 | E Nations, Q | 90 |
| 7 | 9.10.94 | Lithuania | Zagreb | 2-0 | 0 | E Nations, Q | 90 |
| 8 | 16.11.94 | Italy | Palermo | 2-1 | 2 | E Nations, Q | 90 |
| 9 | 25.3.95 | Ukraine | Zagreb | 4-0 | 2 | E Nations, Q | 90 |
| 10 | 29.3.95 | Lithuania | Vilnius | 0-0 | 0 | E Nations, Q | 90 |
| 11 | 26.4.95 | Slovenia | Zagreb | 2-0 | 1 | E Nations, Q | Subbed 89 |
| 12 | 11.6.95 | Ukraine | Kiev | 0-1 | 0 | E Nations, Q | 90 |
| 13 | 3.9.95 | Estonia | Rijeka | 7-1 | 3 | E Nations, Q | 90 |
| 14 | 8.10.95 | Italy | Split | 1-1 | 1 | E Nations, Q | 90 |
| 15 | 15.11.95 | Slovenia | Ljubljana | 2-1 | 1 | E Nations, Q | 90 |
| 16 | 13.3.96 | South Korea | Zagreb | 3-0 | 0 | Friendly | 90 |
| 17 | 10.4.96 | Hungary | Osijek | 4-1 | 1 | Friendly | 90 |

# PREVIOUS TOURNAMENTS

## FRANCE 1960

### QUARTER-FINALS

*22 May 1960, Bucharest*

| | | | |
|---|---|---|---|
| Romania | 0 | Czechoslovakia | 2 |
| | | Masopust, Bubnik | |

*29 May 1960, Bratislava*

| | | | |
|---|---|---|---|
| Czechoslovakia | 3 | Romania | 0 |
| Bubnik, Bubernik [2] | | | |

CZECHOSLOVAKIA *qualify for semi-finals in France, 5-0 on aggregate.*

*8 May 1960, Lisbon*

| | | | |
|---|---|---|---|
| Portugal | 2 | Yugoslavia | 1 |
| Matateu, Santana | | Kostic | |

*22 May 1960, Belgrade*

| | | | |
|---|---|---|---|
| Yugoslavia | 5 | Portugal | 1 |
| Kostic [2], Sekularac, Galic, Cebinac | | Cavem | |

YUGOSLAVIA *qualify for semi-finals in France, 6-3 on aggregate.*

*13 December 1959, Paris*

| | | | |
|---|---|---|---|
| France | 5 | Austria | 2 |
| Vincent [2], Fontaine [3] | | Pichler, Horak | |

*27 March 1960, Vienna*

| | | | |
|---|---|---|---|
| Austria | 2 | France | 4 |
| Probst, Nemec | | Rahis, Kopa, Heutte, Marcel | |

FRANCE *qualify for semi-finals in France 9-4 on aggregate.*

| | | |
|---|---|---|
| Spain | | USSR |

USSR *qualify for semi-finals in France, after Spain withdrew.*

### SEMI-FINALS

*6 July 1960, Paris*

| | | | |
|---|---|---|---|
| France | 4 | Yugoslavia | 5 |
| Heutte [2], Wisnieski, Vincent | | Jerkovic [2], Galic, Knez, Zanetic | |

*6 July 1960, Marseille*

| | | | |
|---|---|---|---|
| Czechoslovakia | 0 | USSR | 3 |
| | | Ivanov [2], Ponedelnik | |

## THIRD-PLACE PLAY-OFF

*9 July 1960, Marseille*

| France | 0 | Czechoslovakia | 2 |
| | | Bubnik, Pavlovic | |

## FINAL

*10 June 1960, Paris*

| USSR | 2 | Yugoslavia | 1 |
| Ponedelnik, Metreveli | | Galic | |

*USSR:* Yashin, Tchekeli, Kroutikov, Voinov, Maslenkin, Netto, Metreveli, Ivanov, Ponedelnik, Bubukin, Meshki.

*Yugoslavia:* Vidinic, Durkovic, Jusufi, Zanetic, Mladenovic, Perusic, Sekularac, Jerkovic, Galic, Matus, Kostic.

## TOP SCORERS

| Bubernik [Czechoslovakia] | 5 |
| Fontaine [France] | 5 |
| Vincent [France] | 5 |
| Galic [Yugoslavia] | 4 |

# SPAIN 1964

## QUARTER-FINALS

*4 December 1963, Luxembourg*

| Luxembourg | 3 | Denmark | 3 |
| H.Klein [2], Pilot | | Madsen [3] | |

*10 December 1963, Copenhagen*

| Denmark | 2 | Luxembourg | 2 |
| Madsen [2] | | Leonard, Schmit | |

*Replay*
*18 December 1963, Amsterdam*

| Denmark | 1 | Luxembourg | 0 |
| Madsen | | | |

DENMARK *qualify for semi-finals in Spain.*

*11 March 1964, Seville*

| Spain | 5 | Republic of Ireland | 1 |
| Marcelino [2], Amancio [2], Fuste | | McEvoy | |

*8 April 1964, Dublin*

| Republic of Ireland | 0 | Spain | 2 |
| | | Zaballa [2] | |

SPAIN *qualify for semi-finals in Spain, 7-1 on aggregate.*

*25 April 1964, Paris*

| France | 1 | Hungary | 3 |
| Cossou | | Tichy [2], Albert | |

*23 May 1964, Budapest*

| Hungary | 2 | France | 1 |
| Bene, Sipos | | Combin | |

HUNGARY *qualify for semi-finals in Spain, 5-2 on aggregate*

*13 May 1964, Stockholm*

| Sweden | 1 | USSR | 1 |
| Hamrin | | Ivanov | |

*27 May 1964, Moscow*

| USSR | 3 | Sweden | 1 |
| Ponedelnik [2], Voronin | | Hamrin | |

USSR *qualify for semi-finals in Spain, 4-2 on aggregate.*

## SEMI-FINALS

*17 June 1964, Madrid*

| Spain | 2 | Hungary | 1 |
| Pereda, Amancio | | Bene | |

*After extra time*

*17 June 1964, Barcelona*

| USSR | 3 | Denmark | 0 |
| Ponedelnik, Ivanov, Voronin | | | |

## THIRD-PLACE PLAY-OFF

*30 June 1964, Barcelona*

| Hungary | 3 | Denmark | 1 |
| Novak [2], Bene | | Bertelsen | |

*After extra time*

## FINAL

*21 June 1964, Madrid*

| Spain | 2 | USSR | 1 |
| Marcelino, Pereda | | Khusainov | |

*Spain:* Iribar, Rivilla, Calleja, Fuste, Olivella, Zoco, Amancio, Pereda, Marcelino, Suarez, Lapetra.

*USSR:* Yashin, Chustikov, Mudrik, Voronin, Shesternev, Anitchkin, Chislenko, Ivanov, Ponedelnik, Kornaev, Khusainov.

**TOP SCORERS**

| | |
|---|---|
| Madsen [Denmark] | 11 |
| Bene [Hungary] | 5 |
| Amancio [Spain] | 4 |
| Ponedelnik [USSR] | 4 |
| Tichy [Hungary] | 4 |
| Orlando [Italy] | 4 |
| Cantwell [Republic of Ireland] | 4 |

# ITALY 1968

## QUARTER-FINALS

*6 April 1968, Sofia*

| Bulgaria | 3 | Italy | 2 |
|---|---|---|---|
| Dermendjiev, Kotkov, Jekov | | Own goal, Prati | |

*20 April 1968, Naples*

| Italy | 2 | Bulgaria | 0 |
|---|---|---|---|
| Prati, Domenghini | | | |

ITALY *qualify for semi-finals in Italy, 4-3 on aggregate.*

*4 May 1968, Budapest*

| Hungary | 2 | USSR | 0 |
|---|---|---|---|
| Farkas, Gorocs | | | |

*11 May 1968, Moscow*

| USSR | 3 | Hungary | 0 |
|---|---|---|---|
| Own goal, Byshovets, Khurtsilava | | | |

USSR *qualify for semi-finals in Italy, 3-2 on aggregate.*

*3 April 1968, Wembley*

| England | 1 | Spain | 0 |
|---|---|---|---|
| R.Charlton | | | |

*8 May 1968, Madrid*

| Spain | 1 | England | 2 |
|---|---|---|---|
| Amancio | | Hunter, Peters | |

ENGLAND *qualify for semi-finals in Italy, 3-1 on aggregate*

*24 April 1968, Marseille*

| France | 1 | Yugoslavia | 1 |
|--------|---|------------|---|
| Di Nallo | | Musemic | |

*24 April 1968, Belgrade*

| Yugoslavia | 5 | France | 1 |
|------------|---|--------|---|
| Petkovic [2], Musemic [2], Dzajic | | Di Nallo | |

YUGOSLAVIA *qualify for semi-finals in Italy, 6-2 on aggregate.*

## SEMI-FINALS

*5 June 1968, Naples*

| Italy | 0 | USSR | 0 |
|-------|---|------|---|

*After extra time*

ITALY *won on the toss of a coin.*

*5 June 1968, Florence*

| Yugoslavia | 1 | England | 0 |
|------------|---|---------|---|
| Dzajic | | | |

## THIRD-PLACE PLAY-OFF

*8 June 1968, Rome*

| England | 2 | USSR | 0 |
|---------|---|------|---|
| Hurst, R.Charlton | | | |

## FINAL

*8 June 1968, Rome*

| Italy | 1 | Yugoslavia | 1 |
|-------|---|------------|---|
| Domenghini | | Dzajic | |

*Italy:* Zoff, Burgnich, Facchetti, Ferrini, Guarneri, Castano, Domenghini, Juliano, Anastasi, Lodetti, Prati.

*Yugoslavia:* Pantelic, Fazlagic, Damsanovic, Pavlovic, Paunovic, Holcer, Petkovic, Acimovic, Musemic, Trivic, Dzajic.

*After extra time*

## FINAL REPLAY

*10 June 1968, Rome*

| Italy | 2 | Yugoslavia | 0 |
|-------|---|------------|---|
| Riva, Anastasi | | | |

*Italy:* Zoff, Burgnich, Facchetti, Rosato, Guarneri, Salvadore, Domenghini, Mazzola, Anastasi, De Sisti, Riva.

*Yugoslavia:* Pantelic, Fazlagic, Damsanovic, Pavlovic, Paunovic, Holcer, Hosic, Acimovic, Musemic, Trivic, Dzajic.

## TOP SCORERS

| | |
|---|---|
| Riva [Italy] | 7 |
| Farkas [Hungary] | 6 |
| R.Charlton [England] | 5 |
| Di Nallo [France] | 5 |
| Van Himst [Belgium] | 5 |
| Fratila [Romania] | 5 |
| Kunzli [Switzerland] | 5 |
| Frenzel [East Germany] | 5 |
| Muller [West Germany] | 5 |
| Domenghini [Italy] | 5 |
| Mazzola [Italy] | 5 |

# BELGIUM 1972

## QUARTER-FINALS

*29 April 1972, Budapest*

| | | | |
|---|---|---|---|
| Hungary | 1 | Romania | 1 |
| Branikovits | | Satmareanu | |

*14 May 1972, Bucharest*

| | | | |
|---|---|---|---|
| Romania | 2 | Hungary | 2 |
| Dobrin, Neagu | | Szoke, Kocsis | |

*Replay*

*17 May 1972, Belgrade*

| | | | |
|---|---|---|---|
| Hungary | 2 | Romania | 1 |
| Szoke, Kocsis | | Neagu | |

HUNGARY *qualify for semi-finals in Belgium.*

*29 April 1972, Wembley*

| | | | |
|---|---|---|---|
| England | 1 | West Germany | 3 |
| Lee | | Muller, Hoeness, Netzer | |

*13 May 1972, Berlin*

| | | | |
|---|---|---|---|
| West Germany | 0 | England | 0 |

WEST GERMANY *qualify for semi-finals in Belgium, 3-1 on aggregate.*

*29 April 1972, Milan*

| | | | |
|---|---|---|---|
| Italy | 0 | Belgium | 0 |

*13 May 1972, Brussels*

| Belgium | 2 | Italy | 1 |

Van Moer, Van Himst — Riva

BELGIUM *qualify for semi-finals in Belgium, 2-1 on aggregate.*

*13 April 1972, Belgrade*

| Yugoslavia | 0 | USSR | 0 |

*13 May 1972, Moscow*

| USSR | 3 | Yugoslavia | 0 |

Banishevsky, Kolotov, Kozinkevich

USSR *qualify for semi-finals in Belgium, 3-0 on aggregate.*

## SEMI-FINALS

*14 June 1972, Antwerp*

| Belgium | 1 | West Germany | 2 |

Polleunis — Muller [2]

*14 June 1972, Brussels*

| USSR | 1 | Hungary | 0 |

Konkov

## THIRD-PLACE PLAY-OFF

*17 June 1972, Liege*

| Belgium | 2 | Hungary | 1 |

Van Himst, Lambert — Ku

## FINAL

*18 June 1972, Brussels*

| West Germany | 3 | USSR | 0 |

Muller [2], Wimmer

*West Germany:* Maier, Hottges, Schwarzenbeck, Beckenbauer, Breitner, Hoeness, Wimmer, Netzer, Heynckes, Muller, Kremers.

*USSR:* Rudakov, Dzodzuashvili, Khurtsilava, Kaplichny, Istomin, Troshkin, Kolotov, Baidachni, Konkov (Dolmatov), Banishevsky (Kozinkevich), Onishenko.

## TOP SCORERS

| Muller [West Germany] | 11 |
| Chivers [England] | 5 |
| Kreische [East Germany] | 5 |
| Cruyff [Holland] | 5 |
| Keizer [Holland] | 5 |

# YUGOSLAVIA 1976

## QUARTER-FINALS

*24 April 1976, Zagreb*

| | | | |
|---|---|---|---|
| Yugoslavia | 2 | Wales | 0 |
| Vukotic, Popivoda | | | |

*22 May 1976, Cardiff*

| | | | |
|---|---|---|---|
| Wales | 1 | Yugoslavia | 1 |
| Evans | | Katalinski | |

YUGOSLAVIA *qualify for semi-finals in Yugoslavia, 3-1 on aggregate.*

*24 April 1976, Bratislava*

| | | | |
|---|---|---|---|
| Czechoslovakia | 2 | USSR | 0 |
| Moder, Panenka | | | |

*22 May 1976, Kiev*

| | | | |
|---|---|---|---|
| USSR | 2 | Czechoslovakia | 2 |
| Burjak, Blochin | | Moder [2] | |

CZECHOSLOVAKIA *qualify for semi-finals in Yugoslavia, 4-2 on aggregate.*

*24 April 1976, Madrid*

| | | | |
|---|---|---|---|
| Spain | 1 | West Germany | 1 |
| Santillana | | Beer | |

*22 May 1976, Munich*

| | | | |
|---|---|---|---|
| West Germany | 2 | Spain | 0 |
| Hoeness, Toppmoller | | | |

WEST GERMANY *qualify for semi-finals in Yugoslavia, 3-1 on aggregate.*

*25 April 1976, Rotterdam*

| | | | |
|---|---|---|---|
| Holland | 5 | Belgium | 0 |
| Rensenbrink [3], Rijsbergen, Neeskens | | | |

*22 May 1976, Brussels*

| | | | |
|---|---|---|---|
| Belgium | 1 | Holland | 2 |
| Van Gool | | Rep, Cruyff | |

HOLLAND *qualify for semi-finals in Yugoslavia, 7-1 on aggregate.*

## SEMI-FINALS

*16 June 1976, Zagreb*

| | | | |
|---|---|---|---|
| Czechoslovakia | 3 | Holland | 1 |
| Ondrus, Nehoda, Vesely | | Ondrus (o.g.) | |

*After extra time*

*17 June 1976, Belgrade*

| | | | |
|---|---|---|---|
| Yugoslavia | 2 | West Germany | 4 |
| Popivoda, Dzajic | | Flohe, D.Muller [3] | |

*After extra time*

## THIRD-PLACE PLAY-OFF

*19 June 1976, Zagreb*

| | | | |
|---|---|---|---|
| Yugoslavia | 2 | Holland | 3 |
| Katalinski, Dzajic | | Geels [2], W.van der Kerkhof | |

*After extra time*

## FINAL

*20 June 1976, Belgrade*

| | | | |
|---|---|---|---|
| Czechoslovakia | 2 | West Germany | 2 |
| Svehlik, Dobias | | D.Muller, Holzenbein | |

*After extra time*

*Czechoslovakia won 5-3 on penalties.*

*Czechoslovakia:* Viktor, Dobias (Vesely), Pivarnik, Ondrus, Capkovic, Gogh, Moder, Panenka, Svenlik (Jurkemik), Masny, Nehoda.

*West Germany:* Maier, Vogts, Beckenbauer, Schwarzenbeck, Dietz, Bonhof, Wimmer (Flohe), D.Muller, Beer (Bongartz), Hoeness, Holzenbein.

## TOP SCORERS

| | |
|---|---|
| Givens [Republic of Ireland] | 8 |
| Nyilasi [Hungary] | 6 |
| Panenka [Czechoslovakia] | 6 |
| Macdonald [England] | 5 |
| Cruyff [Holland] | 5 |
| Katalinski [Yugoslavia] | 5 |

# ITALY 1980

## FINAL PHASE, GROUP ONE

*11 June 1980, Rome*

| | | | |
|---|---|---|---|
| West Germany | 1 | Czechoslovakia | 0 |
| Rummenigge | | | |

*11 June 1980, Naples*

| | | | |
|---|---|---|---|
| Holland | 1 | Greece | 0 |
| Kist | | | |

*14 June 1980, Naples*

| West Germany | 3 | Holland | 2 |
| K.Allofs [3] | | Rep, W.van der Kerkhof | |

*14 June 1980, Rome*

| Czechoslovakia | 3 | Greece | 1 |
| Panenka, Vizek, Nehoda | | Anastopoulos | |

*17 June 1980, Milan*

| Czechoslovakia | 1 | Holland | 1 |
| Nehoda | | Kist | |

*17 June 1980, Turin*

| West Germany | 0 | Greece | 0 |

## FINAL TABLE

| | P | W | D | L | F | A | Pts |
|---|---|---|---|---|---|---|---|
| **WEST GERMANY** | 3 | 2 | 1 | 0 | 4 | 2 | 5 |
| Czechoslovakia | 3 | 1 | 1 | 1 | 4 | 3 | 3 |
| Holland | 3 | 1 | 1 | 1 | 4 | 4 | 3 |
| Greece | 3 | 0 | 1 | 2 | 1 | 4 | 1 |

WEST GERMANY *qualify for final.*

CZECHOSLOVAKIA *qualify for third-place play-off.*

## FINAL PHASE, GROUP TWO

*12 June 1980, Turin*

| Belgium | 1 | England | 1 |
| Ceulemans | | Wilkins | |

*12 June 1980, Milan*

| Italy | 0 | Spain | 0 |

*15 June 1980, Milan*

| Belgium | 2 | Spain | 1 |
| Gerets, Cools | | Quini | |

*15 June 1980, Turin*

| Italy | 1 | England | 0 |
| Tardelli | | | |

*18 June 1980, Naples*

| England | 2 | Spain | 1 |
| Brooking, Woodcock | | Dani | |

218

*18 June 1980, Rome*

Italy 0 Belgium 0

## FINAL TABLE

|  | P | W | D | L | F | A | Pts |
|---|---|---|---|---|---|---|---|
| **BELGIUM** | 3 | 1 | 2 | 0 | 3 | 2 | 4 |
| Italy | 3 | 1 | 2 | 0 | 1 | 0 | 4 |
| England | 3 | 1 | 1 | 1 | 3 | 3 | 3 |
| Spain | 3 | 0 | 1 | 2 | 2 | 4 | 1 |

BELGIUM *qualify for final.*

ITALY *qualify for third-place play-off.*

## THIRD-PLACE PLAY-OFF

*21 June 1980, Naples*

| Italy | 1 | Czechoslovakia | 1 |
|---|---|---|---|
| Graziani | | Jurkemik | |

*After extra time*
*Czechoslovakia won 9-8 on penalties.*

## FINAL

*22 June 1980, Rome*

| West Germany | 2 | Belgium | 1 |
|---|---|---|---|
| Hrubesch [2] | | Van der Eycken | |

*West Germany:* Schumacher, Briegel, Forster, Dietz, Schuster, Rummenigge, Hrubesch, Muller, Allofs, Stielike, Kaltz.

*Belgium:* Pfaff, Gerets, Millecamps, Meeuws, Renquin, Cools, Van der Eycken, Van Moer, Mommens, Van der Elst, Ceulemans.

## TOP SCORERS

| Keegan [England] | 7 |
|---|---|
| Van der Elst [Belgium] | 5 |
| Mavros [Greece] | 5 |
| Fischer [West Germany] | 5 |
| Allofs [West Germany] | 5 |

# FRANCE 1984

## FINAL PHASE, GROUP ONE

*12 June 1984, Paris*

| France | 1 | Denmark | 0 |
|---|---|---|---|
| Busk [o.g.] | | | |

*13 June 1984, Lens*

| Belgium | 2 | Yugoslavia | 0 |
|---|---|---|---|
| Katanec [o.g.], Grun | | | |

*16 June 1984, Nantes*

| France | 5 | Belgium | 0 |
|---|---|---|---|
| Platini [3], Giresse, Fernandez | | | |

*16 June 1984, Lyon*

| Denmark | 5 | Yugoslavia | 0 |
|---|---|---|---|
| Arnesen [2], Berggren, Elkjaer, Lauridsen | | | |

*19 June 1984, St Etienne*

| France | 3 | Yugoslavia | 2 |
|---|---|---|---|
| Platini [3] | | Sestic, Stojkovic | |

*19 June 1994, Strasbourg*

| Denmark | 3 | Belgium | 2 |
|---|---|---|---|
| Arnesen, Brylle, Elkjaer | | Ceulemans, Vercauteren | |

### FINAL TABLE

| | P | W | D | L | F | A | Pts |
|---|---|---|---|---|---|---|---|
| **FRANCE** | 3 | 3 | 0 | 0 | 9 | 2 | 6 |
| **DENMARK** | 3 | 2 | 0 | 1 | 8 | 3 | 4 |
| Belgium | 3 | 1 | 0 | 2 | 4 | 8 | 2 |
| Yugoslavia | 3 | 0 | 0 | 3 | 2 | 10 | 0 |

FRANCE *and* DENMARK *qualify for semi-finals.*

## FINAL PHASE, GROUP TWO

*14 June 1994, Strasbourg*

| West Germany | 0 | Portugal | 0 |
|---|---|---|---|

*14 June 1984, St Etienne*

| Spain | 1 | Romania | 1 |
|---|---|---|---|
| Carrasco | | Boloni | |

*17 June 1984, Marseille*

| | | | |
|---|---|---|---|
| Spain | 1 | Portugal | 1 |
| Santillana | | Sousa | |

*17 June 1984, Lens*

| | | | |
|---|---|---|---|
| West Germany | 2 | Romania | 1 |
| Voller [2] | | Coras | |

*20 June 1994, Paris*

| | | | |
|---|---|---|---|
| Spain | 1 | West Germany | 0 |
| Maceda | | | |

*20 June 1994, Nantes*

| | | | |
|---|---|---|---|
| Portugal | 1 | Romania | 0 |
| Nene | | | |

## FINAL TABLE

| | P | W | D | L | F | A | Pts |
|---|---|---|---|---|---|---|---|
| **SPAIN** | 3 | 1 | 2 | 0 | 3 | 2 | 4 |
| **PORTUGAL** | 3 | 1 | 2 | 0 | 2 | 1 | 4 |
| West Germany | 3 | 1 | 1 | 1 | 2 | 2 | 3 |
| Romania | 3 | 0 | 1 | 2 | 2 | 4 | 1 |

SPAIN *and* PORTUGAL *qualify for semi-finals.*

## SEMI-FINALS

*23 June 1984, Marseille*

| | | | |
|---|---|---|---|
| France | 3 | Portugal | 2 |
| Domergue [2], Platini | | Jordao [2] | |

*After extra time*

*24 June 1984, Lyon*

| | | | |
|---|---|---|---|
| Spain | 1 | Denmark | 1 |
| Maceda | | Lerby | |

*After extra time*
*Spain won 5-4 on penalties.*

## FINAL

*27 June 1984, Paris*

| | | | |
|---|---|---|---|
| France | 2 | Spain | 0 |
| Platini, Bellone | | | |

*France:* Bats, Battiston (Amoros), Le Roux, Bossis, Domergue, Giresse, Platini, Tigana, Fernandez, Lacombe (Genghini), Bellone.
*Spain:* Arconada, Urquiaga, Salva (Roberto), Gallego, Camacho, Francisco, Julio Alberto (Sarabia), Senor, Victor, Carrasco, Santillana.

## TOP SCORERS

| | |
|---|---|
| Platini [France] | 8 |
| Voller [West Germany] | 6 |
| Santillana [Spain] | 6 |
| Rummenigge [West Germany] | 6 |
| Elkjaer [Denmark] | 6 |

# WEST GERMANY 1988

## FINAL PHASE, GROUP ONE

*10 June 1988, Dusseldorf*

| West Germany | 1 | Italy | 1 |
|---|---|---|---|
| Brehme | | Mancini | |

*11 June 1988, Hanover*

| Spain | 3 | Denmark | 2 |
|---|---|---|---|
| Michel, Butragueno, Gordillo | | Laudrup, Povlsen | |

*14 June 1988, Gelsenkirchen*

| West Germany | 2 | Denmark | 0 |
|---|---|---|---|
| Klinsmann, Thon | | | |

*14 June 1988, Frankfurt*

| Italy | 1 | Spain | 0 |
|---|---|---|---|
| Vialli | | | |

*17 June 1988, Munich*

| West Germany | 2 | Spain | 0 |
|---|---|---|---|
| Voller [2] | | | |

*17 June 1988, Cologne*

| Italy | 2 | Denmark | 0 |
|---|---|---|---|
| Altobelli, De Agostini | | | |

## FINAL TABLE

| | P | W | D | L | F | A | Pts |
|---|---|---|---|---|---|---|---|
| WEST GERMANY | 3 | 2 | 1 | 0 | 5 | 1 | 5 |
| ITALY | 3 | 2 | 1 | 0 | 4 | 1 | 5 |
| Spain | 3 | 1 | 0 | 2 | 3 | 5 | 2 |
| Denmark | 3 | 0 | 0 | 3 | 2 | 7 | 0 |

WEST GERMANY *and* ITALY *qualify for semi-finals.*

## FINAL PHASE, GROUP TWO

*12 June 1988, Stuttgart*

| Republic of Ireland | 1 | England | 0 |
|---|---|---|---|
| Houghton | | | |

*12 June 1988, Cologne*

| USSR | 1 | Holland | 0 |
|---|---|---|---|
| Rats | | | |

*15 June 1988, Dusseldorf*

| Holland | 3 | England | 1 |
|---|---|---|---|
| Van Basten [3] | | Robson | |

*15 June 1988, Hanover*

| Republic of Ireland | 1 | USSR | 1 |
|---|---|---|---|
| Whelan | | Protasov | |

*18 June 1988, Frankfurt*

| USSR | 3 | England | 1 |
|---|---|---|---|
| Aleinikov, Mikhailichenko, Pasulko | | Adams | |

*18 June 1988, Gelsenkirchen*

| Holland | 1 | Republic of Ireland | 0 |
|---|---|---|---|
| Kieft | | | |

### FINAL TABLE

| | P | W | D | L | F | A | Pts |
|---|---|---|---|---|---|---|---|
| **USSR** | 3 | 2 | 1 | 0 | 5 | 2 | 5 |
| **HOLLAND** | 3 | 2 | 0 | 1 | 4 | 2 | 4 |
| Republic of Ireland | 3 | 1 | 1 | 1 | 2 | 2 | 3 |
| England | 3 | 0 | 0 | 3 | 2 | 7 | 0 |

USSR *and* HOLLAND *qualify for semi-finals.*

### SEMI-FINALS

*21 June 1988, Hamburg*

| Holland | 2 | West Germany | 1 |
|---|---|---|---|
| R.Koeman, Van Basten | | Matthaus | |

*22 June 1988, Stuttgart*

| USSR | 2 | Italy | 0 |
|---|---|---|---|
| Litovchenko, Protasov | | | |

**FINAL**

*25 June 1988, Munich*

Holland             2      USSR              0

Gullit, Van Basten

*Holland:* Van Breukelen, Van Aerle, Van Tiggelen, Wouters, R.Koeman, Rijkaard, Vanenburg, Gullit, Van Basten, Muhren, E.Koeman.

*USSR:* Dassayev, Khidiatulin, Aleinikov, Mikhailichenko, Litovchenko, Demianenko, Belanov, Gotsmanov (Baltacha), Protasov (Pasulko), Zavarov, Rats.

**TOP SCORERS**

| | |
|---|---|
| Altobelli [Italy] | 7 |
| Claesen [Belgium] | 7 |
| Van Basten [Holland] | 7 |
| Ekstrom [Sweden] | 6 |
| Anastopoulos [Greece] | 5 |
| Gullit [Holland] | 5 |
| Lineker [England] | 5 |
| Thom [East Germany] | 5 |
| Vialli [Italy] | 5 |

# SWEDEN 1992

**FINAL PHASE, GROUP ONE**

*10 June 1992, Stockholm*

Sweden            1      France           1

Eriksson                Papin

*11 June 1992, Malmo*

Denmark          0      England         0

*14 June 1992, Malmo*

France             0      England `       0

*14 June 1992, Stockholm*

Sweden            1      Denmark      0

Brolin

*17 June 1992, Stockholm*

Sweden            2      England         1

Eriksson, Brolin         Platt

*17 June 1992, Malmo*

| Denmark | 2 | France | 1 |
|---|---|---|---|
| Larsen, Elstrup | | Papin | |

**FINAL TABLE**

|  | P | W | D | L | F | A | Pts |
|---|---|---|---|---|---|---|---|
| **SWEDEN** | 3 | 2 | 1 | 0 | 4 | 2 | 5 |
| **DENMARK** | 3 | 1 | 1 | 1 | 2 | 2 | 3 |
| France | 3 | 0 | 2 | 1 | 2 | 3 | 2 |
| England | 3 | 0 | 2 | 1 | 1 | 2 | 2 |

SWEDEN *and* DENMARK *qualify for semi-finals.*

**FINAL PHASE, GROUP TWO**

*12 June 1992, Gothenburg*

| Holland | 1 | Scotland | 0 |
|---|---|---|---|
| Bergkamp | | | |

*12 June 1992, Norrkoping*

| Germany | 1 | CIS | 1 |
|---|---|---|---|
| Hassler | | Dobrovolski | |

*15 June 1992, Norrkoping*

| Germany | 2 | Scotland | 0 |
|---|---|---|---|
| Riedle, Effenberg | | | |

*15 June 1992, Gothenburg*

| Holland | 0 | CIS | 0 |
|---|---|---|---|

*18 June 1992, Norrkoping*

| Scotland | 3 | CIS | 0 |
|---|---|---|---|
| McStay, McClair, McAllister | | | |

*18 June 1992, Gothenburg*

| Holland | 3 | West Germany | 1 |
|---|---|---|---|
| Rijkaard, Witschge, Bergkamp | | Klinsmann | |

**FINAL TABLE**

|  | P | W | D | L | F | A | Pts |
|---|---|---|---|---|---|---|---|
| **HOLLAND** | 3 | 2 | 1 | 0 | 4 | 1 | 5 |
| **GERMANY** | 3 | 1 | 1 | 1 | 4 | 4 | 3 |
| Scotland | 3 | 1 | 0 | 2 | 3 | 3 | 2 |
| CIS | 3 | 0 | 2 | 1 | 1 | 4 | 2 |

HOLLAND *and* GERMANY *qualify for semi-finals.*

**SEMI-FINALS**

*21 June 1992, Stockholm*

| Sweden | 2 | Germany | 3 |
|---|---|---|---|
| Brolin, Andersson | | Hassler, Riedle [2] | |

*22 June 1992, Gothenburg*

| Denmark | 2 | Holland | 2 |
|---|---|---|---|
| Larsen [2] | | Bergkamp, Rijkaard | |

*After extra time*
*Denmark won 5-4 on penalties.*

**FINAL**

*26 June 1992, Gothenburg*

| Denmark | 2 | Germany | 0 |
|---|---|---|---|
| Jensen, Vilfort | | | |

*Denmark:* Schmeichel, Sivebaek (Christiansen), Nielsen, Olsen, Christofte, Jensen, Povlsen, Laudrup, Piechnik, Larsen, Vilfort.

*Germany:* Illgner, Reuter, Brehme, Kohler, Buchwald, Hassler, Riedle, Helmer, Sammer (Doll), Effenberg (Thon), Klinsmann.

**TOP SCORERS**

| | |
|---|---|
| Papin [France] | 11 |
| Pancev [Yugoslavia] | 10 |
| Van Basten [Holland] | 8 |
| Bergkamp [Holland] | 7 |
| Knup [Switzerland] | 6 |
| Christensen [Denmark] | 6 |

# THE QUALIFIERS' PREVIOUS RECORD IN ALL EUROPEAN CHAMPIONSHIP GAMES

## GROUP A

## ENGLAND

**1958-60**

Did not participate

**1962-64**

*First round*

| | | | | |
|---|---|---|---|---|
| 3.10.62 | England | 1 | France | 1 |
| | Flowers (pen) | | Goujon | |
| 27.2.63 | France | 5 | England | 2 |
| | Wisnieski (2), Douis, Cossou (2) | | Smith, Tambling | |

*England knocked out, 6-3 on aggregate.*

**1966-68**

*Group 8*

| | | | | |
|---|---|---|---|---|
| 22.10.66 | Northern Ireland | 0 | England | 2 |
| | | | Hunt, Peters | |
| 16.11.66 | England | 5 | Wales | 1 |
| | Hurst (2), R. Charlton, | | W. Davies | |
| | J. Charlton, own goal | | | |
| 15.4.67 | England | 2 | Scotland | 3 |
| | Hurst, J. Charlton | | McCalliog, Law, Lennox | |
| 21.10.67 | Wales | 0 | England | 3 |
| | | | Ball, R. Charlton, Peters | |
| 22.11.67 | England | 2 | Northern Ireland | 0 |
| | R. Charlton, Hurst | | | |
| 24.2.68 | Scotland | 1 | England | 1 |
| | Hughes | | Peters | |

*England qualify for quarter-finals as winners of Group 8.*

*Quarter-final*

| | | | | |
|---|---|---|---|---|
| 3.4.68 | England | 1 | Spain | 0 |
| | R. Charlton | | | |
| 8.5.68 | Spain | 1 | England | 2 |
| | Amancio | | Peters, Hurst | |

*England qualify for semi-finals, 3-1 on aggregate.*

*Semi-final in Italy*

| | | | | |
|---|---|---|---|---|
| 5.6.68 | Yugoslavia | 1 | England | 0 |
| | Dzajic | | | |

*Third-place play-off*

| | | | | |
|---|---|---|---|---|
| 8.6.68 | England | 2 | USSR | 0 |
| | R. Charlton, Hurst | | | |

**1970-72**

*Group 3*

| | | | | |
|---|---|---|---|---|
| 3.2.71 | Malta | 0 | England<br>Peters | 1 |
| 21.4.71 | England<br>Lee, Chivers, Hurst | 3 | Greece | 0 |
| 12.5.71 | England<br>Chivers (2), Lawler, Lee,<br>Clarke (pen) | 5 | Malta | 0 |
| 13.10.71 | Switzerland<br>Jeandupeux, Kunzli | 2 | England<br>Chivers, Hurst, own goal | 3 |
| 10.11.71 | England<br>Summerbee | 1 | Switzerland<br>Odermatt | 1 |
| 1.12.71 | Greece | 0 | England<br>Chivers, Hurst | 2 |

*England quality for quarter-finals as winners of Group 3.*

*Quarter-final*

| | | | | |
|---|---|---|---|---|
| 29.4.72 | England<br>Lee | 1 | West Germany<br>Hoeness, Netzer (pen), Muller | 3 |
| 13.5.72 | West Germany | 0 | England | 0 |

*England knocked out, 3-1 on aggregate.*

**1974-76**

*Group 1*

| | | | | |
|---|---|---|---|---|
| 20.11.74 | England<br>Channon, Bell (2) | 3 | Czechoslovakia | 0 |
| 20.11.74 | England | 0 | Portugal | 0 |
| 16.4.75 | England<br>Macdonald (5) | 5 | Cyprus | 0 |
| 11.5.75 | Cyprus | 0 | England<br>Keegan | 1 |
| 30.10.75 | Czechoslovakia<br>Nehoda, Gallis | 2 | England<br>Channon | 1 |
| 19.11.75 | Portugal<br>Rui Rodrigues | 1 | England<br>Channon | 1 |

*Czechoslovakia qualify for quarter-finals, England second in Group 1.*

**1978-80**

*Group 1*

| | | | | |
|---|---|---|---|---|
| 20.9.78 | Denmark<br>Simonsen (pen), Arnesen, Rontved | 3 | England<br>Latchford, Keegan (2), Neal | 4 |
| 25.10.78 | Rep of Ireland<br>Daly | 1 | England<br>Latchford | 1 |
| 7.2.79 | England<br>Keegan, Latchford (2), Watson | 4 | Northern Ireland | 0 |
| 6.9.79 | Bulgaria | 0 | England<br>Keegan, Watson, Barnes | 3 |
| 9.9.79 | England<br>Keegan | 1 | Denmark | 0 |
| 17.10.79 | Northern Ireland<br>Moreland (pen) | 1 | England<br>Francis (2), Woodcock (2),<br>Nicholl (og) | 5 |

| 22.11.79 | England | 2 | Bulgaria | 0 |
| | Watson, Hoddle | | | |
| 6.2.80 | England | 2 | Rep of Ireland | 0 |
| | Keegan (2) | | | |

*England qualify for finals in Italy as winners of Group 1.*

*Final Group 2, in Italy*

| 12.6.80 | Belgium | 1 | England | 1 |
| | Ceulemans | | Wilkins | |
| 15.6.80 | Italy | 1 | England | 0 |
| | Tardelli | | | |
| 18.6.80 | Spain | 1 | England | 2 |
| | Dani (pen) | | Brooking, Woodcock | |

*Belgium qualify for final, England third in Group 2.*

**1982-84**

*Group 3*

| 22.9.82 | Denmark | 2 | England | 2 |
| | Hansen (pen), Olsen | | Francis 2 | |
| 17.11.82 | Greece | 0 | England | 3 |
| | | | Woodcock (2), Lee | |
| 15.12.82 | England | 9 | Luxembourg | 0 |
| | Moes (og), Coppell, Woodcock, | | | |
| | Blissett (3), Chamberlain, | | | |
| | Hoddle, Neal | | | |
| 30.3.83 | Greece | 0 | England | 0 |
| 27.4.83 | England | 2 | Hungary | 0 |
| | Francis, Withe | | | |
| 21.9.83 | England | 0 | Denmark | 1 |
| | | | Simonsen (pen) | |
| 12.10.83 | Hungary | 0 | England | 3 |
| | | | Hoddle, Lee, Mariner | |
| 16.11.83 | Luxembourg | 0 | England | 4 |
| | | | Robson (2), Mariner, Butcher | |

*Denmark qualify for finals, England second in Group 3.*

**1986-88**

*Group 4*

| 15.10.86 | England | 3 | Northern Ireland | 0 |
| | Lineker (2), Waddle | | | |
| 12.11.86 | England | 2 | Yugoslavia | 0 |
| | Mabbutt, Anderson | | | |
| 1.4.87 | Northern Ireland | 0 | England | 2 |
| | | | Robson, Waddle | |
| 29.4.87 | Turkey | 0 | England | 0 |
| 14.10.87 | England | 8 | Turkey | 0 |
| | Barnes (2), Lineker (3), | | | |
| | Robson, Beardsley, Webb | | | |
| 11.11.87 | Yugoslavia | 1 | England | 4 |
| | Katanec | | Beardsley, Barnes, Robson, | |
| | | | Adams | |

*England qualify for finals in West Germany as winners of Group 4.*

*Final Group 2, in West Germany*

| | | | | |
|---|---|---|---|---|
| 12.6.88 | England | 0 | Rep of Ireland | 1 |
| | | | Houghton | |
| 15.6.88 | England | 1 | Holland | 3 |
| | Robson | | Van Basten (3) | |
| 18.6.88 | England | 1 | USSR | 3 |
| | Adams | | Aleinikov, Mikhailichenko, | |
| | | | Pasulko | |

*USSR and Holland qualify for semi-finals, England last in Group 2.*

**1990-92**

*Group 7*

| | | | | |
|---|---|---|---|---|
| 17.10.90 | England | 2 | Poland | 0 |
| | Lineker (pen), Beardsley | | | |
| 14.11.90 | Rep of Ireland | 1 | England | 1 |
| | Cascarino | | Platt | |
| 27.3.91 | England | 1 | Rep of Ireland | 1 |
| | Dixon | | Quinn | |
| 1.5.91 | Turkey | 0 | England | 1 |
| | | | Wise | |
| 16.10.91 | England | 1 | Turkey | 0 |
| | Smith | | | |
| 13.11.91 | Poland | 1 | England | 1 |
| | Szewczyk | | Lineker | |

*England qualify for finals in Sweden as winners of Group 7.*

*Final Group 1, in Sweden*

| | | | | |
|---|---|---|---|---|
| 11.6.92 | Denmark | 0 | England | 0 |
| 14.6.92 | France | 0 | England | 0 |
| 17.6.92 | Sweden | 2 | England | 1 |
| | Eriksson, Brolin | | Platt | |

*Sweden and Denmark qualify for semi-finals, England last in Group 1.*

**1994-96**

*As hosts, England qualified automatically for the finals in 1996.*

# SWITZERLAND

**1958-60**

*Did not participate*

**1962-64**

*First round*

| | | | | |
|---|---|---|---|---|
| 11.11.62 | Holland | 3 | Switzerland | 1 |
| | Van der Linden, Swart, Groot | | Hertig | |
| 31.3.63 | Switzerland | 1 | Holland | 1 |
| | Allemann | | Kruijver | |

*Switzerland knocked out, 4-2 on aggregate.*

**1966-68**

*Group 6*

| | | | | | |
|---|---|---|---|---|---|
| 2.11.66 | Romania<br>Dridea, Fratila (3) | 4 | Switzerland<br>Kunzli, Odermatt | 2 |
| 24.5.67 | Switzerland<br>Kunzli (2), Quentin (2),<br>Blattler (2), Odermatt | 7 | Romania<br>Dobrin | 1 |
| 8.11.67 | Switzerland<br>Blattler (2), Kunzli, Durr,<br>Odermatt | 5 | Cyprus | 0 |
| 18.11.67 | Switzerland<br>Quentin, Kunzli | 2 | Italy<br>Riva (2) | 2 |
| 23.12.67 | Italy<br>Mazzola, Riva, Domenghini (2) | 4 | Switzerland | 0 |
| 17.2.68 | Cyprus<br>Melis, Pamboulis | 2 | Switzerland<br>Own goal | 1 |

*Italy qualify for quarter-finals, Switzerland third in Group 6.*

**1970-72**

*Group 3*

| | | | | | |
|---|---|---|---|---|---|
| 16.12.70 | Greece | 0 | Switzerland<br>K. Muller | 1 |
| 20.12.70 | Malta<br>Theobald | 1 | Switzerland<br>Quentin, Kunzli | 2 |
| 21.4.71 | Switzerland<br>K. Muller, Citherlet, Blattler,<br>Kunzli, Quentin | 5 | Malta | 0 |
| 12.5.71 | Switzerland<br>Odermatt | 1 | Greece | 0 |
| 13.10.71 | Switzerland<br>Jeandupeux | 2 | England<br>Chivers, Hurst, own goal | 3 |
| 10.11.71 | England<br>Summerbee | 1 | Switzerland<br>Odermatt | 1 |

*England qualify for quarter-finals, Switzerland second in Group 3.*

**1974-76**

*Group 6*

| | | | | | |
|---|---|---|---|---|---|
| 1.12.74 | Turkey<br>Ismail, B. Mehmet | 2 | Switzerland<br>Schild | 1 |
| 30.4.75 | Switzerland<br>K. Muller | 1 | Turkey<br>Alparslan | 1 |
| 11.5.75 | Rep of Ireland<br>Martin, Treacy | 2 | Switzerland<br>K. Muller | 1 |
| 21.5.75 | Switzerland<br>Elsener | 1 | Rep of Ireland | 0 |
| 12.10.75 | Switzerland | 0 | USSR<br>Muntjian | 1 |
| 12.11.75 | USSR<br>Konov, Onischenko (2),<br>Veremeyev | 4 | Switzerland<br>Risi | 1 |

*USSR qualify for quarter-finals, Switzerland last in Group 6.*

**1978-80**

*Group 4*

| | | | | |
|---|---|---|---|---|
| 11.9.78 | Switzerland<br>Tanner | 1 | Holland<br>Wildschut, Brandts, Geels | 3 |
| 15.11.78 | Poland<br>Boniek, Ogaza | 2 | Switzerland | 0 |
| 28.3.79 | Holland<br>Kist, Metgod, Peters | 3 | Switzerland | 0 |
| 5.5.79 | Switzerland | 0 | East Germany<br>Lindemann, Streich | 2 |
| 22.5.79 | Switzerland<br>Herbert Hermann, Zappa | 2 | Iceland | 0 |
| 9.6.79 | Iceland<br>Gudlaugsson | 1 | Switzerland<br>Ponte, Heinz Hermann | 2 |
| 12.9.79 | Switzerland | 0 | Poland<br>Terlecki (2) | 2 |
| 13.10.79 | East Germany<br>Weber, Hoffmann (3), Schnupase | 5 | Switzerland<br>Barberis, Pfister | 2 |

*Holland qualify for finals, Switzerland fourth in Group 4.*

**1982-84**

*Group 1*

| | | | | |
|---|---|---|---|---|
| 6.10.82 | Belgium<br>Ludi (og), Coeck, Van der Bergh | 3 | Switzerland | 0 |
| 17.11.82 | Switzerland<br>Sulser, Egli | 2 | Scotland | 0 |
| 30.3.83 | Scotland<br>Wark, Nicholas | 2 | Switzerland<br>Egli, Heinz Hermann | 2 |
| 14.5.83 | Switzerland | 0 | East Germany | 0 |
| 12.10.83 | East Germany<br>Richter, Ernst, Streicher | 3 | Switzerland | 0 |
| 9.11.83 | Switzerland<br>Schallibaum, Brigger,<br>Geiger | 3 | Belgium<br>Van den Bergh | 1 |

*Belgium qualify for finals, Switzerland second in Group 1.*

**1986-88**

*Group 2*

| | | | | |
|---|---|---|---|---|
| 24.9.86 | Sweden<br>Ekstrom (2) | 2 | Switzerland | 0 |
| 29.10.86 | Switzerland<br>Bregy | 1 | Portugal<br>Fernandes | 1 |
| 15.11.86 | Italy<br>Donadoni, Altobelli (2) | 3 | Switzerland<br>Brigger, Weber | 2 |
| 15.4.87 | Switzerland<br>Egli, Bregy (3, 1 pen) | 4 | Malta<br>Busuttil | 1 |
| 17.6.87 | Switzerland<br>Halter | 1 | Sweden<br>Ekstrom | 1 |
| 17.10.87 | Switzerland | 0 | Italy | 0 |
| 11.11.87 | Portugal | 0 | Switzerland | 0 |
| 15.11.87 | Malta<br>Busuttil | 1 | Switzerland<br>Zwicker | 1 |

*Italy qualify for finals, Switzerland fourth in Group 2.*

**1990-92**

*Group 2*

| 12.9.90 | Switzerland | 2 | Bulgaria | 0 |
| | Hottiger, Bickel | | | |
| 17.10.90 | Scotland | 2 | Switzerland | 1 |
| | Robertson, McAllister | | Knup | |
| 14.11.90 | San Marino | 0 | Switzerland | 4 |
| | | | A. Sutter, Chapuisat, Knup, | |
| | | | Chassot | |
| 3.4.91 | Switzerland | 0 | Romania | 0 |
| 1.5.91 | Bulgaria | 2 | Switzerland | 3 |
| | Kostadinov, Sirakov | | Knup (2), Turkyilmaz | |
| 5.6.91 | Switzerland | 7 | San Marino | 0 |
| | Knup (2), Hottiger, B. Sutter, | | | |
| | Hermann, Ohrel, Turkyilmaz | | | |
| 11.9.91 | Switzerland | 2 | Scotland | 2 |
| | Chapuisat, Hermann | | Durie, McCoist | |
| 13.11.91 | Romania | 1 | Switzerland | 0 |
| | Mateut | | | |

*Scotland qualify for finals, Switzerland second in Group 2.*

For details on how Switzerland qualified for Euro 96, see pages 31-3.

# HOLLAND

**1958-60**

*Did not participate*

**1962-64**

*First round*

| 11.11.62 | Holland | 3 | Switzerland | 1 |
| | Van der Linden, Swart, Groot | | Hertig | |
| 31.3.63 | Switzerland | 1 | Holland | 1 |
| | Allemann | | Kruijver | |

*Holland qualify for second round, 4-2 on aggregate.*

*Second round*

| 11.9.63 | Holland | 1 | Luxembourg | 1 |
| | Nuninga | | May | |
| 30.10.63 | Luxembourg | 2 | Holland | 1 |
| | Dimmer (2) | | Kruijver | |

*Holland knocked out, 3-2 on aggregate.*

**1966-68**

*Group 5*

| 7.9.66 | Holland | 2 | Hungary | 2 |
| | Pijs, Cruyff | | Molnar, Meszoly | |
| 30.11.66 | Holland | 2 | Denmark | 0 |
| | Swart, Van der Kuylen | | | |
| 5.4.67 | East Germany | 4 | Holland | 3 |
| | Frenzel (3), Vogel | | Mulder (2), Keizer | |
| 10.5.67 | Hungary | 2 | Holland | 1 |
| | Meszoly, Farkas | | Suurbier | |

| 13.9.67 | Holland Cruyff | 1 | East Germany | 0 |
| 4.10.67 | Denmark Bjerre (2, 1 pen), Sondergaard | 3 | Holland Suurbier, Israel | 2 |

*Hungary qualify for quarter-finals, Holland third in Group 5.*

**1970-72**

*Group 7*

| 11.10.70 | Holland Israel | 1 | Yugoslavia Dzajic | 1 |
| 11.11.70 | East Germany P. Ducke | 1 | Holland | 0 |
| 24.2.71 | Holland Lippens, Keizer (2), Cruyff (2), Suurbier | 6 | Luxembourg | 0 |
| 4.4.71 | Yugoslavia Jerkovic, Dzajic | 2 | Holland | 0 |
| 10.10.71 | Holland Hulshoff, Keizer (2) | 3 | East Germany Vogel (2) | 2 |
| 17.11.71 | Luxembourg | 0 | Holland Cruyff (3), Keizer, Pahlplatz, Hulshoff, Hoekema, Israel | 8 |

*Yugoslavia qualify for quarter-finals, Holland second in Group 7.*

**1974-76**

*Group 5*

| 25.9.74 | Finland Rahja | 1 | Holland Cruyff (2), Neeskens | 3 |
| 20.11.74 | Holland Rensenbrink, Cruyff (2) | 3 | Italy Boninsegna | 1 |
| 3.9.75 | Holland Van der Kuylen (3), Lubse | 4 | Finland Paatelainen | 1 |
| 10.9.75 | Poland Lata, Gadocha (2), Szarmach | 4 | Holland W. van der Kerkhoff | 1 |
| 15.10.75 | Holland Neeskens, Geels, Thijssen | 3 | Poland | 0 |
| 22.11.75 | Italy Capello | 1 | Holland | 0 |

*Holland qualify for quarter-finals as winners of Group 5.*

*Quarter-final*

| 25.4.76 | Holland Risbergen, Rensenbrink (3), Neeskens (pen) | 5 | Belgium | 0 |
| 22.5.76 | Belgium Van Gool | 1 | Holland Rep, Cruyff | 2 |

*Holland qualify for semi-finals, 7-1 on aggregate.*

*Semi-final, in Yugoslavia*

| 16.6.76 | Czechoslovakia Ondrus, Nehoda, Moder | 3 | Holland Ondrus (og) | 1 |

*After extra time.*

*Third-place play-off*

| 19.6.76 | Holland | 3 | Yugoslavia | 2 |
|---|---|---|---|---|
| | Geels (2), W. van der Kerkhoff | | Katalinski, Dzajic | |

*After extra time.*

**1978-80**

*Group 4*

| 20.9.78 | Holland | 3 | Iceland | 0 |
|---|---|---|---|---|
| | Krol, Brandts, Rensenbrink | | | |
| 11.10.78 | Switzerland | 1 | Holland | 3 |
| | Tanner | | Wildschut, Brandts, Geels | |
| 15.11.78 | Holland | 3 | East Germany | 0 |
| | Kische (og), Geels (2, 1 pen) | | | |
| 28.3.79 | Holland | 3 | Switzerland | 0 |
| | Kist, Metgod, Peters | | | |
| 2.5.79 | Poland | 2 | Holland | 0 |
| | Boniek, Mazur (pen) | | | |
| 5.9.79 | Iceland | 0 | Holland | 4 |
| | | | Metgod, W. van der Kerkhoff, Nanninga (2) | |
| 17.10.79 | Holland | 1 | Poland | 1 |
| | Stevens | | Rudy | |
| 21.11.79 | East Germany | 2 | Holland | 3 |
| | Schnupase, Streich (pen) | | Thijssen, Kist, R. van der Kerkhoff | |

*Holland qualify for finals as winners of Group 4.*

*Final Group 1, in Italy*

| 11.6.80 | Holland | 1 | Greece | 0 |
|---|---|---|---|---|
| | Kist (pen) | | | |
| 14.6.80 | West Germany | 3 | Holland | 2 |
| | Aloffs (3) | | Rep (pen), W. van der Kerkhoff | |
| 17.6.80 | Czechoslovakia | 1 | Holland | 1 |
| | Nehoda | | Kist | |

*West Germany qualify for final, Holland third in Group 1.*

**1982-84**

*Group 7*

| 1.9.82 | Iceland | 1 | Holland | 1 |
|---|---|---|---|---|
| | Edvaldsson | | Schoenaker | |
| 22.9.82 | Holland | 2 | Rep of Ireland | 1 |
| | Schoenaker, Gullit | | Daly | |
| 18.12.82 | Malta | 0 | Holland | 6 |
| | | | Ophof (pen), Van Kooten (2), Hovenkamp, Schoenaker (2) | |
| 17.2.83 | Spain | 1 | Holland | 0 |
| | Senior (pen) | | | |
| 7.9.83 | Holland | 3 | Iceland | 0 |
| | R. Koeman, Gullit, Houtman | | | |
| 12.10.83 | Rep of Ireland | 2 | Holland | 3 |
| | Waddock, Brady (pen) | | Gullit (2), Van Basten | |

| 16.11.83 | Holland | 2 | Spain | 1 |
| | Houtman, Gullit | | Santillana | |
| 17.12.83 | Holland | 5 | Malta | 0 |
| | Vanenburg, Wijnstekers, | | | |
| | Rijkaard (2), Houtman | | | |

*Spain qualify for finals having scored more goals than Holland.*

## 1986-88

### Group 5

| 15.10.86 | Hungary | 0 | Holland | 1 |
| | | | Van Basten | |
| 19.11.86 | Holland | 0 | Poland | 0 |
| 21.12.86 | Cyprus | 0 | Holland | 2 |
| | | | Gullit, Bosman | |
| 25.3.87 | Holland | 1 | Greece | 1 |
| | Van Basten | | Saravakos | |
| 29.4.87 | Holland | 2 | Hungary | 0 |
| | Gullit, Muhren | | | |
| 14.10.87 | Poland | 0 | Holland | 2 |
| | | | Gullit (2) | |
| 9.12.87* | Holland | 4 | Cyprus | 0 |
| | Bosman (3), R. Koeman (pen) | | | |
| 16.12.87 | Greece | 0 | Holland | 3 |
| | | | R. Koeman, Gilhaus (2) | |

*Holland beat Cyprus 8-0 on 28 October 1987, but the match was ordered to be replayed after the Cyprus goalkeeper was injured when something was thrown from the crowd.

*Holland qualify for finals as winners of Group 5*

### Final Group 2, in West Germany

| 12.6.88 | Holland | 0 | USSR | 1 |
| | | | Rats | |
| 15.6.88 | England | 1 | Holland | 3 |
| | Robson | | Van Basten (3) | |
| 18.6.88 | Rep of Ireland | 0 | Holland | 1 |
| | | | Kieft | |

*USSR and Holland qualify for semi-finals.*

### Semi-final

| 21.6.88 | West Germany | 1 | Holland | 2 |
| | Matthaus (pen) | | R. Koeman (pen), Van Basten | |

### Final

| 25.6.88 | Holland | 2 | USSR | 0 |
| | Gullit, Van Basten | | | |

## 1990-92

### Group 6

| 17.10.90 | Portugal | 1 | Holland | 0 |
| | Rui Aguas | | | |
| 21.11.90 | Holland | 2 | Greece | 0 |
| | Bergkamp, Van Basten | | | |
| 19.12.90 | Malta | 0 | Holland | 8 |
| | | | Van Basten (5, 1 pen), Winter, | |
| | | | Bergkamp (2) | |

236

| 13.3.91 | Holland | 1 | Malta | 0 |
| | Van Basten (pen) | | | |
| 17.4.91 | Holland | 2 | Finland | 0 |
| | Van Basten, Gullit | | | |
| 5.6.91 | Finland | 1 | Holland | 1 |
| | Holmgren | | De Boer | |
| 16.10.91 | Holland | 1 | Portugal | 0 |
| | Witschge | | | |
| 4.12.91 | Greece | 0 | Holland | 2 |
| | | | Bergkamp, Blind | |

*Holland qualify for finals as winners of Group 6.*

**1990-92**

*Final Group 2, in Sweden*

| 12.6.92 | Holland | 1 | Scotland | 0 |
| | Bergkamp | | | |
| 15.6.92 | Holland | 0 | CIS | 0 |
| 18.6.92 | Holland | 3 | Germany | 1 |
| | Rijkaard, Witschge, Bergkamp | | Klinsmann | |

*Holland and Germany qualify for semi-finals.*

*Semi-final*

| 22.6.92 | Holland | 2 | Denmark | 2 |
| | Bergkamp, Rijkaard | | Larsen (2) | |

*After extra time.*

*Denmark won 5-4 on penalties.*

For details on how Holland qualified for Euro 96, see pages 38-41 and 53.


# SCOTLAND

**1958-60**

Did not participate

**1962-64**

Did not participate

**1966-68**

*Group 8*

| 22.10.66 | Wales | 1 | Scotland | 1 |
| | R. Davies | | Law | |
| 16.11.66 | Scotland | 2 | Northern Ireland | 1 |
| | Murdoch, Lennox | | Nicholson | |
| 15.4.67 | England | 2 | Scotland | 3 |
| | Hurst, J. Charlton | | McCalliog, Law, Lennox | |
| 21.10.67 | Northern Ireland | 1 | Scotland | 0 |
| | Clements | | | |
| 22.11.67 | Scotland | 3 | Wales | 2 |
| | Gilzean (2), McKinnon | | R. Davies, Durban | |
| 24.2.68 | Scotland | 1 | England | 1 |
| | Hughes | | Peters | |

*England qualify for quarter-finals, Scotland second in Group 8.*

**1970-72**

*Group 5*

| | | | | |
|---|---|---|---|---|
| 11.11.70 | Scotland<br>O'Hare | 1 | Denmark | 0 |
| 3.2.71 | Belgium | 3 | Scotland | 0 |
| 21.4.71 | Portugal<br>Own goal, Eusebio | 2 | Scotland | 0 |
| 9.6.71 | Denmark<br>F. Laudrup | 1 | Scotland | 0 |
| 13.10.71 | Scotland<br>O'Hare, Gemmill | 2 | Portugal<br>Rui Rodrigues | 1 |
| 10.11.71 | Scotland<br>O'Hare | 1 | Belgium | 0 |

*Belgium qualify for quarter-finals, Scotland third in Group 5.*

**1974-76**

*Group 4*

| | | | | |
|---|---|---|---|---|
| 20.11.74 | Scotland<br>Bremner | 1 | Spain<br>Claramunt (pen), R. Martinez | 2 |
| 5.2.75 | Spain<br>Megido | 1 | Scotland<br>Jordan | 1 |
| 1.6.75 | Romania<br>Georgescu | 1 | Scotland<br>McQueen | 1 |
| 3.9.75 | Denmark | 0 | Scotland<br>Harper | 1 |
| 29.10.75 | Scotland<br>Rioch, Dalglish, MacDougall | 3 | Denmark<br>Bastrup | 1 |
| 17.12.75 | Scotland<br>Rioch | 1 | Romania<br>Crisan | 1 |

*Spain qualify for quarter-finals, Scotland third in Group 4.*

**1978-80**

*Group 2*

| | | | | |
|---|---|---|---|---|
| 20.9.78 | Austria<br>Pezzey, Schachner, Kreuz | 3 | Scotland<br>McQueen, A. Gray | 2 |
| 25.10.78 | Scotland<br>Dalglish (2), Gemmill (pen) | 3 | Norway<br>Aas, Larsen-Okland | 2 |
| 29.11.78 | Portugal<br>Alberto | 1 | Scotland | 0 |
| 7.6.79 | Norway | 0 | Scotland<br>Jordan, Dalglish, Robertson,<br>McQueen | 4 |
| 17.10.79 | Scotland<br>Gemmill | 1 | Austria<br>Krankl | 1 |
| 21.11.79 | Belgium<br>Van der Elst, Voordeckers | 2 | Scotland | 0 |
| 19.12.79 | Scotland<br>Robertson | 1 | Belgium<br>Van den Burgh,<br>Van der Elst (2) | 3 |
| 26.3.80 | Scotland<br>Dalglish, Gray, Archibald,<br>Gemmill (pen) | 4 | Portugal<br>Gomes | 1 |

*Belgium qualify for finals, Scotland fourth in Group 2.*

**1982-84**

*Group 1*

| | | | | |
|---|---|---|---|---|
| 13.10.82 | Scotland<br>Wark, Sturrock | 2 | East Germany | 0 |
| 17.11.82 | Switzerland<br>Sulser, Egli | 2 | Scotland | 0 |
| 15.12.82 | Belgium<br>Van den Burgh, Van der Elst (2) | 3 | Scotland<br>Dalglish (2) | 2 |
| 30.3.83 | Scotland<br>Wark, Nicholas | 2 | Switzerland<br>Egli, Heinz Hermann | 2 |
| 12.10.83 | Scotland<br>Nicholas | 1 | Belgium<br>Vercauteren | 1 |
| 16.11.83 | East Germany<br>Kreer, Streich | 2 | Scotland<br>Bannon | 1 |

*Belgium qualify for finals, Scotland last in Group 1.*

**1986-88**

*Group 7*

| | | | | |
|---|---|---|---|---|
| 10.9.86 | Scotland | 0 | Bulgaria | 0 |
| 15.10.86 | Rep of Ireland | 0 | Scotland | 0 |
| 12.11.86 | Scotland<br>Cooper (2, 1 pen), Johnston | 3 | Luxembourg | 0 |
| 18.2.87 | Scotland | 0 | Rep of Ireland<br>Lawrenson | 1 |
| 1.4.87 | Belgium<br>Claessen (3), Vercauteren | 4 | Scotland<br>McStay | 1 |
| 14.10.87 | Scotland<br>McCoist, McStay | 2 | Belgium | 0 |
| 11.11.87 | Bulgaria | 0 | Scotland<br>Mackay | 1 |
| 2.12.87 | Luxembourg | 0 | Scotland | 0 |

*Republic of Ireland qualify for finals, Scotland fourth in Group 7.*

**1990-92**

*Group 2*

| | | | | |
|---|---|---|---|---|
| 12.9.90 | Scotland<br>Robertson, McCoist | 2 | Romania<br>Camataru | 1 |
| 17.10.90 | Scotland<br>Robertson, McAllister | 2 | Switzerland<br>Knup | 1 |
| 14.11.90 | Bulgaria<br>Todorov | 1 | Scotland<br>McCoist | 1 |
| 27.3.91 | Scotland<br>Collins | 1 | Bulgaria<br>Kostadinov | 1 |
| 1.5.91 | San Marino | 0 | Scotland<br>Strachan (pen), Durie | 2 |
| 11.9.91 | Switzerland<br>Chaupuisat, Hermann | 2 | Scotland<br>Durie, McCoist | 2 |
| 16.10.91 | Romania<br>Hagi (pen) | 1 | Scotland | 0 |
| 13.11.91 | Scotland<br>McStay, Gough, Durie, McCoist | 4 | San Marino | 0 |

*Scotland qualify for finals as winners of Group 2.*

| 12.6.92 | Holland<br>Bergkamp | 1 | Scotland | 0 |
| 15.6.92 | Scotland | 0 | Germany<br>Riedle, Effenberg | 2 |
| 18.6.92 | Scotland<br>McStay, McClair, McAllister (pen) | 3 | CIS | 0 |

*Holland and Germany qualify for semi-finals, Scotland third in Group 2.*

For details on how Scotland qualified for Euro 96, see pages 50-53.

# GROUP B

# SPAIN

**1958-60**

*First round*

| 28.6.58 | Poland<br>Pol, Brychczy | 2 | Spain<br>Suarez (2), De Stefano (2) | 4 |
| 14.10.58 | Spain<br>Gensana, De Stefano, Gento | 3 | Poland | 0 |

*Spain qualify for quarter-finals, 7-2 on aggregate.*

*Quarter-finals*

| | Spain | | USSR | |

*Spain withdrew.*

**1962-64**

*First round*

| 1.11.62 | Spain<br>Guillot (3), Veloso, Collar,<br>own goal | 6 | Romania | 0 |
| 25.11.62 | Romania<br>Tataru, Manolache, Constantin | 3 | Spain<br>Veloso | 1 |

*Spain qualify for second round, 7-3 on aggregate.*

*Second round*

| 30.5.63 | Spain<br>Amancio | 1 | Northern Ireland<br>Irvine | 1 |
| 30.10.63 | Northern Ireland | 0 | Spain<br>Gento | 1 |

*Spain qualify for quarter-finals, 2-1 on aggregate.*

*Quarter-final*

| 11.3.64 | Spain<br>Amancio (2), Marcelino (2),<br>Fuste | 5 | Rep of Ireland<br>McEvoy | 1 |
| 8.4.64 | Rep of Ireland | 0 | Spain<br>Zaballa (2) | 2 |

*Spain qualify for semi-finals, 7-1 on aggregate.*

*Semi-finals in Spain*

| 17.6.64 | Spain | 2 | Hungary | 1 |
|---|---|---|---|---|
| | Pereda, Amancio | | Bene | |

*Final*

| 21.6.64 | Spain | 2 | USSR | 1 |
|---|---|---|---|---|
| | Pereda, Marcelino | | Khusainov | |

## 1966-68

*Group 1*

| 23.10.66 | Rep of Ireland | 0 | Spain | 0 |
|---|---|---|---|---|
| 7.12.66 | Spain | 2 | Rep of Ireland | 0 |
| | Pirri, Jose Maria | | | |
| 1.3.67 | Turkey | 0 | Spain | 0 |
| 31.5.67 | Spain | 2 | Turkey | 0 |
| | Grosso, Gento | | | |
| 1.10.67 | Czechoslovakia | 1 | Spain | 0 |
| | Horvath | | | |
| 22.10.67 | Spain | 2 | Czechoslovakia | 1 |
| | Pirri, Garate | | Kuna | |

*Spain qualify for quarter-finals as winners of Group 1.*

*Quarter-final*

| 3.4.68 | England | 1 | Spain | 0 |
|---|---|---|---|---|
| | R. Charlton | | | |
| 8.5.68 | Spain | 1 | England | 2 |
| | Amancio | | Peters, Hunter | |

*Spain knocked out, 3-1 on aggregate.*

## 1970-72

| 11.11.70 | Spain | 3 | Northern Ireland | 0 |
|---|---|---|---|---|
| | Rexach, Pirri, Luis | | | |
| 9.5.71 | Cyprus | 0 | Spain | 2 |
| | | | Pirri, Violeta | |
| 30.5.71 | USSR | 2 | Spain | 1 |
| | Kolotov, Shevchenko | | Rexach | |
| 27.10.71 | Spain | 0 | USSR | 0 |
| 24.11.71 | Spain | 7 | Cyprus | 0 |
| | Pirri (2), Quino (2), Aguilar, | | | |
| | Lora Rojo | | | |
| 16.2.72 | Northern Ireland | 1 | Spain | |
| | Morgan | | Rojo | |

*USSR qualify for quarter-finals, Spain second in Group 4.*

## 1974-76

*Group 4*

| 25.9.74 | Denmark | 1 | Spain | 2 |
|---|---|---|---|---|
| | Nygaard (pen) | | Claramunt (pen), | |
| | | | R. Martinez | |
| 20.11.74 | Scotland | 1 | Spain | 2 |
| | Bremner | | Quini (2) | |
| 5.2.75 | Spain | 1 | Scotland | 1 |
| | Megido | | Jordan | |

| 17.4.75 | Spain | 1 | Romania | 1 |
| | Velasquez | | Crisan | |
| 12.10.75 | Spain | 2 | Denmark | 0 |
| | Pirri, Capon | | | |
| 16.11.75 | Romania | 2 | Spain | 2 |
| | Georgescu (pen), Iordanescu | | Villar, Santillana | |

*Spain qualify for quarter-finals as winners of Group 4.*

*Quarter-finals*

| 24.4.76 | Spain | 1 | West Germany | 1 |
| | Santillana | | Beer | |
| 22.5.76 | West Germany | 2 | Spain | 0 |
| | Hoeness, Toppmoller | | | |

*Spain knocked out, 3-1 on aggregate.*

## 1978-80

*Group 3*

| 4.10.78 | Yugoslavia | 1 | Spain | 2 |
| | Halilhodzic | | Juanito, Santillana | |
| 15.11.78 | Spain | 1 | Romania | 0 |
| | Asensi | | | |
| 13.12.78 | Spain | 5 | Cyprus | 0 |
| | Asensi, Del Bosque, | | | |
| | Santillana (2), R. Cano | | | |
| 4.4.79 | Romania | 2 | Spain | 2 |
| | Georgescu (2, 1 pen) | | Dani (2) | |
| 10.10.79 | Spain | 0 | Yugoslavia | 1 |
| | | | Surjak | |
| 9.12.79 | Cyprus | 1 | Spain | 3 |
| | Vrahimis | | Villar, Santillana, Saura | |

*Spain qualify for finals as winners of Group 3.*

*Final Group 2, in Italy*

| 12.6.80 | Italy | 0 | Spain | 0 |
| 15.6.80 | Belgium | 2 | Spain | 1 |
| | Gerets, Cools | | Quini | |
| 18.6.80 | England | 2 | Spain | 1 |
| | Brooking, Woodcock | | Dani (pen) | |

*Italy and Belgium qualify for semi-finals, Spain fourth in Group 2.*

## 1982-84

*Group 7*

| 27.10.82 | Spain | 1 | Iceland | 0 |
| | Pedraza | | | |
| 17.11.82 | Rep of Ireland | 3 | Spain | 3 |
| | Grimes, Stapleton (2) | | Maceda, own goal, Victor | |
| 16.02.83 | Spain | 1 | Holland | 0 |
| | Senor (pen) | | | |
| 27.4.83 | Spain | 2 | Rep of Ireland | 0 |
| | Santillana, Rincon | | | |
| 15.5.83 | Malta | 2 | Spain | 3 |
| | Busuttil (2) | | Senor, Carrasco, Gordillo | |
| 29.5.83 | Iceland | 0 | Spain | 1 |
| | | | Maceda | |

| 16.11.83 | Holland | 2 | Spain | 1 |
| | Moutman, Gullit | | Santillana | |
| 21.12.83 | Spain | 12 | Malta | 1 |
| | Santillana (4), Rincon (4), | | Demanuele | |
| | Maceda (2), Sarabia, Senor | | | |

*Spain qualify for finals as winners of Group 7.*

*Final Group 2, in France*

| 14.6.84 | Romania | 1 | Spain | 1 |
| | Boloni | | Carrasco (pen) | |
| 17.6.84 | Portugal | 1 | Spain | 1 |
| | Sousa | | Santillana | |
| 20.6.84 | West Germany | 0 | Spain | 1 |
| | | | Maceda | |

*Spain and Portugal qualify for semi-finals.*

*Semi-final*

| 24.6.84 | Denmark | 1 | Spain | 1 |
| | Lerby | | Maceda | |

*After extra time.*

*Spain won 5-4 on penalties.*

*Final*

| 27.6.84 | France | 2 | Spain | 0 |
| | Platini, Bellone | | | |

**1986-88**

*Group 1*

| 12.11.86 | Spain | 1 | Romania | 0 |
| | Michel | | | |
| 3.12.86 | Albania | 1 | Spain | 2 |
| | Muca | | Arteche, Joaquin | |
| 1.4.87 | Austria | 2 | Spain | 3 |
| | Linzmaier, Polster | | Eloy (2), Carrasco | |
| 29.4.87 | Romania | 3 | Spain | 1 |
| | Piturca, Mateut, Ungureanu | | Caldere | |
| 14.10.87 | Spain | 2 | Austria | 0 |
| | Michel (pen), Sanchis | | | |
| 18.11.87 | Spain | 5 | Albania | 0 |
| | Bakero (3), Michel (pen), | | | |
| | Llorente | | | |

*Spain qualify for finals as winners of Group 1.*

*Final Group 1, in West Germany*

| 11.6.88 | Denmark | 2 | Spain | 3 |
| | M. Laudrup, Povlsen | | Michel, Butragueno, | |
| | | | Gordillo | |
| 14.6.88 | Italy | 1 | Spain | 0 |
| | Vialli | | | |
| 17.6.88 | West Germany | 2 | Spain | 0 |
| | Voller (2) | | | |

*West Germany and Italy qualify for semi-finals, Spain third in Group 1.*

**1990-92**

*Group 1*

| | | | | |
|---|---|---|---|---|
| 10.10.90 | Spain | 2 | Iceland | 1 |
| | Butragueno, Carlos | | Si. Jonsson | |
| 14.11.90 | Czechoslovakia | 3 | Spain | 2 |
| | Danek (2), Moravcik | | Roberto, Carlos | |
| 19.12.90 | Spain | 9 | Albania | 0 |
| | Butragueno (4), Carlos (2), | | | |
| | Amor, Hierro, Bakero | | | |
| 20.2.91 | France | 3 | Spain | 1 |
| | Sauzee, Papin, Blanc | | Bakero | |
| 25.9.91 | Iceland | 2 | Spain | 0 |
| | Orlygsson, Sverrisson | | | |
| 12.10.91 | Spain | 1 | France | 2 |
| | Abelardo | | Fernandez, Papin | |
| 13.11.91 | Spain | 2 | Czechoslovakia | 1 |
| | Abelardo, Michel (pen) | | Nemecek | |
| | Albania | | Spain | |

*Match cancelled.*

*France qualify for finals, Spain third in Group 1.*

For details on how Spain qualified for Euro 96, see pages 27-30.

# BULGARIA
**1958-60**

*First round*

| | | | | |
|---|---|---|---|---|
| 31.5.59 | Yugoslavia | 2 | Bulgaria | 0 |
| | Galic, Tasic | | | |
| 25.10.59 | Bulgaria | 1 | Yugoslavia | 1 |
| | Diev | | Mujic | |

*Bulgaria knocked out, 3-1 on aggregate.*

**1962-64**

*First round*

| | | | | |
|---|---|---|---|---|
| 7.11.62 | Bulgaria | 3 | Portugal | 1 |
| | G. Asparoukhov (2), Diev | | Eusebio | |
| 16.12.62 | Portugal | 3 | Bulgaria | 1 |
| | Hernani (2), Coluna | | C. Iliev | |

*Replay*

| | | | | |
|---|---|---|---|---|
| 23.1.63 | Bulgaria | 1 | Portugal | 0 |
| | G. Asparoukhov | | | |

*Second round*

| | | | | |
|---|---|---|---|---|
| 29.10.63 | Bulgaria | 1 | France | 0 |
| | Diev | | | |
| 26.10.63 | France | 3 | Bulgaria | 1 |
| | Goujon (2), Herbin | | Yakimov | |

*Bulgaria knocked out, 3-2 on aggregate.*

**1966-68**

*Group 2*

| | | | | |
|---|---|---|---|---|
| 13.11.66 | Bulgaria<br>Jekov (2), Tzanev (2) | 4 | Norway<br>Hasund (2) | 2 |
| 11.6.67 | Sweden | 0 | Bulgaria<br>Dermendjiev, Jekov | 2 |
| 29.6.67 | Norway | 0 | Bulgaria | 0 |
| 12.11.67 | Bulgaria<br>Mitkov, Kotkov, Asparoukhov | 3 | Sweden | 0 |
| 26.11.67 | Bulgaria<br>Dermendjiev | 1 | Portugal | 0 |
| 17.12.67 | Portugal | 0 | Bulgaria | 0 |

*Bulgaria qualify for quarter-finals as winners of Group 2.*

*Quarter-final*

| | | | | |
|---|---|---|---|---|
| 6.4.68 | Bulgaria<br>Dermendjiev, Kotkov, Jekov | 3 | Italy<br>Own goal, Prati | 2 |
| 20.4.68 | Italy<br>Prati, Domenghini | 2 | Bulgaria | 0 |

*Bulgaria knocked out, 4-3 on aggregate.*

**1970-72**

*Group 2*

| | | | | |
|---|---|---|---|---|
| 15.11.70 | Bulgaria<br>Atanasov | 1 | Norway<br>Fuglset | 1 |
| 19.5.71 | Bulgaria<br>Petkov, B. Kolev, Velitchkov | 3 | Hungary | 0 |
| 9.6.71 | Norway<br>Iversen | 1 | Bulgaria<br>Vasilev, Jekov, Bonev (2, 1 pen) | 4 |
| 25.9.71 | Hungary<br>Vidats, Juhasz | 2 | Bulgaria | 0 |
| 10.11.71 | France<br>Loubet, Lech | 2 | Bulgaria<br>Bonev (pen) | 1 |
| 4.12.71 | Bulgaria<br>Michailov, Jekov | 2 | France<br>Blanchet | 1 |

*Hungary qualify for quarter-finals, Bulgaria second in Group 2.*

**1974-76**

*Group 8*

| | | | | |
|---|---|---|---|---|
| 13.10.74 | Bulgaria<br>Bonev, Denev (2) | 3 | Greece<br>Antoniadis, Papaioannou,<br>Glezos | 3 |
| 18.12.74 | Greece<br>Sarafis, Antoniadis | 2 | Bulgaria<br>Kolev | 1 |
| 27.4.75 | Bulgaria<br>Kolev (pen) | 1 | West Germany<br>Ritschel (pen) | 1 |
| 11.6.75 | Bulgaria<br>Dimitrov, Denev, Panov,<br>Bonev, Milanov | 5 | Malta | 0 |
| 19.11.75 | West Germany<br>Heynckes | 1 | Bulgaria | 0 |
| 21.12.75 | Malta | 0 | Bulgaria<br>Panov, Iordanov | 2 |

*West Germany qualify for quarter-finals, Bulgaria third in Group 8.*

**1978-80**

*Group 1*

| | | | | |
|---|---|---|---|---|
| 11.10.78 | Denmark<br>B. Nielsen, Lerby | 2 | Bulgaria<br>Panov, Iliev | 2 |
| 29.11.78 | Bulgaria | 0 | Northern Ireland<br>Armstrong, Caskey | 2 |
| 2.5.1979 | Northern Ireland<br>C. Nicholl, Armstrong | 2 | Bulgaria | 0 |
| 19.5.79 | Bulgaria<br>Tsvetkov | 1 | Rep of Ireland | 0 |
| 6.6.79 | Bulgaria | 0 | England<br>Keegan, Watson, Barnes | 3 |
| 17.10.79 | Rep of Ireland<br>Martin, Grealish, Stapleton | 3 | Bulgaria | 0 |
| 31.10.79 | Bulgaria<br>Kostadinov, Tsvetkov (2) | 3 | Denmark | 0 |
| 22.11.79 | England<br>Watson, Hoddle | 2 | Bulgaria | 0 |

*England qualify for finals, Bulgaria fourth in Group 1*

**1982-84**

*Group 4*

| | | | | |
|---|---|---|---|---|
| 27.10.82 | Bulgaria<br>Velitchkov, Nikolov | 2 | Norway<br>Thoresen (pen), Larsen-Okland | 2 |
| 17.11.82 | Bulgaria | 0 | Yugoslavia<br>Stojkovic | 1 |
| 27.3.83 | Wales<br>J. Charles | 1 | Bulgaria | 0 |
| 7.9.83 | Norway<br>Hareide | 1 | Bulgaria<br>Mladenov, Sirakov | 2 |
| 16.11.83 | Bulgaria<br>Gochev | 1 | Wales | 0 |
| 21.12.83 | Yugoslavia<br>Susic (2), Radanovic | 3 | Bulgaria<br>Iskrenov, Dimitrov | 2 |

*Yugoslavia qualify for finals, Bulgaria third in Group 4.*

**1986-88**

*Group 7*

| | | | | |
|---|---|---|---|---|
| 10.9.86 | Scotland | 0 | Bulgaria | 0 |
| 19.11.86 | Belgium<br>Janssen | 1 | Bulgaria<br>Tanev | 1 |
| 1.4.87 | Bulgaria<br>Sadkov, Tanev (pen) | 2 | Rep of Ireland<br>Stapleton | 1 |
| 30.4.87 | Luxembourg<br>Langers | 1 | Bulgaria<br>Sadkov, Sirakov, Tanev, Kolev | 4 |
| 20.5.87 | Bulgaria<br>Sirakov, Iordanov (pen), Kolev | 3 | Luxembourg | 0 |
| 23.9.87 | Bulgaria<br>Sirakov, Tanev | 2 | Belgium | 0 |
| 14.10.87 | Rep of Ireland<br>McGrath, Moran | 2 | Bulgaria | 0 |
| 11.11.87 | Bulgaria | 0 | Scotland<br>Mackay | 1 |

*Rep of Ireland qualify for finals, Bulgaria second in Group 7*

**1990-92**

*Group 2*

| | | | | |
|---|---|---|---|---|
| 20.9.90 | Switzerland<br>Hottiger, Bickel | 2 | Bulgaria | 0 |
| 17.10.90 | Romania | 0 | Bulgaria<br>Sirakov, N. Todorov (2) | 3 |
| 14.11.90 | Bulgaria<br>N. Todorov | 1 | Scotland<br>McCoist | 1 |
| 27.3.91 | Scotland<br>Collins | 1 | Bulgaria<br>Kostadinov | 1 |
| 1.5.91 | Bulgaria<br>Kostadinov, Sirakov | 2 | Switzerland<br>Knup (2), Turkyilmaz | 3 |
| 22.5.91 | San Marino | 0 | Bulgaria<br>Ivanov, Sirakov, Penev (pen) | 3 |
| 16.10.91 | Bulgaria<br>Own goal, Stoichkov (pen),<br>Yankov, Iliev | 4 | San Marino | 0 |
| 20.11.91 | Bulgaria<br>Sirakov | 1 | Romania<br>A. Popescu | 1 |

*Scotland qualify for finals, Bulgaria fourth in Group 2.*

For details on how Bulgaria qualified for Euro 96, see pages 46-9.

# ROMANIA
**1958-60**

*First round*

| | | | | |
|---|---|---|---|---|
| 2.11.58 | Romania<br>Constantin, Oiada, Dinulescu | 3 | Turkey | 0 |
| 26.4.59 | Turkey<br>Lefter (2, 1 pen) | 2 | Rómania | 0 |

*Romania qualify for quarter-finals, 3-2 on aggregate.*

*Quarter-final*

| | | | | |
|---|---|---|---|---|
| 22.5.60 | Romania | 0 | Czechoslovakia<br>Masopust, Bubnik | 2 |
| 29.5.60 | Czechoslovakia<br>Bubernik (2), Bubnik | 3 | Romania | 0 |

*Romania knocked out, 5-0 on aggregate.*

**1962-64**

*First round*

| | | | | |
|---|---|---|---|---|
| 1.11.62 | Spain<br>Guillot (3), Veloso, Collar,<br>own goal | 6 | Romania | 0 |
| 25.11.62 | Romania<br>Tataru, Manolache, Constantin | 3 | Spain<br>Veloso | 1 |

*Romania knocked out, 7-3 on aggregate.*

## 1966-68

### Group 6

| | | | | |
|---|---|---|---|---|
| 2.11.66 | Romania<br>Dridea, Fratila (3) | 4 | Switzerland<br>Kunzli, Odermatt | 2 |
| 26.11.66 | Italy<br>Mazzola, De Paoli | 3 | Romania<br>Dobrin | 1 |
| 3.12.66 | Cyprus<br>Kostakis | 1 | Romania<br>Dridea (2), Lucescu,<br>Fratila (2) | 5 |
| 23.4.67 | Romania<br>Lucescu, Martinovici,<br>Dumitriu (3), Ionescu (2) | 7 | Cyprus | 0 |
| 24.5.67 | Switzerland<br>Kunzli (2), Quentin (2),<br>Blattler (2), Odermatt | 7 | Romania<br>Dobrin | 1 |
| 25.6.67 | Romania | 0 | Italy<br>Bertini | 1 |

*Italy qualify for finals, Romania second in Group 6.*

## 1970-72

### Group 1

| | | | | |
|---|---|---|---|---|
| 11.10.70 | Romania<br>Dumitrache (2), Nunweiler | 3 | Finland | 0 |
| 11.11.70 | Wales | 0 | Romania | 0 |
| 16.5.71 | Czechoslovakia<br>Vesely | 1 | Romania | 0 |
| 22.9.71 | Finland | 0 | Romania<br>Iordanescu, Lupescu,<br>Dembrovschi, Lucescu (pen) | 4 |
| 14.11.71 | Romania<br>Dembrovschi, Lucescu | 2 | Czechoslovakia<br>Jan Capkovic | 1 |
| 24.11.71 | Romania<br>Lupescu, Lucescu | 2 | Wales | 0 |

*Romania qualify for quarter-finals as winners of Group 1.*

### Quarter-final

| | | | | |
|---|---|---|---|---|
| 29.4.72 | Hungary<br>Branikovits | 1 | Romania<br>Satmareanu | 1 |
| 14.5.72 | Romania<br>Dobrin, Neagu | 2 | Hungary<br>Szoke, Kocsis | 2 |

### Replay

| | | | | |
|---|---|---|---|---|
| 17.5.72 | Hungary<br>Kocsis, Szoke | 2 | Romania<br>Neagu | 1 |

## 1974-76

### Group 4

| | | | | |
|---|---|---|---|---|
| 13.10.74 | Denmark | 0 | Romania | 0 |
| 17.4.75 | Spain<br>Velasquez | 1 | Romania<br>Crisan | 1 |
| 11.5.75 | Romania<br>Georgescu (2), Crisan (2),<br>Lucescu, Dinu | 6 | Denmark<br>Dahl | 1 |

| 16.11.75 | Romania | 1 | Scotland | 1 |
| | Georgescu | | McQueen | |
| 16.11.75 | Romania | 2 | Spain | 2 |
| | Georgescu (pen), Iordanescu | | Villar, Santillana | |
| 17.12.75 | Scotland | 1 | Romania | 1 |
| | Rioch | | Crisan | |

*Spain qualify for quarter-finals, Romania second in Group 4.*

**1978-80**

*Group 3*

| 25.10.78 | Romania | 3 | Yugoslavia | 2 |
| | Sames (2), Iordanescu (pen) | | Petrovic, Desnica | |
| 15.11.78 | Spain | 1 | Romania | 0 |
| | Asensi | | | |
| 4.4.79 | Romania | 2 | Spain | 2 |
| | Georgescu (2, 1 pen) | | Dani (2) | |
| 13.5.79 | Cyprus | 1 | Romania | 1 |
| | Kaiafas | | Augustin | |
| 31.10.79 | Yugoslavia | 2 | Romania | 1 |
| | Zl. Vujovic, Sliskovic | | Raducanu | |
| 18.11.79 | Romania | 2 | Cyprus | 0 |
| | Multescu, Raducanu | | | |

*Spain qualify for finals, Romania third in Group 3.*

**1982-84**

*Group 5*

| 1.5.82 | Romania | 3 | Cyprus | 1 |
| | Vaetus, Camataru, Boloni | | Vrahmis | |
| 8.9.82 | Romania | 2 | Sweden | 0 |
| | Andone, Klein | | | |
| 4.12.82 | Italy | 0 | Romania | 0 |
| 16.4.83 | Romania | 1 | Italy | 0 |
| | Boloni | | | |
| 15.5.83 | Romania | 0 | Czechoslovakia | 1 |
| | | | L. Vizek | |
| 9.6.83 | Sweden | 0 | Romania | 1 |
| | | | Camataru | |
| 12.11.83 | Cyprus | 0 | Romania | 1 |
| | | | Boloni | |
| 30.11.83 | Czechoslovakia | 1 | Romania | 1 |
| | Luhovy | | Geolgau | |

*Romania qualify for finals as winners of Group 5.*

*Final Group 2, in France*

| 14.6.84 | Romania | 1 | Spain | 1 |
| | Boloni | | Carrasco | |
| 17.6.84 | West Germany | 2 | Romania | 1 |
| | Voller (2) | | Coras | |
| 20.6.84 | Portugal | 1 | Romania | 0 |
| | Nene | | | |

*Spain and Portugal qualify for semi-finals, Romania fourth in Group 2.*

249

**1986-88**

*Group 1*

| | | | | |
|---|---|---|---|---|
| 10.9.86 | Romania<br>Iovan (2), Lacatus, Hagi | 4 | Austria | 0 |
| 12.11.86 | Spain<br>Michel | 1 | Romania | 0 |
| 25.3.87 | Romania<br>Piturca, Boloni, Hagi,<br>Belodedici, Bumbescu | 5 | Albania<br>Muca | 1 |
| 29.4.87 | Romania<br>Piturca, Mateut, Ungureanu | 3 | Spain<br>Caldere | 1 |
| 28.10.87 | Albania | 0 | Romania<br>Klein | 1 |
| 18.11.87 | Austria | 0 | Romania | 0 |

*Spain qualify for finals, Romania second in Group 1.*

**1990-92**

*Group 2*

| | | | | |
|---|---|---|---|---|
| 12.9.90 | Scotland<br>Robertson, McCoist | 2 | Romania<br>Camataru | 1 |
| 17.10.90 | Romania | 0 | Bulgaria<br>Sirakov, Todorov (2) | 3 |
| 5.12.90 | Romania<br>Sabau, Mateut, Raducioiu,<br>Lupescu, Badea, Petrescu | 6 | San Marino | 0 |
| 27.3.91 | San Marino<br>Pasolini (pen) | 1 | Romania<br>Hagi (pen), Raducioiu,<br>D. Timofte | 3 |
| 3.4.91 | Switzerland | 0 | Romania | 0 |
| 16.10.91 | Romania<br>Hagi (pen) | 1 | Scotland | 0 |
| 13.11.91 | Romania<br>Mateut | 1 | Switzerland | 0 |
| 20.11.91 | Bulgaria<br>Sirakov | 1 | Romania<br>A. Popescu | 1 |

*Scotland qualify for finals, Romania third in Group 2.*

For details on how Romania qualified for Euro 96, see pages 23-6.

# FRANCE

**1958-60**

*First round*

| | | | | |
|---|---|---|---|---|
| 1.10.58 | France<br>Kopa, Fontaine (2),<br>Cisowski (2), Vincent (2) | 7 | Greece<br>Ifantis | 1 |
| 3.12.58 | Greece<br>Papaemanuil | 1 | France<br>Bruey | 1 |

*France qualify for quarter-finals, 8-2 on aggregate*

*Quarter-final*

| 13.12.59 | France | 5 | Austria | 2 |
| | Fontaine (3), Vincent (2) | | Horak, Pichler | |
| 27.3.60 | Austria | 2 | France | 4 |
| | Nemec, Probst | | Marcel, Rahis, Heutte, | |
| | | | Kopa (pen) | |

*France qualify for semi-finals, 9-4 on aggregate.*

*Semi-final in France*

| 6.7.60 | France | 4 | Yugoslavia | 5 |
| | Vincent, Heutte (2), Wisnieski | | Galic, Zanetic, Knez, | |
| | | | Jerkovic (2) | |

*Third-place play-off*

| 9.7.60 | France | 0 | Czechoslovakia | 2 |
| | | | Bubnik, Pavlovic | |

## 1962-64

*First round*

| 20.10.62 | England | 1 | France | 1 |
| | Flowers (pen) | | Goujon | |
| 27.2.63 | France | 5 | England | 2 |
| | Wisnieski (2), Douis, Cossou (2) | | Smith, Tambling | |

*France qualify for second round, 6-3 on aggregate.*

*Second round*

| 29.10.63 | Bulgaria | 1 | France | 0 |
| | Diev | | | |
| 26.10.63 | France | 3 | Bulgaria | 1 |
| | Goujon (2), Herbin | | Yakimov | |

*France qualify for quarter-finals, 3-2 on aggregate.*

*Quarter-final*

| 25.4.64 | France | 1 | Hungary | 3 |
| | Cossou | | Albert, Tichy (2) | |
| 23.5.64 | Hungary | 2 | France | 1 |
| | Sipos, Bene | | Combin | |

*France knocked out, 5-2 on aggregate.*

## 1966-68

*Group 7*

| 22.10.66 | France | 2 | Poland | 1 |
| | Di Nallo, Lech | | Grzegorczyk | |
| 11.11.66 | Belgium | 2 | France | 1 |
| | Van Himst (2) | | Lech | |
| 26.11.66 | Luxembourg | 0 | France | 3 |
| | | | Herbet, Revelli, Lech | |
| 17.9.67 | Poland | 1 | France | 4 |
| | Brychczy | | Herbin, Di Nallo (2), Guy | |
| 28.10.67 | France | 1 | Belgium | 1 |
| | Herbin | | Claessen | |
| 23.12.67 | France | 3 | Luxembourg | 1 |
| | Loubet (3) | | J. Klein | |

*France qualify for quarter-finals as winners of Group 7.*

251

*Quarter-final*

| | | | | |
|---|---|---|---|---|
| 6.4.68 | France | 1 | Yugoslavia | 1 |
| | Di Nallo | | Musemic | |
| 24.4.68 | Yugoslavia | 5 | France | 1 |
| | Petkovic (2), Musemic (2), Dzajic | | Di Nallo | |

*France knocked out, 6-2 on aggregate.*

## 1970-72

*Group 2*

| | | | | |
|---|---|---|---|---|
| 11.11.70 | France | 3 | Norway | 1 |
| | Floch, Lech, Mezy | | Nielsen | |
| 24.4.71 | Hungary | 1 | France | 1 |
| | Kocsis (pen) | | P. Revelli | |
| 8.9.71 | Norway | 1 | France | 3 |
| | Olsen | | Vergnes, Loubet, Blanchet | |
| 9.10.71 | France | 0 | Hungary | 2 |
| | | | Bene, Zambo | |
| 10.11.71 | France | 2 | Bulgaria | 1 |
| | Lech, Loubet | | Bonev (pen) | |
| 4.12.71 | Bulgaria | 2 | France | 1 |
| | Jekov, Michailov | | Blanchet | |

*Hungary qualify for quarter-finals, France third in Group 2.*

## 1974-76

*Group 7*

| | | | | |
|---|---|---|---|---|
| 12.10.74 | Belgium | 2 | France | 1 |
| | Martens, Van der Elst | | Coste | |
| 16.11.74 | France | 2 | East Germany | 2 |
| | Guillou, Gallice | | Sparwasser, Kreische | |
| 25.5.75 | Iceland | 0 | France | 0 |
| 3.9.75 | France | 3 | Iceland | 0 |
| | Guillou (2), Berdoll | | | |
| 12.10.75 | East Germany | 2 | France | 1 |
| | Streich, Vogel | | Bathenay | |
| 15.11.75 | France | 0 | Belgium | 0 |

*Belgium qualify for quarter-finals, France third in Group 7.*

## 1978-80

*Group 5*

| | | | | |
|---|---|---|---|---|
| 1.9.78 | France | 2 | Sweden | 2 |
| | Berdoll, Six | | Nordgren, Gronhagen | |
| 7.10.78 | Luxembourg | 1 | France | 3 |
| | Michaux | | Six, Tresor, Gemmrich | |
| 25.2.79 | France | 3 | Luxembourg | 0 |
| | Petit, Emon, Larios | | | |
| 4.2.79 | Czechoslovakia | 2 | France | 0 |
| | Panenka, Stambachr | | | |
| 5.9.79 | Sweden | 1 | France | 3 |
| | Backe | | Lacombe, Platini, | |
| | | | Battiston | |
| 17.11.79 | France | 2 | Czechoslovakia | 1 |
| | Pecout, Rampillon | | Kozak | |

*Czechoslovakia qualify for finals, France second in Group 5.*

**1982-84**

France qualify for finals as hosts.

*Final Group 1, in France*

| | | | | |
|---|---|---|---|---|
| 12.6.84 | France<br>Own goal | 1 | Denmark | 0 |
| 13.6.84 | France<br>Platini (3, 1 pen), Giresse,<br>Fernandez | 5 | Belgium | 0 |
| 19.6.84 | France<br>Platini (3) | 3 | Yugoslavia<br>Sestic, Stojkovic (pen) | 2 |

*France and Denmark qualify for semi-finals.*

*Semi-final*

| | | | | |
|---|---|---|---|---|
| 23.6.84 | France<br>Domergue (2), Platini | 3 | Portugal<br>Jordao (2) | 2 |

*Final*

| | | | | |
|---|---|---|---|---|
| 27.6.84 | France<br>Platini, Bellone | 2 | Spain | 0 |

**1986-88**

*Group 3*

| | | | | |
|---|---|---|---|---|
| 10.9.86 | Iceland | 0 | France | 0 |
| 11.10.86 | France | 0 | USSR<br>Belanov, Rats | 2 |
| 19.11.86 | East Germany | 0 | France | 0 |
| 29.4.87 | France<br>Micciche, Stopyra | 2 | Iceland | 0 |
| 16.6.87 | Norway<br>Mordt, Andersen | 2 | France | 0 |
| 9.9.87 | USSR<br>Mikhailichenko | 1 | France<br>Toure | 1 |
| 14.10.87 | France<br>Fargeon | 1 | Norway<br>Sundby | 1 |
| 18.11.87 | France | 0 | East Germany<br>Ernst | 1 |

*USSR qualify for finals, France third in Group 3.*

**1990-92**

*Group 1*

| | | | | |
|---|---|---|---|---|
| 5.9.90 | Iceland<br>Edvaaldsson | 1 | France<br>Papin, Cantona | 2 |
| 13.10.90 | France<br>Papin (2) | 2 | Czechoslovakia<br>Skuhravy | 1 |
| 17.11.90 | Albania | 0 | France<br>Boli | 1 |
| 20.2.91 | France<br>Sauzee, Papin, Blanc | 3 | Spain<br>Bakero | 1 |
| 30.3.91 | France<br>Sauzee (2), Papin (2, 1 pen),<br>own goal | 5 | Albania | 0 |
| 4.9.91 | Czechoslovakia<br>Nemecek | 1 | France<br>Papin (2) | 2 |

253

| 12.10.91 | Spain | 1 | France | 2 |
| | Abelardo | | Fernandez, Papin | |
| 20.11.91 | France | 3 | Iceland | 1 |
| | Simba, Cantona (2) | | Sverrisson | |

*France qualify for finals as winners of Group 1.*

*Final Group 1, in Sweden*

| 10.6.92 | Sweden | 1 | France | 1 |
| | J. Eriksson | | Papin | |
| 14.6.92 | England | 0 | France | 0 |
| 17.6.92 | France | 1 | Denmark | 2 |
| | Papin | | Larsen, Elstrup | |

*Sweden and Denmark qualify for semi-finals, France third in Group 1.*

For details on how France qualified for Euro 96, see pages 23-6.

# GROUP C

# GERMANY
As WEST GERMANY

**1958-60**

Did not participate

**1962-64**

Did not participate

**1966-68**

*Group 4*

| 8.4.67 | West Germany | 6 | Albania | 0 |
| | G. Muller (4), Lohr (2) | | | |
| 3.5.67 | Yugoslavia | 1 | West Germany | 0 |
| | Skoblar | | | |
| 7.10.67 | West Germany | 3 | Yugoslavia | 1 |
| | Seeler, G. Muller, Lohr | | Zambata | |
| 17.12.67 | Albania | 0 | West Germany | 0 |

*Yugoslavia qualify for quarter-finals, West Germany second in Group 4.*

**1970-72**

*Group 8*

| 17.10.70 | West Germany | 1 | Turkey | 1 |
| | G. Muller (pen) | | Kamuran | |
| 17.2.71 | Albania | 0 | West Germany | 1 |
| | | | G. Muller | |
| 25.4.71 | Turkey | 0 | West Germany | 3 |
| | | | G. Muller (2), Koppel | |
| 12.6.71 | West Germany | 2 | Albania | 0 |
| | Netzer, Grabowski | | | |
| 10.10.71 | Poland | 1 | West Germany | 3 |
| | Gadocha | | G. Muller (2), Grabowski | |
| 17.11.71 | West Germany | 0 | Poland | 0 |

*West Germany qualify for quarter-finals as winners of Group 8.*

*Quarter-final*

| 29.4.72 | England<br>Lee | 1 | West Germany<br>Netzer (pen), Hoeness,<br>G. Muller | 3 |
| 13.5.72 | West Germany | 0 | England | 0 |

*West Germany qualify for semi-finals, 3-1 on aggregate.*

*Semi-final, in Belgium*

| 14.6.72 | Belgium<br>Polleunis | 1 | West Germany<br>G. Muller (2) | 2 |

*Final*

| 18.6.72 | West Germany<br>G. Muller (2), Wimmer | 3 | USSR | 0 |

## 1974-76

### Group 8

| 20.11.74 | Greece<br>Delikaris, Eleftherakis | 2 | West Germany<br>Cullmann, Wimmer | 2 |
| 22.12.74 | Malta | 0 | West Germany<br>Cullmann | 1 |
| 27.4.75 | Bulgaria<br>Kolev (pen) | 1 | West Germany<br>Ritschel (pen) | 1 |
| 11.10.75 | West Germany<br>Keynckes | 1 | Greece<br>Delikaris | 1 |
| 19.11.75 | West Germany<br>Heynckes | 1 | Bulgaria | 0 |
| 28.2.76 | West Germany<br>Worm (2), Heynckes (2),<br>Vogts, Beer (2, 1 pen),<br>Holzenbein | 8 | Malta | 0 |

*West Germany qualify for quarter-finals as winners of Group 8.*

*Quarter-final*

| 24.4.76 | Spain<br>Santillana | 1 | West Germany<br>Beer (2) | 2 |
| 22.5.76 | West Germany<br>Hoeness, Toppmoller | 2 | Spain | 0 |

*West Germany qualify for semi-finals, 4-1 on aggregate.*

*Semi-finals, in Yugoslavia*

| 17.6.76 | Yugoslavia<br>Popivoda, Dzajic | 2 | West Germany<br>Flohe, D. Muller (3) | 4 |

*Final*

| 20.6.76 | Czechoslovakia<br>Svehlik, Dobias | 2 | West Germany<br>D. Muller, Holzenbein | 2 |

*After extra time.*

*Czechoslovakia won 5-3 on penalties.*

## 1978-80

### Group 7

| 25.2.79 | Malta | 0 | West Germany | 0 |
| 1.4.79 | Turkey | 0 | West Germany | 0 |

| 2.5.79 | Wales | 0 | West Germany | 2 |
| | | | Zimmermann, Fischer | |
| 17.10.79 | West Germany | 5 | Wales | 1 |
| | Fischer (2), Kaltz, | | Curtis | |
| | Rummenigge, K.H. Forster | | | |
| 22.12.79 | West Germany | 2 | Turkey | 0 |
| | Fischer, Rummenigge | | | |
| 27.2.80 | West Germany | 8 | Malta | 0 |
| | K. Allofs (2), Fischer (2), | | | |
| | Bonhof (pen), Rummenigge, | | | |
| | Keisch, own goal | | | |

*West Germany qualify for finals as winners of Group 7.*

*Final Group 1, in Italy*

| 11.6.80 | West Germany | 1 | Czechoslovakia | 0 |
| | Rummenigge | | | |
| 14.6.80 | West Germany | 3 | Holland | 2 |
| | K. Allofs (3) | | Rep (pen), W. van der Kerkhof | |
| 17.6.80 | West Germany | 0 | Greece | 0 |

*West Germany qualify for final as winners of Group 1.*

*Final*

| 22.6.80 | West Germany | 2 | Belgium | 1 |
| | Hrubesch (2) | | Vandereycken | |

## 1982-84

*Group 6*

| 17.11.82 | Northern Ireland | 1 | West Germany | 0 |
| | Stewart | | | |
| 30.3.83 | Albania | 1 | West Germany | 2 |
| | Targaj (pen) | | Voller, Rummenigge (pen) | |
| 23.4.83 | Turkey | 0 | West Germany | 3 |
| | | | Rummenigge (2, 1 pen), | |
| | | | Dremmler | |
| 27.4.83 | Austria | 0 | West Germany | 0 |
| 5.10.83 | West Germany | 3 | Austria | 0 |
| | Rummenigge, Voller (2) | | | |
| 26.10.83 | West Germany | 5 | Turkey | 1 |
| | Voller (2), | | Hasan | |
| | Rummenigge (2, 1 pen), | | | |
| | Stielicke | | | |
| 16.11.83 | West Germany | 0 | Northern Ireland | 1 |
| | | | Whiteside | |
| 20.11.83 | West Germany | 2 | Albania | 1 |
| | Rummenigge, Strack | | Tomori | |

*West Germany qualify for finals as winners of Group 6.*

*Final Group 2, in France*

| 14.6.84 | West Germany | 0 | Portugal | 0 |
| 17.6.84 | West Germany | 2 | Romania | 1 |
| | Voller (2) | | Coras | |
| 20.6.84 | Spain | 1 | West Germany | 0 |
| | Maceda | | | |

*Spain and Portugal qualify for semi-finals, West Germany third in Group 2.*

**1986-88**

West Germany qualify for finals as hosts.

*Final Group 1, in West Germany*

| | | | | |
|---|---|---|---|---|
| 10.6.88 | West Germany<br>Brehme | 1 | Italy<br>Mancini | 1 |
| 14.6.88 | West Germany<br>Klinsmann, Thon | 2 | Denmark | 0 |
| 17.6.88 | West Germany<br>Voller (2) | 2 | Spain | 0 |

*West Germany qualify for semi-finals as winners of Group 1.*

*Semi-final*

| | | | | |
|---|---|---|---|---|
| 21.6.88 | West Germany<br>Matthaus (pen) | 1 | Holland<br>R. Koeman (pen), Van Basten | 2 |

**1990-92**

As GERMANY

*Group 5*

| | | | | |
|---|---|---|---|---|
| 31.10.90 | Luxembourg<br>Girres, Langers | 2 | Germany<br>Klinsmann, Bein, Voller | 2 |
| 1.5.91 | Germany<br>Matthaus | 1 | Belgium | 0 |
| 5.6.91 | Wales<br>Rush | 1 | Germany | 0 |
| 16.10.91 | Germany<br>Moller, Voller, Riedle, Doll | 4 | Wales<br>Bodin (pen) | 1 |
| 20.11.91 | Belgium | 0 | Germany<br>Voller | 1 |
| 18.12.91 | Germany<br>Matthaus (pen), Buchwald,<br>Riedle, Hassler | 4 | Luxembourg | 0 |

*Germany qualify for finals, as winners of Group 5.*

*Final Group 2, in Sweden*

| | | | | |
|---|---|---|---|---|
| 12.6.92 | CIS<br>Dobrovolski (pen) | 1 | Germany<br>Hassler | 1 |
| 15.6.92 | Scotland | 0 | Germany<br>Riedle, Effenberg | 2 |
| 18.6.92 | Holland<br>Rijkaard, Witschge, Bergkamp | 3 | Germany<br>Klinsmann | 1 |

*Holland and Germany qualify for semi-finals.*

*Semi-final*

| | | | | |
|---|---|---|---|---|
| 21.6.92 | Sweden<br>Brolin (pen), K. Andersson | 2 | Germany<br>Hassler, Riedle (2) | 3 |

*Final*

| | | | | |
|---|---|---|---|---|
| 26.6.92 | Denmark<br>Jensen, Vilfort | 2 | Germany | 0 |

For details on how Germany qualified for Euro 96, see pages 46-9.

# CZECH REPUBLIC (As CZECHOSLOVAKIA)

**1958-60**

*Preliminary round*

| | | | | |
|---|---|---|---|---|
| 5.4.59 | Rep of Ireland<br>Tuohy, Cantwell (pen) | 2 | Czechoslovakia | 0 |
| 10.5.59 | Czechoslovakia<br>Stacho (pen), Bubernik,<br>Pavlovic, Dolinsky | 4 | Rep of Ireland | 0 |

*Czechoslovakia qualify for first round, 4-2 on aggregate.*

*First round*

| | | | | |
|---|---|---|---|---|
| 23.9.59 | Denmark<br>Petersen, Hansen | 2 | Czechoslovakia<br>Kacani, Dolinsky | 2 |
| 18.10.59 | Czechoslovakia<br>Bubernik (2), Scherer (2),<br>Dolinsky | 5 | Denmark<br>Kramer | 1 |

*Czechoslovakia qualify for quarter-finals, 7-3 on aggregate.*

*Quarter-final*

| | | | | |
|---|---|---|---|---|
| 22.5.60 | Romania | 0 | Czechoslovakia<br>Masopust, Bubnik | 2 |
| 29.5.60 | Czechoslovakia<br>Bubernik (2), Bubnik | 3 | Romania | 0 |

*Czechoslovakia qualify for semi-finals, 5-0 on aggregate.*

*Semi-final, in France*

| | | | | |
|---|---|---|---|---|
| 6.7.60 | USSR<br>Ivanov (2), Ponedelnik | 3 | Czechoslovakia | 0 |

*Third-place play-off*

| | | | | |
|---|---|---|---|---|
| 9.7.60 | France | 0 | Czechoslovakia<br>Bubnik, Pavlovic | 2 |

**1962-64**

*First round*

| | | | | |
|---|---|---|---|---|
| 24.11.62 | East Germany<br>Liebrecht, Erler | 2 | Czechoslovakia<br>Kucera | 1 |
| 31.3.63 | Czechoslovakia<br>Masek | 1 | East Germany<br>Ducke | 2 |

*Czechoslovakia knocked out, 3-2 on aggregate.*

**1966-68**

*Group 1*

| | | | | |
|---|---|---|---|---|
| 21.5.67 | Rep of Ireland | 0 | Czechoslovakia<br>Szikora, V. Masny | 2 |
| 18.6.67 | Czechoslovakia<br>Jurkanin, Adamec (2) | 3 | Turkey | 0 |
| 1.10.67 | Czechoslovakia<br>Horvath | 1 | Spain | 0 |
| 22.10.67 | Spain<br>Pirri, Garate | 2 | Czechoslovakia<br>Kuna | 1 |
| 15.11.67 | Turkey | 0 | Czechoslovakia | 0 |

| 22.11.67 | Czechoslovakia | 1 | Rep of Ireland | 2 |
| | Own goal | | Treacy, O'Connor | |

*Spain qualify for quarter-finals, Czechoslovakia second in Group 1.*

## 1970-72

*Group 1*

| 7.10.70 | Czechoslovakia | 1 | Finland | 1 |
| | Albrecht | | Paatelainen | |
| 21.4.71 | Wales | 1 | Czechoslovakia | 3 |
| | R. Davies (pen) | | Jan Capkovic (2), Taborsky | |
| 16.5.71 | Czechoslovakia | 1 | Romania | 0 |
| | F. Vesely | | | |
| 16.6.71 | Finland | 0 | Czechoslovakia | 4 |
| | | | Jan Capkovic, Pollak, Karko (2) | |
| 27.10.71 | Czechoslovakia | 1 | Wales | 0 |
| | Kuna | | | |
| 14.11.71 | Romania | 2 | Czechoslovakia | 1 |
| | Dembrovschi, Lucescu | | Jan Capkovic | |

*Romania qualify for quarter-finals, Czechoslovakia second in Group 1*

## 1974-76

*Group 1*

| 30.10.74 | England | 3 | Czechoslovakia | 0 |
| | Channon, Bell (2) | | | |
| 20.4.75 | Czechoslovakia | 4 | Cyprus | 0 |
| | Panenka (3), Masny | | | |
| 30.4.75 | Czechoslovakia | 5 | Portugal | 0 |
| | Bicovsky (2), Nehoda (2), Petras | | | |
| 30.10.75 | Czechoslovakia | 2 | England | 1 |
| | Nehoda, Gallis | | Channon | |
| 12.11.75 | Portugal | 1 | Czechoslovakia | 1 |
| | Nene | | Ondrus | |
| 23.11.75 | Cyprus | 0 | Czechoslovakia | 3 |
| | | | Nehoda, Bicovsky, Masny | |

*Czechoslovakia qualify for quarter-finals as winners of Group 1.*

*Quarter-final*

| 24.4.76 | Czechoslovakia | 2 | USSR | 0 |
| | Moder, Panenka | | | |
| 22.5.76 | USSR | 2 | Czechoslovakia | 2 |
| | Burjak, Blochin | | Moder (2) | |

*Czechoslovakia qualify for semi-finals, 4-2 on aggregate.*

*Semi-final, in Yugoslavia*

| 16.6.76 | Czechoslovakia | 3 | Holland | 1 |
| | Ondrus, Nehoda, Moder | | Ondrus (og) | |

*After extra time.*

*Final*

| 20.6.76 | Czechoslovakia | 2 | West Germany | 2 |
| | Svehlik, Dobias | | D. Muller, Holzenbein | |

*After extra time.*

*Czechoslovakia won 5-3 on penalties.*

**1978-80**

*Group 5*

| | | | | |
|---|---|---|---|---|
| 4.10.78 | Sweden | 1 | Czechoslovakia | 3 |
| | Borg (pen) | | Masny (2), Nehoda | |
| 4.2.78 | Czechoslovakia | 2 | France | 0 |
| | Panenka, Stambachr | | | |
| 1.5.79 | Luxembourg | 0 | Czechoslovakia | 3 |
| | | | Masny, Gajdusek, Stambachr | |
| 10.10.79 | Czechoslovakia | 4 | Sweden | 1 |
| | Nehoda, Kozak, Vizek (2) | | Svensson | |
| 17.11.79 | France | 2 | Czechoslovakia | 1 |
| | Pecout, Rampillon | | Kozak | |
| 24.11.79 | Czechoslovakia | 4 | Luxembourg | 0 |
| | Panenka, Masny (2), Vizek | | | |

*Czechoslovakia qualify for finals as winners of Group 5.*

*Final Group 1, in Italy*

| | | | | |
|---|---|---|---|---|
| 11.6.80 | West Germany | 1 | Czechoslovakia | 0 |
| | Rummenigge | | | |
| 14.6.80 | Czechoslovakia | 3 | Greece | 1 |
| | Panenka, Vizek, Nehoda | | Anastopoulos | |
| 17.6.80 | Czechoslovakia | 1 | Holland | 1 |
| | Nehoda | | Kist | |

*Czechoslovakia finish second in Group 1 and qualify for third-place play-off.*

*Third-place play-off*

| | | | | |
|---|---|---|---|---|
| 21.6.80 | Italy | 1 | Czechoslovakia | 1 |
| | Graziani | | Jurkemik | |

*After extra time.*

*Czechoslovakia won 9-8 on penalties.*

**1982-84**

*Group 5*

| | | | | |
|---|---|---|---|---|
| 6.10.82 | Czechoslovakia | 2 | Sweden | 2 |
| | Janecka (2) | | Jingblad, Eriksson | |
| 13.11.82 | Italy | 2 | Czechoslovakia | 2 |
| | Altobelli, own goal | | Sloup, Chaloupka | |
| 27.3.83 | Cyprus | 1 | Czechoslovakia | 1 |
| | Theophanous | | Bicovsky | |
| 16.4.83 | Czechoslovakia | 6 | Cyprus | 0 |
| | Danek (2), Vizek (2), Prokes, Jurkemik | | | |
| 15.5.83 | Romania | 0 | Czechoslovakia | 1 |
| | | | Vizek (pen) | |
| 21.9.83 | Sweden | 1 | Czechoslovakia | 0 |
| | Corneliusson | | | |
| 16.11.83 | Czechoslovakia | 2 | Italy | 0 |
| | Rada (2, 1 pen) | | | |
| 30.11.83 | Czechoslovakia | 1 | Romania | 1 |
| | Luhovy | | Geolgau | |

*Romania qualify for finals, Czechoslovakia third in Group 5.*

**1986-88**

*Group 6*

| | | | | |
|---|---|---|---|---|
| 15.10.86 | Czechoslovakia<br>Janecka, Knoflicek, Kula | 3 | Finland | 0 |
| 12.11.86 | Czechoslovakia | 0 | Denmark | 0 |
| 29.4.87 | Wales<br>Rush | 1 | Czechoslovakia<br>Knoflicek | 1 |
| 3.6.87 | Denmark<br>Molby | 1 | Czechoslovakia<br>Hasek | 1 |
| 9.9.87 | Finland<br>Hjelm, Lluis, Tiainen | 3 | Czechoslovakia | 0 |
| 11.11.87 | Czechoslovakia<br>Knoflicek, Bilek | 2 | Wales | 0 |

*Denmark qualify for finals, Czechoslovakia second in Group 6.*

**1990-92**

*Group 1*

| | | | | |
|---|---|---|---|---|
| 26.9.90 | Czechoslovakia<br>Danek | 1 | Iceland | 0 |
| 13.10.90 | France<br>Papin (2) | 2 | Czechoslovakia<br>Skuhravy | 1 |
| 14.11.90 | Czechoslovakia<br>Danek (2), Moravcik | 3 | Spain<br>Roberto, Carlos | 2 |
| 1.5.91 | Albania | 0 | Czechoslovakia<br>Kubik, Kuka | 2 |
| 5.6.91 | Iceland | 0 | Czechoslovakia<br>Hasek | 1 |
| 4.9.91 | Czechoslovakia<br>Nemecek | 1 | France<br>Papin (2) | 2 |
| 16.10.91 | Czechoslovakia<br>Kula, Lancz | 2 | Albania<br>Zmijani | 1 |
| 13.11.91 | Spain<br>Abelardo, Michel (pen) | 2 | Czechoslovakia<br>Nemecek | 1 |

*France qualify for finals, Czechoslovakia second in Group 1.*

For details on how the Czech Republic qualified for Euro 96, see pages 38-41.

# ITALY

**1958-60**

Did not participate

**1962-64**

*First round*

| | | | | |
|---|---|---|---|---|
| 2.12.62 | Italy<br>Rivera (2), Orlando (4) | 6 | Turkey | 0 |
| 27.3.63 | Turkey | 0 | Italy<br>Sormani | 1 |

*Italy qualify for second round, 7-0 on aggregate.*

*Second round*

| | | | | |
|---|---|---|---|---|
| 13.10.63 | USSR<br>Ponedelnik, Chislenko | 2 | Italy | 0 |
| 10.11.63 | Italy<br>Rivera | 1 | USSR<br>Gusarov | 1 |

*Italy knocked out, 3-1 on aggregate.*

**1966-68**
*Group 6*

| | | | | |
|---|---|---|---|---|
| 26.11.66 | Italy<br>Mazzola (2), De Paoli | 3 | Romania<br>Dobrin | 1 |
| 22.3.67 | Cyprus | 0 | Italy<br>Domenghini, Facchetti | 2 |
| 25.6.67 | Romania | 0 | Italy<br>Bertini | 1 |
| 1.11.67 | Italy<br>Mazzola (2), Riva (3) | 5 | Cyprus | 0 |
| 18.11.67 | Switzerland<br>Quentin, Kunzli | 2 | Italy<br>Riva (2) | 2 |
| 23.12.67 | Italy<br>Mazzola, Riva,<br>Domenghini (2) | 4 | Switzerland | 0 |

*Italy qualify for quarter-finals as winners of Group 6.*

*Quarter-final*

| | | | | |
|---|---|---|---|---|
| 6.4.68 | Bulgaria<br>Kotkov (pen), Dermendjiev,<br>Jekov | 3 | Italy<br>Own goal, Prati | 2 |
| 20.4.68 | Italy<br>Prati, Domenghini | 2 | Bulgaria | 0 |

*Italy qualify for semi-finals, 4-3 on aggregate.*

*Semi-final, in Italy*

| | | | | |
|---|---|---|---|---|
| 5.6.68 | Italy | 0 | USSR | 0 |

*After extra time.*

*Italy won on the toss of a coin.*

*Final*

| | | | | |
|---|---|---|---|---|
| 8.6.68 | Italy<br>Domenghini | 1 | Yugoslavia<br>Dzajic | 1 |

*Replay*

| | | | | |
|---|---|---|---|---|
| 10.6.68 | Italy<br>Riva, Anastasi | 2 | Yugoslavia | 0 |

**1970-72**
*Group 6*

| | | | | |
|---|---|---|---|---|
| 31.10.70 | Austria<br>Parits | 1 | Italy<br>De Sisti, Mazzola | 2 |
| 8.12.70 | Italy<br>De Sisti, Boninsegna (pen),<br>Prati | 3 | Rep of Ireland | 0 |
| 10.5.71 | Rep of Ireland<br>Conway | 1 | Italy<br>Boninsegna, Prati | 2 |

| 9.6.71 | Sweden | 0 | Italy | 0 |
| 9.10.71 | Italy | 3 | Sweden | 0 |
| | Riva (2), Boninsegna | | | |
| 20.11.71 | Italy | 2 | Austria | 2 |
| | Prati, De Sisti | | Jara, R. Sara | |

*Italy qualify for quarter-finals as winners of Group 6.*

*Quarter-final*

| 29.4.72 | Italy | 0 | Belgium | 0 |
| 13.5.72 | Belgium | 2 | Italy | 1 |
| | Van Moer, Van Himst | | Riva (pen) | |

*Italy knocked out, 2-1 on aggregate.*

**1974-76**

*Group 5*

| 20.11.74 | Holland | 3 | Italy | 1 |
| | Rensenbrink, Cruyff (2) | | Boninsegna | |
| 19.4.75 | Italy | 0 | Poland | 0 |
| 5.6.75 | Finland | 0 | Italy | 1 |
| | | | Chinaglia (pen) | |
| 27.9.75 | Italy | 0 | Finland | 0 |
| 26.10.75 | Poland | 0 | Italy | 0 |
| 22.11.75 | Italy | 1 | Holland | 0 |
| | Capello | | | |

*Holland qualify for quarter-finals, Italy third in Group 5.*

**1978-80**

Italy qualify for finals as hosts.

*Final Group 2, in Italy*

| 12.6.80 | Italy | 0 | Spain | 0 |
| 15.6.80 | Italy | 1 | England | 0 |
| | Tardelli | | | |
| 18.6.80 | Italy | 0 | Belgium | 0 |

*Italy qualify for third-place play-off.*

*Third-place play-off*

| 21.6.80 | Italy | 1 | Czechoslovakia | 1 |
| | Graziani | | Jurkemik | |

*After extra time.*

*Italy lost 9-8 on penalties.*

**1982-84**

*Group 5*

| 13.11.82 | Italy | 2 | Czechoslovakia | 2 |
| | Altobelli, own goal | | Sloup, Chaloupka | |
| 4.12.82 | Italy | 0 | Romania | 0 |
| 12.2.83 | Cyprus | 1 | Italy | 1 |
| | Mavris | | Own goal | |
| 16.4.83 | Romania | 1 | Italy | 0 |
| | Boloni | | | |
| 29.5.83 | Sweden | 2 | Italy | 0 |
| | Sandberg, Stromberg | | | |

| 15.10.83 | Italy | 0 | Sweden | 3 |
| | | | Stromberg (2), Sunesson | |
| 16.11.83 | Czechoslovakia | 2 | Italy | 0 |
| | Rada (2, 1 pen) | | | |
| 22.12.83 | Italy | 3 | Cyprus | 1 |
| | Altobelli, Cabrini, Rossi (pen) | | Tsighis (pen) | |

*Romania qualify for finals, Italy fourth in Group 5.*

**1986-88**

*Group 2*

| 15.11.86 | Italy | 3 | Switzerland | 2 |
| | Own goal, Altobelli (2, 1 pen) | | Brigger, Weber | |
| 6.12.86 | Malta | 0 | Italy | 2 |
| | | | Ferri, Altobelli | |
| 24.1.87 | Italy | 5 | Malta | 0 |
| | Bagni, Bergomi, Altobelli (2), | | | |
| | Vialli | | | |
| 14.2.87 | Portugal | 0 | Italy | 1 |
| | | | Altobelli | |
| 3.6.87 | Sweden | 1 | Italy | 0 |
| | Larsson | | | |
| 17.10.87 | Switzerland | 0 | Italy | 0 |
| 14.11.87 | Italy | 2 | Sweden | 1 |
| | Vialli (2) | | Larsson | |
| 5.12.87 | Italy | 3 | Portugal | 0 |
| | Vialli, Giannini, De Agostini | | | |

*Italy qualify for finals as winners of Group 2.*

*Final Group 1, in West Germany*

| 10.6.88 | West Germany | 1 | Italy | 1 |
| | Brehme | | Mancini | |
| 14.6.88 | Italy | 1 | Spain | 0 |
| | Vialli | | | |
| 17.6.88 | Italy | 2 | Denmark | 0 |
| | Altobelli, De Agostini | | | |

*Italy and West Germany qualify for semi-finals.*

*Semi-final*

| 22.6.88 | USSR | 2 | Italy | 0 |
| | Litovchenko, Protasov | | | |

**1990-92**

*Group 3*

| 17.10.90 | Hungary | 1 | Italy | 1 |
| | Disztl | | R. Baggio (pen) | |
| 3.11.90 | Italy | 0 | USSR | 0 |
| 22.12.90 | Cyprus | 0 | Italy | 4 |
| | | | Vierchowod, Serena (2), | |
| | | | Lombardo | |
| 1.5.91 | Italy | 3 | Hungary | 1 |
| | Donadoni (2), Vialli | | Bognar | |
| 5.6.91 | Norway | 2 | Italy | 1 |
| | Dahlum, Bohinen | | Schillaci | |
| 12.10.91 | USSR | 0 | Italy | 0 |

| 13.11.91 | Italy | 1 | Norway | 1 |
| | Rizzitelli | | Jakobsen | |
| 21.12.91 | Italy | 2 | Cyprus | 0 |
| | Vialli, R. Baggio | | | |

*USSR qualify for finals, Italy second in Group 3.*

*For details on how Italy qualified for Euro 96, see pages 34-7.*

# RUSSIA
As USSR

**1958-60**

*First round*

| 28.9.58 | USSR | 3 | Hungary | 1 |
| | Ilyin, Metreveli, Ivanov | | Gorocs | |
| 27.9.59 | Hungary | 0 | USSR | 1 |
| | | | Voinov | |

*USSR qualify for quarter-finals, 4-1 on aggregate.*

*Quarter-final*

| | Spain | | USSR | |
| *Spain withdrew.* | | | | |

*Semi-final, in France*

| 6.7.60 | USSR | 3 | Czechoslovakia | 0 |
| | Ivanov (2), Ponedelnik | | | |

*Final*

| 10.7.60 | USSR | 2 | Yugoslavia | 1 |
| | Metreveli, Ponedelnik | | Galic | |

**1962-64**

*First round*

Bye as holders

*Second round*

| 13.10.63 | USSR | 2 | Italy | 0 |
| | Ponedelnik, Chislenko | | | |
| 10.11.63 | Italy | 1 | USSR | 1 |
| | Rivera | | Gusarov | |

*USSR qualify for quarter-finals, 3-1 on aggregate.*

*Quarter-final*

| 13.5.64 | Sweden | 1 | USSR | 1 |
| | Hamrin | | Ivanov | |
| 27.5.64 | USSR | 3 | Sweden | 1 |
| | Ponedelnik (2), Voronin | | Hamrin | |

*USSR qualify for semi-finals, 4-2 on aggregate.*

*Semi-final, in Spain*

| 17.6.64 | USSR | 3 | Denmark | 0 |
| | Voronin, Ponedelnik, Ivanov | | | |

*Final*

| 21.6.64 | Spain | 2 | USSR | 1 |
|---|---|---|---|---|
| | Pereda, Marcelino | | Khusainov | |

**1966-68**

*Group 3*

| 11.6.67 | USSR | 4 | Austria | 3 |
|---|---|---|---|---|
| | Malofeyev, Streltsov, Chislenko, Byshovets | | Hof, Wolny, Siber | |
| 16.7.67 | USSR | 4 | Greece | 0 |
| | Banishevski (2), Sabo (pen), Chislenko | | | |
| 30.8.67 | USSR | 2 | Finland | 0 |
| | Chislenko, Khurtsilava | | | |
| 6.9.67 | Finland | 2 | USSR | 5 |
| | Peltonen (pen), Syrjavaara | | Sabo (2, 1 pen), Banishevski, Malofeyev, Maslov | |
| 15.10.67 | Austria | 1 | USSR | 0 |
| | Grausam | | | |
| 31.10.67 | Greece | 0 | USSR | 1 |
| | | | Malofeyev | |

*USSR qualify for quarter-finals as winners of Group 3.*

*Quarter-final*

| 4.5.68 | Hungary | 2 | USSR | 0 |
|---|---|---|---|---|
| | Farkas, Gorocs | | | |
| 11.5.68 | USSR | 3 | Hungary | 0 |
| | Khurtsilava, Byshovets, own goal | | | |

*USSR qualify for semi-finals, 3-2 on aggregate.*

*Semi-final, in Italy*

| 5.6.68 | Italy | 0 | USSR | 0 |
|---|---|---|---|---|

*After extra time.*

*USSR lost on the toss of a coin.*

*Third-place play-off*

| 8.6.68 | England | 2 | USSR | 0 |
|---|---|---|---|---|
| | R. Charlton, Hurst | | | |

**1970-72**

*Group 4*

| 15.11.70 | Cyprus | 1 | USSR | 3 |
|---|---|---|---|---|
| | Haralambous | | Kolotov, Evruyzhikhin, Shevchenko | |
| 30.5.71 | USSR | 2 | Spain | 1 |
| | Kolotov, Shevchenko | | Rexach | |
| 7.6.71 | USSR | 6 | Cyprus | 1 |
| | Fedotov (2), Banishevsky, Evruzhikhin (2), Kolotov | | Michael | |
| 22.9.71 | USSR | 1 | Northern Ireland | 0 |
| | Muntjian (pen) | | | |
| 13.10.71 | Northern Ireland | 1 | USSR | 1 |
| | Nicholson | | Byshovets | |

| 27.10.71 | Spain | 0 | USSR | 0 |

*USSR qualify for quarter-finals as winners of Group 4.*

*Quarter-final*

| 30.4.72 | Yugoslavia | 0 | USSR | 0 |
| 13.5.72 | USSR<br>Kolotov, Banishevsky, Kozinkevich | 3 | Yugoslavia | 0 |

*USSR qualify for semi-finals, 3-0 on aggregate.*

*Semi-finals, in Belgium*

| 14.6.72 | USSR<br>Konkov | 1 | Hungary | 0 |

*Final*

| 18.6.72 | West Germany<br>G. Muller (2), Wimmer | 3 | USSR | 0 |

## 1974-76

*Group 6*

| 30.10.74 | Rep of Ireland<br>Givens (3) | 3 | USSR | 0 |
| 2.4.75 | USSR<br>Kolotov (2 pens), Blochin | 3 | Turkey | 0 |
| 18.5.75 | USSR<br>Blochin, Kolotov | 2 | Rep of Ireland<br>Hand | 1 |
| 12.10.75 | Switzerland | 0 | USSR<br>Muntjian | 1 |
| 12.11.75 | USSR<br>Konkov, Onischenko (2),<br>Veremeyev | 4 | Switzerland<br>Risi | 1 |
| 23.11.75 | Turkey<br>Cemil | 1 | USSR | 0 |

*USSR qualify for quarter-finals as winners of Group 6.*

*Quarter-final*

| 24.4.76 | Czechoslovakia<br>Moder, Panenka | 2 | USSR | 0 |
| 22.5.76 | USSR<br>Burjak, Blochin | 2 | Czechoslovakia<br>Moder (2) | 2 |

*USSR knocked out, 4-2 on aggregate.*

## 1978-80

*Group 6*

| 20.9.78 | USSR<br>Chesnokov, Bessonov | 2 | Greece | 0 |
| 11.10.78 | Hungary<br>Varadi, Szokolai | 2 | USSR | 0 |
| 19.5.79 | USSR<br>Chesnokov, Shengalia | 2 | Hungary<br>Tatar, Pusztai | 2 |
| 4.7.79 | Finland<br>Ismail | 1 | USSR<br>Khapsalis | 1 |
| 12.9.79 | Greece<br>Nikoloudis | 1 | USSR | 0 |

| 31.10.79 | USSR | 2 | Finland | 2 |
| | Andreyev, Gavrilov | | | |

*Greece qualify for finals, USSR fourth in Group 6.*

**1982-84**
*Group 2*

| 13.10.82 | USSR | 2 | Finland | 0 |
| | Baltacha, Andreyev | | | |
| 27.4.83 | USSR | 5 | Portugal | 0 |
| | Cherenkov (2), Rodionov, | | | |
| | Demianenko, Larionov | | | |
| 22.5.83 | Poland | 1 | USSR | 1 |
| | Boniek | | Own goal | |
| 1.6.83 | Finland | 0 | USSR | 1 |
| | | | Blochin | |
| 9.10.83 | USSR | 2 | Poland | 0 |
| | Demianenko, Blochin | | | |
| 13.11.83 | Portugal | 1 | USSR | 0 |
| | Jordao (pen) | | | |

*Portugal qualify for finals, USSR second in Group 2.*

**1986-88**
*Group 3*

| 24.9.86 | Iceland | 1 | USSR | 1 |
| | Sigurvinsson | | Sulakvelidze | |
| 11.10.86 | France | 0 | USSR | 2 |
| | | | Belanov, Rats | |
| 29.10.86 | USSR | 4 | Norway | 0 |
| | Litovchenko, Belanov (pen), | | | |
| | Blochin, Khidatulin | | | |
| 29.4.87 | USSR | 2 | East Germany | 0 |
| | Zavarov, Belanov | | | |
| 3.6.87 | Norway | 0 | USSR | 1 |
| | | | Zavarov | |
| 9.9.87 | USSR | 1 | France | 1 |
| | Mikhailichenko | | Toure | |
| 10.10.87 | East Germany | 1, | USSR | 1 |
| | Kirsten | | Aleinkov | |
| 28.10.87 | USSR | 2 | Iceland | 0 |
| | Belanov, Protasov | | | |

*USSR qualify for finals as winners of Group 3.*

*Final Group 2, in West Germany*

| 12.6.88 | USSR | 1 | Holland | 0 |
| | Rats | | | |
| 15.6.88 | USSR | 1 | Rep of Ireland | 1 |
| | Protasov | | Whelan | |
| 18.6.88 | USSR | 3 | England | 1 |
| | Aleinikov, Mikhailichenko, | | Adams | |
| | Pasulko | | | |

*USSR and Holland qualify for semi-finals.*
*Semi-final*

| 22.6.88 | USSR | 2 | Italy | 0 |
| | Litovchenko, Protasov | | | |

*Final*

| 25.6.88 | Holland | 2 | USSR | 0 |
|---|---|---|---|---|
| | Gullit, Van Basten | | | |

**1990-92**

*Group 3*

| 12.9.90 | USSR | 2 | Norway | 0 |
|---|---|---|---|---|
| | Kanchelskis, O. Kuznetsov | | | |
| 3.11.90 | Italy | 0 | USSR | 0 |
| 17.4.91 | Hungary | 0 | USSR | 1 |
| | | | Mikhailichenko | |
| 29.5.91 | USSR | 4 | Cyprus | 0 |
| | Mostovoi, Mikhailichenko, | | | |
| | Korneev, Aleinikov | | | |
| 28.8.91 | Norway | 0 | USSR | 1 |
| | | | Mostovoi | |
| 25.9.91 | USSR | 2 | Hungary | 2 |
| | Shalimov (pen), | | Kiprich (2) | |
| | Kanchelskis | | | |
| 12.10.91 | USSR | 0 | Italy | 0 |
| 13.11.91 | Cyprus | 0 | USSR | 3 |
| | | | Protasov, Huran, | |
| | | | Kanchelskis | |

*USSR qualify for finals as winners of Group 3.*

As CIS

*Final Group 2, in Sweden*

| 12.6.92 | CIS | 1 | Germany | 1 |
|---|---|---|---|---|
| | Dobrovolski (pen) | | Hassler | |
| 15.6.92 | CIS | 0 | Holland | 0 |
| 18.6.92 | CIS | 0 | Scotland | 3 |
| | | | McStay, McClair, | |
| | | | McAllister (pen) | |

*Holland and Germany qualify for semi-finals, CIS fourth in Group 2.*

For details on how Russia qualified for Euro 96, see pages 50-53.

# GROUP D

# DENMARK
**1958-60**

*First round*

| 23.9.59 | Denmark | 2 | Czechoslovakia | 2 |
|---|---|---|---|---|
| | Petersen, Hansen | | Kacani, Dolinsky | |
| 18.10.59 | Czechoslovakia | 5 | Denmark | 1 |
| | Bubernik (2), Scherer (2), | | Kramer | |
| | Dolinsky | | | |

*Czechoslovakia qualify for quarter-finals, 7-3 on aggregate.*

## 1962-64

*First round*

| | | | | |
|---|---|---|---|---|
| 28.6.62 | Denmark<br>Madsen (3), Clausen,<br>Enoksen, Bertelsen | 6 | Malta<br>Theobald | 1 |
| 8.12.62 | Malta<br>Urpani | 1 | Denmark<br>Madsen, Christensen,<br>Bertelsen | 3 |

*Denmark qualify for second round, 9-2 on aggregate.*

*Second round*

| | | | | |
|---|---|---|---|---|
| 29.6.63 | Denmark<br>Petersen (pen), Madsen,<br>Clausen, Enoksen | 4 | Albania | 0 |
| 30.10.63 | Albania<br>Pano | 1 | Denmark | 0 |

*Denmark qualify for quarter-finals, 4-1 on aggregate.*

*Quarter-final*

| | | | | |
|---|---|---|---|---|
| 4.12.63 | Luxembourg<br>Pilot, H. Klein (2) | 3 | Denmark<br>Madsen (3) | 3 |
| 10.12.63 | Denmark<br>Madsen (2) | 2 | Luxembourg<br>Leonard, Schmit | 2 |

*Replay*

| | | | | |
|---|---|---|---|---|
| 18.12.63 | Denmark<br>Madsen | 1 | Luxembourg | 0 |

*Denmark qualify for semi-finals.*

*Semi-final, in Spain*

| | | | | |
|---|---|---|---|---|
| 17.6.64 | USSR<br>Voronin, Ponedelnik, Ivanov | 3 | Denmark | 0 |

*Third-place play-off*

| | | | | |
|---|---|---|---|---|
| 20.6.64 | Hungary<br>Bene, Novak (2) | 3 | Denmark<br>Bertelsen | 1 |

## 1966-68

*Group 5*

| | | | | |
|---|---|---|---|---|
| 21.9.66 | Hungary<br>Albert (2), Meszoly, Bene,<br>Farkas, Varga | 6 | Denmark | 0 |
| 30.11.66 | Holland<br>Swart, Van der Kuylen | 2 | Denmark | 0 |
| 24.5.67 | Denmark | 0 | Hungary<br>Albert, Bene | 2 |
| 4.6.67 | Denmark<br>Bjerre (pen) | 1 | East Germany<br>Lowe | 1 |
| 4.10.67 | Denmark<br>Bjerre (2, 1 pen), Sondergaard | 3 | Holland<br>Suurbier, Israel | 2 |
| 11.10.67 | East Germany<br>Korner, Pankau (2) | 3 | Denmark<br>Dyreborg, Sondergaard | 2 |

*Hungary qualify for quarter-finals, Denmark fourth in Group 5.*

**1970-72**

*Group 5*

| | | | | |
|---|---|---|---|---|
| 14.10.70 | Denmark | 0 | Portugal<br>Joao | 1 |
| 11.11.70 | Scotland<br>O'Hare | 1 | Denmark | 0 |
| 25.11.70 | Belgium<br>Devrindt (2) | 2 | Denmark | 0 |
| 12.5.71 | Portugal<br>Rui Rodriguez, Eusebio (2),<br>Vitor Baptista (2) | 5 | Denmark | 0 |
| 26.5.71 | Denmark<br>Bjerre | 1 | Belgium<br>Devrindt (2) | 2 |
| 9.6.71 | Denmark<br>F. Laudrup | 1 | Scotland | 0 |

*Belgium qualify for quarter-finals, Denmark fourth in Group 5.*

**1974-76**

*Group 4*

| | | | | |
|---|---|---|---|---|
| 25.9.74 | Denmark<br>Nygaard (pen) | 1 | Spain<br>Claramunt (pen), R. Martinez | 2 |
| 13.10.74 | Denmark | 0 | Romania | 0 |
| 11.5.75 | Romania<br>Georgescu (2), Crisan (2),<br>Lucescu, Dinu | 6 | Denmark<br>Dahl | 1 |
| 3.9.75 | Denmark | 0 | Scotland<br>Harper | 1 |
| 12.10.75 | Spain<br>Pirri, Capon | 2 | Denmark | 0 |
| 29.10.75 | Scotland<br>Dalglish, Rioch, MacDougall | 3 | Denmark<br>Bastrup | 1 |

*Spain qualify for quarter-finals, Denmark fourth in Group 4.*

**1978-80**

*Group 1*

| | | | | |
|---|---|---|---|---|
| 24.5.78 | Denmark<br>M. Jensen, Nielsen, Lerby | 3 | Rep of Ireland<br>Stapleton, Grealish, Daly | 3 |
| 20.9.78 | Denmark<br>Simonsen (pen), Arnesen,<br>Rontved | 3 | England<br>Keegan (2), Latchford, Neal | 4 |
| 11.10.78 | Denmark<br>B. Nielsen, Lerby | 2 | Bulgaria<br>Panov, Iliev | 2 |
| 25.10.78 | Northern Ireland<br>Spence, Anderson | 2 | Denmark<br>H. Jensen | 1 |
| 2.5.79 | Rep of Ireland<br>Daly, Givens | 2 | Denmark | 0 |
| 6.6.79 | Denmark<br>Elkjaer (3), Simonsen | 4 | Northern Ireland | 0 |
| 9.9.79 | England<br>Keegan | 1 | Denmark | 0 |
| 31.10.79 | Bulgaria<br>Kostadinov, Tsvetkov (2) | 3 | Denmark | 0 |

*England qualify for finals, Denmark fifth in Group 1.*

**1982-84**

*Group 3*

| | | | | |
|---|---|---|---|---|
| 22.9.82 | Denmark | 2 | England | 2 |
| | Hansen (pen), J. Olsen | | Francis (2) | |
| 10.11.82 | Luxembourg | 1 | Denmark | 2 |
| | Di Domenico | | Lerby (pen), Berggren | |
| 27.4.83 | Denmark | 1 | Greece | 0 |
| | Busk | | | |
| 1.6.83 | Denmark | 3 | Hungary | 1 |
| | Elkjaer, J. Olsen, | | Nyilasi | |
| | Simonsen (pen) | | | |
| 21.9.83 | England | 0 | Denmark | 1 |
| | | | Simonsen (pen) | |
| 12.10.83 | Denmark | 6 | Luxembourg | 0 |
| | M. Laudrup (3), Elkjaer (2), | | | |
| | Simonsen | | | |
| 26.10.83 | Hungary | 1 | Denmark | 0 |
| | Kiss | | | |
| 16.11.83 | Greece | 0 | Denmark | 2 |
| | | | Elkjaer, Simonsen | |

*Denmark qualify for finals as winners of Group 3.*

*Final Group 1, in France*

| | | | | |
|---|---|---|---|---|
| 12.6.84 | France | 1 | Denmark | 0 |
| | Own goal | | | |
| 16.6.84 | Denmark | 5 | Yugoslavia | 0 |
| | Arnesen (2, 1 pen), Berggren, | | | |
| | Elkjaer, Lauridsen | | | |
| 19.6.84 | Denmark | 3 | Belgium | 2 |
| | Arnesen (pen), Brylle, | | Cuelemans, Vercauteren | |
| | Elkjaer | | | |

*France and Denmark qualify for semi-finals*

*Semi-final*

| | | | | |
|---|---|---|---|---|
| 24.6.84 | Spain | 1 | Denmark | 1 |
| | Maceda | | Lerby | |

*After extra time.*

*Denmark lost 5-4 on penalties.*

**1986-88**

*Group 6*

| | | | | |
|---|---|---|---|---|
| 19.10.86 | Denmark | 1 | Finland | 0 |
| | Bertelsen | | | |
| 12.11.86 | Czechoslovakia | 0 | Denmark | 0 |
| 29.4.87 | Finland | 0 | Denmark | 1 |
| | | | Molby | |
| 3.6.87 | Denmark | 1 | Czechoslovakia | 1 |
| | Molby | | Hasek | |
| 9.9.87 | Wales | 1 | Denmark | 0 |
| | Hughes | | | |
| 14.10.87 | Denmark | 1 | Wales | 0 |
| | Elkjaer | | | |

*Denmark qualify for finals as winners of Group 6.*

*Final Group 1, in West Germany*

| | | | | |
|---|---|---|---|---|
| 11.6.88 | Spain | 3 | Denmark | 2 |
| | Michel, Butragueno, Gordillo | | Laudrup, Povlsen | |
| 14.6.88 | West Germany | 2 | Denmark | 0 |
| | Klinsmann, Thon | | | |
| 17.6.88 | Italy | 2 | Denmark | 0 |
| | Altobelli, De Agostini | | | |

*West Germany and Italy qualify for semi-finals, Denmark fourth in Group 1.*

## 1990-92

*Group 4*

| | | | | |
|---|---|---|---|---|
| 10.10.90 | Denmark | 4 | Faroe Isles | 1 |
| | M. Laudrup (2), Elstrup, Povlsen | | Morkore | |
| 17.10.90 | Northern Ireland | 1 | Denmark | 1 |
| | Clarke | | Bartram (pen) | |
| 14.11.90 | Denmark | 0 | Yugoslavia | 2 |
| | | | Bazdarevic, Jarni | |
| 1.5.91 | Yugoslavia | 1 | Denmark | 2 |
| | Pancev | | Christensen (2) | |
| 5.6.91 | Denmark | 2 | Austria | 1 |
| | Christensen (2) | | E. Ogris | |
| 25.9.91 | Faroe Isles | 0 | Denmark | 4 |
| | | | Christofte (pen), Christensen, Pingel, Vilfort | |
| 9.10.91 | Austria | 0 | Denmark | 3 |
| | | | Own goal, Povlsen, Christensen | |
| 13.11.91 | Denmark | 2 | Northern Ireland | 1 |
| | Povlsen (2) | | Taggart | |

*Denmark qualify for finals as second placed team, Yugoslavia finished first but were banned.*

*Final Group 1, in Sweden*

| | | | | |
|---|---|---|---|---|
| 11.6.92 | Denmark | 0 | England | 0 |
| 14.6.92 | Sweden | 1 | Denmark | 0 |
| | Brolin | | | |
| 11.6.92 | France | 1 | Denmark | 2 |
| | Papin | | Larsen, Elstrup | |

*Sweden and Denmark qualify for semi-finals.*

*Semi-final*

| | | | | |
|---|---|---|---|---|
| 22.6.92 | Holland | 2 | Denmark | 2 |
| | Bergkamp, Rijkaard | | Larsen (2) | |

*After extra time.*

*Denmark won 5-4 on penalties.*

*Final*

| | | | | |
|---|---|---|---|---|
| 26.6.92 | Denmark | 2 | Germany | 0 |
| | Jensen, Vilfort | | | |

For details on how Denmark qualified for Euro 96, see pages 27-30.

# PORTUGAL
**1958-60**

*First round*

| | | | | |
|---|---|---|---|---|
| 21.6.59 | East Germany | 0 | Portugal | 2 |
| | | | Matateu, Coluna | |
| 28.6.59 | Portugal | 3 | East Germany | 2 |
| | Coluna (2), Cavem | | Vogt, Kohle | |

*Portugal qualify for quarter-finals, 5-2 on aggregate.*

*Quarter-final*

| | | | | |
|---|---|---|---|---|
| 8.5.60 | Portugal | 2 | Yugoslavia | 1 |
| | Santana, Matateu | | Kostic | |
| 22.5.60 | Yugoslavia | 5 | Portugal | 1 |
| | Kostic (2), Cebinac, | | Cavem | |
| | Sekularac, Galic | | | |

*Portugal knocked out, 6-3 on aggregate.*

**1962-64**

*First round*

| | | | | |
|---|---|---|---|---|
| 7.11.62 | Bulgaria | 3 | Portugal | 1 |
| | Asparoukhov (2), Diev | | Eusebio | |
| 16.12.62 | Portugal | 3 | Bulgaria | 1 |
| | Hernani (2), Coluna | | Iliev | |

*Replay*

| | | | | |
|---|---|---|---|---|
| 23.1.63 | Bulgaria | 1 | Portugal | 0 |
| | Asparoukhov | | | |

**1966-68**

*Group 2*

| | | | | |
|---|---|---|---|---|
| 13.11.66 | Portugal | 1 | Sweden | 2 |
| | Jaime Graca | | Danielsson (2) | |
| 1.6.67 | Sweden | 1 | Portugal | 1 |
| | Svensson | | Custodio Pinto | |
| 8.6.67 | Norway | 1 | Portugal | 2 |
| | Iversen | | Eusebio (2) | |
| 12.11.67 | Portugal | 2 | Norway | 1 |
| | Torres, Jaime Graca | | Nilsen | |
| 26.11.67 | Bulgaria | 1 | Portugal | 0 |
| | Dermendjiev | | | |
| 17.12.67 | Portugal | 0 | Bulgaria | 0 |

*Bulgaria qualify for quarter-finals, Portugal second in Group 2.*

**1970-72**

*Group 5*

| | | | | |
|---|---|---|---|---|
| 14.10.70 | Denmark | 0 | Portugal | 1 |
| | | | Jacinto Joao | |
| 17.2.71 | Belgium | 3 | Portugal | 0 |
| | R. Lambert (2, 1 pen), Denul | | | |
| 21.4.71 | Portugal | 2 | Scotland | 0 |
| | Own goal, Eusebio | | | |

| | | | | |
|---|---|---|---|---|
| 12.5.71 | Portugal<br>Rui Rodrigues, Eusebio,<br>Vitor Baptista (2), own goal | 5 | Denmark | 0 |
| 13.10.71 | Scotland<br>O'Hare, Gemmill | 2 | Portugal<br>Rui Rodrigues | 1 |
| 21.11.71 | Portugal<br>Peres (pen) | 1 | Belgium<br>Lambert | 1 |

*Belgium qualify for quarter-finals, Portugal second in Group 5.*

### 1974-76

*Group 1*

| | | | | |
|---|---|---|---|---|
| 20.11.74 | England | 0 | Portugal | 0 |
| 30.4.75 | Czechoslovakia<br>Bicovsky (2), Nehoda (2),<br>Petras | 5 | Portugal | 0 |
| 8.6.75 | Cyprus | 0 | Portugal<br>Nene, Moinhos | 2 |
| 12.11.75 | Portugal<br>Nene | 1 | Czechoslovakia<br>Ondrus | 1 |
| 19.11.75 | Portugal<br>Rui Rodrigues | 1 | England<br>Channon | 1 |
| 3.12.75 | Portugal<br>Alves | 1 | Cyprus | 0 |

*Czechoslovakia qualify for quarter-finals, Portugal third in Group 1.*

### 1978-80

*Group 2*

| | | | | |
|---|---|---|---|---|
| 11.10.78 | Portugal<br>Gomes | 1 | Belgium<br>Vercauteren | 1 |
| 15.11.78 | Austria<br>Schachner | 1 | Portugal<br>Nene, Alberto Fonseca | 2 |
| 29.11.78 | Portugal<br>Alberto Fonseca | 1 | Scotland | 0 |
| 9.5.79 | Norway | 0 | Portugal<br>Alves | 1 |
| 17.10.79 | Belgium<br>Van Moer, Van der Elst | 2 | Portugal | 0 |
| 1.11.79 | Portugal<br>Artur, Nene (2) | 3 | Norway<br>Hammer | 1 |
| 21.11.79 | Portugal<br>Reinaldo | 1 | Austria<br>Welzl, Schachner | 2 |
| 26.3.80 | Scotland<br>Dalglish, A. Gray, Archibald,<br>Gemmill (pen) | 4 | Portugal<br>Gomes | 1 |

*Belgium qualify for finals, Portugal third in Group 2.*

### 1982-84

*Group 2*

| | | | | |
|---|---|---|---|---|
| 22.9.82 | Finland | 0 | Portugal<br>Nene, Oliveira | 2 |
| 10.10.82 | Portugal<br>Nene, Gomes | 2 | Poland<br>Krol | 1 |

| 27.4.83 | USSR<br>Cherenkov (2), Rodionov,<br>Demianenko, Larionov | 5 | Portugal | 0 |
| 21.9.83 | Portugal<br>Jordao, Carlos Manuel,<br>own goal, Jose Luis, Oliveira | 5 | Finland | 0 |
| 28.10.83 | Poland | 0 | Portugal<br>Carlos Manuel | 1 |
| 13.11.83 | Portugal<br>Jordao (pen) | 1 | USSR | 0 |

*Portugal qualify for finals as winners of Group 2.*

*Final Group 2, in France*

| 14.6.84 | West Germany | 0 | Portugal | 0 |
| 17.6.84 | Portugal<br>Sousa | 1 | Spain<br>Santillana | 1 |
| 20.6.84 | Portugal<br>Nene | 1 | Romania | 0 |

*Portugal and Spain qualify for semi-finals.*

*Semi-final*

| 23.6.84 | France<br>Domergue (2), Platini | 3 | Portugal<br>Jordao (2) | 2 |

**1986-88**

*Group 2*

| 12.10.86 | Portugal<br>Coelho | 1 | Sweden<br>Stromberg | 1 |
| 29.10.86 | Switzerland<br>Bregy | 1 | Portugal<br>M. Fernandes | 1 |
| 14.2.87 | Portugal | 0 | Italy<br>Altobelli | 1 |
| 29.3.87 | Portugal<br>Jorge Placido (2) | 2 | Malta<br>Mizzi (pen), Busuttil | 2 |
| 23.9.87 | Sweden | 0 | Portugal<br>Gomes | 1 |
| 11.11.87 | Portugal | 0 | Switzerland | 0 |
| 5.12.87 | Italy<br>Vialli, Giannini,<br>De Agostini | 3 | Portugal | 0 |
| 20.12.87 | Malta | 0 | Portugal<br>Frederico | 1 |

*Italy qualify for finals, Portugal third in Group 2.*

**1990-92**

*Group 6*

| 12.9.90 | Finland | 0 | Portugal | 0 |
| 17.10.90 | Portugal<br>Rui Aguas | 1 | Holland | 0 |
| 23.1.91 | Greece<br>Borbokis, Manolas,<br>Tsalouhidis | 3 | Portugal<br>Rui Aguas, P. Futre | 2 |
| 9.2.91 | Malta | 0 | Portugal<br>P. Futre | 1 |

| 20.2.91 | Portugal<br>Rui Aguas, Leal, Paneira (pen),<br>own goal, Cadete | 5 | Malta | 0 |
|---|---|---|---|---|
| 11.9.91 | Portugal<br>Cesar Brito | 1 | Finland | 0 |
| 16.10.91 | Holland<br>Witschge | 1 | Portugal | 0 |
| 20.11.91 | Portugal<br>Joao Pinto | 1 | Greece | 0 |

*Holland qualify for finals, Portugal second in Group 6.*

For details on how Portugal qualified for Euro 96, see pages 42-5.

# TURKEY
## 1958-60
*First round*

| 2.11.58 | Romania<br>Constantin, Oaida, Dinulescu | 3 | Turkey | 0 |
|---|---|---|---|---|
| 26.4.50 | Turkey<br>Lefter (2, 1 pen) | 2 | Romania | 0 |

*Turkey knocked out, 3-2 on aggregate.*

## 1962-64
*First round*

| 2.12.62 | Italy<br>Rivera (2), Orlando (4) | 6 | Turkey | 0 |
|---|---|---|---|---|
| 27.3.63 | Turkey | 0 | Italy<br>Sormani | 1 |

*Turkey knocked out, 7-0 on aggregate.*

## 1966-68
*Group 1*

| 16.11.66 | Rep of Ireland<br>O'Neill, McEvoy | 2 | Turkey<br>Ogun | 1 |
|---|---|---|---|---|
| 22.2.67 | Turkey<br>Ayhan, Ogun | 2 | Rep of Ireland<br>Cantwell | 1 |
| 1.3.67 | Turkey | 0 | Spain | 0 |
| 31.5.67 | Spain<br>Grosso, Gento | 2 | Turkey | 0 |
| 18.6.67 | Czechoslovakia<br>Adamec (2), Jurkanin | 3 | Turkey | 0 |
| 15.11.67 | Turkey | 0 | Czechoslovakia | 0 |

*Spain qualify for quarter-finals, Turkey fourth in Group 1.*

## 1970-72
*Group 8*

| 17.10.70 | West Germany<br>G. Muller (pen) | 1 | Turkey<br>Kamuran | 1 |
|---|---|---|---|---|
| 13.12.70 | Turkey<br>Metin, Cemil | 2 | Albania<br>Ziu | 1 |
| 25.4.71 | Turkey | 0 | West Germany<br>G. Muller (2), Koppel | 3 |

| 22.9.71 | Poland | 5 | Turkey | 1 |
| | Bula, Lubanski (3), Gadocha | | Nihat | |
| 14.11.71 | Albania | 3 | Turkey | 0 |
| | Pernaska (2), Pano | | | |
| 5.12.71 | Turkey | 1 | Poland | 0 |
| | Cemil | | | |

*West Germany qualify for quarter-finals, Turkey third in Group 8.*

## 1974-76

### Group 6

| 20.11.74 | Turkey | 1 | Rep of Ireland | 1 |
| | Own goal | | Givens | |
| 1.12.74 | Turkey | 2 | Switzerland | 1 |
| | Ismail, B. Mehmet | | Schild | |
| 2.4.75 | USSR | 3 | Turkey | 0 |
| | Kolotov (2 pens), Blochin | | | |
| 30.4.75 | Switzerland | 1 | Turkey | 1 |
| | K. Muller | | Alparslan | |
| 29.10.75 | Rep of Ireland | 4 | Turkey | 0 |
| | Givens (4) | | | |
| 23.11.75 | Turkey | 1 | USSR | 0 |
| | Cemil | | | |

*USSR qualify for quarter-finals, Turkey third in Group 6.*

## 1978-80

### Group 7

| 29.11.78 | Wales | 1 | Turkey | 0 |
| | Deacy | | | |
| 18.3.79 | Turkey | 2 | Malta | 1 |
| | Sedat, Fatih | | Spiteri Gonzi | |
| 1.4.79 | Turkey | 0 | West Germany | 0 |
| 28.10.79 | Malta | 1 | Turkey | 2 |
| | E. Farrugia | | Sedat, Mustafa | |
| 21.11.79 | Turkey | 1 | Wales | 0 |
| | Erhan | | | |
| 22.12.79 | West Germany | 2 | Turkey | 0 |
| | Fischer, Zimmermann | | | |

*West Germany qualify for finals, Turkey second in Group 7.*

## 1982-84

### Group 6

| 27.10.82 | Turkey | 1 | Albania | 0 |
| | Arif | | | |
| 17.11.82 | Austria | 4 | Turkey | 0 |
| | Polster, Pezzey, Prohanska (pen), | | | |
| | Schachner | | | |
| 30.3.83 | Northern Ireland | 2 | Turkey | 1 |
| | O'Neill, McClelland | | Nasan | |
| 23.4.83 | Turkey | 0 | West Germany | 3 |
| | | | Rummenigge (2, 1 pen), | |
| | | | Dremmler | |
| 11.5.83 | Albania | 1 | Turkey | 1 |
| | Own goal | | Metin | |

| 12.10.83 | Turkey<br>Selcuk | 1 | Northern Ireland | 0 |
|---|---|---|---|---|
| 26.10.83 | West Germany<br>Voller (2),<br>Rummenigge (2, 1 pen),<br>Stielicke | 5 | Turkey<br>Hasan | 1 |
| 16.11.83 | Turkey<br>Ilyas, Selcuk (2, 1 pen) | 3 | Austria<br>Baumeister | 1 |

*West Germany qualify for finals, Turkey fourth in Group 6.*

**1986-88**

*Group 4*

| 29.10.86 | Yugoslavia<br>Zl. Vujovic (3), Savicevic | 4 | Turkey | 0 |
|---|---|---|---|---|
| 12.11.86 | Turkey | 0 | Northern Ireland | 0 |
| 29.4.87 | Turkey | 0 | England | 0 |
| 14.10.87 | England<br>Lineker (3), Barnes (2),<br>Robson, Beardsley, Webb | 8 | Turkey | 0 |
| 11.11.87 | Northern Ireland<br>Quinn | 1 | Turkey | 0 |
| 16.12.87 | Turkey<br>Yusuf, Feyyaz | 2 | Yugoslavia<br>Radanovic, Katanec,<br>Hadzibegic | 3 |

*England qualify for finals, Turkey fourth in Group 4.*

**1990-92**

*Group 7*

| 17.10.90 | Rep of Ireland<br>Aldridge (3, 1 pen), O'Leary,<br>Quinn | 5 | Turkey | 0 |
|---|---|---|---|---|
| 14.11.90 | Turkey | 0 | Poland<br>Dziekanowski | 1 |
| 17.4.91 | Poland<br>Tarasiewicz, Urban, Kosecki | 3 | Turkey | 0 |
| 1.5.91 | Turkey | 0 | England<br>Wise | 1 |
| 16.10.91 | England<br>Smith | 1 | Turkey | 0 |
| 13.11.91 | Turkey<br>Riza (pen) | 1 | Rep of Ireland<br>Byrne (2), Cascarino | 3 |

*England qualify for finals, Turkey fourth in Group 7.*

For details on how Turkey qualified for Euro 96, see pages 31-3.

# CROATIA

Have never previously competed in the European Championships.

For details on how Croatia qualified for Euro 96, see pages 34-7.

# STATTO'S STATISTICS

## LEAGUE TABLE OF EUROPEAN CHAMPIONSHIP STANDINGS

| | No of entries | Pts | P | W | D | L | F | A | Final Phase |
|---|---|---|---|---|---|---|---|---|---|
| Holland | 9 | 123 | 81 | 51 | 14 | 16 | 177 | 66 | 5 |
| Spain | 10 | 115 | 80 | 45 | 17 | 28 | 161 | 75 | 5 |
| W Germany | 8 | 113 | 70 | 44 | 17 | 9 | 143 | 51 | 7 |
| USSR | 9 | 102 | 74 | 41 | 20 | 13 | 121 | 57 | 6 |
| Italy | 9 | 101 | 71 | 35 | 24 | 12 | 108 | 50 | 4 |
| France | 10 | 97 | 72 | 36 | 20 | 16 | 140 | 78 | 4 |
| Portugal | 10 | 93 | 69 | 35 | 16 | 18 | 104 | 72 | 2 |
| England | 9 | 88 | 63 | 36 | 16 | 11 | 127 | 46 | 5 |
| Romania | 10 | 87 | 68 | 31 | 19 | 18 | 114 | 75 | 2 |
| Denmark | 10 | 87 | 81 | 32 | 17 | 32 | 122 | 117 | 5 |
| Yugoslavia | 9 | 85 | 66 | 37 | 11 | 18 | 128 | 80 | 4 |
| Belgium | 9 | 85 | 71 | 31 | 19 | 21 | 111 | 82 | 3 |
| Czechoslovakia | 9 | 84 | 64 | 34 | 16 | 14 | 119 | 58 | 3 |
| Bulgaria | 10 | 83 | 67 | 31 | 14 | 22 | 108 | 76 | 1 |
| Hungary | 10 | 80 | 73 | 31 | 16 | 26 | 126 | 102 | 2 |
| Scotland | 8 | 77 | 61 | 27 | 16 | 18 | 88 | 62 | 2 |
| Rep of Ireland | 10 | 76 | 70 | 26 | 19 | 25 | 101 | 90 | 1 |
| Austria | 10 | 69 | 64 | 26 | 12 | 26 | 115 | 91 | – |
| Greece | 9 | 68 | 63 | 24 | 14 | 25 | 93 | 86 | 1 |
| Poland | 10 | 65 | 60 | 22 | 18 | 20 | 84 | 73 | – |
| N Ireland | 9 | 64 | 62 | 25 | 12 | 25 | 74 | 76 | – |
| Sweden | 9 | 63 | 58 | 23 | 15 | 20 | 78 | 71 | 1 |
| Switzerland | 9 | 62 | 58 | 21 | 15 | 22 | 93 | 82 | 1 |
| Wales | 9 | 57 | 56 | 21 | 13 | 22 | 70 | 73 | – |
| E Germany | 8 | 52 | 46 | 20 | 12 | 14 | 76 | 57 | – |
| Turkey | 10 | 48 | 56 | 16 | 12 | 28 | 47 | 100 | 1 |
| Norway | 10 | 45 | 62 | 13 | 13 | 36 | 65 | 108 | – |
| Finland | 8 | 35 | 54 | 9 | 12 | 33 | 49 | 106 | – |
| Russia | 1 | 26 | 10 | 8 | 2 | 0 | 34 | 5 | 1 |
| Iceland | 7 | 23 | 48 | 7 | 8 | 33 | 25 | 83 | – |
| Croatia | 1 | 23 | 10 | 7 | 2 | 1 | 22 | 5 | 1 |
| Czech Rep | 1 | 21 | 10 | 6 | 3 | 1 | 21 | 6 | 1 |
| Luxembourg | 9 | 19 | 61 | 4 | 8 | 49 | 31 | 188 | – |
| Albania | 7 | 18 | 43 | 5 | 6 | 32 | 24 | 93 | – |
| Lithuania | 1 | 16 | 10 | 5 | 1 | 4 | 13 | 12 | – |
| Georgia | 1 | 15 | 10 | 5 | 0 | 5 | 14 | 13 | – |
| Slovakia | 1 | 14 | 10 | 4 | 2 | 4 | 14 | 18 | – |
| Cyprus | 8 | 13 | 58 | 2 | 8 | 48 | 22 | 168 | – |
| Ukraine | 1 | 13 | 10 | 4 | 1 | 5 | 11 | 15 | – |
| Latvia | 1 | 12 | 10 | 4 | 0 | 6 | 11 | 20 | – |
| Malta | 8 | 12 | 52 | 2 | 8 | 44 | 21 | 169 | – |
| Israel | 1 | 12 | 10 | 3 | 3 | 4 | 13 | 13 | – |
| Belarus | 1 | 11 | 10 | 3 | 2 | 5 | 8 | 13 | – |
| Slovenia | 1 | 11 | 10 | 3 | 2 | 5 | 13 | 13 | – |
| Moldova | 1 | 9 | 10 | 3 | 0 | 7 | 11 | 27 | – |
| Faroe Isles | 2 | 9 | 18 | 3 | 1 | 14 | 13 | 61 | – |
| Macedonia | 1 | 7 | 10 | 1 | 4 | 5 | 9 | 18 | – |
| Armenia | 1 | 5 | 10 | 1 | 2 | 7 | 5 | 17 | – |

| | No of entries | Pts | P | W | D | L | F | A | Final Phase |
|---|---|---|---|---|---|---|---|---|---|
| Liechtenstein | 1 | 1 | 10 | 0 | 1 | 9 | 1 | 40 | - |
| Azerbaijan | 1 | 1 | 10 | 0 | 1 | 9 | 2 | 29 | - |
| Estonia | 1 | 0 | 10 | 0 | 0 | 10 | 3 | 31 | - |
| San Marino | 2 | 0 | 18 | 0 | 0 | 18 | 3 | 69 | - |

## GOALS IN EACH TOURNAMENT

| | Qualifiers | | Final phase | | Total | | Average Goals/ Games | No. of entries |
|---|---|---|---|---|---|---|---|---|
| | Games | Goals | Games | Goals | Games | Goals | | |
| 1958-60 | 24 | 91 | 4 | 17 | 28 | 108 | 3.05 | 17 |
| 1962-64 | 50 | 158 | 4 | 13 | 54 | 171 | 3.16 | 28 |
| 1966-68 | 98 | 306 | 5 | 7 | 103 | 313 | 3.03 | 31 |
| 1970-72 | 105 | 282 | 4 | 10 | 109 | 292 | 2.67 | 32 |
| 1974-76 | 104 | 289 | 4 | 19 | 108 | 308 | 2.85 | 32 |
| 1978-80 | 108 | 327 | 14 | 27 | 122 | 354 | 2.90 | 32 |
| 1982-84 | 116 | 341 | 15 | 41 | 131 | 382 | 2.91 | 33 |
| 1986-88 | 116 | 279 | 15 | 34 | 131 | 313 | 2.38 | 33 |
| 1990-92 | 123 | 333 | 15 | 32 | 138 | 365 | 2.64 | 34 |
| 1994-96 | 231 | 680 | | | | | 2.94 | 48 |

## LEADING SCORERS IN EACH COMPETITION (QUALIFIERS AND FINALS)

| 1958-60 | 5 goals | Fontaine (France) |
|---|---|---|
| | | Vincent (France) |
| | | Bubernik (Czechoslovakia) |
| 1962-64 | 11 goals | Madsen (Denmark) |
| 1966-68 | 7 goals | Riva (Italy) |
| 1970-72 | 11 goals | G. Muller (West Germany) |
| 1974-76 | 8 goals | Givens (Republic of Ireland) |
| 1978-80 | 7 goals | Keegan (England) |
| 1982-84 | 8 goals | Platini (France) |
| 1986-88 | 7 goals | Claesen (Belgium) |
| | | Altobelli (Italy) |
| | | Van Basten (Holland) |
| 1990-92 | 11 goals | Papin (France) |
| 1994-96 | 12 goals* | Suker (Croatia) |

* Qualifiers only

## OVERALL LEADING SCORERS IN EUROPEAN CHAMPIONSHIP

| Player | Final phase | Qualifiers | Total |
|---|---|---|---|
| Muller (West Germany) | 4 | 12 | 16 |
| Van Basten (Holland) | 5 | 11 | 16 |
| Polster (Austria) | 0 | 15 | 15 |
| Santillana (Spain) | 1 | 12 | 13 |
| Suker (1 for Yugoslavia, 12 for Croatia) | 0 | 13 | 13 |
| Cruyff (Holland) | 0 | 12 | 12 |
| Voller (West Germany) | 4 | 8 | 12 |
| Papin (France) | 2 | 10 | 12 |
| Klinsmann (West Germany & Germany) | 2 | 10 | 12 |
| Madsen (Denmark) | 0 | 11 | 11 |
| Stoichkov (Bulgaria) | 0 | 11 | 11 |

## HIGHEST ATTENDANCES FOR THE FINAL

| | | | |
|---|---|---|---|
| Spain v USSR | 1964 | Madrid | 120,000 |
| Italy v Yugoslavia | 1968 | Rome | 75,500 |
| Holland v USSR | 1988 | Munich | 72,308 |
| Italy v Yugoslavia | 1968 | Rome (Replay) | 60,000 |
| France v Spain | 1984 | Paris | 48,000 |
| West Germany v Belgium | 1980 | Rome | 47,864 |
| West Germany v Czechoslovakia | 1976 | Belgrade | 45,000 |
| West Germany v USSR | 1972 | Brussels | 43,437 |
| Denmark v Germany | 1992 | Gothenburg | 37,800 |
| USSR v Yugoslavia | 1960 | Paris | 17,966 |

## LONGEST RUN WITHOUT A DEFEAT IN THE EUROPEAN CHAMPIONSHIP

| | From | To | |
|---|---|---|---|
| West Germany | 7.10.1967 | 17.11.1982 | 32 games |

## HIGHEST SCORE

| | | |
|---|---|---|
| Spain v Malta | 12-1 | 21.12.83 |

# HAT-TRICKS IN THE EUROPEAN CHAMPIONSHIPS

|  | *Player* | *Goals* | *Opposition* |
|---|---|---|---|
| Austria | Parits | 3 | Rep of Ireland [1972] |
|  | Polster | 3 | Liechtenstein [1996] |
|  | Stoger | 3 | Rep of Ireland [1996] |
| Belgium | Stockman | 3 | Luxembourg [1968] |
|  | Claesen | 3 | Luxembourg [1988] |
|  | Claesen | 3 | Scotland [1988] |
| Croatia | Suker | 3 | Estonia [1996] |
| Czechoslovakia | Panenka | 3 | Cyprus [1976] |
|  | Siegl | 3 | Malta [1996] |
| Denmark | Madsen | 3 | Malta [1964] |
|  | Madsen | 3 | Luxembourg [1964] |
|  | Elkjaer | 3 | Northern Ireland [1980] |
|  | M. Laudrup | 3 | Luxembourg [1984] |
| England | Macdonald | 5 | Cyprus [1976] |
|  | Blissett | 3 | Luxembourg [1984] |
|  | Lineker | 3 | Turkey [1988] |
| Finland | Paatelainen | 4 | San Marino [1996] |
| France | Fontaine | 3 | Austria [1960] |
|  | Loubet | 3 | Luxembourg [1968] |
|  | Platini | 3 | Belgium [1984] |
|  | Platini | 3 | Yugoslavia [1984] |
| East Germany | Frenzel | 3 | Holland [1968] |
|  | Kreische | 4 | Luxembourg [1972] |
|  | Hoffmann | 3 | Switzerland [1980] |
|  | Thom | 3 | Iceland [1988] |
| West Germany | G. Muller | 4 | Albania [1968] |
|  | D. Muller | 3 | Yugoslavia [1976] |
|  | K. Allofs | 3 | Holland [1980] |
| Greece | Sideris | 3 | Austria [1968] |
|  | Mavros | 4 | Finland [1980] |
| Holland | Cruyff | 3 | Luxembourg [1972] |
|  | Van der Kuylen | 3 | Finland [1976] |
|  | Rensenbrink | 3 | Belgium [1976] |
|  | Bosman | 3 | Cyprus [1988] |
|  | Van Basten | 3 | England [1988] |
|  | Van Basten | 5 | Malta [1992] |
|  | Overmars | 3 | Malta [1996] |
| Hungary | Farkas | 3 | East Germany [1968] |
|  | Nyilasi | 5 | Luxembourg [1976] |
|  | Poczik | 3 | Luxembourg [1984] |
| Italy | Orlando | 4 | Turkey [1964] |
|  | Riva | 3 | Cyprus [1968] |
|  | Zola | 3 | Lithuania [1996] |
| Northern Ireland | Best | 3 | Cyprus [1972] |
|  | Clarke | 3 | Faroe Isles [1992] |
| Poland | Zmijewski | 3 | Belgium [1968] |
|  | Lubanski | 3 | Turkey [1972] |
| Portugal | Paulo Alves | 3 | Liechtenstein [1996] |
| Rep of Ireland | Givens | 3 | USSR [1976] |
|  | Givens | 4 | Turkey [1976] |
|  | Aldridge | 3 | Turkey [1992] |
| Romania | Fratila | 3 | Switzerland [1968] |
|  | Dumitriu | 3 | Cyprus [1968] |
|  | Raducioiu | 3 | Azerbaijan [1996] |

# ROLL OF HONOUR

| | | 1st | 2nd | 3rd |
|---|---|---|---|---|
| 1 | West Germany | 2 | 2 | 1 |
| 2 | USSR | 1 | 3 | 0 |
| 3 | Spain | 1 | 1 | 0 |
| 4 | Holland | 1 | 0 | 2 |
| 5 | Czechoslovakia | 1 | 0 | 2 |
| 6 | Denmark | 1 | 0 | 1 |
| 7 | Italy | 1 | 0 | 1 |
| 8 | France | 1 | 0 | 0 |
| 9 | Yugoslavia | 0 | 2 | 0 |
| 10 | Belgium | 0 | 1 | 1 |
| 11 | Hungary | 0 | 0 | 1 |
| | England | 0 | 0 | 1 |
| | Portugal | 0 | 0 | 1 |
| | Sweden | 0 | 0 | 1 |

* NB: Where there was no third-place play-off, both beaten semi-finalists are included.

# THE REFEREES

By Dermot Gallagher

Euro 96 is upon us. It is the third most prestigious football tournament, behind the World Cup and the Olympics, in the world. As with the players it brings the same opportunities for success and disappointment for the refereeing fraternity who will ply their trade throughout England during June. Throughout the group competitions, which resulted in 15 teams plus England achieving their right to exhibit their skills in the finals, many referees were in similar combat – handling high-pressure group matches under strict scrutiny, hoping their ultimate goal of a finals place would be realised.

In the end, 39 of UEFA's top referees were called to Seville during mid-February to undergo fitness tests and discussions aimed at bringing a consistent application of the Laws of the Game to the forthcoming tournament. Referees were encouraged to express their views and UEFA helped to ensure that all present were finely tuned to face all aspects of play – leading to the highest possible standards.

As the course neared its conclusion, it became known that the select 24 would be announced – bringing with it the tension of anticipation. Referees' ages, as with the players, vary greatly. For some, the announcement would be the realisation of their dreams, others would see that in four years time they could still return, but for some the exclusion would not only bring the natural disappointment but in reality it meant the last chapter of the book had been completed.

Emotions among referees are similar to those of any player – and all those were seen when the 24 names were announced. The disappointment etched on the face of a 42-year-old referee was equal to any seen on a top professional footballer who has just heard the final whistle in a semi-final with his team behind. It is a side of the game the public don't see. The commitment and dedication to a game that begins as a hobby quickly turns into a passion that consumes your life. It is a metamorphosis unparalleled. Often referees put the game before both family and career in an attempt to reach for the stars.

For 15 referees – as with many of Europe's finest players who have already been eliminated – this tournament was over. However, as with any side of the game, there have to be winners as well as losers – for 24 referees their first victory was complete. Being fortunate enough to be a member of the 24, along with English colleague David Elleray, attention is now switched forward to appointments and ultimately the tournament itself in June.

March 22 brought the referees' appointments for the individual group matches and each referee was allocated two linesmen and a fourth official from his own country to work throughout European and domestic matches for the rest of the season to create a bond, ensuring a thoroughly professional performance.

The interim period is now taken up with matches bringing their own emotions, challenges and satisfaction, building up to what each of the referees feels will be a fiesta of football played by the finest teams within the finest stadia throughout Europe. Nothing has been left to chance and each of the 24 referees' teams are as professionally prepared, both physically and mentally, to play their part.

All we await now is Spanish referee Manuel Diaz Vega to blow his whistle to commence the England v Switzerland match while the other 23 referees echo: 'Let the tournament begin. It means so much to us all.'

**8.6.96:**

England v Switzerland .................................................... *Manuel Diaz Vega* (Spain)

**9.6.96:**

Spain v Bulgaria .................................................... *Piero Ceccarini* (Italy)

Germany v Czech Republic .................................................... *David Elleray* (England)

Denmark v Portugal .................................................... *Mario Van der Ende* (Holland)

**10.6.96:**

Holland v Scotland .................................................... *Leif Sundell* (Sweden)

Romania v France .................................................... *Hellmut Krug* (Germany)

**11.6.96:**

Italy v Russia .................................................... *Leslie Mottram* (Scotland)

Turkey v Croatia .................................................... *Serge Muhmenthaler* (Switzerland)

**13.6.96:**

Switzerland v Holland .................................................... *Atanas Ouzounov* (Bulgaria)

Bulgaria v Romania .................................................... *Peter Mikkelsen* (Denmark)

**14.6.96:**

Czech Republic v Italy .................................................... *Antonio J Lopez Nieto* (Spain)

Portugal v Turkey .................................................... *Sandor Puhl* (Hungary)

**15.6.96:**

Scotland v England .................................................... *Pierluigi Pairetto* (Italy)

France v Spain .................................................... *Vadim Zhuk* (Belarus)

**16.6.96:**

Russia v Germany .................................................... *Kim Milton Nielsen* (Denmark)

Croatia v Denmark .................................................... *Marc Batta* (France)

**18.6.96:**

Scotland v Switzerland .................................................... *Vaclav Krondl* (Czech Rep)

France v Bulgaria .................................................... *Dermot Gallagher* (England)

Holland v England .................................................... *Gerd Grabher* (Austria)

Romania v Spain .................................................... *Ahmet Cakar* (Turkey)

**19.6.96:**

Russia v Czech Republic .................................................... *Anders Frisk* (Sweden)

Croatia v Portugal .................................................... *Bernd Heynemann* (Germany)

Italy v Germany .................................................... *Guy Goethals* (Belgium)

Turkey v Denmark .................................................... *Nikolai Levnikov* (Russia)

# 1996 EUROPEAN CHAMPIONSHIP OFFICIAL BETTING

| Team | Pre-draw odds | Post-draw odds | Odds at 8 March |
|---|---|---|---|
| Italy | 5/1 | 5/1 | 5/1 |
| Germany | 5/1 | 5/1 | 5/1 |
| England | 11/2 | 7/1 | 7/1 |
| Holland | 6/1 | 9/2 | 9/2 |
| Spain | 6/1 | 7/1 | 7/1 |
| France | 10/1 | 10/1 | 8/1 |
| Portugal | 12/1 | 10/1 | 10/1 |
| Russia | 14/1 | 20/1 | 20/1 |
| Bulgaria | 14/1 | 16/1 | 16/1 |
| Romania | 14/1 | 16/1 | 16/1 |
| Croatia | 16/1 | 12/1 | 12/1 |
| Denmark | 25/1 | 25/1 | 25/1 |
| Czech Republic | 33/1 | 80/1 | 80/1 |
| Scotland | 40/1 | 50/1 | 50/1 |
| Switzerland | 40/1 | 50/1 | 50/1 |
| Turkey | 50/1 | 50/1 | 50/1 |

These odds from Ladbrokes, official bookmaker to Euro 96.

The first official odds were published on Saturday 22 January 1994 within five minutes of the qualifying draw, and Ladbrokes installed Germany as the 9/2 favourites.

The original betting was:

| | |
|---|---|
| 9/2 Germany | 12/1 Russia |
| 5/1 Italy | 14/1 Denmark |
| 6/1 England | 16/1 France |
| 6/1 Holland | 20/1 Spain |

The first eight favourites in the original betting all line up in the final sixteen teams.

Sweden and Belgium were the most fancied teams not to qualify for the finals. Ladbrokes had offered both countries at 25/1.

# EUROPEAN CHAMPIONSHIP FIXTURES 1996

*(including head-to-head results for the first-named team)*

| June | Group | Team | Team | Venue | Time |
|---|---|---|---|---|---|
| Sat 8 | A | England | Switzerland | Wembley | 15.00 |
| | | P15 W10 D2 L3 F40 A12 | | | |
| Sun 9 | B | Spain | Bulgaria | Elland Road | 14.30 |
| | | P2 W2 D0 L0 F15 A0 | | | |
| Sun 9 | C | Germany | Czech Rep | Old Trafford | 17.00 |
| | | P17 W10 D4 L3 F36 A24 | | | |
| Sun 9 | D | Denmark | Portugal | Hillsborough | 19.30 |
| | | P6 W6 D0 L0 F15 A3 | | | |
| Mon 10 | A | Holland | Scotland | Villa Park | 16.30 |
| | | P12 W5 D2 L5 F14 A15 | | | |
| Mon 10 | B | Romania | France | St James' Park | 19.30 |
| | | P6 W3 D1 L2 F10 A7 | | | |
| Tue 11 | C | Italy | Russia | Anfield | 16.30 |
| | | P11 W2 D5 L4 F7 A9 | | | |
| Tue 11 | D | Turkey | Croatia | City Ground | 19.30 |
| | | Never played | | | |
| Thu 13 | A | Switzerland | Holland | Villa Park | 19.30 |
| | | P30 W14 D2 L14 F59 A65 | | | |
| Thu 13 | B | Bulgaria | Romania | St James' Park | 16.30 |
| | | P33 W8 D4 L21 F47 A72 | | | |
| Fri 14 | C | Czech Rep | Italy | Anfield | 19.30 |
| | | P26 W8 D8 L10 F37 A39 | | | |
| Fri 14 | D | Portugal | Turkey | City Ground | 16.30 |
| | | P4 W3 D0 L1 F10 A5 | | | |
| Sat 15 | A | Scotland | England | Wembley | 15.00 |
| | | P107 W40 D24 L43 F168 A188 | | | |
| Sat 15 | B | France | Spain | Elland Road | 18.00 |
| | | P23 W8 D5 L10 F27 A49 | | | |
| Sun 16 | C | Russia | Germany | Old Trafford | 15.00 |
| | | P15 W3 D1 L11 F5 A36 | | | |
| Sun 16 | D | Croatia | Denmark | Hillsborough | 18.00 |
| | | Never played | | | |
| Tue 18 | A | Scotland | Switzerland | Villa Park | 19.30 |
| | | P13 W6 D3 L4 F21 A20 | | | |
| Tue 18 | B | France | Bulgaria | St James' Park | 16.30 |
| | | P17 W6 D4 L7 F27 A22 | | | |
| Tue 18 | A | Holland | England | Wembley | 19.30 |
| | | P12 W4 D5 L3 F18 A14 | | | |
| Tue 18 | B | Romania | Spain | Elland Road | 16.30 |
| | | P12 W4 D4 L4 F15 A18 | | | |
| Wed 19 | C | Russia | Czech Rep | Anfield | 19.30 |
| | | P12 W6 D4 L2 F21 A12 | | | |
| Wed 19 | D | Croatia | Portugal | City Ground | 16.30 |
| | | Never played | | | |
| Wed 19 | C | Italy | Germany | Old Trafford | 19.30 |
| | | P25 W11 D7 L7 F37 A32 | | | |
| Wed 19 | D | Turkey | Denmark | Hillsborough | 16.30 |
| | | P4 W1 D2 L1 F3 A3 | | | |
| Sat 22 | QF | 1st in B | 2nd in A | Anfield | 18.30 |
| Sat 22 | QF | 2nd in B | 1st in A | Wembley | 15.00 |
| Sun 23 | QF | 1st in C | 2nd in D | Old Trafford | 15.00 |
| Sun 23 | QF | 2nd in C | 1st in D | Villa Park | 18.30 |
| Wed 26 | SF | B1 or A2 | C2 or D1 | Old Trafford | 16.00 |
| Wed 26 | SF | B2 or A1 | C1 or D2 | Wembley | 19.30 |
| Sun 30 | Final | | | Wembley | 19.00 |